PERICLES OF ATHENS

PERICLES
OF ATHENS

Vincent Azoulay

TRANSLATED BY JANET LLOYD
FOREWORD BY PAUL CARTLEDGE

Princeton University Press

Avec le soutien du

Princeton and Oxford

Originally published in France as *Périclès: La démocratie athénienne à l'épreuve du grand homme* © Armand Colin, 2010

Copyright © 2014 by Princeton University Press
Requests for permission to reproduce material from this work should be sent to Permissions, Princeton University Press
Published by Princeton University Press, 41 William Street, Princeton, New Jersey 08540
In the United Kingdom: Princeton University Press, 6 Oxford Street, Woodstock, Oxfordshire OX20 1TW

press.princeton.edu

Jacket image: Bronze helmet of Corinthian type, 1873.0910.1. © Trustees of the British Museum.

LIBRARY OF CONGRESS CATALOGING-IN-PUBLICATION DATA

Azoulay, Vincent.
[Périclès. English]
Pericles of Athens / Vincent Azoulay ; translated by Janet Lloyd ; foreword by Paul Cartledge.
pages   cm
Includes bibliographical references and index.
ISBN 978-0-691-15459-6 (hardcover : alk. paper) 1. Pericles, approximately 495 B.C.–429 B.C.
2. Statesmen—Greece—Athens—Biography. 3. Athens (Greece)—Politics and government. I. Title.
DF228.P4A9613 2014   938'.505092—dc23
[B]
2013026887

British Library Cataloging-in-Publication Data is available

This book has been composed in Garamond Premier Pro

Printed on acid-free paper. ∞

Printed in the United States of America

1 3 5 7 9 10 8 6 4 2

To My Parents

❧

For Pauline Schmitt Pantel

CONTENTS

FIGURES

Introducing Azoulay's *Pericles*

Paul Cartledge

There is no shortage of would-be biographies of Pericles, son of Xanthippus of the deme Cholargos (to give him his full, ancient Athenian democratic-citizen nomenclature). But to be frank, not many of them are much good—and that includes the best surviving ancient one, compiled by Plutarch of Chaeronea in about A.D. 100. One hint that Plutarch was not perhaps on the very top of his form here is that the ancient Roman with whom he saw fit to compare or rather contrast the Athenian Greek was Quintus Fabius Maximus Verrucosus, later nicknamed Cunctator ("the Delayer"), the man tasked with rescuing Republican Rome's fortunes after the disastrous defeat inflicted by Hannibal at Cannae in 216 B.C. The careers of Pericles and Fabius simply did not have enough points of significant similarity to make the comparison at all helpful or even interesting.

On the other hand, the fact that pastmaster Plutarch could do no better suggests that writing a good biography of Pericles would have been a pretty hopeless goal for any ancient author. And since Plutarch did at least have at his disposal a large amount of primary written source material not available to or used by any later author, the lot of the modern would-be biographer is even more desperate. Yet this has not deterred a seemingly endless succession of attempts at, if not strictly a Life of Pericles, then at any rate a Life and Times. This latter at least is understandable. The times Pericles lived in—from about 493 to 429 B.C.—and indeed helped to make and shape were deeply interesting, and the family and the city of his birth lay at their very epicenter.

Pericles belonged to the same aristocratic family, the Alcmeonids of Athens, from which had issued the man credited—by Herodotus, the father of Western historiography—with introducing Greece's first democracy, in 508/7 B.C. He lived through the Greco-Persian Wars of 490 (Marathon) and 480–479 (Salamis and Plataea). He sponsored, at the tender age of twenty or so, the earliest surviving tragic drama by Athens's and Greece's first master of that evergreen theatrical genre: the *Persians* of Aeschylus first staged in the Theater of Dionysus at the foot of the Athenian Acropolis in early 472. He was intimately connected with the building program on top of the Acropolis that witnessed the construction preeminently of the Parthenon (447–432). He hobnobbed with leading intellectuals of the day, both Athenian and foreign. His private life—living with a foreign Greek woman to whom he could not legally be married, thanks to a law that he had himself sponsored in 451—was a scandal that writers of comic drama considered a gift. Above all, so far as posterity is concerned, Pericles made such a huge—and hugely favorable—impression on Herodotus's principal successor as a writer of big Greek history, Thucydides of Athens (ca. 455–400?), that Thucydides came near to calling him the uncrowned monarch of Athens, and to writing his history of the Atheno-Peloponnesian War (431–404) in terms of the Athenians' adherence to or failure to adhere to the policies and strategies advocated, so persuasively, by Pericles—as Thucydides understood and presented them.

It was thus Thucydides who posed Plutarch the biographer with his greatest problem, and Thucydides too who ultimately set up the problematic with which Dr. Azoulay grapples in this intriguing, innovative, and justly prize-winning book.[1] For Plutarch found it very hard to reconcile the sober-sided statesmanlike Pericles of Thucydides with the scandalously self-indulgent and bohemian Pericles presented in other contemporary, fifth-century B.C. sources, including both comic drama and law court oratory. Dr. Azoulay, for his part, has several objectives in view, but not the least of them is to deconstruct the image of Pericles that is now standard both in scholarship and in more popular works—namely, that of a game-changer, the "grand homme" and very epitome of not just Athens but also his "age."[2]

Let us therefore start this very brief introduction with that notion of Pericles as secular hero, the ancient Greek answer to Voltaire's Louis XIV: was there, really, a "siècle de Périclès"? One of the many surprises that Dr. Azoulay can spring is to show how recent that notion is—no more ancient, that is, than the era of Voltaire himself. The phrase itself goes no further back than the future Frederick the Great's *Anti-Machiavel* of 1739, published (anonymously) in Amsterdam in 1740 and vigorously distributed by Voltaire himself. But, as Dr. Azoulay ably shows, it is not until very much more recently that it has gained wide currency and been given, supposedly, material content. Not the least of the many valuable historiographical services our author performs is to show how shaky are the foundations of such an intellectual-ideological edifice.

Indeed, the prime virtue of this outstanding book is that it is resolutely historiographical and problematizing. So far from attempting merely to set out "how it actually was" in Pericles' life and lifetime, Dr. Azoulay frames his "biographical odyssey" in terms of a series of—roughly chronologically ordered—problems. He begins (chapter 1) with the problem of how the young Pericles accommodated himself to the illustrious but also notorious families into which he was born: on his mother's side he was an Alcmaeonid, and thus under an ancestral curse going back almost a century and a half, on his father's he was heir to a mega-feud with the no less aristocratic family of Miltiades of Marathon. His second problem (chapters 2 and 3) is that of the twin military and rhetorical bases of his political power—and what "power" meant or could mean in a democracy such as Athens was and, thanks not least to Pericles' own efforts, became. A third problem concerns the power and wealth of Athens as that was expressed both externally and internally: how far was Pericles himself responsible for the imperialism of Athens (chapter 4)? In what way and to what extent did the by Greek standards massive internal revenues of Athens grease the wheels of democracy (chapter 5)? The fourth problem addressed by Dr. Azoulay is that of the relationship not so much between the public and the private as between the personal and the communitarian: in chapter 6 are considered with great finesse Pericles' interactions with relatives and friends; in chapter 7 the unconventional "erotics" of his scandal-ridden career; and in chapter 8 his relations with the gods of the *polis* ("citizen-state") of democratic Athens.[3]

The final chapters are the most explicitly historiographical in content and flavor: As the author states at the start of chapter 11, "One of the primary virtues of a historiographical inquiry is certainly its ability to dispel automatic assumptions and show that traditions do themselves have a history." Chapter 9 explores the vision peddled particularly by Plato and inherited by Plutarch of Pericles as not at all the Thucydidean statesman, but the ultimate demagogue, the vilest mis-leader and immoral corruptor of the ordinary people of Athens. This is a vision that is shown to owe more to snobbery and anti-democratic sentiment than to objective historical evaluation and rational judgment. But it was also a vision that made it hard for Pericles to ascend to the status and stature of "great man," as he did in a complicated process that Dr. Azoulay most skilfully untangles in chapter 11 (fifteenth to eighteenth centuries) and chapter 12 (eighteenth to twenty-first centuries). For Machiavelli and Bodin, Pericles was the very incarnation of democratic instability, for Montaigne a model of trumpery rhetoric, and indeed until after the French Revolution Pericles was deemed and doomed to remain firmly in the historiographical-ideological shadows. No gloriously conquering Alexander, no bravely fighting Cimon, no sagely legislating Solon he. And yet, as noted earlier, it was in the 1730s that the "Age of Pericles" tag first saw the light or, as Dr. Azoulay puts it, that the Periclean "myth" was born.

J.-J. Winckelmann's pioneering art history of "Antiquity" of 1764, *Geschichte der Kunst des Alterthums*, privileged the classical "Periclean" moment of fifth-century Greece and Athens, where and when as he saw it political, social, and intellectual conditions conduced most favorably to fostering eternally valuable aesthetic creativity. But it was the English private scholar and historian George Grote, ex-MP, who did most to establish the story of Athens and Athenian (quasi-parliamentary) democracy as the master-narrative of Western enlightenment in his originally twelve-volume *History of Greece* (1846–1856; esp. vol. VI, ch. XLVII), in the process permanently displacing from that role the rival city of Sparta—whose cause was not helped by its being so fervently embraced by reactionaries and nationalists from William Mitford in the late eighteenth century, through the pedagogues of the Royal Prussian Cadet-Corps of the later nineteenth, to those of the National Socialist elite schools sponsored in Hitler's name by his academic lapdogs in the twentieth.[4]

A central chapter (chapter 10) addresses explicitly the problematic of the "great man" or event-making hero. It would be wrong for me to spoil the party by revealing Dr. Azoulay's own take on that, although I can safely disclose that his Pericles is not that of Evelyn Abbott, author in the "Heroes of the Nations" series of *Pericles and the Golden Age of Athens* (New York/London: G. P. Putnam's Sons, 1891), nor indeed that of Thucydides. I can also add that here, as indeed throughout this book, he writes with great clarity, and with an impressive depth of interpretative sophistication, both qualities that have been expertly captured in this excellent translation by the *doyenne* of nontraducers, Janet Lloyd.

Acknowledgments

On the threshold of this work, I should like to express my great gratitude to Maurice Sartre who, with his communicative enthusiasm, convinced me to embark upon this adventure and whose unfailing support enabled me not to lose my way. I also owe a great deal to the history students of Paris-Est Marne-la-Vallée, who were the first to accompany me as we paced up and down those Periclean paths in the wan early mornings of Bois de L'Etang; their reactions often helped me to refine, develop, and clarify my hypotheses and arguments.

I should also like to thank all those who were patient and kind enough to reread the early versions of this work, helping me to avoid many historical, orthographic, and logical pitfalls—in particular, Marie-Christine Chainais, Pascal Payen, and Jérôme Wilgaux, who allowed me to benefit from their precious expertise. Two long-suffering scholars deserve a special mention: Paulin Ismard, who followed my tentative progress step by step and assumed the friendly role of a critical mirror, and Christophe Brun, who, with his customary humor and his salutary objectivity, toppled many of my firm convictions.

Finally, nothing would have been possible without Cécile Chainais, who was at my side throughout the gestation of this *Pericles* and thanks to whom I discovered the keys to paternity.

PERICLES OF ATHENS

Introduction

Pericles is a familiar figure in school textbooks and books on Greece. He enjoys the rare privilege of, on his own, embodying a whole "age," condensing within his name the peak of Athens's glory and the flowering of the first democracy in history. We know him from a bust made in the Roman period: the impenetrable face seems to defy the efforts of any historian. What angle can one adopt in order to apprehend this bust without prejudice? How can one suggest a new way of looking at a figure so often scrutinized? Confronting a monument such as this clearly involves a risk: that of wandering for ages over wave after wave of historiography, with the risk of never reaching a safe harbor.

Method: A Biographical Inquiry Considered as an Odyssey

Many a pitfall lies in wait for the rash or unsuspecting historian who launches himself into this adventure. First, he needs to steer between two symmetrical perils: idealization and its opposite, relativism. With the ballast of such a weighty laudatory tradition, it is hard for historians of Antiquity to approach Pericles without eminently positive preconceptions. Since the nineteenth century, this figure has often been regarded as one of the principal creators of the "Greek miracle," the very embodiment of "an ideal of beauty crystallized in the marble of Pentelicus," to borrow the famous words of Ernest Renan.[1] Pericles, at the head of a peaceful and harmonious city, appears as the model of a wise and incorruptible leader, just as he is portrayed in the laudatory portrait of him presented by the historian Thucydides.

However, over the past fifty or so years, that enchanted vision has been battered by numerous studies. To be sure, in Pericles' day Athens was the scene of intense political and cultural fervor: direct democracy was lastingly established and meanwhile the Acropolis was covered with grandiose monuments that, in our eyes, still today proclaim that Greece had reached the peak of its glory. All the same, those undeniable successes cannot mask the limitations of the Athenian system. Its democracy had nothing to do with human rights, for it was solely concerned with the rights of citizens. In Pericles' day, the civic community remained an exclusive club from which slaves, metics, and women were all excluded and that, moreover, had no hesitation in tyrannizing its allies within the framework of a maritime empire that became increasingly hegemonic.

So, as the scales abruptly tip the other way, should we now topple the statue of Pericles that tradition has sculpted so carefully? In a switch from miracle to mirage, does the Athenian general (*stratēgos*) deserve to be relegated to a forgotten page of history, as no more than an emblem of a macho, slave-based, and colonialist world—in short, as a prefiguration of the Western imperialism of the nineteenth and twentieth centuries? To do so would be to lurch from Charybdis to Scylla, from unbridled idealization to radical relativism. For in truth, that negative vision is just as reductive as what it replaces, for it judges the ancient city by the yardstick of contemporary realities.

The other reef that a historian must endeavor to avoid in an inquiry such as the present one is anachronism. To condemn Pericles in the name of today's values would be to make a remarkable error in perspective. To reduce the past to the present would be to view one's prey with only one eye, like the *Odyssey*'s Cyclops. The whole perspective is distorted . . . We should bear in mind that slavery was not abolished in Europe until the nineteenth century, and, in France, women did not acquire the right to vote until the end of World War II. But should we, on that account, deny the role played by the Second and the Third Republics in the democratization of the French nation? To gauge the break that occurred in the time of Pericles, we should, in truth, compare it, not to the situation today, but to that which then prevailed in the ancient world. A "one-eyed" view definitely tells us far more about today's obsessions than about fifth-century Athens. Such anachronisms can, in a more insidious fashion, often be traced to the analogies to which historians resort in order to evoke the Greek world and its "great men." It is probably totally pointless to regard Pericles as the leader of a political party—as if any such structures existed in Athens—or to interpret the building site on the Acropolis as the fruit of Keynesian policies *avant la lettre*, with Pericles assuming the mantle of Roosevelt.[2]

Should we, then, simply draw attention to the radical difference of the Greek world, at the risk of boring readers confronted with an Antiquity shrouded in its singularity? If Pericles resembles our contemporary politicians not at all, why continue to take an interest in that figure? Yet is it possible totally to shed the preoccupations of the present day, as we confront the past? Again, it is all a matter of balance. The present book favors an un-Cyclopean, two-eyed view founded upon a constant "toing and froing" between the present and the past. Provided it is kept under control, anachronism may have pedagogic or even heuristic virtues.[3] The narrow path that I intend to follow involves drawing comparisons with the present, without, however, succumbing to the dizzying prospects of analogy.

In this odyssey strewn with pitfalls, there is one last trap that is particularly hard to avoid—namely, personalization, which is an inherent part of all biographical projects. Like the traveler who, enraptured by the siren's songs to the point of losing all recollection of his family and homeland, a biographer often tends to neglect the social and political environment in which his hero moves. By focusing on a single individual, a historian risks leaving in the shadows the role played by the collectivity. That would, to put it mildly, be paradoxical when one is tackling the first democracy in history. It has to be said that the ancient sources do nothing to dispel such an enchantment. By the end of the fifth century, already Thucydides was declaring that "Athens, though in name a democracy, gradually became in fact a government ruled by its foremost citizen" (2.65).

That famous declaration has for many years been taken quite literally, as if the history of the Athenian democracy and the career of its leader could be superposed one upon the other and completely fused.[4] But such personalization is eminently challengeable: Thucydides, himself a *stratēgos*, was far from being as "objective" as a certain line of historiography has long maintained. In so far as historians today are more objective than their famous predecessor, it is fair enough to declare "No, Thucydides is not a colleague,"[5] for the author of *The Peloponnesian War* was heir to a deep-seated tradition that tended to envisage history solely in relation to the great men who, it was supposed, molded it.

So should we tip the scales in the opposite direction and dilute Pericles' own actions with those of the Athenian people? In order to render to Caesar that which is Caesar's and to the people that which is theirs, it would be tempting to write a history of Athens animated by an anonymous collective: in short, to write a history not of Pericles, but of 50,000 citizens. A number of studies on the *stratēgos* do have that tendency and, on the pretext of producing a life of Pericles, in fact sketch in a portrait of fifth-century Athens.[6]

All the same, that would be a simplifying, if not simplistic approach to the problem. Rather than choose between the people and a single individual, it would better to consider that very question as the subject to be studied. Even if Pericles did undeniably weigh heavily upon the city's collective decisions, on the other hand, reading between the lines, the life of the great man illuminates the influence that the Athemian *dēmos* exerted upon its leaders. In order to wield the slightest degree of power, the great man was obliged to take popular expectations into account and to align, adjust, and adapt his own behavior in response to them. It is precisely that complex interaction between the crowd and its leaders that deserves to be placed at the heart of the inquiry.

A project centered on Pericles has to walk a tightrope. We should take care not to idealize Athens but, at the same time, not to deny the rupture introduced by the invention of democracy; if possible, we should also avoid misleading parallels without, however, renouncing certain carefully controlled anachronisms, given that history, even when positivist, always feeds on present-day debates; and finally, we should succumb neither to the illusion of the power of one great man nor to that of the all-powerful masses. Rather, we should inquire into the productive tension that developed between the *stratēgos* and the Athenian community. If we accept those three conditions, we have some hope of plumbing the true historical depths of both Pericles and the city, at the same time emphasizing the profound differences as well as the few resemblances that it has with our own contemporary democratic life.

Instead of launching into a new biography of Pericles, we must instead seek to set this great figure in context, reinserting it into the democratic political culture of the fifth century B.C. Pericles, the man, is surrounded by numerous and sometimes contradictory accounts where, reading between the lines, we find embedded[7] a picture of the social and historical world of classical Athens. Pericles thus seems to operate as a good reagent—to borrow a chemical metaphor—that reveals the multiple aspects of the workings of Athenian democracy.

In order to evaluate the extent and scope of these interactions, we must begin by reconstructing the background against which Pericles' life unfolded. These salient chronological points are necessary in order to seize upon both the disagreements that crystallized around his actions and also the degree to which he left his mark on the destiny of Athens.

CHRONOLOGY: A BRIEF HISTORY OF PERICLES

The city (*polis*), which appeared around the eighth century, constituted a new form of political and territorial organization that rapidly spread throughout the Mediterranean region, from the Black Sea right across to the shores of Andalusia. In the early fifth century, the Greek world was composed of a mosaic of communities that were independent of one another but were linked by their language and their cults. Among them was the city of Athens, which at that time appears to have been a community undergoing serious changes. At the time of Pericles' birth in 494/3 B.C.,[8] the city had recently freed itself from the domination of tyrants who, for the past half-century, had held the reins of power. This was an important change. Once the tyranny had collapsed, in 510 B.C., all forms of personal domination remained for many years discredited—a factor that Pericles had to take into account throughout his career. In 508/7 B.C., this upheaval acquired an institutional form: a series of reforms, inspired by Cleisthenes, introduced profound changes into the political organization of the city, laying down the bases of the democracy that then developed in the course of the fifth century.

Pericles was related to Cleisthenes the reformer and so belonged to an extremely prestigious family. However, very little is known of his youth except that he probably spent a few years in exile, as his father Xanthippus was banished by the Athenian people when he was ostracized. This was a procedure that made it possible temporarily to get rid of any member of the elite considered to be too powerful and so prevent any return to tyranny. That sanction of ostracism lapsed in 485, halfway between the two Persian Wars, in which a fraction of the Greek cities stood against the Persian Empire.

Pericles grew up against the background of this struggle, which was, right from the start, an unequal one. The imbalance between the two worlds was flagrant: on the one side, disunited Greek communities of, at the most, a few thousand citizens, on the other side, the immense Achaemenid Empire, the center of gravity of which was positioned in the high Iranian plateaux but whose domination extended from the shores of the Black Sea, in the West, all the way to Afghanistan in the East, encompassing Egypt in the South. The First Persian War, in 490, was no more than a skirmish from which, to general surprise, the Athenian heavy infantry (the hoplites) emerged as victors. But the Second Persian War was a far greater confrontation. By land and by sea, the Persian forces invaded the territory of continental Greece and, in the face of this threat, no more than thirty-one cities—out of the hundreds that then made up Hellas—united to resist the offensive. Although Sparta was nominally in command of the Greek forces, Athens controlled most of the fleet, the construction of which had been financed by the silver extracted from the Laurium mines, in southern Attica.

It was in this dramatic context that Pericles' father, Xanthippus, was recalled by the Athenians who, in the face of danger, momentarily desisted from their quarrelsome divisions. Led by the *stratēgos* Themistocles, the Greek troops destroyed the Persian fleet in September 480 B.C., in the straits of Salamis, not far from Athens. The Athenian oarsmen, recruited from among the poorest citizens (known as "thetes" in the classification established by

Solon the lawgiver at the start of the sixth century), were responsible for this decisive victory, and this encouraged them to lay claim to a political role in keeping with their military importance. As for Pericles' father, Xanthippus, he lost no time in excelling himself personally in the conflict by leading the Athenian fleet to victory off Cape Mycale, in 479 B.C., in one of the war's last engagements.

At this stage, nothing precise is known about the young Pericles, and it would be another twenty years before he came to the fore of the political scene. Ever since the ostracism of Themistocles, who was accused in 471 B.C. of having treated with the Persian enemy, it had been the *stratēgos* Cimon who exerted the most influence in the city of Athens, thanks to the military prestige that he had acquired within the framework of the Delian League, founded in 478 B.C. After the Second Persian War, Athens had in effect taken the lead in an alliance designed to prevent a return of the Persians to the Aegean. This was centered on the little island of Delos, in the middle of the Cyclades archipelago. Although it began as an alliance freely joined, the league soon developed into an instrument in the service of the Athenians, who exploited the allied cities on the pretext of defending them against the Persian threat. Although the Athenian poorer citizens derived considerable material profit thanks to this advantageous position, their political influence within the city remained limited. To maintain the status quo, Cimon could depend upon the support of the venerable Council of the Areopagus, the seat of the city's most prestigious magistrates: retired archons and members of the traditional Athenian elite.

It was within that roughly sketched-in context that, in 463 B.C., Pericles entered upon the political stage as an opponent of Cimon, laying accusations against him. Once he had kicked this bothersome rival decisively into touch, there followed thirty or so years in the course of which Pericles clearly took over all the major roles in the city, while the democracy gradually became stronger. All the same, his authority at no point went unchallenged. At first he suffered attacks from all those who, led by a relative of Cimon's, Thucydides of Alopeke (who should not be confused with the historian of the same name), opposed the rise to power of the people (the *dēmos*) in the city. Even after the ostracism of this dangerous rival, in 443 B.C., Pericles was assailed by virulent criticisms, as is testified by the attacks launched, in the course of the 430s, against several of those close to him—namely, Anaxagoras the philosopher; Aspasia, Pericles' partner; and the sculptor Phidias.

The mark that Pericles made upon the city was nevertheless undeniable. In the first place, it was he who pressed for the most prestigious magistracies to be open even to the most poverty-stricken of the citizens; next, the census disqualifications that had been established at the beginning of the sixth century were progressively removed, although access to the post of archon continued to be denied to the thetes. It was also thanks to Pericles' initiative that pay, in the form of *misthoi*, was for the first time introduced as remuneration for taking part in civic life. By the end of the 450s, the juries serving in Athenian courts were reimbursed so that the least wealthy citizens could be in a position to serve in lawsuits without fear of losing a day's wages. From being purely a formality, democracy gradually became a reality. Meanwhile, Pericles initiated a policy of major public works, the building of the Parthenon between 447 and 438 B.C. being its most dazzling manifestation; and, finally, he completed the construction of the Long Walls that linked the town to its port, Piraeus, and also built a war-fleet, to the great advantage of the thetes, who manned the triremes and received a wage for this. In this respect, internal democratization and external imperialism kept in step as they developed.

So it was by no means by chance that Pericles also became a passionate defender of Athenian interests within the Delian League. In, at the latest, 454 B.C., at the height of its influence, the federal treasury was transferred to the Acropolis. Now the Athenians could draw on it as they wished, in order to finance the functioning of their democracy. But among their allies, these developments gave rise to discontent that was all the more fervent given that the Persian peril had been dispelled as early as the 460s. With the swearing of the Peace of Callias in 449 B.C., the situation became critical. This treaty drew a final line under the confrontation that began with the Persian Wars, thereby rendering the maintenance of the Delian League pointless. However, Athens refused to dissolve this alliance, from which it acquired substantial profits; and Pericles had no compunction about putting down the uprisings that followed, in Euboea in 446 B.C. and then a long war against Samos, which lasted from 441 to 439.

Meanwhile, over and above these sporadic revolts, the democratic city had to cope with the growing hostility of Sparta and its Peloponnesian allies. Alarmed by Athens's rise to power, the Spartans headed an alliance designed to counter its influence. After a series of clashes between their respective allies, followed by a brief interlude of calm—the "Thirty Years' Peace" of 446 B.C.—tensions rose again until, in 431 B.C., the conflict erupted openly. This was the start of the Peloponnesian War. It was to last for twenty-seven years and end in the defeat of Athens in 404 B.C. It was Pericles who elaborated the strategy that, during the early years, made it possible for the Athenians to resist the Peloponnesians despite the latter's numerical superiority and their redoubtable infantry. Thanks to their own superiority at sea and their impregnable defense system, the Athenians even appeared to be in a good position to triumph. But from 430 onward, a serious "plague" ravaged the city, and one year later Pericles was dead, carried off by this scourge.

Those few milestones trace a complex biographical path, the subtle twists and turns of which it is hard to pinpoint. The fact is that the ancient sources are full of gaps and can seldom convey a clear idea of the role that Pericles played in the evolution of the city of Athens in the mid-fifth century.

SOURCES: THE ANCIENT CONSTRUCTION OF THE FIGURE OF PERICLES

I should first point out that the epigraphical and archaeological sources throw very little light upon the *stratēgos*'s actions. No decree proposed by Pericles has come down to us, and he is mentioned by name in only two inscriptions. The first, engraved more than a century after his death, records that, as *khorēgos*, he financed three tragedies (including *The Persians*) and a satyr play, by Aeschylus. The second, on which Pericles' name was restored by epigraphists, alludes to his involvement in the construction of a fountain in the sanctuary of Eleusis in Attica.[9]

The archaeological evidence leaves the historian equally at a loss. The bust of Pericles that adorns the covers of so many books is merely a marble copy dating from the Roman period. The bronze original, sculpted by Cresilas, a craftsman of Cretan origin, used to stand on the Acropolis, no doubt as a votive offering (a gift to the deity) dedicated after his death by those close to him.[10] Pericles was represented wearing his famous helmet, raised to expose his brow. In this case too, we should remember that it was an idealized image, designed to represent a function—that of *stratēgos*—rather than the individual himself, as a snapshot might do.[11]

To tackle Pericles' actions, historians are thus reduced to consulting literary sources. These are marked by two major features: first, the essential role that is played by a late text, Plutarch's *Life of Pericles*, which gathers together many pieces of evidence dating from the fifth and fourth centuries, whose relative reliability has been demonstrated by historians;[12] second, the two-edged nature of the documentation on the *stratēgos*, some of which is laudatory, some critical.

Topping the list is Herodotus, an author whose loyalties remain hard to pin down. That is not really surprising. In the course of his work devoted to the Persian Wars and their cause, this historian, a younger contemporary of the *stratēgos*, mentions Pericles only once. Despite the absence of any tangible evidence, many interpreters nevertheless portray Herodotus as an enthusiastic partisan of the *stratēgos*.[13] He was living in Athens in the 450–440s and was even thought to have slipped in a discreet laudatory reference to Pericles when he recounted a dream that his mother had had just before the baby's birth.[14] However, there is nothing to support this hypothesis, which rests upon a questionable assumption—namely, that "the father of history must surely have been a friend of the father of democracy." The fact is, though, that in his *Histories* Herodotus gives a critical account, if not of Pericles himself, at least of his ancestors, and does not hesitate to record traditions hostile to the Alcmaeonids and to Pericles' father, Xanthippus.[15] The historian is certainly no totally committed eulogist of Athens. Even if he admired the city that emerged victorious from the Persian Wars, he expressed barely veiled criticisms of the imperialist power that, guided by Pericles, oppressed the Ionian Greeks within the framework of the Delian League. As a native of Halicarnassus, he was well placed to see that his own community had simply exchanged one form of domination for another, when it passed from Persian control into that of the Athenians.

While Herodotus's view of Pericles may lead to some confusion, that is not the case of other contemporary testimonies. The criticism of the comic poets is undeniably bitter, as are the comments of Ion of Chios and Stesimbrotus of Thasos. However, Thucydides, the historian of the Peloponnesian War, was clearly full of admiration.

In Pericles' lifetime, in the theater, comic poets such as Cratinus and Hermippus were quick to depict the *stratēgos* as a ridiculous figure.[16] The comic authors were writing about the contemporary scene, and their often violent and sometimes abusive plays were performed before the entire city, on the occasion of the great religious festivals in honor of Dionysus. Most of those comedies have come down to us only as fragments, but they nevertheless do allow us to sense the virulence of the accusations launched against Pericles. The poets reproached him for his tyrannical behavior and, above all, for connections of his that were harmful to the city. On the stage, Pericles was represented sometimes as an all-powerful leader, sometimes as a puppet manipulated by his friends (such as Damon) or his lovers (such as Aspasia).[17]

All the same, those theatrical works are tricky for a historian to handle: in the first place, for the very reason that they are fragmentary and this often makes it difficult to reconstruct their authors' intentions; second, because they aim to shock and deliberately magnify certain characteristics in order to provoke laughter, in what seems to be a ritualized verbal ranting; and finally, because they inevitably make their criticism personal and always attack clearly identified figures—rather than political and social mechanisms. Attacks *ad personam* are one of the mainsprings of comedy, which defines itself by naming names (*onomasti komoidein*).[18] So it is that Comedy invariably tends to concentrate exclusively on individuals whom it certainly denigrates but nevertheless positions very much centerstage.

The extant fragments of Ion of Chios and Stesimbrotus of Thasos are equally difficult to interpret. Ion of Chios, who was contemporary with Pericles, excelled in a range of public genres, including tragedy and dithyrambs. When he visited Athens, he was a guest of Cimon, whom he describes in flattering terms, whereas he denigrates the behavior of Pericles, particularly at the time of the war against Samos.[19] As for Stesimbrotus of Thasos, he was equally ill-disposed toward the *stratēgos*. In his treatise on *Themistocles, Thucydides, and Pericles*, he launches into a classic attack on these three Athenian political leaders, criticizing both their upbringing and their characters.[20] It is not surprising that he criticized the seemingly high-handed behavior of Pericles; in the Greek world, lifestyles were an integral part of the definition of politics.[21]

These many attacks were the source of a tradition hostile to Pericles. Thucydides (the historian) was indisputably at the origin of an idealized representation of the *stratēgos*.[22] This historian, who was himself a *stratēgos* before he was exiled from Athens in 424, presents, in his *History of the Peloponnesian War*, an idealized account of the actions of Pericles, reconstructing several of his speeches, including the famous funeral oration delivered in 431 in honor of the Athenians killed in the first year of the war. Yet Thucydides gives a detailed account of only the last two years of Pericles' life. In part 1 of his *History*, which contains an account of the *pentēkontaetia*, the fifty-year period between the end of the Persian Wars and the start of the Peloponnesian War, the *stratēgos* is mentioned, fleetingly, only three times: when he beat the Sicyonians and attacked Oiniadae in 454 (1.111.2), when he defeated Euboea in 446 (1.114), and when he crushed the revolt in Samos in 440/39 (1.116–117). In effect, Pericles takes on the foremost roles only at the end of book I and already disappears halfway through book II (2.65) in this work that runs to a total of eight books. Thucydides dwells upon the *stratēgos* only as an actor in the Peloponnesian War and is not concerned to present a detailed account of his life before the outbreak of those hostilities. The historian is, in any case, interested in power and its mechanisms more than individuals themselves—although he does take care to underline the mark that Pericles left on Athenian political life (2.65).[23]

Throughout the fourth century, the ancient sources continue to oscillate between praise and blame, depending on the objectives of the authors and those of their public. With very few exceptions, the attitude of the philosophers is negative. Among Socrates' disciples, Pericles becomes a subject of reflection both political and philosophical, and soon turns into an anti-model.

Antisthenes (445–365), an admirer of Sparta and full of contempt for democracy, criticizes Pericles openly and showers insults upon his companion, Aspasia. As for Plato, he presents the *stratēgos* as a dangerous demagogue who corrupts the masses and is incapable even of raising his own children in a suitable manner. The Socratics thus used Pericles as a foil, within the framework of critical thinking about democracy and its innately vicious functioning.

At the other end of the spectrum, the Attic orators are more inclined to celebrate Pericles, although the *stratēgos* is frequently eclipsed by the brilliant aura surrounding Solon. Their discreet but positive comments may be explained by the fact that they were addressing a popular public rather than a select audience such as that of philosophic circles, in which anti-democratic views could be expressed more freely.[24]

In the last third of the fourth century, Aristotle and his school presented two contrasting pictures of Pericles. In his *Politics*, Aristotle turns the *stratēgos* into the very embodiment of *phronēsis*, prudence—that is to say, the ability to deliberate skilfully in an ever-changing world.[25] Meanwhile, the author of the *Constitution of the Athenians*—whether Aristotle himself or a member of his school—unequivocally criticizes the introduction of the *misthos* and accuses Pericles of having sought by this means to corrupt the masses. In this way, he picks up the Platonic line.

In this succession of ancient texts, there is one that, although late, is a decisive link in the chain: *The Life of Pericles* by Plutarch (A.D. 46 to 125) This Greek gentleman, a native of Chaeronea in Boeotia, composed his *Parallel Lives* in the early second century A.D., at a time when Greece had already long since fallen under Roman domination. When setting up this particular parallel between a Greek and a Roman, Plutarch chose, in the name of the prudence that characterized them both, to compare Pericles and Fabius Maximus. This work, which was influenced by Plato, gathered together, in the form of more or less explicit citations, most of the comic fragments on Pericles, the criticisms of the *stratēgos* made by Ion of Chios and Stesimbrotus of Thasos, and also the hostile remarks of Antisthenes and the Socratics. So Plutarch's handling of the subject inevitably presents today's historians with a delicate problem.

In the first place, his work is marked by a desire to construct a unifying framework—a *Life*—drawing on material that, although abundant, is heterogeneous. This profusion of texts often leads Plutarch to attempt to reconcile the irreconcilable and, in his account, to juxtapose totally opposed traditions. For example, he devotes equal space to, on the one hand, Thucydides' cool analysis of the underlying causes of the Peloponnesian War and, on the other, to the vituperations of the comic poets who delighted in emphasizing the role that Pericles' partner, Aspasia, played in the outbreak of hostilities.

In this combination of as much praise as blame, Plutarch himself conveys a mixed view of Pericles' actions. On the one hand, he is clearly intent on celebrating the man behind the great architectural works—the monuments that, at the time when he was composing his *Lives*,[26] testified to the ancient power of Greece; yet, at the same time, as a good disciple of Plato and an admirer of Cimon, he wanted to denigrate Pericles, the democrat. This tension sometimes makes it difficult to grasp his true intentions. To resolve this contradiction, Plutarch divides the life of his hero into two artificially opposed parts. He suggests that at first Pericles behaved as a demagogue, showering gifts upon the masses and thereby fostering pernicious habits among them (9.1). Then, when his own position was definitively assured, following the ostracism of Thucydides of Alopeke, Pericles is portrayed as radically changing his attitude and, without hesitation, restraining the aspirations of the people, at the risk of incurring its anger (15.2–3).

One further difficulty makes interpreting Plutarch's text a particularly delicate matter. Because he lived at the time of the Caesars, he does not always understand the facts that he claims to describe. He tends to interpret Pericles' actions in the light of his own time, attributing to his hero the behavior or even the authority of a Roman emperor. The fact that the people might exercise truly effective sovereignty never even crosses his mind.

Exhaustive though it is, the *Life of Pericles* does not herald an end to the controversies that surrounded the figure of the *stratēgos*. A few decades after the death of Plutarch, Aelius Aristides (A.D. 117–185), in his speech *Against Plato; in Defence of the Four*, without the slightest reservation, pays emphatic homage to the democratic leader. On the strength of Thucydides' authority, he maintains that Pericles never corrupted the people in the slightest way, contrary to the popular view among Platonists, echoed by Plutarch.[27]

In roughly the same period, Pausanias adopted a radically opposed view in his *Periegesis*, in a passage in which he digressed on the subject of the famous men of the Athenian past. While happy to praise the military exploits of Themistocles, Xanthippus, and Cimon against the Persians (8.52.1–2), he expresses the greatest scorn for the warmongers of the Peloponnesian conflict, "especially the most distinguished of them." His judgment is categorical: "they might be said to be murderers, almost wreckers of Greece."[28] Scandalized by the Greek internal wars, Pausanias does not deign even to mention the name of Pericles and assigns him to a kind of *damnatio memoriae*.

Without any clear suggestion of a cause-and-effect link, the memory of the *stratēgos* thereafter progressively continued to fade right down to the early fifteenth century, at which point the humanist Leonardo Bruni, inspired by the writings of Thucydides and Aelius Aristides, revived it.[29]

From this rapid survey of the sources of Antiquity, it is possible to draw two clear conclusions. The first is somewhat disappointing: to produce a straightforward biography of Pericles involves guesswork or even an illusion, unless one imitates Plutarch and creates an imaginary itinerary that reveals more about the preconceptions of its creator than it does about the trajectory of the *stratēgos*. For what can be said about Pericles' youth prior to 472, the date when he financed Aeschylus's *Persians*? What do we really know of his life between 461 and 450? No linear account of the *stratēgos*'s life is conceivable—unless, that is, one cheats with the information provided and arranges it into a chronological order that, although coherent, is arbitrary. Only the last three years of his existence, from 432 to 429, rise to the surface in this ocean of ignorance, and they do so thanks to the unique shaft of light shed by Thucydides' *Peloponnesian War*.

Does this amount to an insurmountable defect that rules out writing any book about Pericles? Not at all. A perusal of the ancient sources in fact indicates another, surely more fruitful avenue of research. The ancient sources, ranging from Thucydides to Plutarch and from the comic poets to Aelius Aristides, all, in their own ways, ponder the relations established between Pericles the individual and the community in which he lived. Is Pericles an all-powerful figure or simply a ventriloquist who expresses the aspirations of the people? A wide range of answers can be envisaged, and they deserve to be closely scrutinized. And this is the line of investigation that will serve as a guiding thread for the present inquiry, which will be organized into two major parts, the one historical, the other historiographical.

The first section will start with a study of the genealogical, economic, and cultural trump cards that were held by the young Pericles at the point when he stealthily embarked upon his political career (chapter 1). The following two chapters will be devoted to the bases of Pericles' power. These were clearly twofold: his success rested on military glory—as head of the Athenian armies and navies (chapter 2)—and on his expert handling of public discourse—to the point of embodying the orator par excellence who fascinated the Athenians from the Assembly tribune (chapter 3).

As *stratēgos*, Pericles was deeply implicated in the development of Athenian imperialism. With no misgivings at all, he ruthlessly crushed the revolts of the allied cities, adopting in this respect a policy that was widely favored in Athens: possibly his sole originality lay in his theorizing its necessity and establishing imperial power on an unprecedented scale (chapter 4). Within the city, Pericles actively promoted the genesis of a truly democratic economic policy—a policy that was founded on widespread redistributions of the city's wealth to a newly redefined civic community (chapter 5).

Both within the city and beyond it, Pericles responded to the demands of the people or even anticipated them. The pressure that the *dēmos* exerted could be felt at every level. It was because the least of his actions and gestures were all scrutinized and, frequently, criticized that Pericles seems to have kept his relatives, friends, and lovers at a distance. He no doubt hoped in this way to ward off the many attackers who described him as a man who was manipulated, ready to put the interests of those close to him before the well-being of the Athenian people (chapters 6 and 7). Such reproaches were likewise leveled against his attitude toward the city gods, for he was also accused of fostering friendships with impious men (chapter 8).

At Pericles' death, these weighty suspicions faded away: the *stratēgos* now, a least for a part of tradition, came to symbolize a golden age that was gone forever. A number of ancient authors even treated the passing of Pericles as a pivotal moment in the history of Athens, as if his death marked the starting point of the city's decadence—a view that calls for serious qualification (chapter 9).

Having completed this historical journey, it will be necessary to reconsider this whole investigation and return to the question formulated right at the outset—namely, how did the Athenian democracy react to its experience of this great man? In short, we must try to understand Athens as a reflection of Pericles and Pericles as a reflection of Athens (chapter 10).

Pericles was neither a hero nor a nobody. He should be restored to his full complexity, and we should endeavor to free ourselves from a historiography that, over a long period, either ignored him or exposed him to public contempt, before eventually transforming him into a veritable icon of democracy. The Periclean myth is a recent re-creation. Up until the end of the eighteenth century, Pericles was for the most part judged with disdain, if not arrogantly ignored. Blinded by Roman and Spartan models, the men of the Renaissance and the Enlightenment regarded the *stratēgos* as an unscrupulous demagogue who headed a degenerate regime (chapter 11). It was not until the nineteenth century—and, in particular, Thucydides' return to favor—coupled with the advent of parliamentary regimes in Europe—that, progressively, a new Pericles emerged in the writings of historians, where he was now presented as an enlightened bourgeois. Prepared by Rollin and Voltaire and completed by George Grote and Victor Duruy, this slow metamorphosis engendered the figure of an idealized Pericles who, still today, is enthroned in school textbooks on a par with Louis XIV (chapter 12).

CHAPTER 1

An Ordinary Young Athenian
Aristocrat?

In the *Politics*, Aristotle defines the elite by a collection of characteristics that distinguishes it from the common people: good birth (*eugeneia*), wealth (*ploutos*), excellence (*aretē*), and, finally, education (*paideia*).[1] These were the various aspects, combined in different degrees, that defined social superiority in the Greek world. Pericles was clearly abundantly endowed with all those distinctive attributes. However, in a democratic context, such advantages could sometimes turn out to operate as obstacles or even handicaps. Not all forms of superiority were acceptable in themselves, but needed to adopt a form that was tolerated by the *dēmos* for fear of arousing its mistrust or even anger: in Athens, the forms taken by distinction constituted an object of implicit negotiation between members of the elite and the people.

Such compromises were evident at every level. Membership of a prestigious lineage was undeniably an advantage, provided that the people did not doubt the family's attachment to the new regime that Cleisthenes had set in place. Likewise, wealth was a blessing for anyone who wished to launch himself into political life, but only if that fortune was judged to be legitimate by the Athenians and if a considerable proportion of those riches was used to benefit the community as a whole. Finally, the asset of a refined education was of capital importance in a context in which influence was clearly associated with an ability to hold forth in the Assembly; but if that skill was employed in a thoughtless manner it could be taken for a form of cultural arrogance that the average citizen would not tolerate.

Pericles' entrance upon the Athenian political stage took place in the context of this generalized negotiation. His first dextrous steps into public life enabled him to win over the people by demonstrating that his superiority, at once genealogical, economic, and also cultural, was compatible with the democratic ideology and the practices that were taking shape.

THE TRUMP CARDS HELD BY THE YOUNG PERICLES

Eugeneia: An Equivocal Ancestry

At the time of Pericles' birth, strictly speaking, there was in Athens no "aristocracy" in the sense of a system in which hereditary power was held by a few great families. Yet for a long time historians believed that in the Archaic period, the city was managed by a handful of lineages that monopolized all powers. In truth, however, that is a mistaken interpretation of the ancient sources, read through the deforming prism of ancient Rome. The city of Athens was, quite simply, not organized into *genē*. In the Archaic and the Classical periods, *genē* essentially designated families—or groups of families—from which the priest or priestess of a civic cult was chosen; and no more than a marginal political influence seems to have been exerted by those groups.[2]

However, this does not mean that descent counted for nothing in early-fifth-century Athens. There were undoubtedly certain powerful families (*oikiai*) that played a primary role in city life. All Athenians belonged to lineages that it is possible to pick out thanks to the names borne by their members. Pericles was called "the son of Xanthippus," and his eldest son was called "Xanthippus, son of Pericles." The rules for passing a name down resulted in the eldest son acquiring the name of his paternal grandfather, thereby creating an interplay of recognizable echoes and conferring a cumulative aura upon patronyms. Pericles, the younger son of Xanthippus and Agariste, in point of fact came from a doubly prestigious line (figure 1), but was not a member of any kind of "nobility," in the sense that the word still carries today.

His father Xanthippus, son of Ariphron, led the Athenian and other Greek troops to victory in the battle of Cape Mycale, at the end of the Second Persian War. The author of the *Constitution of the Athenians* even calls him the "people's champion" (*prostatēs tou dēmou*),[3] and his influence was considered sufficiently alarming for him to be ostracized by the Athenians in 485 B.C. However, contrary to one deeply rooted historiographical myth, he

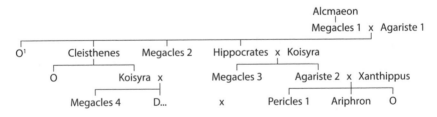

FIGURE 1. Pericles' genealogical tree.

did not belong to the postulated *genos* of the Bouzygae:[4] neither Herodotus nor Thucydides nor even Plutarch have anything to say about this. In reality, the belief rests upon a mistaken reading of a fragment from a comic poet, Eupolis, who had one of his characters declare: "Is there any orator that can be cited now? The best is the Bouzyges, the cursed one [*alitērios*]!"[5] But, according to one ancient commentator, the poet, far from alluding to Pericles, was referring to a certain Demostratus, an orator who played a by no means negligible role in Athens at the time of the Peloponnesian War.[6]

In truth, little is known about Xanthippus's clan except that its lineage was judged sufficiently prestigious for the Alcmaeonids to consent to give it one of their daughters in marriage (Herodotus, 6.131). So initially, it was actually through his maternal descent that Pericles came to the city's notice.[7] The Alcmaeonids were certainly one of the most illustrious Athenian clans, but they did not constitute a *genos* since no hereditary priesthood was associated with them. All the same, theirs was a powerful *oikos* (the term used by Herodotus, 6.125.5), and that was no small matter. Their influence was already evident even before the establishment of Pisistratus's tyranny in 561 B.C. According to tradition, Alcmaeon, the eponymous ancestor of the lineage, was the first Athenian to win the chariot race at Olympia,[8] thereby shedding glory upon his entire lineage. Then, a few years before Pericles' birth—in 508/7 B.C.—another Alcmaeonid, Cleisthenes, initiated a thorough reform of the civic organization, thereby establishing the bases of the future democratic system. And it was Agariste, the niece of Cleisthenes the lawgiver, who married Xanthippus and gave birth to Pericles.[9]

Nevertheless, the Alcmaeonids' reputation was, to say the least, equivocal. Although they enjoyed great fame, it was to some extent of a pernicious nature: they were accused not only of being polluted (*enageis*) by the impiety of their ancestors but also of maintaining suspicious relations with the tyrants of Athens. The accusation of impiety, first, dated from the earliest days of Archaic Athens. In the 630s B.C., a certain Cylon, a victor in the Olympic Games, intoxicated by his success, attempted to seize power in Athens, aided by the tyrant of Megara. His attempt proved to be a lamentable failure: besieged by the Athenians, the conspirators took refuge on the Acropolis, close to the statue (*agalma*) of the goddess, assuming the posture of suppliants who, as such, enjoyed the protection of the gods.[10] Having agreed to leave this sanctuary, following assurances that they would be spared, they were nevertheless massacred, at the instigation of the Alcmaeonids, who, because of this, contracted a taint that would be passed down from generation to generation.

This episode acquired an ambivalent meaning: a glorious one if the emphasis was laid upon the Alcmaeonids' opposition to tyranny, but a shaming one if it was laid upon the impiety implied by the murder of suppliants. Indeed, the Spartans had no hesitation in invoking this old story as grounds for insisting on two occasions that the Alcmaeonids, whom they judged to be embarrassing, should be exiled: the first time was in 510 B.C., when King Cleomenes demanded, successfully, that Cleisthenes be banished (Herodotus, 5.72); the second time was in 431, just before the outbreak of the Peloponnesian War, when the Spartans demanded, this time unsuccessfully, that Pericles be exiled (Thucydides, 1.126.2).[11]

Over and above that original misdeed, the Alcmaeonids were also accused of maintaining equivocal links with tyrants. To be sure, on several occasions they opposed Athenian tyrants, not only at the time of Cylon's abortive attempt but also when Pisistratus seized power.[12] Furthermore, the Alcmaeonid Cleisthenes was one of the main instigators of the fall of Hippias, the city's last tyrant, in 510 B.C. However, far from simply representing resistance to tyrants, the Alcmaeonids were associated with them through close matrimonial relations. Even after clashing with Pisistratus, the Alcmaeonid Megacles had no qualms at all about proposing his own daughter as a wife for him (Herodotus, 1.60). And it should also be said that Megacles himself had married the daughter of yet another tyrant, Cleisthenes of Sicyon, after a determined struggle to win her hand.[13] According to Herodotus, this was the marriage that made the Alcmaeonids famous throughout the whole of Greece.[14] Nor is that all, for Cleisthenes had not always been a fierce opponent of tyrants. Before he was exiled, he worked in close collaboration with the Pisistratids, for he had been elected archon during the period when they were in power.[15] This smoldering reputation dogged the family right down to the Persian Wars: at the time of the Battle of Marathon, in 490, the Alcmaeonids were accused of attempting to betray their country at the point when Hippias, who had lived in exile since 510, made the most of the Persian invasion in an attempt to return to power in the city.[16] And in the course of the years between the Persian Wars, several members of the Alcmaeonid family fell victim to the newly introduced procedure of ostracism, which was designed to remove Athenians who aimed for a return to tyranny.[17]

This dubious notoriety is reflected in a condensed form in the story of Agariste's dream, which Herodotus relates (6.131). According to this historian, just before the birth of the future *stratēgos*, the mother of Pericles dreamed that she gave birth to a lion. If regarded as a sign sent by the gods, the dream seemed a mark of special favor, prefiguring an exceptional destiny for the child about to be born. However, this was a sign that was, to say the least, ambiguous: in the first place, because that dream evoked legends surrounding the births of certain tyrants, in particular that of Cypselus of

Corinth;[18] and second, because the dream's content was in itself equivocal. Ever since Homer, the lion had been associated with royal power and, as such, clashed seriously with the imaginary representations of democracy. In Athens, it sometimes happened that politicians were described as "the people's dogs" because they were the faithful guardians of its interests; however, they could never be compared to lions without running the risk of ostracism![19]

On his mother's side, then, Pericles came from a lineage that was certainly illustrious but whose fame was problematic. To invoke its prestige was to risk being reproached not only for impiety at a religious level but also for tyrannical aspirations at a political level. Within a democratic context, a prestigious birth was certainly a double-edged weapon that had to be handled very carefully indeed, humoring the people's touchiness as much as possible.

Ploutos: An Illegitimate Fortune?

Wealth too seemed an advantage for a young Athenian seeking to enter political life, but at the same time that fortune had to be regarded as legitimate by the *dēmos*. This it certainly was in Pericles' case, even if embarrassing stories continued to circulate about the lust for riches of his maternal family, the Alcmaeonids.

There can be no doubt that Pericles was rich, for he was a beneficiary of the "legitimate inheritance" that he held from his father (*ton patrōion kai dikaion plouton*).[20] What did this consist of? Land, essentially: the young man possessed country property as well as the house in which he lived in Athens itself. That estate was probably situated in the Cholargos deme, a few kilometers to the north of the town, and it was farmed profitably by a well-trusted slave.[21] The size of this property must have been considerable, for at the time of the start of the Peloponnesian War, Pericles promised to hand over "his land and his farms" (*tēn khōran kai tas epauleis*) if the Spartan king Archidamus decided to spare his properties on account of the links of hospitality by which he and Pericles were connected.[22] Thucydides, who was a contemporary of these events, even refers to "his fields and his properties [*tous de agrous tous heautou kai oikias*]"[23]—the plurals used here are significant. Young Pericles' fortune was thus shored up by the possession of land—a form of wealth that was judged to be particularly legitimate in the Athens of the early fifth century.

Another factor enables us to calculate the level of wealth that the family fortune comprised. While still a very young man, in 472 B.C., Pericles was rich enough to be expected to provide a liturgy—that is to say, a type of public service for which only the most affluent Athenians and metics were liable.[24]

In the fourth century, out of several tens of thousands of taxpayers, barely one thousand individuals were liable for liturgies; Demosthenes even declared that no more than sixty individuals contributed liturgies each year (*Against Leptines* [20], 21).[25] Even if those figures represent an underestimate, they do convey some idea of the financial affluence of the young Pericles, who must certainly have been one of the *pentakosiomedimnoi*, the group of the richest men of Athens. Ever since the reforms attributed to Solon, the lawgiver, at the beginning of the sixth century B.C., the citizens had been divided into four census classes. These may well have been based on agricultural incomes, and the *pentakosiomedimnoi* constituted the very top category. The right to participate in civic institutions depended partly upon this classification, for the Council of the Areopagus was at that time open only to the two top census classes.

Wealthy though he was, Pericles had to face a number of troubling rumors about the manner in which his Alcmaeonid ancestors had acquired their fortune and had used it.[26] An early anecdote recounted by Herodotus testifies to this latent hostility. In the mid-sixth century, Alcmaeon, son of Megacles, had assisted King Croesus when the latter went to consult the Delphic oracle. When the Lydian sovereign summoned him to Sardis in order to recompense his services, he offered him as much gold as he could carry away on his person. Thereupon, Alcmaeon had himself fitted out with made-to-measure clothes and boots that would accommodate as much gold as possible. Worse still, he had no compunction about rolling in a heap of gold powder so as to fill his hair with it, and he even stuffed his mouth with the precious metal, "resembling anything on earth rather than a human being, with his mouth crammed full and his entire body bulging."[27] Alcmaeon consequently became a figure of fun to Croesus and thereafter also to Herodotus's readers. This anecdote portrayed the Alcmaeonids as individuals with an inexhaustible thirst for the riches obtainable from Eastern rulers, even at the cost of their dignity as citizens. Alcmaeon's attitude rebounded upon his descendants: at the end of his digression on the Alcmaeonids, Herodotus took care to remind his readers that Alcmaeon was an ancestor of Pericles, the son of Xanthippus (6.131.2).

That was not the only shady story that circulated about the Alcmaeonids' wealth. The Alcmaeonid Cleisthenes, who was rich enough to finance the reconstruction of the temple of Apollo in Delphi after this had been burned down in 548 B.C., was accused by hostile gossip (Herodotus, 5.66) of having corrupted the Delphic Pythia, bribing her with the family fortune to ensure that his lineage always received favorable oracles.

Pericles' ancestors thus formed an object of suspicion on the score not only of the origin of their fortune, but also the way that they handled it.

Wealth, like birth, was an advantage that, to be effective, had to appear legitimate in the eyes of the Athenian people.

Paideia: A Rhetorical Athlete

One last element lay at the root of the superiority to which members of the Athenian elite laid claim: education (*paideia*). This was a capital asset that was not inherited, but acquired. Far from being innate, eloquence resulted from a lengthy apprenticeship. As one comic fragment put it, "Speaking is a gift of nature, speaking well a product of art [*tekhnē*]."[28] It was therefore essential to benefit from a careful—and often costly—education in order to acquire such competence as was indispensable in a democracy in which speech was playing an increasingly important role.

Pericles received a thorough education in rhetoric and clearly preferred oratorical exertion to physical exertions. That, at least, is what is suggested by a spicy dialogue reported by Stesimbrotus of Thasos and recorded by Plutarch,[29] in which Archidamus, the king of Sparta, questions Pericles' main opponent, Thucydides, the son of Melesias, wanting to know which of the two men is the better at wrestling. Somewhat embarrassed, Thucydides apparently replied: "Whenever I throw him in wrestling, he disputes the fall, and carries his point, and persuades the very men who saw him fall." To discredit his adversary, Thucydides here resorts to two arguments that were often employed to denigrate the sophists, the masters of eloquence who offered their lessons to the highest bidders: on the one hand, their excessive evaluation of speech over action and, on the other, their obvious disdain for physical prowess.[30] Pericles thus found himself dismissed as a mere manipulative sophist. Quite apart from its polemical aspect, this anecdote drew attention to the exceptional quality of the education received by Pericles, to whom two famous teachers were attributed, one a foreigner, Anaxagoras of Clazomenae, the other an Athenian, Damon of Oa.[31]

The former, Anaxagoras, developed a rationalist or even secular line of thought that valued experimentation. It was he, according to Plato's *Phaedrus*, who taught Pericles rhetoric.[32] However, the links between the two men are so tenuous that some historians doubt whether they even existed.[33] In the case of the latter, Damon, we are on firmer ground. This Athenian initiated Pericles into *mousikē*, a combination of arts linked with music, singing, and dancing.[34] The comic poets even represent him as the principal teacher of Xanthippus's son. In a fragment preserved by Plutarch, Damon is addressed as follows: "First, then, reply to me, please, for it is said that you are the Chiron who raised Pericles."[35] His influence over the young man was thus compared to that of the fabled centaur, Chiron, who educated so many Greek heroes, including Achilles and Jason!

How can we explain how it was that a musician was so important in Pericles' education? Here, we must be careful to avoid any anachronism. Among the Greeks, *mousikē* had absolutely nothing to do with "art for art's sake." *Mousikē* was linked to mathematics and poetry and it exerted considerable power over its listeners, thereby influencing city life in the same way as public speaking did.[36] So *mousikē* and politics were more closely linked than one might imagine, and the Athenians seem to have been perfectly well aware of the fact. Indeed, they may have condemned Damon to exile on that very account: several *ostraka* found by archaeologists lend a measure of credibility to the episode that Plutarch relates, without, however, producing any formal proof.[37]

The fate of Damon certainly reflects how tricky it was to cope with culture in a democratic context. While a solid grasp of rhetoric and music was indispensable in order to shine in the Assembly, if there was the slightest hint of it being used for anti-democratic ends, it was liable to arouse mistrust among the people. Herein, perhaps, lies the explanation for the diametrically opposed choice that some members of the elite made where *paideia* was concerned. According to Stesimbrotus of Thasos, Cimon "acquired no literary education, nor any other liberal and distinctively Hellenic accomplishment; he lacked entirely the Attic cleverness and fluency of speech; in his outward bearing there was much nobility and truthfulness; the fashion of the man's spirit was, rather, Peloponnesian."[38]

For Cimon, this was a way not only of getting closer to the Spartans but also of reducing the cultural distance that separated him from the Athenian people. And this strategy of inverted distinction did, in effect, clearly contribute to the great popularity that this *stratēgos* enjoyed among his fellow citizens.

Although birth, wealth, and education constituted undeniable trump cards, they were certainly no guarantee of political success to those who held them. Those who enjoyed such genealogical, economic, and cultural assets needed to make use of them without upsetting the *dēmos*. As he gradually made his way into political life, Pericles was acutely aware of this need.

A Gradual Entry into Political Life

The *Khorēgia* of Aeschylus's Persians: Victory through Singing

Pericles tested out those various assets for the first time in 472 B.C., when he was just twenty-one or twenty-two years old. Thanks to an inscription engraved in the fourth century (*IG* II² 2318), which lists the victors in the

Great Dionysia, we know that in that year he was designated a *khorēgos* and that he, in association with Aeschylus, was declared the victor. We thus know that Pericles was responsible for financing the tetralogy composed by the poet (three tragedies and one satyr play), which included *The Persians*, the most ancient tragedy to be preserved *in toto* and which set on stage Themistocles' victory at Salamis.

What was the exact nature of this civic gesture? A *khorēgos*'s task was to recruit the best candidates for a chorus, which comprised between twelve and fifteen people; he also had to employ a professional to train the chorus-members, and provide a venue (a *khorēgeion*) sufficiently spacious for the chorus to rehearse its complex moves in comfort. Finally, his mission included providing material support for the entire cast and meeting the costs of the actual performance, in particular those of the masks and costumes. These were by no means negligible expenses: as far as we know, they ran to between 3,000 and 5,000 drachmas in the case of a tragic *khorēgia*.[39] The fact that Pericles served as a *khorēgos* certainly indicates that he had already inherited the family fortune; by this date, Xanthippus must already have been dead.

We still need to understand exactly why Pericles felt obliged to take on this heavy responsibility when he had barely come of age. Of course, he may not have had any choice in the matter, for any wealthy Athenian could expect to have a *khorēgia* imposed upon him. All the same, it sometimes happened that citizens forestalled this so as not to appear to be forced into the task and also because they hoped that political advantages would accrue to them. The ambiguity of the system that obtained in Athens lay in the fact that liturgies—which included the *khorēgia*—were at once obligations imposed by the city and, at the same time, a means of winning popularity for the individuals who carried out those obligations with munificence.

If this duty, despite its costliness, carried a political advantage, it was because in consequence the *khorēgos* won esteem among his fellow-citizens. In the first place, before the dramatic representations took place, the *khorēgos* would occupy a prestigious position in the religious procession (*pompē*) that opened the Dionysia festival. He had the right to wear special clothing that made him stand out in the crowd; both Alcibiades and Demosthenes took care to make the most of this privilege. Furthermore, during the performance, the *khorēgos* did not necessarily remain silent. In the early fifth century, he himself might even act as the chorus leader and perform in the *orchēstra*;[40] according to this hypothesis, Pericles himself may have led the chorus in *The Persians* and delivered the speech praising Athens that Aeschylus assigned to the chorus-leader! In that case, the young man would have been speaking in the name of the collectivity for the very first time, thereby anticipating his future role as orator. This may also help us to understand the importance that *mousikē* held in the education of this young man.

Finally, when the performance was over, the *khorēgos* would increase his prestige still further if he was victorious in the dramatic competition that brought the Dionysia to a close. The names of the victors, who were selected by a panel of ten judges, were announced before the whole community assembled in the theater. The laureates, crowned with ivy, were presented with a prestigious prize: a bronze tripod for the tragic choruses and possibly a ram for the winning poets. Sometimes the *khorēgoi* would present offerings to the gods in order to keep the memory of their success alive: Themistocles was said to have had a *pinax* (a wooden tablet) painted, to celebrate his victory in the tragedy competition, as *khorēgos* for the poet Phrynichus, in 477 B.C.

One further factor may have decided Pericles to volunteer as a *khorēgos* in 472. By preempting any summons addressed to him, the young man made a sensational entrance on to the public stage, even before reaching the age when he could hope for a magistracy. The fact was that Athenian citizens had to wait until they were thirty years old before they could assume even a minor city post. Making sure of a *khorēgia* was a way of getting around that age-limit and seizing an early start in the race to make a name for himself among the Athenians.[41]

Basking in the prestige of this triumph in the Dionysia, young Pericles made his mark in the post-Salamis Athens. All the same, though, his *khorēgia* should not be interpreted as a deliberately political gesture or a way of advertising his support for Themistocles, who was then facing growing opposition that, one year later, would lead to his ostracism. Although *The Persians* does praise the victor at Salamis indirectly, there is nothing to prove that Pericles had any say in the content of the play, which was the concern solely of the poet. Besides, it was the eponymous Archon that drew lots in order to assign a *khorēgos* to a dramatist.[42] It was thus purely by chance that the young man found himself collaborating with a well-established author—namely, Aeschylus, who, since 485/4 B.C.,[43] had already won several victor's crowns. That first action needs to be evaluated correctly for, far from being a prefiguration of his political future, the 472 *khorēgia* was an opportunity for Pericles to highlight his wealth and his culture and, at the same time, show that he was using them for the greatest benefit of the community.

The Lawsuit against Cimon: Presenting Himself as an Opponent

After that first burst of glory, Pericles remained in the shadows for several years. Was it for fear of being ostracized as his father, Xanthippus, had been? That is Plutarch's version of the matter (*Pericles*, 7.1), but it is not possible to corroborate what he says. However, the young man did not remain inactive, for he proved his attachment to the city on the battlefield: again according to Plutarch, "he was courageous in warfare and willingly risked his life."[44] His real entry into political life was deferred for a while, but eventually it came about following an extremely spectacular lawsuit. As the Pseudo-Aristotle notes in his *Constitution of the Athenians* (27.1): "Having first distinguished himself when still a young man he challenged the audits of Cimon, who was a general."[45]

This came about in 463 B.C., when Pericles had just turned thirty. At this time, Cimon held great influence in the city, particularly since Themistocles had been ostracized in 471. Cimon, who was elected repeatedly as *stratēgos*, was at this time playing a prominent part in every military campaign. He led the expedition that came to the aid of Sparta after the Helots, dependents of the Spartans, taking advantage of the great earthquake that occurred in 464, had revolted against their masters. By 465, he was already to be found heading the siege of Thasos, an island in the northern Aegean that was trying to free itself from the Delian League.

In 463, while the campaign against Thasos dragged on, Cimon had to face a lawsuit centering on his rendering of accounts, an obligation that affected all magistrates.[46] The *stratēgos* was accused of accepting bribes from the king of Macedon, who was anxious to protect his kingdom from Athenian attacks. The prosecution, which was led by Pericles, came to nothing, for an obvious enough reason: up until the reforms of Ephialtes, passed by vote in the following year, renderings of accounts were all judged by the Areopagus, which was the principal supporter of Cimon's policies!

Over and above the issue of this trial, which proved favorable to Cimon, this anecdote testifies to the general role played by prosecutions in the construction of political reputations: prosecutions were above all the business of young ambitious men. While assuming the position of a prosecutor was a way to make one's name swiftly, in the long run it was a difficult position to maintain. To remain a prosecutor for too long was to risk being regarded as a sycophant, a professional prosecutor.[47] While such "sycophants" were necessary to the functioning of democracy, given the absence of any public prosecution service in Athens, they were at the same time detested because they acted for their own personal profit, in that they could receive a percentage of the fines imposed if the verdict was guilty.[48]

The reasons why Pericles involved himself personally in this process remain to be determined. Was he motivated by purely political aspirations, as an honest defender of the interests of the people? That is by no means certain. Between Cimon's lineage and that of Pericles, there was a long tradition of rivalry or even animosity that dated from the mid-sixth century, when their respective ancestors had battled to win the hand in marriage of Agariste, the daughter of the tyrant of Sicyon, a struggle in which the Alcmaeonid Megacles had emerged as victor. Furthermore, in 493, the Alcmaeonids had accused Miltiades, Cimon's father, of exercising tyranny in the Chersonese.[49] Finally, in 489, Xanthippus brought a second lawsuit against Miltiades, following the disastrous expedition to Paros: Pericles' father had identified himself with the antipathies of his in-laws, to the point of himself being tarred by the Alcmaeonids' sinister reputation.[50] In the lawsuit brought against Cimon, it is therefore hard to determine the respective parts played by private quarrels and political motivations.

However, the fact is that, after this unsuccessful political debut, Pericles seems rapidly to have acquired influence by helping to establish "the reforms of Ephialtes" in the very next year, which marked a decisive step forward in the process of the city's democratization. Nevertheless, despite the declarations to be found in the fourth-century sources, the young man's collaboration in this important institutional change is far from certain.

The Reforms of Ephialtes: Overshadowed by Pericles

In 462, Cimon set off, with a large force of hoplites, to help the Spartans, who were engaged in a struggle against the revolt of their Helots. Making the most of his absence, the Athenians adopted sweeping political reforms at the instigation of the democratic leader, Ephialtes. Most of the powers of the Areopagus, the old aristocratic council of Athens, were redistributed among popular institutions—the Assembly, the Council, and the law courts—thereby sparking off the effective democratization of the city. On his return, Cimon was unable to reverse the situation and eventually was even ostracized.

Although the ancient authors do all mention the role played in this episode by Ephialtes, they tend to treat him as a mere puppet who implemented the intentions of others. According to the *Constitution of the Athenians*, Ephialtes was secretly manipulated by Themistocles; but that is chronologically impossible, for Themistocles had been ostracized almost ten years previously! And when Plutarch mentions the reform (*Pericles*, 9.4), he portrays Ephialtes as a handy screen for the illustrious Pericles, who could already be glimpsed in Xanthippus's young son. Relegated to the shadows cast by two great men—Themistocles upstream and Pericles downstream—Ephialtes was soon eclipsed in the political memory of Athens.[51]

That effacement can certainly be explained by the reformer's premature disappearance. Soon after carrying off this great political victory, Ephialtes was killed "by night, in circumstances that remain obscure."[52] According to a tradition that goes back to Idomeneus of Lampsacus, a close disciple of Epicurus, Pericles was not uninvolved in this sordid affair. It is suggested that he "cunningly assassinated [or arranged for the assassination of] Ephialtes, the demagogue, who had been his friend and companion in political action, simply because he was jealous and envied Ephialtes' popularity [*doxa*]."[53] But, as Plutarch suggests, in all probability, those were mere baseless rantings. This serious allegation, reported one hundred and fifty years after the event, is certainly intended to blacken the reputation of Pericles, the "demagogue." But, quite apart from its doubtful veracity, Idomeneus's accusation reflects a more general tendency of the ancient sources: they are prone to credit famous men with all important actions, whether positive or negative, that occurred in their own lifetimes.

In effect, the Epicurean polemicist simply adopts the line of thinking used by the ancient authors in their analyses of Ephialtes' reforms themselves: given that some of them ascribe to Pericles a secret influence in this episode, why not postulate his complicity in Ephialtes' assassination?

From this point of view, Idomeneus's line of argument is no more well-founded—or ill-founded—than the suggestions of the Pseudo-Aristotle or those of Plutarch. All these theories about plots are, by their very nature, impossible to prove. In truth, this entire historiographical construction centered on Pericles should be considered as doubtful: not only is the implication that Pericles had a hand in murdering Ephialtes highly improbable, but his supposed role in the reforms introduced in 462 B.C. is equally hypothetical.[54]

When they deny Ephialtes the status of a protagonist, it is in truth the Athenian people that the ancient authors are leaving in the shadows so as to focus exclusively on the dazzling aura surrounding the great man. It was not until the 450s—or even the early 440s—that Pericles truly set his mark on Athenian political life. It was only after this gradual entry into political life that he began to be elected *stratēgos* on a regular basis.

CHAPTER 2

The Bases of Periclean Power:
The *Stratēgos*

"Pericles son of Xanthippus, the foremost man of the Athenians at that time, wielding greatest influence both in speech and in action, came forward and advised them."[1] Those are the words with which the historian Thucydides introduces the Athenian leader at the moment when, in 431 B.C., the city is about to engage in war against Sparta. At this point, the historian defines the two domains that constitute the basis of the superiority of a statesman: speech and action. And it was indeed as an orator in the Assembly, expert in handling *logos*, and as a *stratēgos* in warfare, well accustomed to military command, that Pericles dominated Athenian political life for twenty or so years.

Military leader and orator: those are the two indissociable aspects of Periclean power. They rest upon a common basis, the office of a *stratēgos*. It was as a *stratēgos*, reelected time after time, that Pericles led the Athenians in warfare, showered with all the laurels of military glory; and it was also as a *stratēgos* that he was in a position to participate in the deliberations of the Council, influence its decisions and, in its name, propose the decrees that were then submitted to the vote in the Athenian Assembly.

Let us begin by shedding some light upon the institutional and military mainsprings of Pericles' authority. After describing the function of a *stratēgos* and considering the reasons why the role played by this office was so crucial in Athens, it will be necessary to analyze the way in which Pericles set up a veritable policy for glory, even to the point of singing the praises of his own successes. His valor as head of the army and navy was, however, contested by his political opponents. It has to be said that the *stratēgos* had elaborated a new military ethos that to some extent broke away from the heroic ideal peculiar to members of the Athenian elite. Throughout his life, Pericles refused to engage in warfare unless it was absolutely necessary, even at the risk of being accused of cowardice by his opponents. This rule of behavior was applied in the most spectacular fashion at the start of the Peloponnesian

War, when Pericles persuaded the Athenians to take refuge inside the town without doing battle with the Peloponnesian hoplites. It was certainly an effective strategy, but it was swiftly challenged.

THE REELECTED *STRATĒGOS*: A POPULAR MAGISTRATE

The Function of *Stratēgos*

The office of *stratēgos*, created right at the end of the sixth century, in 501–500, rapidly became the essential magistracy of classical Athens. The way that it operated was closely linked with the isonomic regime set in place by the reforms of Cleisthenes. The *stratēgoi* made up a college of ten magistrates, one for each tribe, and each elected for one year (*Constitution of the Athenians*, 22.2–3). Their number and their designation therefore depended closely upon the new organization of the civic body into the ten tribes that had been created in 508/7.

Usually, the *stratēgoi* were recruited from among the well-to-do citizens; and the simple reason for this was that, to have a chance of being elected, one had to be capable of winning the confidence of the Athenians and this involved a certain degree of education, which was, by definition, costly. All the same, nowhere does any source suggest that any census-qualification affected the right to aim for a post as a *stratēgos*.[2] In that there was no legal barrier that limited access to such a post, this new type of magistracy complied fully with the democratic practices that had been evolving progressively ever since 507 B.C.

The function of *stratēgoi* was to command the Athenian army, as indeed the etymology of the word suggests (*stratos*, the army, and *agein*, to lead). Once the Persian Wars were over, *stratēgoi* definitively supplanted the post of archon that had previously served this purpose: the polemarch was now marginalized and limited to ritual and legal functions.[3] What is the explanation for the *stratēgoi*'s rapid rise to power? The fact that they had a double advantage over the other Athenian magistrates: not only were they elected by the Assembly (which strengthened their popular legitimacy), but, furthermore, they could be renewed in their post. Ever since 487, archons had, on the contrary, been selected by lot, and they could not remain in power for more than one year, after which they were admitted to the Council of the Areopagus as figures that were, to be sure, prestigious but who, ever since Ephialtes' reforms in 462/461, had lacked any real powers.

Over and above their military vocation, the *stratēgoi* held a measure of ex officio political power. Although they could probably not convene the

Assembly on their own initiative,[4] on the other hand they did have the right to attend Council meetings, to speak in them, and, in so doing, to propose convening the *Ekklēsia* through action on the part of the *prutaneis* (the rotating Council leaders). This gave them influence over the political life of the city, especially given that their voices possessed particular weight in that they stemmed from the legitimacy of election—unlike those of members of the *Boulē*, who were selected each year simply by the drawing of lots.

It was in the fifth century that the *stratēgoi* played their most notable role. Of the fourteen political leaders known in the fifth century, as many as thirteen occupied this function, whereas in the fourth century that tendency was to be reversed: of the twenty-six politicians identified in that period, only six were elected as *stratēgoi*.[5] In the fourth century, the *stratēgos*'s function evolved into a specialized magistracy of an increasingly technical nature, as the *Constitution of the Athenians* testifies.[6] From that time onward, an increasing number of politicians no longer considered it useful to assume the function of a military leader, and this consequently lost its aura.[7]

In the fifth century, in contrast, *stratēgoi* were by no means mere technicians. According to the *Constitution of Athenians*, citizens had no hesitation in electing "generals with no experience of war but promoted on account of their family reputation" (26.1). It was a development that sometimes caused veritable military disasters. The tragic poet Sophocles, who was a *stratēgos* at the time of the expedition to Samos in 441/0 B.C.,[8] was the very embodiment of a *stratēgos* preoccupied with love rather than with death, with *eros* more than with *thanatos*. His contemporary, Ion of Chios, records having encountered him in Chios, on his way to Lesbos, "in his capacity as *stratēgos*." Having been invited to a private banquet (*sumposion*), Sophocles is said to have organized a scurrilous ruse in order to get to embrace the handsome young lad employed to serve the wine. Having succeeded in his aim, the poet was said to have exclaimed: "My dear hosts, I have been working on my strategic skills ever since Pericles claimed that, even if I know all about poetry, I know nothing of strategy. But is it not true that this stratagem of mine has been successful?"[9] Blinded, as he was, by the delights of the *sumposion*, the poet was clearly failing to distinguish the private sphere from the public, and love affairs from the conduct of warfare. This was precisely something that Pericles took care not to do, for once he had entered political life, he refused to attend even the most modest private banquet.[10] The episode also shows to what extent the magistracy of a *stratēgos* was unspecialized, even though the people did in fact take care to elect true specialists in military matters to the college of the ten *stratēgoi*—men such as the military experts Myronides and Phormion.

Among all the fifth-century *stratēgoi*, Pericles stands out as having had a quite exceptional career.

An Exceptional *Stratēgos*

Pericles was exceptional on two counts: first, the numerous times that he was reelected as *stratēgos*. He occupied the post at least fifteen times and consequently exerted a lasting influence on the destiny of the city. His first attested election took place in 448/7 and then, between 443/2 and 429/8 B.C., he was, according to Plutarch, reelected fourteen times in succession.[11] Second, Pericles may have distinguished himself from his colleagues through the manner of his elections: according to some historians, he was sometimes elected by all the Athenians (*ex hapantōn*), not solely by the members of his own tribe (*kata phulas*). This was a great honor for, in the early fifth century, elections in principle took place separately within each of the tribes. In certain years, the Akamantis tribe, to which Pericles belonged, seems to have provided the college of *stratēgoi* with two representatives. For example, in 441/440 Pericles and Glaukon both appear in the list provided by the Atthidographer, Androtion, despite the fact that they were both members of the same tribe.[12]

Since the late nineteenth century, most historians have believed that *stratēgoi* were appointed according to two different methods: while the first nine were elected by their tribes, the tenth was elected *ex hapantōn*, by the entire body of Athenians. This *stratēgos*, chosen by the entire civic community would, for that very reason, have enjoyed greater prestige than his colleagues; and it is thought that Pericles was not alone in being elected in this distinctive fashion. It is believed that, after the War of Samos in 440/439, the *stratēgos* Phormion was likewise elected in this fashion and that this soldier of genius was reelected *ex hapantōn* in 430/429 at the very time when Pericles was relieved of his responsibilities and subjected to an extremely heavy fine.[13]

However, the hypothesis of a twofold system of election remains tenuous. It is based on an extract from the *Constitution of the Athenians* (61.1) that attests that in Aristotle's day the *stratēgoi* were elected no longer by their tribes but by the people as a whole. But this passage does not record the point at which this change took place. It could very well have happened as early as the first half of the fifth century, which would explain the simultaneous presence of *stratēgoi* from the same tribe, without implying the coexistence of two different modes of election.[14] As early as Pericles' time, *stratēgoi* may have been elected by the community as a whole, and this would have bestowed upon them reinforced popular legitimacy, although it would at the same time have deprived them of the chance to stand out individually from the rest of the other *stratēgoi*.

Exceptional though Pericles' career as a *stratēgos* was, he was never invested with the preeminent position of running the business of the city on his own, as some historians have claimed. That hypothesis is based on an overhasty reading of a passage in Thucydides in which the historian mentions Pericles' return to grace soon after being removed from office in 430 B.C.: at this point the Athenians elected him *stratēgos* yet again and entrusted him with "all affairs" (*panta ta pragmata*) (2.65.4). Some interpreters have regarded this as proof that Pericles was now designated *stratēgos autokratōr* and have assumed that he had regularly held this special position in the past. However, there is nothing to support that conjecture. In Athens, "full powers" such as those were attributed only for a special mission, on a particular occasion. What Thucydides probably means to say here is nothing more than that "the Athenians had full confidence in him in all matters."[15] One might even say that, in a period of warfare, *panta ta pragmata* would refer only to a city's "military affairs"—in other words, to precisely the business for which a *stratēgos* was responsible.

The fact remains that Pericles' longevity as a *stratēgos* truly was extraordinary, given the brutal events that affected the democratic city in this period. What can be the explanation for that permanence at the head of Athenian affairs? Although it is not the only factor involved here, this string of reelections may be explained in particular by Pericles' numerous military successes. The fact is that victory was not only the aim of all *stratēgoi*, who were elected precisely to wage a war and to win it; it was also one of the motors of their continuing hold on power: victory enveloped a victorious leader in a charisma that, in return, guaranteed him popular support.

The Victorious *Stratēgos*: The Paths of Glory

The Charisma of Victory

In the course of his long career at the head of the Athenian armies and navies, Pericles won many battles. Although not himself a specialist in warfare, as Phormion was, he took care to surround himself with competent individuals, relying in particular on the aid of "Menippus, his friend and second-in-command as *stratēgos* [*hupostratēgountos*]."[16] Thanks to the latter's skills, Pericles won many victories—no fewer than nine according to Plutarch: "Being now near his end, the best of the citizens and those of his friends who survived were sitting around him holding discourse of his excellence and power, how great they had been, and estimating all his achievements and the number of his trophies,—there were nine of these which he had set up as the city's victorious general" (*Pericles*, 38.3). Among these successes there were three that particularly struck the minds of his contemporaries. One century later, the orator Lycurgus of Athens recalled that Pericles "had conquered Samos, Euboea and Aegina,"[17] all of them victories won over recalcitrant allies in the Delian League.

However, military successes were not enough. News of them needed to spread. Pericles publicized his own successes with masterly skill. His talent as a propagandist shone out in the full glare of publicity after the victory over Samos in 440/439. On this occasion, Pericles was chosen by the Athenians to deliver, in the public cemetery, the *dēmosion sēma*, the funeral oration for the soldiers who had died for their country. Thanks to his oratorical skill, this was a chance not only to celebrate the citizens who had fallen in battle, but at the same time implicitly to convey the part that he himself had played in the final victory. A number of famous phrases from this speech have been preserved for us by Plutarch and Aristotle,[18] and we know that his eulogy aroused so much admiration that "as he came down from the tribune, . . . the women clasped his hand and fastened wreaths and fillets on his head, as though he was some victorious athlete [*hōsper athlēten nikēphoron*]" (*Pericles*, 28.4). Thanks to the charm of his eloquence, Pericles was showered with a glory that likened him to the victors in athletic games. The comparison is certainly apt: the athletes who won crowns received extraordinary honours from their city—in particular, honorific statues that were raised to them in the public squares,[19] and thanks to the prestige that this bestowed upon them, some became important political leaders, one being the famous Milo of Croton, at the end of the sixth century.

To celebrate his victory over the Samians, Pericles also made the most of another comparison that was equally flattering to him. Ion of Chios tells us that he compared this success of his to Agamemnon's capture of Troy, even going so far as to proclaim himself superior to the *Iliad*'s king: "he had the most astonishingly great thoughts of himself for having subjected the Samians; whereas Agamemnon was all of ten years in taking a barbarian city, he had in nine months' time reduced the foremost and most powerful people of Ionia" (Plutarch, *Pericles*, 28.5). In this brief summary, Pericles presented himself in the guise of an epic hero, thereby appropriating the aura associated with the Homeric poems.[20]

This strategy of heroization involved not only words but also images. Even though it may not have been consecrated until after his death, in 429, the bronze effigy of Pericles set up on the Acropolis glorified his function of *stratēgos* far more emphatically than his own true features would have. Placed among the sanctuary's most prominent monuments,[21] this standing statue corresponded to a well-known type of representation of a *stratēgos*: it featured both nudity and a raised Corinthian helmet placed on the statue's head.[22] The helmet evoked Pericles' function as *stratēgos*— namely, military strategy—while the nudity likened him to the heroes, or even the gods, in accordance with the iconographic conventions of the day. The effigy thus celebrated the memory of Pericles as a great man who had defended his country.

However, such forms of self-glorification attracted virulent criticism from his political opponents, who were bent on minimizing the extent of his military successes and condemning the shameless publicity that he bestowed upon them.

A Disputed Military Reputation

At a strictly military level, Pericles was in no way an exceptional *stratēgos*. In fact, he came off badly in comparison with certain of his predecessors and colleagues, so much so that Plutarch even presents him as living off the military successes of others: "The victories of Cimon and the trophies of Myronides and Leocrates, and the many successes of Tolmides, made it the privilege of Pericles, during his administration, to enrich the city with holidays and public festivals, rather than to enlarge and protect her dominion by war."[23] So was Pericles really a mediocre *stratēgos* who exploited the victories achieved by his colleagues? Although that would probably be an exaggerated conclusion to draw, his merits certainly were less dazzling than those of other *stratēgoi* who were more familiar with military manoeuvres.[24]

His opponents belittled him not only for his modest warrior talents but also for the way that he publicized his own rare victories. After the war against Samos and the funerary speech that he delivered, he fell victim to the biting irony of Elpinike, Cimon's sister. According to a report probably made by Ion of Chios,[25] she criticized him for having "lost us many brave citizens, not in a war with Phoenicians or Medes, like my brother Cimon, but in the subversion of an allied and kindred [*suggenē*] city."[26] Pericles appears to have learned his lesson from those bitter criticisms. In the funerary speech that he delivered in 431, after the first campaigning season of the Peloponnesian War, he certainly refrained from launching into pompous praises for his own actions. According to Thucydides, he explicitly refused to appeal to Homer—as he had at the time of the war against Samos, in order to exalt the Athenian dead: "We shall need no Homer to sing our praise nor any other poet whose verses may perhaps delight for the moment but whose presentation of the facts will be discredited by the truth."[27] Perhaps this was also his way of confirming that Athens no longer needed to invoke the glorious precedents of the past in order to celebrate the battles of the present: in a kind of prefiguration of the quarrel between the Ancients and the Moderns, the city now presented itself as a model for others to follow, not simply an imitator.

Those were not the only criticisms leveled at Pericles where military matters were concerned. His opponents also blamed him for having sometimes prevented his political rivals from fighting in the best of conditions, even to the point of endangering the whole city. For example, he was said to have forbidden Cimon to take part in the battle of Tanagra, in 457, in order to prevent this troublesome rival from returning to favor. Cimon, the hero of Eurymedon, who had been living in exile for five years, had on this occasion hoped to reintegrate himself into the Athenian forces and thereby prove his devotion to his country, which was then at war with the Spartans. Having obstructed him, Pericles was obliged to show exceptional heroism himself, so as to wipe out the memory of the services offered by his rival: "For which reason, it is thought, Pericles fought most sturdily in that battle and was the most conspicuous of all in exposing himself to danger."[28]

In similar fashion, Pericles is said to have done his utmost to prevent Cimon's son, Lakedaimonius, from covering himself with glory in battle. According to Stesimbrotus of Thasos, in 433 B.C. Pericles sent Lakedaimonius to assist Corcyra, which was then in difficulty, facing Corinthian interference, but Pericles provided him with only 10 triremes, thereby rendering his task impossible.[29]

So was Pericles simply a sordid manipulator, striving to belittle the merits of his rivals in order to magnify his own and to be the only one to tread the paths of glory? We should beware of drawing overhasty conclusions that are based solely on a reading of Plutarch. In the first place, Lakedaimonius was not the only *stratēgos* sent on this mission to Corcyra: Cimon's son was accompanied by two of his colleagues, as is attested both by Thucydides and by an inscription recording the expenses devoted to this venture.[30] Furthermore, it was the people of Athens who decided on the despatch of these *stratēgoi*, not Pericles himself. The fact nevertheless remains that, in a context of perpetual rivalry between political and military leaders such as this, it was in each leader's interest to see that his rivals basked in as little glory as possible on the battlefields.

There was yet another, even more radical criticism that Pericles had to face. Throughout his career, the *stratēgos* favored a way of waging war that broke radically with the traditional customs and codes. Whenever possible, he tried to avoid fighting, thereby sometimes attracting accusations of cowardice or even treachery from opponents who found themselves short of arguments.

A Reflective *Stratēgos*: A Deliberate Rejection of Heroism

Pericles *Cunctator*?

In military matters, Pericles was inevitably bound not to benefit from more than a limited degree of charisma, by reason of the proverbial circumspection that caused Plutarch to compare him to Fabius Maximus, the *Cunctator* (delayer), the Roman consul who obstinately refused to confront the Carthaginians following the defeat at Trasimene in 217 B.C., in order to give the Romans time to reorganize their forces.

Nothing was more alien to Pericles than the kind of rashness displayed by military leaders who were in quest of glory, even at the risk of imperiling the city: "nor did he envy and imitate those who took great risks, enjoyed brilliant good fortune and so were admired as great generals."[31] In this respect, he deliberately turned his back on the heroic ideal that favored combat in all circumstances, even if it meant paying the ultimate price, in accordance with the ambivalent model set by Achilles.[32]

Pericles stood in opposition to one other *stratēgos* in particular. This was Tolmides, the son of Tolmaeus (whose very name sets out its own agenda, since *tolmē* means "rashness" in Greek). Tolmides was keen to invade Boeotia in 447, and at this point he was well placed to win over the people "on account of his previous good fortune and of the exceeding great honour bestowed upon him for his wars [*dia to timasthai . . . ek tōn polemikōn*]" (*Pericles*, 18.2). It was a frantic quest for glory that eventually ended in disaster, for the battle of Coronea was a serious defeat for Athens, in the course of which Cleinias, the father of the handsome Alcibiades, was killed.[33]

Pericles adopted the same prudent behavior in 440, at the time of the war against Samos. He preferred to embark on a lengthy siege rather than throw himself into an ill-prepared attack. As Plutarch explains, he wished to conquer the town "at the price of money and time, rather than of the wounds and deadly perils of his fellow-citizens" (*Pericles*, 27.1–2). However, such circumspection greatly aggravated the Athenians "in their impatience of delay and eagerness to fight" (ibid.). Eventually, the *stratēgos* was obliged to devise a stratagem to distract their impatience.

The fact is that, in a Greece marked by the culture of the *agōn*, Pericles' prudence was often interpreted by his opponents as pusillanimous or even as cowardly. Although effective in the long run, his rejection of direct confrontation—and of the laurels that could thereby be swiftly won—was bound to arouse strong resistance in the city. In a way, the death of Pericles perfectly symbolized the position that he had adopted: for the *stratēgos* did not perish on the field of battle, laden with honors, but was struck down by the "plague" and died in his bed, obstinately remaining confined within the city and refusing to enter into direct combat with the Spartan enemy.

All the same, it would be mistaken to make Pericles out to be a gentle lamb, let alone a bleating pacifist who rejected any form of conflict. What the *stratēgos* rejected was not warfare in itself, but rather a particular way of waging it—that is to say, ill-prepared and without taking into consideration the balance of power between the forces involved. After all, Pericles shamelessly put down the revolts of his allies,[34] and himself played a crucial role in unleashing the Peloponnesian War, as Thucydides confirms: "Being the most powerful man of his time and the leader of the State [*agōn tēn politeian*], he was opposed to the Lacedaemonians in all things, and *would not let the Athenians make concessions, but kept urging them on to the war*."[35] Besides, we know of the accusations that the comic poets brought against him, judging him to be responsible for starting the war in order to distract attention away from misdemeanors of his own.[36] Although he recommended a firm attitude when facing the Spartans, he was not willing to set off to war regardless of the conditions that obtained. If it is victory that one seeks, one has to prepare for war![37] That was the line of behavior adopted by the *stratēgos* who, at the start of the Peloponnesian War developed a strategy that was certainly effective but was, at the same time, much contested in the Athenian ranks.

The Peloponnesian War: The Originality of Pericles' Military Strategy

When hostilities against Sparta broke out in 431, Pericles managed to convince his fellow-citizens generally to take refuge behind their walls, rather than clash head-on with the Peloponnesian troops, who outnumbered them and were better trained. It is true that the city benefited from its exceptional defensive position. Even before Pericles entered upon the political scene, the Athenians had begun to fortify their city and to link the urban core (*astu*) to their port, Piraeus, in such a way as to render the whole impregnable. The construction of the Long Walls had been launched by Cimon,[38] although the work on the northern wall was not completed until after his ostracism (462/457). As for the southern wall, which doubled the earlier rampart, this was built at Pericles' suggestion, between 452 and 431 B.C. (it is not possible to be more specific).[39] Themistocles, Cimon, and Pericles all played their parts in these developments, and by the time they were completed, the town of Athens had become a kind of fortified island supplied with food from territory that included the cities of the Delian League as well as the Attic countryside.

Periclean strategy constituted a coherent whole. It was founded upon the abandonment of the rural territory, the avoidance of fighting on land and the prowess of the navy, and it involved a number of closely related elements: direct confrontation on land with the enemy's army, which was undeniably more powerful than the Athenian one, was to be avoided; the Athenian navy was to be used, rather than the hoplites; outside the city territory, military operations were to be conducted using the fleet; the allegiance of the allies was to be maintained but without seeking to extend the Athenian Empire; the city was to rely on the products that were accessible thanks to Athenian sea power; and, finally, properties situated in the *khōra* were to be abandoned so as to concentrate on defending the maritime supply routes and the town of Athens (*astu*).[40]

It was this last decision that aroused the most resistance among the Athenians. For a largely rural population, the idea of abandoning the territory to the ravages of the enemy was hard to accept; moreover, this tactic was the more painful since the Athenians maintained a special relationship with their own land. They regarded themselves as autochthonous, the descendants of Erichthonius, who was the son of the Attic land and Hephaestus.[41] For them, to abandon the *khōra* was to leave their life-giving mother defenseless.

This opposition, magnified by the outbreak of the plague in Athens in 430,[42] threatened the authority of the *stratēgos*, as is attested both by Thucydides' account and by fragments from the contemporary comic poets. In his play, the *Moirai* (*The Fates*), performed at the Lenaean Festival, in 430 B.C., the comic poet Hermippus deplored Pericles' policy as follows:

> Thou king of the Satyrs, why, pray, wilt thou not
> Take the spear for thy weapon, and stop the dire talk
> With the which, until now, thou conductest the war,
> While the soul of a Teles is in thee?
> If the tiniest knife is but laid on the stone
> To give it an edge, thou gnashest thy teeth,
> As if bitten by fiery Cleon.[43]

This passage delights in dwelling upon the implied cowardice of Pericles, who, in this context, is transformed into a latter-day Dionysus who prefers to lead a theatrical chorus rather than his men into battle. The comparison may well testify to Pericles' interest in drama, but is designed above all to discredit the *stratēgos*, depicting him as a man concerned above all to promote his own pleasure rather than defend his city.

Despite this underlying anger, Pericles' prudent strategy was followed by the Athenians even after the death of its promoter, for the fact was that it chimed with the interests of the majority of the citizens. Had that not been the case, Pericles, despite all his oratorical skills, would not have been able to carry the Assembly with him for more than a few months. In truth, his policy did suit the realities facing the Athenian democracy and also its imaginary representations. In the first place, in a city where one-fifth of the citizens possessed no land at all and almost two-thirds of them owned only fields of less than one hectare (around 2.5 acres), the abandonment of the *khōra* was the lesser evil.[44] Only the large and medium-sized landowners, whom Aristophanes defended, were seriously affected by the Spartans' devastation of the fields and their crops.[45] As Pericles himself proclaimed in his speech to the Athenians in 430, "You should make light of them [the houses and the land], regarding them . . . as a mere flower-garden or ornament of a wealthy estate."[46] Furthermore, far from avoiding all conflict, Pericles simply chose one particular form of warfare—naval confrontation—rather than another—namely, hoplite combat. By favoring the oarsmen rather than the hoplites, the *stratēgos* followed in the footsteps of Themistocles, who valued the poorest of the citizens (the thetes), to the disadvantage of the hoplite class and the cavalrymen.[47]

It was because his policies responded to a profoundly democratic requirement that Pericles, despite forceful criticism, was in the end able to resist the resentments of the Athenian people and convince it of the correctness of his views—and to do so not solely thanks to his talents as an orator capable of bewitching his fellow citizens.[48] The fact nevertheless remains that his expertise in public speaking certainly was a valuable asset to him in his pursuit of political authority.

CHAPTER 3

The Bases of Periclean Power:
The Orator

In the funeral oration that Pericles delivered in 431, to honor the citizens who had fallen during the first year of the Peloponnesian War, he praised the city, emphasizing the role that speech played in deliberations and decision-taking: "We Athenians decide public questions for ourselves or at least endeavor to arrive at a sound understanding of them in the belief that it is not debate that is a hindrance to action, but rather not to be instructed by debate before the time comes for action."[1] Unlike the laconic Spartans, the Athenians indeed never hesitated to enter upon long discussions prior to voting, in the meetings of the Assembly that took place on the Pnyx hill forty times a year.

Speak before doing anything and reflect before taking action: this characterization of Athens is to some extent valid for Pericles himself who, under cover of his celebration of the whole city, was implicitly praising himself. Thucydides often describes the *stratēgos* as an orator who enlightens the crowd and influences the decisions that it takes. The art of speaking—or not speaking—was clearly a second basis upon which Periclean power rested.

In this Athenian city rapidly moving toward democratization, persuasive oratory was now playing a key role. In this respect, Pericles remained the incarnation, par excellence, of an orator endowed with a power of rhetoric that combined both authority and pedagogy. The ancient sources never cease to dwell upon his quasi-divine oratorical power, employing a selection of metaphors the effects of which need to be assessed. When Pericles addressed the people from the tribune of the Assembly, he abided by extremely elaborate codes of oratory. The rhetoric and gestures that he adopted made him a measured orator whose imperturbability was nevertheless interpreted by his opponents as arrogance or even aristocratic disdain.

Pericles was a past master not only of public speaking but also of the art of remaining silent or, to be more precise, of getting his political allies to speak in his place: in order not to saturate the crowds with his own presence, often he would remain in the background so as to make his own rare public appearances more solemn and striking. The combination of all these facets of his behavior rendered his hold over the people well nigh irresistible.

PERICLES AND RHETORIC: KNOWING HOW TO SPEAK

Rhetoric and Democracy

The Athenian democracy respected the principle of *isēgoria*: equal access to public speech for all citizens. At the start of every Assembly meeting, after the Pnyx had been purified by a sacrifice, the herald (*kērux*) stepped out before the Athenians, said a prayer and pronounced a curse on any orator who attempted to mislead the people, and then asked, "Who wishes to speak?". Whoever came forward placed upon his head a myrtle crown that made him unassailable, and spoke directly to the people, proposing a decree to be voted upon. Any citizen could, in his turn, speak in answer to the preceding orator. The Assembly thus proceeded like a competition (*agōn*) in public speaking, with the city gods looking on.

In truth, these egalitarian principles masked powerful internal hierarchies. In the first place, according to the orator Aeschines, Athenian law ruled that turns for speaking be determined by the speakers' respective ages: the oldest citizens had the right to speak first and this lent a particular force to their words.[2] Second, not many Athenians dared to speak in public. Unless a man had mastered the art of oratory, he would soon expose himself to ridicule or even to *thorubos*, the kind of general tumult often mentioned in the speeches of the Attic orators.[3] Furthermore, speaking in public involved a legal risk: the orator was responsible before the magistrates for the motions for which he requested the people's assent. Even if his point of view triumphed in the Assembly, he might then be pursued by his opponents within the framework of a legal trial in which he was accused of illegality, a *graphē paranomōn* that may have been instituted by Ephialtes' reforms of 462/1. If found guilty by the judges, the orator had to pay a heavy fine or was even condemned to *atimia*, total or partial privation of his civic rights. So nobody came forward to speak without carefully weighing up the pros and cons.

Stepping up to the tribune involved personal initiative, and the risk was all the greater given that the orator could not count on the support of any structured political formation. Although historians are often inclined to reduce Athenian political life to confrontation between two camps—the aristocrats and the democrats—we know of no official political party possessed of a clearly defined policy and stable organization in Athens.[4] Although influential men were surrounded by factions that supported them, these were always precarious and informal. Coalitions would form and disintegrate depending on the circumstances and the questions debated.

Within such a fluctuating framework, mastery of the art of oratory represented an essential trump card for anyone bold enough to ascend to the tribune. That is why the lessons of the sophists were so successful among the Athenian elite of the second half of the fifth century. The mission of these itinerant sages was, in return for considerable fees, to teach a person how to handle speech, whatever the circumstances. In the course of his long stay in Athens, the Sicilian sophist, Gorgias, from Leontini, is even said to have defined rhetoric as follows: "the ability to persuade with speeches either judges in the law courts or citizens in the Assembly or an audience at any other meeting that may be held on public affairs."[5] As can be imagined, in Athens the demand for such skills was particularly great. "To control the people with one's tongue"[6] was precisely the aim of Athenian orators schooled by the sophists.

Pericles mastered this art of persuasion (*peithō*) to the highest degree. The *stratēgos* dominated his opponents by his speech—and solely by his speech. In a city marked by its semi-literacy, Pericles was still fully a man of oral communication. Unlike the orators of the fourth century such as Demosthenes or Aeschines, he left to posterity no written texts, apart from his decrees. So it is only through the filter of other authors—in particular, Thucydides—that we can attempt to evaluate the nature of Pericles' rhetoric and its amazing persuasive force.

Pericles the Demagogue

A reading of *The Peloponnesian War* enables one to appreciate the full measure of Pericles' oratory. In this work, the historian records three long speeches delivered by the *stratēgos*. The first relates to the declaration of war; the second, dated 431, is the funerary oration in which Pericles celebrates an Athens still confident and domineering; the third, one year later, in 430, is the harangue that he addressed to a rowdy assembly at the time when the city, ravaged by the plague, had to endure the devastation of its territory.

Clearly, these extremely sophisticated if not sophistic speeches[7] certainly do not bear authentic witness to Pericles' eloquence. Thucydides may well have been present when these three rhetorical tours de force were delivered, but he reconstructed them many years later, leaving his own stamp upon them at a time when he had long since been living in exile. So these samples of Periclean eloquence are in all likelihood partly Thucydidean. Indeed, the historian himself half-admits to this at the beginning of his work: "The speeches are given in the language in which, as it seemed to me, the several speakers would express, on the subjects under consideration, the sentiments most befitting the occasion, though at the same time I have adhered as closely as possible to the general sense of what was actually said."[8]

Despite this partial rewriting, *The Peloponnesian War* makes it possible to appreciate the two complementary facets of Pericles' oratorical skill: authority and pedagogy. According to Thucydides, the *stratēgos* did not hesitate to counter the crowd's anger and even chided it severely. This authoritarian dimension had a pedagogic aim. In his speeches to the Assembly, the *stratēgos* frequently addressed the people as he would a capricious child who would change its mind depending on the circumstances.[9] This uncompromising speech-making won the historian's admiration: "he restrained the multitude while respecting their liberties, and led them rather than was led by them, because he did not resort to flattery, with a view to pleasing them [*pros hēdonēn*], seeking power by dishonest means, but was able, in the strength of his high reputation, to oppose them and even provoke their wrath" (2.65.8). The fact is that Pericles stood out as being radically different from his successors who, according to Thucydides, sought in their speeches only to flatter the people, without any attempt to instruct it.[10]

Of course, this is an idealized description. Although contemporary sources are in agreement when they emphasize Pericles' oratorical skills, they certainly do not all praise him for them. Pericles is often criticized for his ability to turn black into white—and, in particular, to persuade his listeners that he had won a fight when, in fact, he had lost it[11]—and he is often depicted as an orator who, though extraordinary, is alarming. The comic poets compare his eloquence now to a kind of bestial seduction, now to a divine enchantment, resorting to a double play of revealing metaphors.

First, consider the animal metaphor: in Eupolis's *Demes*, Pericles' wit is compared to the sting of a wasp or a bee: "Pericles was the most eloquent man in the world. When he appeared he was like a good sprinter. His words set him ten feet ahead of the other orators. He spoke rapidly, but as well as this rapidity, a kind of Persuasion [*Peithō*] clung to his lips, for he was the only orator who left his prick [*kentron*] in the ears of those who heard him" (fr. 102 K.-A.). Here, the poet assimilates Periclean rhetoric to a sting striking the listener in order to blunt his perceptions (the metaphor also clearly plays on sexual connotations).[12]

Now for the divine metaphor: according to Plutarch, it was on account of his extraordinary eloquence that Pericles was nicknamed "the Olympian" by the comic poets: "they spoke of him as 'thundering' and 'lightning' when he harangued his audience, and as "wielding a dread thunderbolt [*keraunon*] in his tongue.'"[13] This metaphor attributes a quasi-divine power to the speech of the *stratēgos*. A thunderbolt, the divine attribute par excellence, could strike a person down and could bind those whom it touched, constricting them in unbreakable bonds from which it was absolutely impossible to escape.[14] The poet Cratinus possibly resorted to the same analogy in his play titled *The Ploutoi* (The Spirits of Wealth), composed in 430/429 B.C. for the Lenaean Festival, in which he assimilated Pericles to Zeus "binding the rebel Titans in unbreakable bonds [*desmoi*]."[15]

Periclean eloquence thus possesses a disquieting power that links it now to the beasts, now to the gods. In both cases, the *stratēgos* was set apart from common humanity, either for better or for worse. When the comic writers presented him in this way, they intended to arouse in the public admiration as well as suspicion.[16]

One reason why Periclean rhetoric was effective, even terrifying, is that it observed a number of oratorical and gestural codes that served to magnify its impact and renown even further.

PERICLES AT THE TRIBUNE: KNOWING HOW TO BEHAVE

Oratorical Codes and Political Innuendo

In the Assembly, as in the *Agora*, Pericles' behavior was, according to Plutarch, marked by order and balance. "He not only had . . . a spirit that was solemn and a discourse that was lofty and free from popular and reckless effrontery, but also a composure of countenance that never relaxed into laughter, a gentleness of carriage and cast of attire that suffered no emotion to disturb it while he was speaking, a modulation of voice that was far from boisterous [*athorubon*], and many similar characteristics which struck all his hearers with wondering amazement [*thaumastōs*]."[17] Plutarch, the moralist, presents Pericles as the very embodiment of a model orator, in sharp contrast to demagogues such as Cleon.

According to the author of the *Constitution of the Athenians*, the death of Pericles in fact ushered in new oratorical codes: "When Pericles died, Nicias, who died in Sicily, held the headship of the men of distinction and the head of the People was Cleon, son of Cleaenetus, who was thought to have done the most to corrupt the people by his impetuous outbursts and was the first person to use bawling and abuse on the platform, all other persons speaking in an orderly fashion."[18] Thucydides described Cleon as "the most violent of the citizens of his day," and Aristophanes declared him to be a "thief, brawler, roaring as Cycloborus roars."[19] To the horror of members of the traditional elite but in keeping with democratic ideology, Cleon broke with the current conventions. Although the origin of his wealth and his way of addressing the public shocked some of the Athenian elite, they in no way offended the sensibilities of the people, as was proved by his brilliant career and his numerous reelections to the post of *stratēgos*.

Cleon initiated a new mode of communication between the leaders and the *dēmos*, and it was destined to enjoy a fine future. In the fourth century, the orator Aeschines reminisced about a time in the past when orators spoke in a more measured fashion, with one hand placed beneath a fold in their clothing—the *himation*—thereby conveying their moderation and distinction:

> So decorous were those public men of old, Pericles, Themistocles and Aristides (who was called by a name most unlike that by which Timarchus here is called), that to speak with the arm outside the cloak, as we all do nowadays as a matter of course, was regarded then as an ill-mannered thing and they carefully refrained from doing it. . . . See now, fellow-citizens, how unlike to Timarchus were . . . those men of old whom I mentioned a moment ago. They were too modest to speak with the arm outside the cloak, but this man, not long ago, yes, only the other day, in an assembly of the people, threw off his cloak and leaped about like a gymnast, half-naked.[20]

Quite apart from its nostalgic tone, this passage shows how much oratorical gestures and techniques had changed since the age of Pericles. But even if he praises the eloquence of the past, the better to draw attention to the lack of dignity of Timarchus, his opponent, Aeschines in no way calls for a return to the conventions of the past that—in any case—would no longer have suited the fourth-century audience.

Pericles thus founded his oratorical successes upon a way of addressing the people that was somewhat out of date. All the same, the reason he fascinated his listeners so much was not just because he was the last representative of a form of eloquence that was on the way out. Far from invariably respecting well-trodden paths, as an orator he broke away from the customary codes of behavior, in that he never responded with violence to attacks launched against him. Throughout his career, Pericles manifested an unrivaled ability to suffer outrageous assaults without striking back. This set him apart from his contemporaries and lent a particular solemnity to his words.

Periclean Imperturbability: An Ambiguous Solemnity

At the Assembly's tribune, Pericles was several times confronted by the people's anger, but never betrayed the slightest annoyance. This imperturbability was highlighted in 430 B.C., when the Athenians accused him of being responsible for the many disasters that had struck them. As Plutarch, following Thucydides, points out: "Pericles was moved by no such things, but gently and silently underwent the ignominy and the hatred [*tēn adoxian kai tēn epekhtheian*]."[21] Far from being dictated by the circumstances, this imperturbability was a deliberate strategy on the part of the Athenian leader, who observed this line of conduct not only in the Assembly but also when in the Agora, engaging in the exchanges of daily life. Plutarch records a particularly striking episode: "Once, at a time when he had been abused and insulted all day long by a certain lewd fellow of the baser sort, he endured it all quietly, though it was in the market place, where he had urgent business to transact, and towards evening went away homewards unruffled, the fellow following along and heaping all manner of contumely upon him. When he was about to go indoors, it being now dark, he ordered a servant to take a torch and escort the fellow in safety back to his own home."[22] Rather than react as any citizen normally would, Pericles remained unmoved and refused to lose his temper despite repeated insults. This was, to put it mildly, an unusual reaction. Faced with such a torrent of insults, the normal reaction would have been to respond to the affront by giving as good as he got—a form of negative reciprocity—or else to set the matter before the judges, for to insult serving magistrates was behavior liable to heavy punishment.[23] Not only did the *stratēgos* refrain from replying but he chose to respond to the humiliation with a kindness—in accordance with a positive form of reciprocity: he had the offender escorted back to his home.

In Plutarch's account, Pericles thus stands out by reason of his imperturbable behavior, at the risk of compromising his honor as a citizen and his dignity as a magistrate.[24] It is tempting to link this phlegmatic attitude with his sculpted effigy, which represents him as impassive, parading a serenity untouched by emotion, as if whoever commissioned the sculpture (either himself or his relatives) wished to emphasize this particularly detached way of behaving and appearing.[25]

This representation of a Pericles of bronze, draped in all his dignity, was, however, not devoid of a measure of ambiguity. His opponents suggested that this carefully studied pose was simply a disguised form of arrogance. A refusal to respond to insults might well pass for a manifestation of an excessive distance, for it was a way of refusing to communicate with ordinary citizens, even in an aggressive mode. Such was the reproach expressed by Ion of Chios, who was always quick to criticize the *stratēgos*, to the advantage of Cimon: "The poet Ion, however, says that Pericles had a presumptuous [*hupotuphon*] and somewhat arrogant manner of address and that into his haughtiness [*megalaukhiais*] there entered a good deal of disdain and contempt for others; he praises, on the other hand, the tact, complaisance and elegant address which Cimon showed in his social intercourse."[26]

When he displayed such emotional detachment, Pericles shocked his contemporaries as much as he fascinated them: when solemnity (*semnotēs*) was not tempered by a dose of affability, it always risked being taken badly and considered to reflect an anti-democratic stance.[27] That is precisely the gist of a line by the comic poet Cratinus, who presents Pericles as "a man full of haughtiness and frowning brows [*anelktais ophrusi semnon*]."[28] Weird though it might seem, in Athens, certain facial expressions conveyed well-established political meanings. Frowning eyebrows were considered as an external sign of oligarchical or even tyrannical aspirations. So when the orator Demosthenes wanted to discredit his opponent Aeschines, he reproached him not only for his sumptuous clothing and his imposing trailing train but also for his frowning brows: "But since he has perpetrated wrongs without number, he has become *mighty supercilious* [*tas ophrus anespake*]. . . . Behold him, pacing the market-place with the stately stride of Pythocles, his long robe reaching to his ankles, his cheeks puffed out, as one who should say 'One of Philip's most intimate friends, at your service!' He has joined the clique that wants to get rid of democracy."[29] As a reflection of a misplaced solemnity, frowning brows—here rendered as "superciliousness"—could be interpreted as a manifestation of overweening scorn. So when he dwelt on this seemingly anodyne facial detail, Cratinus was launching a particularly grave accusation against Pericles.[30]

When Pericles addressed the people with such imposing solemnity, he was bound to attract virulent criticism from all those bent on representing such behavior as tyrannical haughtiness. To counter that suspicion, the *stratēgos* devised a new stratagem to protect himself from similar accusations: he would take care to limit his public declarations and appearances so as not to have the people tire of him.

PERICLES OFFSTAGE: KNOWING HOW TO KEEP QUIET

The Art of Delegation

Whoever intervened on every point on the political stage, was bound, eventually, to aggravate his fellow-citizens. In his *Precepts of Statecraft* (811E), Plutarch enjoys reminding his readers of this fact: "Those who strip for every political activity . . . soon cause themselves to be criticized by the multitude; they become unpopular and arouse envy when they are successful, but joy when they meet with failure." Pericles seems to have been deeply aware of this danger. In the course of his career, he limited the number of his public interventions by getting his friends to speak in his place. It was often those close to him who, in the Assembly, stepped up to the tribune to propose the decrees that Pericles wished to submit for public approval. In this way, his authority was protected from envy yet without being any the less effective. As Plutarch, again, remarks: "Pericles made use of Menippus for the position of general, humbled the Council of the Areopagus by means of Ephialtes, passed the decree against the Megarians by means of Charinus, and sent Lampon out as founder of Thurii. For, when power seems to be distributed among many, not only does the weight of hatreds and enmities become less troublesome, but there is also greater efficiency in the conduct of affairs."[31]

So Pericles resorted to a practice that was well-attested in the fourth century. At that time, certain citizens had no compunction whatever about selling their names and proposing decrees of which they were not the true authors: "[Stephanos] was not yet a public speaker, but thus far merely a pettifogger, one of those who stand beside the platform and shout, who prefer indictments and informations for hire, and who let their names be inscribed on motions made up by others."[32] Seen in this light, it is perhaps not simply by chance that no decree proposed by Pericles is attested epigraphically among the dozens that cover the period in which he is said to have wielded such decisive influence.

Cleverly delegating power in order to strengthen his own authority, Pericles made use of a number of "straw men," who functioned as so many lightning conductors that distracted the people's hatred. In this way, Metiochus (or Metichus), totally unknown in any other respect,[33] is described by Plutarch as the clumsy victim of his own activism. This understudy of Pericles seems to have become the target of the comic authors, who mocked him mercilessly: "Metiochus, you see, is general, Metiochus inspects the roads, Metiochus inspects the bread and Metiochus inspects the flour, Metiochus takes care of all things and Metiochus will come to grief."[34] As Plutarch correctly points out, "He was one of Pericles' followers and seems to have used the power gained through him in such a way as to arouse odium and envy [*epiphthonōs*]" (*Precepts of Statecraft*, 811F).

The same applies to the seer Lampon, another of the *stratēgos*'s trusted followers.[35] The scene unfolds in 444/3 B.C., when the Greek world was finally enjoying some respite from warfare. After trying in vain to convene a pan-Hellenic congress (*Pericles*, 17.1), Pericles made the most of the "Thirty Years' Peace" signed with Sparta and its allies and launched an ambitious project: the founding of a new colony at Thurii, in Magna Graecia, on the site of the ancient Sybaris. Even though the Dorian cities of the Peloponnese did not take part, the expedition was a propagandist success, involving numerous Greeks such as the architect Hippodamus of Miletus, the historian Herodotus of Halicarnassus, and the sophist Protagoras of Abdera. Rather than take any leading role, Pericles sheltered behind Lampon in carrying out this operation: the seer, placed at the head of the colonists, even acted as one of the founders (*oikistēs*) of the colony (Diodorus, 12.10.3–4). However, this sudden notoriety of his made him the butt of attacks from the comic poets, as can be seen from several fragments of Cratinus.[36] Concealed behind Lampon, Pericles was sheltered from attack at the very moment when he had to confront the increasingly virulent opposition of Thucydides of Alopeke; less than one year later, his opponent was ostracized, having failed to come to grips with the *stratēgos* lying low in the shadows, carefully concealed behind his political allies.

A Strategy of Light and Darkness

To preserve his authority, Pericles felt it necessary to secure a shadowy zone for himself: "Pericles, seeking to avoid the satiety which springs from continual intercourse, made his approaches to the people by intervals, as it were, not speaking on every question, nor addressing the people on every occasion, but offering himself like the Salaminian trireme, as Critolaus says, for great emergencies" (*Pericles*, 7.5). Skilfully handled, this measure of obscurity was not solely designed to disarm the envy of the people; it also had the advantage of imparting a particular dignity to Pericles' rare appearances.

In a very attenuated way, such behavior was reminiscent of a "hidden king," who reigned in his palace, sheltered from the eyes of the masses. Being shut away and kept secret indeed constituted means whereby royal authority was strengthened—this voluntary seclusion being the essential element in the "imperial mysteries" that the Greeks could observe from their contact with the palaces of eastern potentates. In his account of the Persian Wars, Herodotus had, precisely, described how the Median king, Deiokes, had adapted an imposing ceremonial that cut him off from his subjects in such a way that he remained surrounded by a quasi-divine aura. Many decades later, Xenophon likewise emphasized the role played by ceremony in the construction of the authority of Cyrus, the founder of the Persian Empire: the great king chose to live partly cloistered away, so as to appear only at particularly ritualized and majestic moments. To some extent, Pericles appropriated certain elements of that Eastern tradition, adapting it to the democratic context—just as he seems to have been inspired by the architecture of the Persian Empire when he built the Odeon on the slopes of the Acropolis.[37]

In truth, the fourth-century Athenians were not fooled by such strata-
gems and were wary of men who calculated their public appearances too
carefully. When accused of speaking in the *Ekklēsia* in too parsimonious a
fashion, Aeschines, for example, found himself obliged to justify his behavior
to his fellow-citizens: "You blame me if I come before the people not constantly but only at intervals ... [yet] the fact that a man speaks only at intervals marks him as a man who takes part in politics because of the call of the
hour and for the common good; whereas to leave no day without its speech
is the mark of a man who is making a trade of it and talking for pay."[38] So, to
convince his audience that he was behaving as a perfect democrat, Aeschines
presented himself as an ordinary citizen—not a professional orator—who
spoke in the Assembly only from time to time, as circumstances demanded.
He hoped in this way to disarm critics who regarded his fleeting appearances
as a sign of his unconfessed and unconfessable oligarchic aspirations.

Even if such calculated reticence sometimes aroused suspicions, it clearly
benefited Pericles. His measured appearances impressed the masses all the
more because they evoked not just an imperial ceremony, but possibly even
a form of religious epiphany. That is the implication of the comparison that
Plutarch draws between, on the one hand, Pericles and, on the other, the
Salaminian and Paralian triremes—two sacred vessels used only for exceptional events. Plutarch makes his meaning clear in his *Precepts of Statecraft*
when, without actually naming Pericles, he declares: "Just as the Salaminia
and the Paralus ships at Athens were not sent out to sea for every service, but
only for necessary and important missions, so the statesman should employ
himself for the most momentous and important matters, *as does the King
of the Universe*."[39] Political leaders and deities in the same boat! It is in this
context of a quasi-divine apparition that the nickname given to Pericles—he
was called "the Olympian"—deserves to be analyzed.[40]

In this interplay of shadow and light, there were inevitably both winners
and losers. Metiochus, about whom nothing is known, or even Ephialtes, reduced to a mere silhouette, are the forgotten ones in this story of light and
darkness. Having been exposed to the full glare of publicity, they were condemned to remain in the glorious shadow of Pericles, the past master of both
speech and silence.

CHAPTER 4

Pericles and Athenian Imperialism

The power of Pericles, founded on speech as much as on action, developed within the framework of an Athenian city that, from 450 onward, was caught up in a rapid process of democratization. Yet the increasing liberty of the *dēmos* was accompanied by the enslavement of its allies within the framework of the Delian League. This league, founded in 478 B.C., progressively became an instrument in the service of Athens. The democratization of the city progressed at the same rate as its increasing power over its allies.

What exactly was the role that Pericles played in the establishment of Athenian imperialism? Did he try to check the imperial dynamic or did he, on the contrary, act as its catalyst? And, anyway, is it possible to speak already of Athenian imperialism at the time when the *stratēgos* was exercising a decisive influence on the destiny of the city? Today historians are still arguing about these questions. Some represent Pericles' "reign" as the pivotal moment in the construction of Athenian imperialism, while other scholars, on the contrary, endeavor to exonerate the *stratēgos* from all responsibility in this matter, either by emphasizing his personal moderation or by maintaining that the cusp of imperialism was reached only after his death.

However, it will not do to look no further than that alternative. The *stratēgos* was swept up in a dynamic that, both upstream and downstream, shaped far more than his own individual actions, for it had already involved what was, broadly speaking, a policy embraced by Cimon and it would affect Cleon's rise to power. Pericles was simply continuing an imperialist system that was initiated before him and that went on after him, a system that was backed by a general consensus both among the Athenian elite and also more widely in the city of Athens.

Pericles took part in running the empire with no misgivings at all. His military exploits in Euboea, Samos, and Aegina were all against rebellions that he simply crushed with a considerable degree of bloody force. If there was any specifically Periclean aspect to the situation, it lay not in imperial practices but rather in what he said about them. Pericles was probably the first to theorize the need for Athenian imperialism and publicly display the city's domination over the league allies by organizing the construction of the Odeon and the Parthenon.

Pericles and the Establishment of the Athenian Empire

The Delian League: From *Summakhia* to *Arkhē*

In 478 B.C., at the end of the Second Persian War, the Athenians, with the co-operation of a large number of the cities dotted around the Aegean, founded a league (a *summakhia*), the seat of which was the small and sacred island of Delos. According to Thucydides (1.95.1), membership was at that time voluntary. The cities spontaneously chose to unite their forces under the leadership of Athens, in order to prevent the Persians returning to the Aegean. To this end, members had to contribute to the war effort in proportion to their resources, either directly, with ships and soldiers, or indirectly, by paying tribute (*phoros*) representing the monetary equivalent of the ships to be supplied (Thucydides, 1.98.3). The overwhelming majority of the cities chose the second option: as far as we can tell from the *stēlē* on which the contributions of the league's member cities were recorded in 454, only thirteen or fourteen of the contributing cities were still paying tribute in the form of triremes or military contingents. In short, Athens did the fighting, while the allies paid.

Also according to Thucydides, the total sum of tribute was fixed at 460 talents in 478 by the Athenian Aristides. In order to calculate the contributions of each of the cities, Aristides no doubt took over the framework of the Achaemenid system of taxation that was set in place after the revolt of Ionia in 493: to a certain extent, the allies had simply switched masters. However, at this juncture, the members of the alliance were still deciding on its general policies all together, with each contributor possessing a vote in the league's council (*sunedrion*).

A number of crucial dates mark out the Delian League's development and its slide into imperialism. First there was the battle of Eurymedon, fought between 469 and 466 B.C. by the Athenian fleet, commanded by the *stratēgos* Cimon. This great victory de facto sealed the end of the Persian threat in the Aegean. Next came the peace negotiated by Callias between the Athenians and the Persians in 449 B.C. Following the failure of the Athenian expedition to Egypt, the Athenians sent Callias as an ambassador to Susa, where a peace treaty was signed, with the Persians agreeing to leave the Aegean and the cities of Asia Minor under the control of the Athenians, while the Athenians, for their part, undertook not to launch any more expeditions against the royal territories. The peace of Callias thus, de facto, if not *de iure*, put an end to the Persian threat.[1]

After the peace had been signed, the Delian League no longer had as much *raison d'être*, and that is perhaps why the levying of tribute was suspended in 448 B.C.[2] However, that respite was short-lived, and the Athenians then continued to receive a *phoros* even though the Persian threat had disappeared. These taxes were resented all the more because in the late 450s the league's treasury had been transferred to Athens. The sum to be paid as tribute was fixed every four years by the Athenian *ekklēsia*, which summoned all the allies at the time of the great Panathenaea, in order to reveal to them the sum that they were to pay annually. All of this is attested by Cleinias's decree.[3]

It was therefore certainly not by chance that several major revolts broke out within this league that now had no purpose. In 447/6 Euboea revolted against Athens, which, after putting down the uprising, imposed democratic systems on the island and installed cleruchies, garrisons of Athenian soldiers, who settled there.[4] It was at this point that the city of Histiaea became the cleruchy of Oreos. In 440/39, the island of Samos was pacified after a long siege, as was then the city of Byzantium. The vocabulary used to speak of the league and its members now changed: the Athenians spoke no longer of their *hēgemonia* but of their *arkhē*—their domination—and they now referred to the league members as *hupēkooi*, dependents, not allies.[5] During the Peloponnesian War, the revolts multiplied, prompting the Athenians to exact heavy reprisals. In 427, Mytilene was forced back into the league and the island of Lesbos was subjected to heavy repression. In 425, tribute was almost tripled in order to cope with the heavy expenses of warfare. Athenian imperialism had now reached its peak. It was not until the disastrous result of the Sicilian expedition (415–413 B.C.) and, above all, the last years of the war that Athens's grip loosened; the league was finally dissolved at the end of the conflict, in 404 B.C.

Did Pericles play a role in the imperial metamorphosis of the Delian League? Did he, as leader of the people, act as a catalyst in the aggressive tendencies of the Athenians or did he, on the contrary, try to keep them in check? In order to resolve that alternative, we must first determine a crucial question: exactly when was the league transformed into an empire (figure 2)?

The Slide into Imperialism: A Periclean Turning Point?

Precisely when did Athens increase its power over the members of the Delian League to the point of turning them into mere subjects, or even "slaves"? Among historians, this tricky question eludes a consensus. Specialists on the Athenian Empire disagree on the dating of the complex epigraphical evidence. A number of decrees testifying to the growing imperialism of Athens have been found, but it has not been possible to date them precisely, on account of their lamentable state of preservation. While most epigraphists place the date of their engraving between 450 and 440, some specialists defend a later dating, around 430/420.[6] One might remain unmoved by this erudite battle were it not for the fact that what is at stake here is crucial for an understanding of the nature of the Periclean empire and the role that Pericles himself played in its development. There are two possibilities: if these inscriptions go back to the mid-fifth century, the hardening of Athenian imperialism must have taken place under Pericles and probably at his instigation; if, on the contrary, they were not engraved until the time of the Peloponnesian War, "only the war forced the Athenians to tighten their grip on the Aegean world,"[7] so Pericles, who died at the beginning of the conflict, was in no way implicated in the process.[8]

To be quite frank, the second alternative does not seem credible. Whatever the date of the decrees in question, there is plenty of other evidence of the Athenian descent into imperialism as early as the middle of the fifth century. On this basis, it might seem logical to detect signs of specifically Periclean policies, particularly since some authors who were contemporaries of the *stratēgos* make this their justification for taking a hard line in this matter. One such is Stesimbrotus of Thasos, a native of an island placed under Athenian control, who certainly criticizes Pericles for his cruel behavior toward the people of Thasos and contrasts this to the supposed moderation of Cimon.[9] In reality, that contrast does not withstand scrutiny. What strikes one upon reading the sources that are available is above all how quickly the Delian League was transformed into an empire placed at the service of Athens. In fact, this happened as early as the time when Cimon dominated the political life of the city. So it was probably under his leadership that the first of the allies' revolts was repressed. As early as 475, the city of Carystus, in Euboea, was forced, against its will, to join the league. In 470 or 468, Naxos revolted, and, as Thucydides declares, "this was the first allied city to be enslaved [*edoulōthē*] in violation of the established rule" (1.98.4). However, the first rebellion of any magnitude was that of Thasos, between 465 and 463. It took the Athenians two years to overcome this city that possessed, on the continent, mineral resources and forests that were eminently desirable.[10] When the conflict was over, the city precinct was razed to the ground and its navy was confiscated. The people of Thasos became tribute-payers to Athens and lost their liberty. Very soon, the Athenians also insisted that the cities that had revolted, once they rejoined the alliance, should solemnly swear

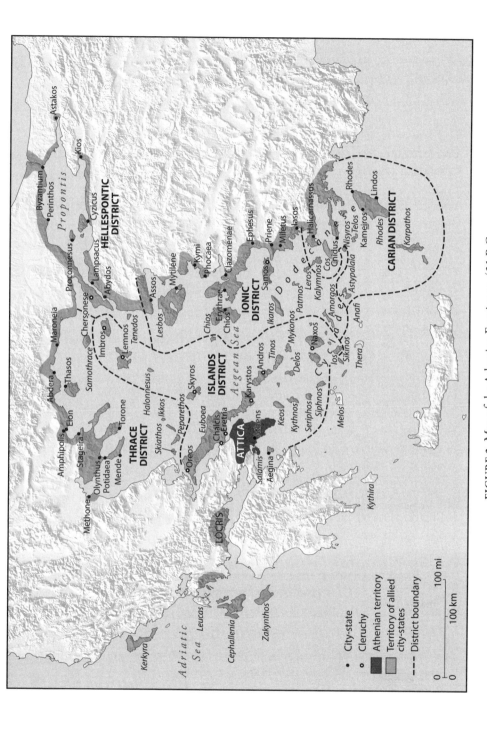

FIGURE 2. Map of the Athenian Empire ca. 431 B.C.

never again to secede, as we know from an inscription in Erythrae, a city in Asia Minor that rejoined the league some time between 465 and 450 B.C.[11]

An aggressive imperialist thrust was thus initiated as early as the second third of the fifth century. No Athenian leader could afford to resist it if he wished for the support of the people. In this context, Cimon repressed the revolts of the allies as regularly as did Pericles after him. It was Cimon who was in charge of the lengthy siege of Thasos in 465–463 and also he who decisively promoted the development of cleruchies, the Athenian garrisons that were installed in allied territories.[12] Apart from a few minor disagreements, the political leaders clearly shared in common the conviction that the empire constituted the guarantee of Athenian sociopolitical stability. There may have been disagreement about the methods to be adopted, but there was none where the principle was concerned: the empire was vital for Athens, so, if necessary, the allies had to be repressed by force. Moreover, the transfer of the Delian League's treasury, often interpreted as the ultimate symbol of the hardening attitude of imperialism, may quite possibly have taken place before 454—the date when it is actually mentioned—indeed, it may have been carried out even prior to the victory of Eurymedon, at the beginning of the 460s.[13]

All the same, it would be exaggerated to detect no change at all in Athenian politics during the years between 440 and 430. However, such developments probably owed nothing to Pericles himself but everything to the transformation of the geopolitical context and, in particular, the establishment of peace, de facto if not *de iure*, with Persia. With the signing of the peace of Callias in 449, Athenian domination in effect became radically illegitimate in the eyes of the allies/subjects: the league was now subject to a whole spate of revolts, which were countered by increasing repression.

Faced with mounting challenges, Pericles unhesitatingly resorted to force and was, as a result, sometimes accused of cruelty. This practical experience of his, marked by a series of bloody incidents, now led him, at the theoretical level, to develop his lucid thinking about the empire and the need to maintain it.

PERICLES FACED BY THE ALLIES: IMPERIAL PRACTICES AND REPRESENTATIONS

The Recourse to Force: Periclean Cruelty

Still today, certain historians seek to palliate the image of Pericles' actions in the face of the allies. Donald Kagan, in his biography, emphasizes the relative moderation of the *stratēgos*'s behavior in this episode.[14] "Save Private Pericles!": the *stratēgos* cannot possibly have been cruel and risk besmirching the Greek miracle with an indelible stain! That is an eminently ideological attitude and it should be analyzed in relation to the biographer's own political background. In this respect, his political trajectory is instructive: having started out as a liberal—in the American sense of the term—Kagan became a Republican in the 1970s and then, in the 1990s, was one of the founders of a neo-conservative "think tank" ("Project for the New American Century"). Meanwhile, one of his sons became John McCain's advisor on foreign policy. So it is perfectly logical that, as an apostle of American interventionism abroad, Kagan should present us with a Pericles who is both firm yet temperate and is the epitome of moderation when faced with undisciplined and recalcitrant allies.[15]

However, that supposed moderation is a fiction. During the years in which he played a leading role, Pericles made sure that the allies' revolts were shamelessly repressed, sometimes even with cruelty. In truth, the *stratēgos* was intimately associated with the repressive policies of Athens. Significantly enough, Thucydides, who only mentions Pericles three times in his long account of the *pentēkontaetia* (the period of almost fifty years [478–431] that separated the end of the Persian Wars from the outbreak of the Peloponnesian War) twice mentions his direct involvement in forcing the allies to toe the line.

The Euboean Revolt

First, the historian describes his participation in the punishment of Euboea, in 446 B.C.: "The Athenians again crossed over into Euboea under the command of Pericles and subdued the whole of it; the rest of the island they settled by agreement, but expelled the Histiaeans from their homes and themselves occupied their territory."[16] That was how Pericles wreaked his revenge on those who, having captured an Athenian vessel, massacred the entire crew.[17] The city was turned into a cleruchy and the rest of the Euboean cities were placed under strict supervision, as is attested epigraphically by two decrees concerning Eretria and Chalcis.[18]

The comic poets dwelt upon this bloody episode—in particular, in Aristophanes' *Clouds*, a play that was staged for the first time in 423 B.C. Referring to Euboea, the poet has one of the characters say: "We have stretched it enough, we and Pericles!"[19] The treatment meted out to the rebels was so traumatic that it was still haunting the Athenian conscience nearly forty years later. When the Peloponnesian War ended, at the news of the defeat at Aigos Potamoi, in 405, the Athenians were gripped by terror, fearing now to see the allies, so long tyrannized, seeking revenge for the exactions that they had suffered. And in the long list of outrages, the crushing of the Euboean revolt figured prominently: "That night, no one slept, all mourning, not for the lost alone, but far more for their own selves, thinking that they would suffer such treatment as they had visited upon the Melians, colonists of the Lacedaemonians, after reducing them by siege, and upon the Histiaeans and Scionaeans and Toronaeans and Aeginetans and many other Greek peoples" (Xenophon, *Hellenica*, 2.2.3). The repression of Euboea in 446, led by Pericles, thus symbolized all the harshness of Athenian imperialism, to the point of leaving an indelible mark on the civic conscience.

The Samos Affair

Pericles' second intervention left just as deep a scar. In 440–439 B.C.,[20] taking advantage of an altercation between Samos and Miletus over the possession of Priene, in Asia Minor, the Athenians embarked on a long war against the Samians, who had defected and left the Delian League. We need not dwell on the ins-and-outs of the conflict but should note that this war turned out to be extremely costly for Athens, both in men and in money. In money, first: an inscription records the total sum of the expenses for the war. The final sum was as high as 1,400 talents, more than three years' accumulated tribute, which was later paid back solely by the Samians![21] But the war was also costly in men and was marked by an extreme violence that struck the imagination of ancient authors. Two stories focus on the cruelty of the conflict; it was a violence that was initially reciprocal but for which, later on, the Athenians alone were held responsible.

The first episode was recorded in the fourth century by Douris of Samos, who was well placed to know of the affair since he was a native of the rebel island.[22] In the course of the conflict, some Athenian prisoners were captured by the Samian rebels, who tattooed their faces with an owl. Gratuitous cruelty? Not at all. The rebels were simply paying back the Athenians who, earlier, had marked the faces of enemy prisoners with the prow of a Samian ship, the *Samaina*.[23] By recording this incident, Douris clearly intended to underline the Athenians' initial responsibility in this unleashing of violence. However, the episode took on another, less immediate significance. By tattooing their prisoners in this way, both groups of belligerents turned them into monetary symbols and consequently into interchangeable merchandise—for, just as the owl was the monetary symbol of Athens, the *Samaina* was that of Samos (figure 3).[24]

Furthermore, this story may reveal the true cause of this bloody conflict. Over and above the reasons alleged by the ancient sources, the main objective of the repression led by Pericles may have been to impose upon Samos the use of Athenian coins. The Samians appear to have refused to apply Clearchus's

(a)

(b)

FIGURE 3. A coin war: (a) Athenian silver tetradrachm, minted 449 B.C. 17.07 grams. Owl facing right. SNG Copenhagen 31. Photo © Marie-Lan Nguyen. (b) Silver tetradrachm, minted in Zancle (Messana) by the Samians between 493 and 489 B.C., showing, on the reverse, the prow of a Samian ship (*Samaina*). Image © Hirmer Fotoarchiv.

decree, which was probably passed in the early 440s and imposed upon all the allies the use of Athenian weights and measures and silver currency.

However that may be, the Samos affair shows us a Pericles who resorted to unbridled violence, as the outcome of the conflict testifies. After the Athenians' victory, the Samians "were reduced by siege and agreed to a capitulation, pulling down their walls, giving hostages and consenting to pay back by instalments the money spent upon the siege" (Thucydides 1.117.3). All this was altogether normal; Athens applied victors' rights and deprived the Samians of all attributes of sovereign power: its ramparts, its fleet, and its currency. What was less normal though was the cruelty that, again according to Douris of Samos, Pericles inflicted upon the Samian elite: "To these details, Douris the Samian adds stuff for tragedy, accusing the Athenians and Pericles of great cruelty. But he appears not to speak the truth when he says that Pericles had the Samian trierarchs and marines brought into the marketplace of Miletus and crucified there, and that then, when they had already suffered grievously for ten days, he gave orders to break their heads in with clubs and make an end of them, and then cast their bodies forth without funeral rites."[25] In Douris's version, the horror of the tortures—inflicted in Miletus, not in Athens—had been intended to serve as a lesson addressed to the entire empire. But this account aimed above all to emphasize not only the cruelty of Pericles, but his impiety: to deprive bodies of the funeral rites was a grave transgression, the full implications of which are revealed in Sophocles' *Antigone*. It may be that Douris is overdramatizing (*epitragoidein*) the events, as Plutarch, being concerned to protect the reputation of the Athenian *stratēgos*, claims; but in any case, Douris's testimony underlines the existence of a tradition hostile to Pericles that deliberately emphasizes his intolerable cruelty.[26]

In fact, such a sinister reputation already surrounded Pericles' father, Xanthippus. Right at the end of the *Histories*, at a strategic point in his text, Herodotus produces an equivocal image of Pericles' father: guided by vengeance, Xanthippus had the Persian governor Artaÿctes crucified at Sestos, after having his son stoned to death before his eyes.[27] Perhaps this was a way for the historian, himself a native of Halicarnassus, implicitly to cast blame upon the actions of the son by means of an account of his father's behavior. Herodotus presented Xanthippus as the initiator of a strategy of terror that reached its zenith under Pericles.[28]

Such cruelty was further amplified with the outbreak of the Peloponnesian War in 431, as is shown by the expulsion of the Aeginetans in the first year of the conflict. Here too, it was probably Pericles who initiated that repression.

The Expulsion of the Aeginetans

Within a context of exacerbated tensions, the *stratēgos* decided to punish the Aeginetans even though they had not, in fact, revolted against Athens. That, at least, is the version favored by Plutarch: "By way of soothing the multitude who ... were distressed over the war, he won their favor by distributions of moneys and proposed allotments (*kai klēroukhias egraphen*) of conquered lands; the Aeginetans, for instance, he drove out entirely and parcelled out their island among the Athenians by lot."[29] There were, in truth, several reasons why Aegina was punished in this way. In the first place, it had always been an undisciplined ally that had been late in joining the league (in around 459 B.C.), and it was, furthermore an ancient naval power that was a longstanding rival of the Athenians.[30] Second, the Athenians accused the Aeginetans of having provoked the war and encouraged the Spartans' hatred of Athens (Thucydides, 2.27.1); and last, the Athenians were in need of a sure base for themselves, within reach of the Peloponnese.

Although Thucydides does not accuse Pericles directly, there can be no doubt that he was implicated in this business. One of the only statements actually attributed to Pericles—for he left no writings of his own—refers precisely to the fate of the island, "urging the removal of Aegina as 'the eye-sore of the Piraeus,' "[31] and evoking the sticky substance that gathers on the lids of an infected eye. In this way, Pericles assimilated the island of Aegina to a bodily secretion that the Athenians were invited to suppress by means of an appropriate treatment. The metaphorical scorn reflected the real violence to which the Aeginetans were subjected at the beginning of the Peloponnesian War.

Pericles' career, from the Euboean affair in 446 down to the expulsion of the Aeginetans, definitely suggests an unchanging attitude toward the allies. However, in this respect, the *stratēgos* was no better and no worse than anyone else and was by no means original. He was simply continuing a policy that was initiated before him—*pace* the admirers of Cimon such as Ion of Chios and Stesimbrotus of Thasos—a policy that was also continued after him, whatever the critics of Cleon, such as Thucydides, have to say.[32] But what distinguished Pericles was the lucidity that he acquired from this experience of warfare punctuated by brutal episodes. The *stratēgos* developed a deep line of thought on the empire and the necessity of maintaining it. It was a choice that he theorized in words and materialized in grandiose monuments.

The Spectacle of Force and Pericles' Presentation of It

The Theorization of Imperialism: A Necessary Injustice

If there is one original aspect to Pericles' attitude to imperialism, it lies not so much in his practice as in the way that he represented the empire both to others and to himself. In the speech that he made in 430, faced with the anger of the Athenian people, the *stratēgos* set out a particularly lucid analysis of the Delian League and the way that it worked:

You may reasonably be expected, moreover, to support the dignity which the city has attained through empire—a dignity in which you all take pride—and not to avoid its burdens, unless you resign its honours also. Nor must you think that you are fighting for the simple issue of slavery or freedom; on the contrary, *loss of empire is also involved and danger from the hatred incurred in your sway*. From this empire, however, it is too late for you ever to withdraw, if any one at the present crisis, through fear and shrinking from action does indeed seek thus to play the honest man; *for by this time the empire you hold is like a tyranny, which it may seem wrong to have assumed, but which, certainly, it is dangerous to let go*. Men like these would soon ruin a city if they should win others to their views, or if they should settle in some other land and have an independent city all to themselves (Thucydides, 2.63.1–3).

The *stratēgos* conceded that it was perhaps unjust to change the Delian League into an empire at the service of Athens. However, there could be no question of reversing the decision, for to do so would be to accept slavery, *douleia*.[33] His reasoning is subtle: it is necessary to defend an empire, even one that is acquired by coercion, for it would be too dangerous to give it up. If the allies cease to be in thrall to Athens, they will not remain neutral but will switch over to the enemy in order to wreak vengeance for the tribulations that they have suffered. In his speech, Pericles, rather then retreating on the subject of imperialism, goes into the attack. However unjust it was, the people must continue to act tyrannically toward the members of the League.[34] There can be no question of dismounting once one's steed is already charging.

Convinced of the necessity of the empire, Pericles furthermore undertook to lend legitimacy to the power of Athens by means of monuments that, over and above their proclaimed purpose, gave material expression to the city's new imperial status.

The Odeon and Xerxes' Tent: From One Empire to Another

The Odeon, constructed between 446 and 430 B.C., was associated so closely with Pericles that Cratinus, the comic poet, had one of his characters declare: "The squill-head Zeus! Lo! Here he comes, the Odeon like a cap upon his cranium, now that for good and all the ostracism is o'er."[35] The Odeon as headgear: what better way of expressing the link that bound the monument and the *stratēgos* together?

Today, this building is little known, for the archaeological excavations were never completed. But in Antiquity, it was considered one of the most impressive monuments in a city that was rich in architectural marvels (figure 4). The

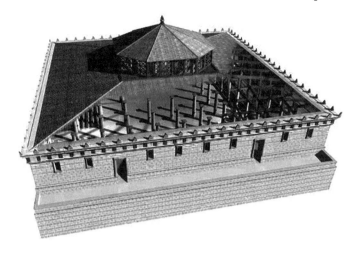

FIGURE 4. The Odeon of Pericles (ca. 443–435 B.C.): a virtual reconstruction. Image © the University of Warwick. Created by the THEATRON Consortium.

precinct in which it stood could accommodate huge crowds: this Odeon, flanking the theater of Dionysus, which was at that time built of wood, appeared as an immense hypostyle construction—with multiple colonnades—of 4,000 square meters in area (around 43,000 square feet). It was the largest public building in Athens and the first theater in Antiquity ever provided with a roof.

At an architectural level, the Odeon was freely inspired by Xerxes' tent, which had been brought back to Athens, as booty, after the victory at Plataea, which the Greeks won over the Persians in 479 B.C.[36] According to Plutarch: "The Odeon, which was arranged internally with many tiers of seats and many pillars, and which had a roof made with a circular slope from a single peak, they say was an exact reproduction of the Great King's pavilion, and this too was built under the superintendence of Pericles" (*Pericles*, 13.5). One should, incidentally, not be misled by the vocabulary, Xerxes' "pavilion" or "tent" resembled a real palace that could be dismantled and transported elsewhere and that adopted the form of the imperial residences of Persepolis. Its true model was the Apadana and the palace of a hundred columns, a reception hall built by Xerxes himself.[37] In adopting such an architectural style, Pericles was modeling his Odeon on the great imperial architecture of the Achaemenids.

This strange mimicry had two symmetrical functions. It was intended, within the urban setting of the city itself, to commemorate the Athenian victory in the Persian Wars. Better still, by creating this hall for spectacles, the Athenians were manipulating the despotic symbolism associated with Xerxes' tent and adapting it to democratic purposes. Whereas the original

FIGURE 5. Tribute-bearers (maybe Ionians) from the ceremonial staircase (northern stairway) of the Apadana (Iran: Persepolis, end of the sixth century B.C.). In *Persepolis and Ancient Iran* with an introduction by Ursula Schneider, Oriental Institute. © 1976 by The University of Chicago. Image courtesy of the Oriental Institute of the University of Chicago.

pavilion had, in principle, been reserved for the exclusive enjoyment of the Great King, the Odeon was conceived as an edifice open to all, constructed for the pleasure of the entire population. However, this architectural choice probably conveyed a quite different message to the foreigners who passed through Athens. The edifice must have struck them as a veritable imperialist manifesto.[38] The Odeon, which imitated the splendors of Achaemenid architecture, returned the allies to the status of subjects and reminded them that they had, in truth, simply swapped masters. We should furthermore bear in mind that it was on the staircase leading to the Apadana, the throne-room in Persepolis, on which the Odeon drew freely for inspiration, that the long cohorts of tributary peoples had been represented, bringing their contributions to the Great King, in a lengthy procession (figure 5). Nor was that association solely metaphorical: in Athens, the allies of the Delian League were obliged to pass in front of Pericles' Odeon when they came to deposit their tribute in the theater of Dionysus.[39] This edifice brilliantly symbolized their new status as tribute-bearers, strictly in line with the imperial Achaemenid heritage.[40]

The same reasoning may be applied to the city's most famous monument, the Parthenon, for in many respects this too testified to the hardening of Athenian imperialism.

The Parthenon: A Marble Symbol of Athenian Imperialism

There can be little doubt that the great building program launched in Athens after 450 was associated with imperial dynamics. Pericles' opponents would even reproach him for having misapplied imperial revenues in order to realize his monumental policy and, especially, to build the Parthenon with its statue of Athena Parthenos: "Hellas is insulted with a dire insult and manifestly subjected to tyranny when she sees that, with her own enforced contributions for the war, we are gilding and bedizening our city, which, for all the world like a wanton woman, adds to her wardrobe precious stones and costly statues and temples worth their millions" (Plutarch, *Pericles*, 12.2). To be sure, this declaration calls for a measure of qualification. For it is by no means certain that the Parthenon was built with the money obtained from the allies.[41] All the same, the fact remains that, in the imaginary representations of the Athenians and of their allies, this building remained closely associated with the onward march of the empire, for was it not used to shelter the league's treasury, which was transferred to Athens in 454 B.C., at the latest?

It is, moreover, this practical necessity—namely, to find a place for the treasury—that explains the strange layout of the monument. The fact is that, ordinarily, a Greek temple was built in accordance with a stereotyped schema: a vestibule (*pronaos*), then a central hall containing the cult statue (*naos*), and, finally, a back room (*opisthodomos*), for the use of the temple staff. In comparison to this canonical arrangement, the structure of the Parthenon is, to say the least, unusual—and for two reasons: in the first place, the huge dimensions of the *naos* contrast strongly with the limited area taken up by the *pronaos* and the *opisthodomos* (figure 6). The fact was that the central hall had to be spacious enough to house the immense statue of Athena Parthenos. Then, an extra room, with four columns, was set between the *naos* and the *opisthodomos*: a hall that gave its name to the edifice as a whole, the Parthenon, " the room for the virgin."[42] It was in this space that the city treasures were stored, in particular the treasury of the Delian League. This extra room that housed the allies' tribute was thus the very symbol of Athenian imperialism. It is surely not merely by chance that the four columns that

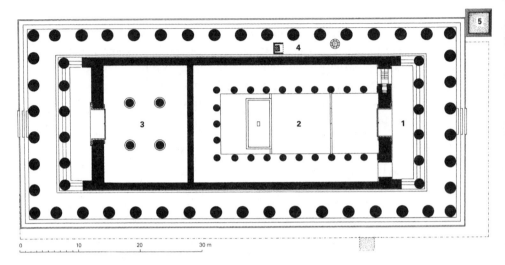

FIGURE 6. Athens, Acropolis, the Parthenon (ca. 447–437 B.C.): plan of the temple. Drawing by M. Korres. Courtesy of the Media Center for Art History at Columbia University.

supported the roofing of this room were in the Ionic style. Incorporating this Ionic style at the very heart of a Doric edifice was a way for the Athenians to give material expression to their domination over a league made up chiefly of Ionian cities.

Far from being a temple,[43] the Parthenon was a treasury and a monument that glorified imperialism and symbolized the hardening or even petrification of Athenian domination. In this respect, the chronology is significant: the construction of the Parthenon began in 447, one year before the great Euboean revolt, and it was completed in 438, one year after the Samos affair.

In truth, there is nothing specifically Periclean about the management of the empire, except a particular way of theorizing about its necessity, and its presentation. Although we should perhaps not impute to Pericles in particular the responsibility for the city's slide into imperialism, Pericles certainly did take over this new order without compunction, both in practice and in the representations that he promoted. Now we must evaluate to what degree the imperial dynamic and democratization of the city went hand in hand. Let us do so by analyzing the bases of the Periclean economy.

CHAPTER 5

A Periclean Economy?

Today, an "economy" means the production, distribution, and consumption of goods, both material and immaterial. But this term, which was forged in Athens in the classical period, had a sense that was very different from its contemporary one. In the fourth century, *oikonomia* defined, first, the way of managing an *oikos*, an agricultural property. It was only by extension that the term came to designate the management of the resources of a city, or even an empire. This mismatch between *oikonomia* and "economy," the ancient formulation and the modern definition, for a long time led historians to doubt the existence, in the Greek world, of any economic sphere separate from all other social activities.

One group of ancient historians thus maintains that the cities knew of nothing more than a primitive form of economy, characterized by the preponderant part played by agriculture, the role of self-subsistence, the limited place of crafts and money, and an absence of major exchange systems. That view has long since been challenged by experts who, on the contrary, emphasize the dynamism of the ancient economy. In this battle between "primitivists" and "modernists" that started at the end of the nineteenth century, the Athens of Pericles constitutes a particularly animated scene of disagreement.

The fact is that, in the course of the fifth century, the democratic city experienced a phase of extraordinary prosperity. Its silver coinage was developing so rapidly that the little Athenian "owls" became the common currency of a large part of the Greek world. Its port, Piraeus, became the major seat of exchange for the eastern Mediterranean. However, historians are not in agreement as to the nature of the economic prosperity of Athens: did it result from an internal dynamic, in particular a rational management of resources both private and public, or was it no more than a by-product of Athens's exploitation of the Delian League? What were the bases of the Athenian economy under Pericles? Was this an economy based on the revenues that Athens obtained from the hegemonic position that it acquired, or did its vitality spring from the rise of new economic ways of proceeding within the city? And, in any case, is it really possible to assign to Pericles a specific role in any such evolution?

To find answers to these questions, we must begin by focusing upon the private sphere: can we detect the existence of any Periclean *oikonomia*—that is to say, any specific way of managing an *oikos* and one's own personal assets? According to the ancient authors, the *stratēgos* administered his own patrimony extremely carefully, radically rejecting extravagant behavior and the kind of practices that led one into debt and that were then favored by the Athenian elite.

When we pass from the private sector to the civic level, the questions change. They now concentrate on the part that the empire played in the economic dynamism of Athens. Even if it is clear that the Athenians drew substantial benefits, both direct and indirect, from the empire, this does not mean that their prosperity stemmed solely from the tribute that they levied on their subject cities. Today, most historians think that the policy of "major constructions" associated with the name of Pericles was financed only partly by the league treasury, which was transferred to Athens before 454.

Whatever the exact degree of the economic exploitation of the allies, the city also profited from other large revenues—what the Greeks called *prosodoi*. The Athenians took to using these sums of money in a new way: they redistributed part of them to the community in the form of wages and civic allowances. Perhaps this was the true specificity of the Periclean economy: a new way of redistributing wealth to beneficiaries who, in return, became more strictly controlled. In this major development, Pericles certainly played a decisive role.

PERICLES AND A RATIONAL MANAGEMENT OF THE *OIKOS*: THE BIRTH OF A "MARKET ECONOMY"

The *Oikonomia Attikē*

Etymologically, *oikonomia* designates the controlled management (*nomos* comes from *nemein*, with the root meaning "distribute" and so "manage") of a household. Far from identifying with the modern notion of an economy, initially it concerned only the private sphere and, above all, affected only agricultural activity, to the detriment of other forms of production and distribution, such as artisan activity and commerce.

It is true that agriculture constituted the essential part of the wealth that was produced in the Greek world—as much as 80 percent of its total value.[1] This predominance of agricultural activity has sometimes led historians to represent the Greek economy as a static world, characterized by technological stagnation and an ideal of self-sufficiency. But was that really the case? It is certainly what one might think, reading ancient history sources that set such a high value upon the *autourgos*, the citizen who worked on his land with his own bare hands within the framework of direct exploitation. Yet that representation corresponds only partly to the reality.

In plenty of cities, the majority of citizens did not possess a property large enough to assure the viability of such an ideal of self-sufficiency. In Athens, the only city for which it is feasible to guess at a few figures, fewer than one citizen out of three was in a position to live off his own land. Close on two-thirds of the civic population either owned no land at all or else not enough for them to live off; most citizens owned plots of land less than one hectare in area (that is, less than 2.5 acres) and were consequently forced to engage in other activities, as craftsmen or as wage-earning agricultural laborers, in order to make a living.[2] So only a fraction of the citizen population lived off its land, a number that corresponded to the number of those who, in the fifth century, belonged to the census class of *zeugitae*. To these should be added a tiny elite composed of large-scale landowners, such as Cimon and Pericles—probably no more than one thousand individuals in all—who owned estates of over 20 hectares (that is, 50 acres), which were in many cases run by specialized managers (see later).

Two conclusions may be drawn from that summary. First, the model of small-scale landowners was far from dominant in Athens; and second, self-sufficiency is not the appropriate term to describe the lifestyle of either large-scale landowners or landless citizens. While the latter were obliged to find something to live off by buying in from outside, the former had to profit from their surpluses by selling them in some local, regional, or international market. Selling surpluses, buying what was lacking and paying taxes: that is an accurate enough definition of the *oikonomia attikē* that was characteristic of the fifth-century democracy of which Pericles is the ambiguous symbol.

Pericles in His *Oikos*: Agriculture Destined for the Marketplace

As we have seen,[3] Pericles was a large-scale landowner and the heir to a family possessed of great wealth. According to Plutarch, far from living glued to his estate, the *stratēgos* managed his *oikos* in strict symbiosis with the market, selling his agricultural produce outside the city: "The wealth which was legally his, . . . so that it might not cause him much trouble and loss of time when he was busy with higher things, he set into such orderly dispensation as he thought was easiest and most exact. This was to sell his annual products all together in the lump, and then to buy in the market each article as it was needed" (*Pericles*, 16.3–4). Such buying and selling practices depended on confidence in the way the market functioned, for they implied retaining no stocks at all and relying throughout the year on continuous supplies from the agora. Such marketing operations also presupposed not only the existence of local or even regional markets but also an in-depth monetarization of Athenian society. Purchases were made using silver currency, which of course had first to be acquired from sales. We should remember that minted coins, invented in the sixth century, had spread rapidly throughout the whole of Greece, but particularly in Athens, and that ever since the early fifth century the city had been able to mint many issues of coins, thanks to its intensive exploitation of the Laurium district, in southern Attica. Pericles therefore had no compunction about resorting to money, unlike some of the traditional elite, who blamed this tool for dissolving traditional social relations by bringing fortunes into circulation and thereby upsetting status-based hierarchies.[4]

Pericles' *oikonomia* was also characterized by another distinctive feature, this time involving the management of "human capital." The *stratēgos* chose not to manage his property himself, preferring to delegate the task to Euangelos, a slave (*oiketēs*) whom he had previously trained. In this way, Pericles showed his attachment to the aristocratic ideal of *skholē*, leisure, freeing time to devote himself to political and military activities. This practice of delegation was in no sense a sign of aristocratic disdain for agricultural work. Rather, it testified to a desire for rational specialization: the estate was entrusted to a strictly efficient man[5] who devoted himself full time to it and could even show inventiveness at the level of agricultural techniques.

Pericles' attitude toward his *oikos* reflects not so much the development of market-agriculture—that would be an exaggerated claim—but rather of "marketable agriculture"—that is to say, agriculture whose products were destined for the marketplace.[6] In this respect, the Periclean *oikonomia* testifies to a world that certainly did not operate within a closed space, on the model of self-sufficiency. But now we need to understand the reasons that led Pericles to act in this way. Was his behavior prompted by a desire for gain or by avarice (of which he was accused by some of his own relatives) or was it, rather, an effective way for the *stratēgos* to hold on to his patrimony, meanwhile maintaining his allegiance to the people?

The Periclean Mode of Management: Marked on the One Hand by a Refusal to Borrow and on the Other by a Rejection of Speculation

Pericles adopted a mode of managing his *oikos* that enabled him never to spend more than he produced. By selling the whole of his agricultural produce on the market, in one fell swoop, the *stratēgos* was in a position to know exactly how much capital he had at his disposal and so to proceed to make his purchases. He was now able to calculate exactly how much he could spend in order to meet both his private needs and his public commitments, such as liturgies, without drawing on his patrimony or running into debt.[7] As Plutarch explains, his family "murmured at his expenditure for the day merely and under the most exact restrictions, there being no surplus of supplies at all, as in a great house and under generous circumstances, but every outlay and intake proceeding by count and measure."[8]

This attitude toward accounting differed radically from the usual practices of members of the civic elite who, for the most part, preferred to run into debt rather than calculate their expenses. Wealthy Athenians felt no compunction about borrowing and pledging their land as collateral, in order to maintain their rank in society, as can be seen from the numerous pledged boundary markers (*horoi*) found in Attica and dating from the fourth and third centuries B.C. Strictly speaking, such boundary stones were placed in the fields in order to announce to one and all that this particular field was pledged to a mortgage or a guarantee.[9] Far from being a sign of the endemic indebtedness of the small-scale Athenian peasantry—which may well have existed in the fifth century but is not documented—these boundary stones instead testified to a system of credit and mortgages that operated within a group of affluent citizens. As specialists have shown, debtors and creditors were all members of the same elite, so it was not poverty that drove borrowers to mortgage their land; rather, the need to finance heavy prestige expenses, such as dowries and liturgies, or else a desire to make productive investments.[10] This was precisely the kind of sumptuary or speculative behavior that Pericles wished to avoid, so anxious was he to cover his expenses without risk of encroaching on his patrimony.

Pericles' attitude was certainly marked by a measure of rationality, but there was nevertheless a negative aspect to it. In the eyes of many members of the elite, it smacked of stinginess to the point of creating serious tensions within his own family. His children bitterly resented the mediocre lifestyle that he imposed on the entire household. As Plutarch reports, his son Xanthippus was a "natural big spender [*phusei te dapanēros*] and was married to a young and extravagant woman" (*Pericles*, 36.1). So he did not take at all kindly to the fact that Pericles was so parsimonious with his allowances.[11] Xanthippus was steeped in an ethic of aristocratic generosity and regarded his father's carefully calculated moderation as pure avarice.

In reality, Pericles was above all determined not to be placed in the position of a debtor, a situation that he reckoned to be incompatible with the authority that he was keen to maintain. In this respect, an anecdote reported by Plutarch provides a striking illustration of his horror of debt. Exasperated at not receiving enough money from his father, "Xanthippus eventually sent to one of his father's friends and got money, pretending that Pericles had bade him do it. When the friend afterwards demanded repayment of the loan, Pericles not only refused it, but brought a suit against him to boot. So the young fellow Xanthippus, incensed at this, fell to abusing his father" (*Pericles*, 36.1–2). Because he refused to incur any debts, the *stratēgos* apparently had no hesitation in quarreling not only with one of his friends, but even with his own son!

The historical truth of this episode is far from well established, but the anecdote does testify to the hostility that Pericles' behavior aroused among members of the Athenian elite, who were accustomed to a quite different attitude to expenditure. When stripped of its polemical aspect, this episode also reveals the deep-seated reasons for Pericles' attitude. His mode of expenditure stemmed neither from avarice nor from speculation, but constituted a way of protecting his patrimony, by ruling out resorting to loans. Its aim was to defend his authority by avoiding being placed in a position of indebtedness.

Nevertheless, the *stratēgos's* behavior is still astonishing, for it seems to defy the most elementary economic rationality. If Pericles refused to fall into debt, well and good. But that does not explain why he proceeded to sell all his produce *in one go*: to sell everything at once ruled out the possibility of obtaining the best prices, if only because, by pouring all his surpluses into the market, Pericles automatically drove prices down, to his own disadvantage. The iron law of the market would have favored him selling his products as circumstances dictated—for example, at points when gaps needed to be bridged and the price of cereals was soaring. It is therefore hard to portray Pericles as a model of novel and rational economic behavior. While the Aristotelian school defined the *oikonomia attikē* by the twofold action of selling and buying,[12] it certainly did not recommend selling all one's produce at once!

So how is it possible to explain this strange decision that not only alienated his closest relatives but also deprived him of substantial profits? In truth, in behaving in this way, Pericles was obeying rationality of a political rather than an economic nature. Because all forms of speculation were liable to damage the people—who depended on cereals for their survival—the *stratēgos* was absolutely determined not to pass for a profiteer or even a monopolist, however much this harmed his own interests. Pericles wished to be the protector of the *dēmos* even in the manner in which he managed his own property.

Although he was sometimes accused of avarice in the private sphere, the *stratēgos* had a fine reputation for generosity in the public sphere. Throughout his career, he manifested an unfailing concern for the well-being of the people, not only through the liturgies that he delighted in providing with munificence (see earlier, chapter 1), but above all by passing on to the *dēmos* the profits that resulted from the exploitation of the empire.

PERICLES AND THE EXPLOITATION OF THE EMPIRE: THE DEVELOPMENT OF AN ECONOMY BASED ON REVENUES

Under Pericles' leadership, the Athenians derived from the functioning of the Delian League both direct benefits in the shape of pay and cleruchies, and indirect ones thanks to Athens's control of commercial routes.

The Direct Benefits of Imperialism: Military Pay and Cleruchies

Military pay constituted one means of enrichment for the city: the empire made it possible, de facto, to feed a by no means negligible proportion of the civic population. According to Plutarch, Pericles sent out "sixty triremes annually, on which large numbers of the citizens sailed about for eight months under pay [*emmisthoi*], practising and at the same time acquiring the art of seamanship" (*Pericles*, 11.4). Was this an innovatory move on the part of the *stratēgos*? That is a matter for debate, for it was a practice that may have gone back to Cimon or even to Aristides.[13]

Whatever the case may be, soldiers and oarsmen, thetes, but also metics, were certain of being remunerated well enough when they enrolled on the Athenian triremes. At the cost of one drachma per day for every man who embarked, Athens supported over 10,000 citizens and metics during those eight months of seafaring.[14] If Plutarch is to be believed, that already represented an expenditure of over 400 talents a year and it was all funded by the league's treasury!

Remaining in the domain of the military and the direct administration of the empire, we must, as the author of *Constitution of the Athenians* suggests,[15] add to this all the pay for sixteen hundred bowmen, twelve hundred cavalrymen, and five hundred guards for the arsenals located in Athens. The empire furthermore mobilized seven hundred magistrates who were despatched throughout the league to control it and protect Athenian interests. These were specialized employees such as the *hellēnotamiai*, the league treasurers, and the *episkopoi* (the overseers), whose salaries were, in all probability, directly financed by the federal treasury.[16] All this represented no fewer than 4,000 men who, at that time, were all Athenian citizens. If the oarsmen are added to these, the total amounts to almost 15,000 individuals supported directly by the empire, the majority of whom were Athenians, out of a population of between 40,000 and 50,000 citizens.

Thanks to Pericles, citizens benefited from the empire in other ways too. The *stratēgos* increased the number of cleruchies—that is to say, the installation of military garrisons in the territories of allied cities. This was part of a tradition that had been initiated well before his time and was then developed by Cimon.[17] "He [Pericles] despatched a thousand settlers to the [Thracian] Chersonesus, and five hundred to Naxos, and to Andros half that number, and a thousand to Thrace, to settle with the Bisaltae, and others to Italy, when the site of Sybaris was settled, which they named Thurii."[18] But the list provided by Plutarch is incomplete: cleruchies were also sent to Chalcis and Histiaea after the revolt in Euboea,[19] and to Sinope and Amisos on the Black Sea (*Pericles*, 20.2), to Aegina (*Pericles*, 23.2), and to Astakos in the Propontis.

What exactly was a cleruchy? It was composed of Athenian citizens who were installed, as a garrison, on a portion of the allied territory that had been confiscated for their use. The cleruchs, who retained their original citizenship, had to remain, under arms, in the lands that the allies cultivated for them and from which they received the income. So these were not peasant-soldiers, but soldier-landlords of the occupied territory. In all likelihood, they did not become owners of the land but simply enjoyed the usufruct, in the name of the city of Athens as a whole.[20]

This system certainly helped the poorest of the Athenians, the thetes and the *zeugitae*, who were the principal beneficiaries of these territorial initiatives: the decree that founded the city of Brea, in Thrace (between 446 and 438), testifies explicitly to the role that fell to them in this type of operation.[21] The cleruchs in this way became eligible for the archonship, at least they did once this prestigious magistracy was opened to admit the third census class, from 457 B.C. onward. It would, however, be wrong to treat the cleruchies simply as a way of benefiting the poorest citizens. Everything leads us to believe that wealthy Athenians were also beneficiaries, although they were not forced to reside in the garrisons.[22]

Over and above their direct exploitation of the empire, the Athenians enjoyed other, more indirect, benefits from their hegemonic position at the heart of the Delian League. By constructing a vast commercial zone that was, if not unified, at least under Athenian control, the city confirmed its position as the economic center of the Aegean world at the time of Pericles.

The Indirect Benefits of Imperialism: The Control of Commercial Routes

Thanks to its powerful navy, very early on in the fifth century, Athens obtained control of the wheat route that led to the Pontus Euxinus, today's Black Sea, the location of one of the principal granaries of the Greek world—the kingdom of the Bosporus. Much was at stake here: cereals (*sitos*) formed the basis of the staple diet of the Greeks of Antiquity—almost three-quarters of their daily nutritional intake[23]—and, as Attica was, for ecological reasons, deficient in grain,[24] every year the city was obliged to import almost 25,000 tons of cereals in order to feed its large population.[25] That is why, ever since the foundation of the league, the Athenians had taken care to control the stopping-off points along this vital commercial route, at a time when navigation was mostly a matter of hopping from one Aegean island to another: Lemnos and Imbros remained under Athenian control throughout the Classical period; Skyros was captured in 475; and the revolt of Thasos was mercilessly crushed in 465–463.

This policy was pursued and strengthened in the years when Pericles played a major role in the city. First, the *stratēgos* encouraged the creation of the colonies of Brea, in Thrace—between 446 and 438—and Amphipolis in Chalcidice in 437, both so as to distribute land to Athenian citizens and also in order to secure supplies of cereals for Athens (Thucydides, 4.102). Next, he launched an expedition to the Chersonesus, a narrow spit of land that controlled the routes through the straits. According to Plutarch, this was the most popular of all his military ventures (*Pericles*, 19.1). This campaign, which may have begun in 447 B.C., made it possible to set up cleruchies[26] and to establish control of the straits leading to the rich wheat-lands of the Pontus Euxinus. Finally, Pericles may have led a military expedition to the Black Sea, if we are to believe Plutarch, who, however, is the only author to mention this little-known episode (*Pericles*, 20.1). This campaign, probably launched between 438 and 432, after the Samos War, testifies to the *stratēgos*'s concern to ensure cereal supplies to the city.

This preoccupation of his found expression in the elaboration of an ad hoc legal framework and the creation of a specific magistracy, probably in Pericles' time. An Athenian decree drawn up between 432 and 426 for Methone in Pieria (on the Macedonian coast at the end of the Thermaic Gulf) reveals the existence of "guardians of the Hellespont," the *hellespontophulakes*. The text authorized the city of Methone each year to import a fixed quantity of grain, for which it had to apply to these magistrates.[27] The "guardians of the Hellespont" in this way controlled all the convoys of grain in the Hellespont (today known as the Dardanelles), for the allied cities had first to apply to them for authorization to transport wheat directly to their own territories. Even if, as it happened, those arrangements suited the allied cities, they nevertheless show how very intrusive Athens's control of the trading of cereals was. No city was allowed free passage in the straits leading to the Black Sea: the Athenians were determined not only to safeguard their own supplies and prevent these deliveries from being diverted by the enemy, but possibly also to make supplies to the allies dependent on their loyalty.[28] Thanks to the empire, the Athenians in this way benefited from guaranteed supplies of cereals that enabled them to feed their large population at a strictly controlled price, at the same time manipulating an effective means of making the allies toe the line.

At an economic level, there was yet another consequence to this imperial dynamic: in the course of the fifth century, in step with its increase of military power, Athens became the commercial hub in the eastern Mediterranean. Under Pericles, Piraeus became the spot on to which the riches of the "whole world" converged. As the *stratēgos* himself emphatically stated, according to Thucydides, in the funeral oration of 431 B.C., "Our city is so great that all the products of all the earth flow in upon us, and ours is the happy lot to gather in the good fruits of other lands with as much home-felt security of enjoyment as we do those of our own soil."[29] This position at a crossroads was a great financial advantage to the city. All the imports and exports that passed through Piraeus were subject to 2 percent taxation: the *pentekostē*, the tax of one-fiftieth, brought in large sums of money that filled the coffers of Athens, making it possible to pursue an ambitious policy of redistribution (see later).

Finally, the city benefited from one more trump card that was linked to its hegemonic position. To cover certain military expenses, the city raised tribute (*phoros*) the total sum of which is known to us from 454 onward, thanks to great lists engraved in stone. These monumental inscriptions, situated on the Acropolis, consigned one-sixtieth of the sums paid by each member of the league to the goddess Athena, as "first fruits" (*aparkhē*).[30] These sums paid by the allies were partly diverted by the Athenians, who used them for purposes other than their original one, which had been to prevent the Persians from returning to the Aegean. It has to be said that the extent of that diversion of funds is, still today, a matter of controversy.

The Treasury of the Delian League Placed at the Service of Athens?

According to Plutarch, Pericles' enemies accused him of having drawn on the treasury of the allies to finance the great works on the Acropolis that were undertaken from 449 B.C. (*Pericles*, 12.2). This is the famous passage that led to those great works, in particular the construction of the Parthenon, being regarded as the petrified symbol of Athenian imperialism.[31] Several other sources also testify to the size of the sums mobilized for this vast building project: according to Diodorus Siculus, who probably draws his information from the fourth-century historian Ephorus, the Athenians spent 4,000 talents (out of a total of 10,000) on building simply the Propylaea and on funding the siege of Potidaea (432–429 B.C.). In Thucydides' work, Pericles himself suggests a comparable sum.[32] However, some historians question not the use of the league's treasury to finance the great building works, but the degree to which the allies were made to contribute. Did the *phoros* cover the entire costs of the monumental building policy initiated by Pericles, or did it contribute only a part of it?

The core of the problem lies in the exact status of the league treasury at the point when it was transferred to the Acropolis, no later than 454: was it at this point amalgamated with the treasury of the goddess—that is to say, the city treasury—or did it remain distinct, stored in a separate coffer? The *Athenian Tribute Lists*, which recorded the sum of one-sixtieth of the contributions of all the members of the league, seem to favor the latter alternative: after all, why keep a scrupulous record of the total *aparkhē* offered to the goddess (one-sixtieth) if the whole of the treasury fell to her in any case?[33]

There is one further element that favors this hypothesis. Athens was sufficiently prosperous to finance the essential part of the works with its own funds and to do so despite the scale of the expenses simultaneously incurred not only in the town (for new constructions in the Agora and the erection of Pericles' Odeon), but also in the *khōra*, for the building of the *Telesterion* of Eleusis, the sanctuaries of Nemesis in Rhamnous and of Demeter and Kore at Thorikos, and even the construction of the temple of Poseidon on Cape Sunium.[34] The city had abundant financial resources at its disposal, thanks to the income accumulated from the exploitation of the Laurium mines, commercial taxes such as the *pentekostē*, and the tenth part levied on booty that systematically swelled the city treasury. In his play *The Wasps* (656–660), Aristophanes underlines the composite nature of Athens's financial resources, which accrued both from the exploitation of the empire and from its own economic dynamism: "And not with pebbles precisely ranged, but roughly thus on your fingers count / The tribute paid by the subject States, and just consider its whole amount; / And then, in addition to this, compute the many taxes and one-per-cents, / The fees and the fines, and the silver mines, the markets and harbours, and sales and rents. / If you take the total result of the lot, it will reach two thousand talents or near."

For those two reasons, on the one hand the probable maintenance of two distinct coffers and, on the other, Athens's own economic dynamism, some historians believe that only the *aparkhē* was used to finance the constructions on the Acropolis—that is to say, about seven talents per year.[35]

Adalberto Giovannini even maintains that this allocation was decided by Athens and its allies together in 454, at the point when the treasury was transferred to the Acropolis on account of the military threat hanging over Delos. That, he thinks, was the precise moment that Athena Polias replaced Delian Apollo as the tutelary deity of the League. The reconstruction of the goddess's temple would in these circumstances logically enough involve the allies' participation. Clearly, this argument rests upon an irenic and idealized view of the international relations that prevailed; it nevertheless has the huge advantage of not reducing the Athenian system purely to a simple matter of an economy based on imperial revenues.

Far from living off the empire like a parasite, the city possessed an economic dynamism of its own, quite independent of its exploitation of the allies. When Athens embarked on an expensive policy of redistribution of wealth, it did so drawing partly on its own funds. In the period when Pericles was repeatedly elected as *stratēgos*, the Athenians were indeed setting up a full-scale system of redistributions not only by means of its great constructional undertakings but also through the general introduction of civic pay. It was probably here that the true originality of the Periclean economy lay.

PERICLES AND THE *MISTHOI*: THE ESTABLISHMENT OF A POLICY OF REDISTRIBUTION

The Social Impact of the Great Works: The Establishment of a State Socialism?

If we are to believe the famous passage from Plutarch, those great works provided *misthoi*, wages, for a great many skilled professions:

> It was true that his military expeditions supplied those who were in the full vigour of manhood with abundant resources from the common funds, and in his desire that the unwarlike throng of common labourers should neither have no share at all in the public receipts, nor yet get fees for laziness and idleness, he boldly suggested to the people projects for great constructions, and designs for works which would call many arts into play and involve long periods of time, in order that the stay-at-homes, no whit less than the sailors and sentinels, might have a pretext for getting a beneficial share of the public wealth. The materials to be used were stone, bronze, ivory, gold, ebony and cypress-wood; the arts which elaborate and work up these materials were those of carpenter, moulder, bronze-smith, stone-cutter, dyer, worker in gold and ivory, painter, embroiderer, embosser, to say nothing of the forwarders and furnishers of the material, such as factors, sailors and pilots by

sea, and, by land, wagon-makers, trainers of yoked beasts, and drivers. There were also rope-makers, weavers, leather-workers, road-builders, and miners. And since each particular art, like a general with the army under his separate command, kept its own throng of unskilled and untrained labourers in compact array, to be as instrument unto player and as body unto soul in subordinate service, it came to pass that for every age, almost, and every capacity, the city's great abundance was distributed and scattered abroad by such demands.[36]

Despite a tenacious tradition that denies the historical reality, Pericles clearly took measures that were advantageous to craftsmen, as Max Weber was one of the first to recognize.[37] The great construction works benefited all those who, to varying degrees, were involved on the building sites, and they did so regardless of the status of the workers.[38] There were many non-citizens present on those public building sites, as can be deduced, with very little risk of error, by extrapolating from the construction accounts relating to another Athenian temple, the Erechtheum. The accounts preserved are those for the years 409/8 and 408/7 B.C., but the actual building had commenced as early as 421. In 408, the building site employed 107 individuals, mostly stonemasons and carpenters. Their legal statuses varied considerably, since epigraphists have worked out that there were definitely 23 citizens, 42 metics, and 20 slaves among them. All the various components of the Athenian population were thus represented on the building site. However, those statutory differences were not reflected at the level of wages, for every worker received one drachma per day, although the slaves no doubt handed their wages over to their master, who in most cases would himself be working on the same building site.[39]

Let us now try to evaluate the aims and the scope of those great building works. Some historians have interpreted them in terms of modern economic behavior. Was it a matter of relaunching economic activity? Was it an attempt to establish a veritable "State socialism," as Gustave Glotz claimed in his day?[40] It seems to me that that would be to adopt a misleading point of view and to slip into anachronism, for the Greek cities in truth had no economic policies, as such. If a city intervened in economic life, it was above all so as to increase its *prosodoi*, its revenues, even if it did then redistribute them among members of the community; it was not ever a matter of investing and increasing economic activity; in the Greek world, growth and the fight against unemployment were not, as such, political objectives.

The monumental policy initiated by Pericles in truth had a twofold purpose: In the first place, it was intended to adorn the city with imposing monuments and, once and for all, wipe out the outrages of the Persian Wars. So the primary ambition of the "great works" was at once political and symbolic. Second, the intention was to proceed to share the common benefits between all the members of the community. In this respect, these building sites were part of a policy to redistribute wealth to the people on a scale never before seen in history.

Although the redistributions that stemmed from the great works benefited both the citizens and the metics who worked side by side on the building sites, Pericles also promoted measures destined to benefit solely the Athenians, for it was they who were the principal supporters of his policies and, as malicious gossip did not fail to point out, he needed to make sure that they would vote for him.

The Creation of Civic Pay

In the first place, the *stratēgos* is said to have increased the number of banquets and religious spectacles laid on for his fellow-citizens and he did so at a by no means negligible cost.[41] It was a way to win the favor of the poorest citizens who, on the occasion of a sacrifice, would receive a portion of the sacrificed animals. The *stratēgos* was said, for the same reason, to have created a public fund, the *theorikon,* grants from which were designed to cover the costs of citizens who attended the festivals of Dionysus. According to one late text, "Given that many wished to go to the theatre so competition for places was fierce among both citizens and foreigners, Pericles wished to please the people and the poor and decreed that city revenues should be devoted to the festivals."[42] The assertion should nevertheless be considered with a degree of caution, for the *theorikon* is not attested until the mid-fourth century, so some historians doubt that its creation should be attributed to Pericles.[43]

What is certain, on the other hand, is that the *stratēgos* submitted to the Assembly the proposal that a number of grants, receiving of *misthoi*, should be created as remuneration for citizens for the time that they devoted to serving the city. These *misthoi* were so closely associated with the actions of Pericles that, in the *Gorgias*, Socrates confides to Callicles: "What I for my part hear is that Pericles has made the Athenians idle, cowardly, talkative, and avaricious, by starting the system of public payments [*misthophoria*]."[44]

Clearly, the *stratēgos* did play a pivotal role in this development that enabled the poorest citizens to take part in the functioning of democracy without fear of forfeiting their means of livelihood.

But again, we should consider what this innovation really amounted to. In the first place, contrary to Plato's assertion, the *stratēgos* did not introduce such payment for *all* public services. Only the dicasts, the judges of the people's lawsuits, benefited from them, and possibly the council members;[45] attendance at the *ekklēsia* was not remunerated until the beginning of the fourth century. Furthermore, initially, the sum paid as *misthos* was not enough to compensate for the loss of even the most modest of wages. Not only were the 6,000 dicasts only paid when they were actually sitting, and this did not happen every day,[46] but the two obols initially paid as compensation and even the three later paid under Cleon, by no means equaled the pay of a skilled manual worker, which was at least three times greater (about one drachma per day).

Despite those limitations, the establishment of this kind of pay marked a further stage of the city's democratization, at a date that is hard to specify; the measure was probably introduced after the reforms of Ephialtes, in 462, which certainly gave more power to the lawcourts, and probably before the death of Cimon in 451, if it is true that the compensation system was introduced, as Plutarch claims, in a context of rivalry between Cimon and Pericles.[47]

Whatever the exact number of these payments introduced by Pericles, as a result of them citizenship became a privilege that found expression in the pecuniary gain of those who received them. From then on, the Athenians became keen to restrict the number of those who potentially possessed such rights. Access to the first *misthoi* coincided with restrictions on citizenship.

Redistributions and Redefinition of the Civic Body

In 451, the Athenian political community was redefined more strictly. Not only were women and domiciled foreigners excluded, as was customary elsewhere in Greece, but now the city also rejected bastards (*nothoi*) with only one Athenian parent or who were born from an extramarital liaison between Athenians.[48] In the wake of Aristotle and echoing his words, Plutarch explicitly attributed this initiative to the *stratēgos*:

> Many years before this, when Pericles was at the height of his political career and had sons born in wedlock, . . . he proposed a law that only those should be reckoned Athenians whose parents on both sides were Athenians. And so, when the king of Egypt sent a present to the people of forty thousand measures of grain, and this had to be divided up among the citizens, there was a great crop of prosecutions against citizens of illegal birth by the law of Pericles, who had up to that time escaped notice and been overlooked.[49]

This restrictive measure, earlier mentioned by the author of the *Constitution of the Athenians*, Pseudo-Aristotle, should be understood bearing several parameters in mind. The first was of a political and ideological order: the new law chimed with one of the founding Athenian myths—namely, that of autochthony. From the mid-fifth century onward, Athenians took to calling themselves "autochthonous," born from the very soil of Attica, unlike most of the rest of the Greeks, who were considered to be the descendants of invaders, such as the Spartans, who were said to be descended from the Dorians.[50] In rejecting those of "mixed blood," the Athenian citizens were emphasizing their own prestigious origin, their *eugeneia*, thereby collectively laying claim to a distinctive attribute, birth, which had, in principle, been the preserve solely of the aristocracy.[51] This illustrious birth of theirs moreover constituted one of the bases upon which the Athenians relied to claim their hegemony over the rest of the Greeks. In the eyes of the Athenians, their noble ancestry justified their domination within the framework of the Delian League.

Within the city, that law may have reflected a certain hardening in the Athenians' attitude to the growing influence of its metics.[52] It is difficult to put a precise figure to the domiciled foreigners in Athens, but in the second half of the fifth century, they represented between one-fifth and one-half of the city's citizen population—between 10,000 and 20,000 individuals.[53] Socially, they were well integrated and some of them were probably married to Athenians—and to Athenian women—producing children who, by law, had citizen status. The law of 451 was intended to exclude "those with mixed blood" from the civic community.[54] However, there is no indication that this should be regarded as the result of an identity-crisis on the part of alarmed or xenophobic Athenians, for there is no mention of any such fear in the ancient sources; again, that would be to transfer certain contemporary anxieties onto the societies of the past.

The purpose of the measure introduced by Pericles seems to have been above all of a socioeconomic nature: it was voted in so as to limit the number of potential beneficiaries of the civic redistributions of wealth "because of the excessive number of citizens," as the *Constitution of the Athenians* explains (26.3–4). Was it prompted by any particular event? Plutarch's assertion should be viewed with caution: it is by no means certain that the vote on this measure was linked to the gift of wheat from the Egyptian Psammetichus, for the consignment from the pharaoh was sent in 445/4 B.C., six years after the introduction of the law on citizenship. All the same, even if he is mistaken about the details, Plutarch the moralist hits on the basic truth: the reason why the Athenians decided to redefine their civic body certainly was because it was necessary to regulate the sharing of the city's wealth, in particular, the distribution of the many instances of compensatory pay that had just been approved—for the members of the *heliaea* and of the *boulē*—and all the types of advantages that stemmed from the increasing imperialism of the city. A restrictive redefining of the circle of potential beneficiaries now became a matter of the first importance.

Progressively, a democracy that was more radical but also more closed upon itself was thus being set in place. At the same time as the Athenians began to receive pay for participating in the city institutions, they hardened the criteria governing the attribution of citizenship. There is really nothing surprising about this: *mutatis mutandis* and to introduce a cautious anachronism, that measure of 451 evokes the early days of the Social Republic in France, at the end of the nineteenth century, when the first redistributive measures voted in under the Third Republic went hand in hand with a stricter differentiation between nationals and foreigners. At the very moment when the first social laws were passed, new techniques of documentation and police control were set in place—in particular, the invention of passports and identity cards.[55]

Through a historical irony, after the deaths of his two legitimate sons, Pericles was finally forced to beg the people to waive this law in the case of his own bastard son. Now without a male heir, the *stratēgos* wanted Pericles the younger, born from his union with Aspasia, to be allowed to enter a phratry—an essential move in the process of acquiring citizenship—in order for him to be entered in the deme register and to inherit his father's fortune and social network. He was claiming that an exception should be made for his own family—he who liked to present himself as a man unaffected by the influence of family and friends. This tension that had grown between the *oikos* and the *polis*, relatives and the city, now needs to be examined.

CHAPTER 6

Pericles and His Circle:
Family and Friends

In most human societies, an individual counts for nothing outside the several groups to which he or she belongs. The individual's place in society depends largely on the influence of his or her family circle and his or her network of friends. The Greek cities were no exception to that rule: there were no "self-made men" in Antiquity! In Athens as elsewhere, one's family and friends were indispensable sources of support for anyone desiring a political career. All the same, in a democratic context, what was normally a trump card could turn out to be a handicap. To come from an illustrious family, make a brilliant marriage, and have powerful friends was potentially to be suspected of acting contrary to the interests of the people or even of aspiring to tyranny.

In fifth-century Athens, a politician thus had to resolve a complex equation. Although he needed his circle of family and friends in order to acquire power, he also had to take precautions against the suspicion that his entourage was bound to arouse. This delicate balance was hard to maintain, as the case of Pericles shows. On the one hand, the *stratēgos* behaved like any other member of the elite, shamelessly making the most of his social networks and establishing alliances with other powerful families, but on the other, he wished to appear to be a man wholly devoted to the people's cause, even to the point of neglecting the most important family rituals.

Not content to hold his kin (*suggeneis*) at a distance, Pericles more generally neglected the traditional forms of friendship (*philia*) and the sociability that was associated with them. So as not to arouse the people's jealousy, the *stratēgos* even avoided private banquets and such friendly entertainments. But even this did not prevent him from being attacked for his equivocal friendships and, in particular, his hospitality toward foreigners and even foreign women. The friends of Pericles, who were often mocked by the comic poets and sometimes were even dragged before the courts, paid the price for the people's mistrust of Pericles. Around Pericles' circle of friends there circulated stories that revealed the people's desire to monitor his family and friendly connections, even though these were indispensable for establishing and maintaining their leader's authority.

PERICLES AND HIS *OIKOS*: THE POLITICAL WAYS OF EXPLOITING KINSHIP

The Matrimonial Strategies of the Athenian Elite: Pericles' Nameless Wife

Kinship was the basis of a diffuse and lasting solidarity, whether it was vertical (between ancestors and descendants) or horizontal (between husband and wife). In this respect, Pericles could rely not only on his prestigious ancestors (see earlier, chapter 1), but also on the matrimonial alliances that he contracted within the Athenian elite. Plutarch refers tersely to Pericles' successive unions: "His own wife was near of kin to him and had been wedded first to Hipponicus, to whom she bore Callias, surnamed the Rich; she bore also, as the wife of Pericles, Xanthippus and Paralus. Afterwards, since their married life was not agreeable, he legally bestowed her upon another man, with her own consent, and himself took Aspasia, and loved her exceedingly" (Plutarch, *Pericles*, 24.5). This account illuminates the main characteristics of marriage within the Athenian elite. It testifies both to the structure of Greek marriage and also to its more or less explicit purposes.

In the first place, it reflects the domination of men over women. Marriage was a private contract between men in which the woman was a passive object: Pericles' wife was, exceptionally, only taken into account when she was passed on to a third husband. A telling sign of this inferiority is her anonymity. It is only by dint of a series of reinvestigations and hypotheses that Pierre Brulé has managed to restore her name to her. Pericles' wife seems to have been named Deinomache and is believed to have been the grand-daughter of Cleisthenes, the lawgiver.[1]

Second, this marriage illustrates the principle of endogamy that prevailed within the Athenian elite and that was further accentuated by the 451 law on citizenship. Pericles' wife belonged to a circle of close relatives. According to Pierre Brulé's reconstruction, Deinomache was the grand-daughter of Cleisthenes, while Pericles was the grandson of one of Cleisthenes' brothers, so his mother was the lawgiver's niece. Moreover, his wife's father was none other than his own mother's brother and so was Pericles' uncle; so Pericles and his wife were first cousins (see figure 1).

Pericles' marriage provides a splendid illustration of the way in which kinship structures functioned in Athens. The ideal marriage was a union with one's closest relative. We even get the impression that Deinomache's first marriage was dissolved so that Pericles could "recover" the woman who was his cousin. However, we should not overemphasize this characteristic, for exogamy and endogamy by no means excluded one another. "The flexibility of the Athenian matrimonial system allowed those involved to choose between the advantages of endogamy and exogamy according to whatever was in their best interest."[2]

Over and above the structural elements—masculine domination and the principle of endogamy—this account also illuminates the two principal aims of marriage. First, its explicit objective: to produce legitimate children. With Pericles, Deinomache gave birth to Xanthippus and Paralus. From this point of view, Cleisthenes' grand-daughter seems to have been endowed with a remarkable procreative ability: quite apart from the daughters that she may have had, she provided sons for every one of her successive husbands! Next, the implicit objective: this string of unions served to forge alliances between members of the Athenian elite. Deinomache, initially married to Hipponicus II, was then passed on to Pericles, and was finally given to Cleinias—as if she were nothing but a fine trousseau. Her first husband, Hipponicus II, was himself endowed with a particularly impressive pedigree. Through his father, he was descended from the priestly Kerykes group, which provided one of the two priests who celebrated the mysteries of Eleusis. Through his mother, he was also related to the Cimonid family, as the son of Elpinike, Cimon's sister. However, Pericles had no cause to envy him since he, himself, like his wife, was part of the great Alcmaeonid family. As for Cleinias, the last of Deinomache's husbands, he belonged to one of the wealthiest families in Athens and could proudly claim descent from the heroes Eurysakes and Ajax.[3]

The effect of these successive marriages was to create more or less diffuse links of solidarity between the various spouses. So, after the death of Cleinias—the last of Deinomache's husbands—in the battle of Coronea in 447, Pericles became the guardian of the latter's orphaned sons, most notably the scandalous Alcibiades. This widening circle undeniably represented an advantage where political matters were concerned, as Plutarch noted after mentioning the death of Xanthippus at the time of the plague of 430 B.C.: "Pericles lost his sister also at that time, and of his relatives and friends the largest part, and those who were most serviceable to him in his administration of the city" (*Pericles*, 36.4).

However, we should not exaggerate the political impact of this network of alliances. Even if they were related, some members of the elite did not hesitate to clash openly within the public space. One example is provided by Pericles and his opponent Cimon, both of whom were part of the same network of alliances: Cimon had married a woman who came from the *oikos* of the Alcmaeonids, Isodike; and his sister, Elpinike, was the mother of the first husband of Pericles' wife. As for the *stratēgos*'s eldest son, Xanthippus, he married a daughter of Teisandrus, a member of the elder branch of the family of Miltiades and Cimon. Yet this close interlacing of relations did not prevent the two men from clashing time and again in the Assembly.[4] How can this animosity be explained? The fact is that, in the course of the fifth century, the people's rise to power had deeply upset the organized interplay of traditional alliances. In order to win the support of the *dēmos*, some members of the elite, Pericles among them, did not hesitate to set aside their kinship network, at least in their speeches, if not in their actions.

Without a Family? Pericles between *Oikos* and *Polis*

Even if, in practice, Pericles was not averse to relying on the support of his relatives, he nevertheless adopted in public a mode of behavior that tended to deny or at least marginalize their role. The *stratēgos* presented himself as a man more or less estranged from his family circle. In the first place, as we have seen, he separated from his wife and transferred her to the *oikos* of Cleinias; second, his relations with his legitimate heirs, particularly his elder son, Xanthippus, were severely fraught. It is hard to credit the rumors spread by Stesimbrotus of Thasos, according to whom the *stratēgos* slept with his daughter-in-law, the wife of his son. However, the fact remains that Pericles refused to advantage his own children and to treat them as "Daddy's boys," in all probability not so much out of stinginess as in order not to affront the people.[5] Perhaps we can thus interpret the choice of the name that he gave to his second son, Paralus. This could be seen as a way of showing an interest in the navy and so to manifest his allegiance to the thetes who manned the triremes. The Paralian was in effect the name of one of the city's two sacred ships.[6]

More radically still, throughout his political career, Pericles refused to take part in even the most elementary rituals of family sociability. He would no longer attend the wedding banquets that provided the cement par excellence that welded together the bond of kinship. Plutarch mentions only one exception to this rule: apparently, Pericles did attend the wedding of Euryptolemus, his cousin, but he stayed only until the libations—the first phase of the ritual. In the first place, this was a way of preserving his dignity and his solemn bearing. By attending too many banquets and taking part in too many festive celebrations, one risked slipping into drunkenness and possibly attracting ridicule.[7] For the *stratēgos,* though, it was above all a matter of avoiding the ceremonies in which families flaunted their power, their wealth, and their networks of relations to such a degree that sumptuary laws had been introduced so as to maintain a modicum of order by dint of limiting the number of guests that could be invited.[8]

In similar fashion, the *stratēgos* chose not to respect the current funerary conventions, even when his own children were carried off by death: "he did not give up nor yet abandon his loftiness and grandeur of spirit because of his calamities, nay, *he was not even seen to weep or to perform the funeral rites even at the grave of one of his close relatives* [*tōn anangkaiōn*], until indeed he lost the very last one of his own legitimate sons, Paralus" (Plutarch, *Pericles*, 36.4: translation B. Perrin, modified). At this point, we need to assess the degree of transgression that such behavior implied. To be sure, at the death of a relative, the men were expected to hold back their tears, unlike the women, who would express their grief in ritualized lamentations. The funeral procession (*ekphora*) had to pass through the city before sunrise and not include too many participants.[9] Nevertheless, it was unheard of for a relative, let alone a father, to withdraw from this crucial moment in the funerary ritual. On the contrary, the closest relatives were expected not only to be present but furthermore to lead the funerary procession![10]

If Pericles chose not to accompany members of his own family to their entombment, it may not have been solely on account of his remarkable fortitude, as Plutarch suggests, but also above all because he wished to avoid affronting the people. In the same way as a wedding ceremony, a funeral procession presented an opportunity for a public demonstration of an *oikos*'s power, as is attested by the many regulations imposed upon such manifestations, even as early as the archaic period.

All the same, Pericles' strange behavior cannot be explained solely by his desire not to affront the *dēmos*. We should regard it, more positively, as a way for the *stratēgos* to present himself as the parent of all Athenians: by setting aside his real family links, he could devote himself entirely to imaginary kinship relations that linked him with all his fellow-citizens through the device of the myth of autochthony that was now back in favor.[11] This, we should remember, converted all the citizens to brothers born from the same mother, the soil of Attica. The Athenians imagined themselves to be collectively endowed with a prestigious ancestry and consequently to stand on a footing of equality with one another;[12] the hierarchies of birth gave way before the belief of an origin common to all. In this context, the law of 451 on citizenship made sense, voted in, as it was, on Pericles' initiative. It chimed with the Athenian myth of autochthony, transforming the city into an endogamous community with no foreign additions.[13] There can be no doubt that the *stratēgos*'s entire policy aimed to place civic fraternity above real kinship.

However, for the *stratēgos* there was a psychological if not political price to pay for denying the importance of the family. In Athens, as elsewhere, such a rejection was hard to maintain to the bitter end. When, in 430, he learned of the death of his last legitimate heir, Paralus, the imperturbable *stratēgos* was brutally overcome by emotion and "broke out into wailing, and shed a multitude of tears, although he had never done any such thing in all his life before" (Plutarch, *Pericles*, 36.5). For a long time, he remained prostrate with grief in his *oikos*, rather than going to speak in the Assembly (*Pericles*, 37.1), and when he eventually reassumed his place as *stratēgos*, it was in order to request that his private interests be placed above the law of the city: he urged that the law on bastards (*nothoi*) that he himself had proposed in the past should be annulled "in order that the name and lineage [*genos*] of his house might not altogether expire through lack of succession" (37.2). The Athenians, whose hearts were touched, eventually allowed him "to enrol his illegitimate son in the phratry-lists and to give him his own name—Pericles" (ibid.).

This tension between *oikos* and *polis*, the private sphere and the public space, extended for the most part to the whole of Pericles' entourage. Not content to set his family at a distance, the *stratēgos* also appeared to break with his friends so as not to provoke the *phthonos* (envy) of the people.

PERICLES AND *PHILIA*: HARMFUL FRIENDSHIPS

The Friend of All and Yet of None

According to Plutarch, when Pericles entered political life he decided to adopt a transparent mode of public behavior and to set his old circle of friends at a distance: "Straightway he made a different ordering in his way of life. On one street only in the city was he to be seen walking—the one that took him to the market-place and the council-chamber. Invitations to dinner and all such friendly and familiar intercourse he declined, so that during the long period that elapsed while he was at the head of the city, there was not a single friend [*ton philon*] to whose house he went to dine" (*Pericles*, 7.4). As a stalwart member of the elite, Plutarch deplored the decision that led the young Pericles to cut himself off from his former *philoi*—that is to say, the elite circle in which he had been raised (*Pericles*, 7.5). Yet the *stratēgos*'s behavior did make sense in the increasingly democratic framework of the mid-fifth century. Perpetually placed before the eyes of the people, Pericles had decided ostensibly to reject his private friendships and the sociability that went with them. In this respect, his avoidance of private banquets—the *sumposion*—was a crucial element in the system that he adopted. In that it was a microcosm that shut out the external world, the *sumposion* was an object of suspicion to the *dēmos*, which was excluded from it. A group of banqueters functioned as an alternative community, more or less cut off from the civic and democratic order, as is clear from the works titled *Symposium* written by Plato and Xenophon. It was certainly not by chance that, a few years after Pericles' death, those jovial groups of banqueters became involved in the oligarchic revolutions that shook the Athenian city.[14]

Throughout his career, Pericles set the friendship of the people before his personal relationships. In any case, his public commitments were so absorbing that he could not always spare the time to devote to his friends, even the closest of them. According to an anecdote related by Plutarch, Anaxagoras of Clazomenae reproached him for this neglect of the elementary rules of *philia*: "At a time when Pericles was absorbed in business, Anaxagoras lay on his couch all neglected, in his old age, starving himself to death, his head already muffled for departure, and when the matter came to the ears of Pericles, he was struck with dismay and ran at once to the poor man and besought him most fervently to live, bewailing not so much that great teacher's lot as his own, were he now to be bereft of such a counsellor in the conduct of the city. Then Anaxagoras—so the story goes—unmuffled his head and said to him, 'Pericles, even those who need a lamp pour oil therein'" (*Pericles*, 16.7). So it was as a result of insufficient leisure time (*skholē*) as much as by his choice that the *stratēgos* cut himself off from his friends. Having devoted his career to the public interest, the *stratēgos* no longer had time to maintain a sociable life among his friends, with all that this, in the long term, involved in the way of reciprocal gestures and exchanges of favors.

To judge from Plutarch's account, Pericles' career was thus characterized by his marginalization of his private friendships, so as to maintain contacts solely with the *dēmos*. Some historians, such as W. R. Connor, have detected in this a radical innovation that reflects the democratic mutations that were taking place in the democracy during the fifth century. Until Pericles arrived on the scene, politicians were happy to depend on support in their affairs from their networks of *philoi*. But Connor suggests that a new political style emerged with Pericles, based on an austere lifestyle in which one's friends were deliberately relegated to the remote fringes of political life.[15] However, such a contrast is to a large extent exaggerated. In the first place, upstream, even before Pericles appeared upon the scene, Themistocles had, according to Aelian,[16] already behaved in this fashion. Second, downstream, Pericles' successors continued to make use of their circles of friends in order to secure their own power.[17] When Alcibiades arrived in Piraeus in 407 B.C., after eight years in exile, his first reflex was anxiously to look around for his close relatives; only when sure that they were indeed present, did he disembark and make his way to the town, to be elected *stratēgos autokratōr.*[18]

This enables us to qualify Plutarch's testimony. It probably reflects a democratic commonplace—namely, the leader's devotion to the people's interests alone, rather than the real practices of the elite. In fact, Pericles does not seem in practice to have renounced his many friendships. Rightly or wrongly, he was even accused by his enemies of maintaining a whole galaxy of more or less embarrassing *philoi.*

Pericles' Circle?

The ancient sources attribute to Pericles a whole gallery of "friends," as numerous as they were prestigious: among the Athenians, Damon, Phidias, and Sophocles; among the foreigners, Anaxagoras of Clazomenae, Aspasia of Miletus, Protagoras of Abdera, Hippodamus of Miletus, Kephalus of Syracuse, the Spartan king Archidamus, and many others too.[19] Pericles would therefore have been surrounded by a vast group of poets, philosophers, sophists, architects, and artists, all of whom helped him to make Athens "the school of Greece," to borrow the expression said by Thucydides to have been used by Pericles in his funeral speech.

However, historians have questioned the existence of a veritable "Pericles' circle"—with all that such a notion presupposes in the way of stability and allegiance—and they are skeptical for two reasons. In the first place, not all those ties of friendship are attested. The relations established between Pericles on the one hand and Hippodamus of Miletus and Protagoras of Abdera on the other are, to put it mildly, nebulous.[20] As for Kephalus of Syracuse, the father of the orator Lysias, even if he was indeed acquainted with Pericles, there is no evidence to suggest that he was a close friend of the *stratēgos.*[21] It was clearly a posteriori that the ancient authors reconstructed those friendly relations between a number of famous fifth-century figures, gathering them around the figure of Pericles like bees clustered around their queen. Besides, even such friends as are reliably confirmed lack the stability required to constitute a veritable "circle." Damon was ostracized early on; Phidias, an itinerant artist, was often away from Athens, carried to wherever his work took him—for example, to Olympia, where he worked from 437 to 433, sculpting the monumental statue of Zeus; and as for Anaxagoras, Plutarch himself stresses the fact that his relations with Pericles were frequently interrupted for long periods.

Even if, strictly speaking, there was no "Pericles' circle," that did not stop the *stratēgos*'s opponents from criticizing him for it. In truth, the supposed

Pericles' circle was in the first place a creation by his enemies, who hoped in this way to instill suspicions in the minds of Athenians, for in the Greek world, it was tyrants that were known to maintain a circle around themselves, a court entirely devoted to singing their praises. And was this not, after all, the kind of relationship that was suggested by sources that recorded that the *stratēgos*'s companions (*hetairoi*) were called "the new Pisistratids" (*Pericles*, 16.1)?

Whatever the case may be, the members of Pericles' circle came under constant attack, both on the comic stage and in the city courts. The target, through them, was clearly Pericles himself. Plutarch explicitly recognizes this when he describes the accuser who had Anaxagoras dragged before the court for impiety, probably in the early 430s: "He [Diopeithes] targeted Pericles, through Anaxagoras."[22] The opponents of Pericles were pursuing two contrary objectives when they criticized his entourage. Sometimes, they sought to present the *stratēgos* as an all-powerful man, reigning over the courtiers who groveled at his feet; at other times, they depicted him as a mere puppet, surreptitiously manipulated by a set of *éminences grises* or even foreign powers.

The accusations launched against the sculptor Phidias fell into the first of those two categories. He was depicted as Pericles' right-hand man, ready to do anything to execute his base demands. Rumor had it that the sculptor even acted as a pimp, to serve the pleasures of the *stratēgos*-tyrant: "making assignations for Pericles with free-born women who would come ostensibly to see the works of art."[23] Furthermore, the sculptor too was dragged before the courts, probably for embezzlement, following a scandal the mud from which also bespattered Pericles. In his play *The Peace*, performed in 421 B.C., Aristophanes picked up on this affair (but, unfortunately, only in vague terms), even suggesting that it was one of the causes of the Peloponnesian War.[24]

For the most part, though, Pericles was depicted not as a manipulating master, but as a man who was himself manipulated by his friends. For example, some sources represent Damon of Oa as the *stratēgos*'s eminence grise. According to the *Constitution of the Athenians*, it was he who persuaded Pericles to introduce pay for jurors.[25] Plutarch develops this theme, depicting Damon as the mentor of Xanthippus's son: "Damon seems to have been a consummate sophist, but to have taken refuge behind the name of music in order to conceal [*epikruptomenos*] from the multitude his real power, and he associated with Pericles, that political athlete, as it were, in the capacity of coach and trainer. However, Damon was not left unmolested in this use of his lyre as a screen, but was ostracized for being a great schemer and a friend of tyranny."[26] Damon consequently became the embodiment of a man of secrets or even plots, a shadowy counselor who handled his pupil, Pericles, like a puppet. The discovery of four potsherds bearing Damon's name testifies, if not to the truth of the anecdote, at least to the influence that Athenians ascribed to Damon.[27]

According to his detractors, Pericles was manipulated above all by foreigners, even—worse still—by female ones. He was certainly reputed to maintain numerous friendly relations outside the civic circle, as the comic poet Cratinus relates in a fragment cited by Plutarch: "Come, oh Zeus, patron of foreigners [*xenios*] and head of State [*Caranius*]!"[28] Pericles, who is often described as an Olympian, is here assimilated to Zeus *Xenios*, the god who protects and welcomes in foreigners. For the poet, this was a transparent way of deploring the links that bound the *stratēgos* to foreigners domiciled in the city. Aspasia came from Miletus, Chrysilla from Corinth, Anaxagoras from Clazomenae, and Kephalus from Syracuse. These relations were potentially dangerous ones. The *stratēgos*'s enemies could blame him for setting the interests of his foreign friends above those of the Athenian people.

In this respect, the outbreak of the Peloponnesian War placed Pericles in a particularly delicate position, for the *stratēgos* maintained links of hospitality (*xenia*) with the Spartan king Archidamus, who led his troops in an assault on Athens and laid waste its territory. At this point, Pericles solemnly promised, before the Assembly, that he would give the city his own properties should the Spartan leader leave them intact on account of the *xenia* that linked them.[29] The *stratēgos* was thus forced to take preemptive action so as not to be regarded as a corrupt man who allowed the city territory to be laid waste, knowing that he himself had nothing to fear personally with respect to his land. In the context of war, conventional aristocratic hospitality became incompatible with the obligations dictated by the civic world.[30]

However, his enemies concentrated most of their attacks on another of the *stratēgos*'s equivocal relationships. His love for Aspasia was deplored on many occasions. He was even accused of starting the Peloponnesian War for the sake of her lovely eyes. This was a matter of slipping from friendship into love or, to be more exact, from *philia* into *eros*.

CHAPTER 7

Pericles and *Eros*: Caught between Civic Unity and Political Subversion

Eros, not love: this terminological choice is no mere flirtatious quibble. It is intended to draw attention to how far apart the two terms are. In the Greek world, *eros* did not correspond to any romantic sentiment, nor did it bear any similarity to the wishy-washy notion nowadays conjured up by "love." Whether homosexual or heterosexual, *eros* was first and foremost a connective force or, at times, a disconnective one.[1]

First, as a connective force: *eros* linked individuals together, as indeed did *philia*, friendship. However, whereas friendship presupposed a form of equality between the partners, *eros* functioned in a hierarchical and asymmetrical fashion. The erotic link depended on a form of reciprocity that was structurally inegalitarian, for it always brought together a free citizen, who was in the dominant position, and a woman or an *erōmenos*—an adolescent—whose status was inferior. When transposed into a political framework, *eros* retained those same characteristics: it encouraged the development of hierarchical links between on the one hand, the citizens, and on the other, the city.

Next, as a force for disconnection: *eros* possessed a terrifying power capable of turning the normal functioning of social life upside down. Not content with snapping the very limbs of lovers,[2] it was capable of destabilizing even the best-established forms of social balance. *Eros* could destroy relations of *philia* or lead to adultery or even to treason; it then threatened the very survival of the city, which is why *eros* and politics often worked together, for better or worse.

Pericles' life combined those two contradictory aspects of *eros*. First, the power of connection: the *stratēgos* was an ardent defender of a veritable civic eroticism, to the point of urging the Athenians to cherish their city as a lover cherishes his loved one. According to Pericles, the citizens should behave themselves as a community of active lovers, linked together by their common love for their country. Yet, far from leaving the people and their city to this loving tête-à-tête, the leader came and involved himself in that relationship.

According to the ancient authors, Pericles aroused desire in the crowd both by his rhetoric and by his behavior, as his protégé Alcibiades was later to do. There was thus an erotic dimension to his authority. The citizens loved not only their city but also their leader. Next, a power of disconnection, for Pericles' story also testifies to the subversive power of *eros*. The *stratēgos* was accused of having experimented with the entire range of heterosexual unions, even to the point of placing the city in danger through his multiple and transgressive love affairs. His opponents denounced him for having not only behaved as a seducer, perverting the wives of other citizens, but also for being a man seduced and manipulated by beautiful foreign women.

Aspasia became the target of the barrage of criticisms aimed at Pericles. Presented, as she was, now as a *hetaira* or even a prostitute, now as a legitimate wife and a skilled mistress of rhetoric, this enigmatic woman deserved the whole study finally devoted to her in M. M. Henry's *Prisoner of History: Aspasia of Miletus and Her Biographical Tradition* (Oxford, UK: Oxford University Press, 1995). The ancient sources often portray her as a warmonger, a new Helen of Troy, bewitching Pericles and getting him to unleash the conflict against the Spartans. That biased image needs to be evaluated in the light of the prejudices that surrounded all women whose legal status was uncertain.

THE DEMOCRATIC AMOROUS TRIANGLE: THE CITY, THE LEADER, AND THE PEOPLE

Athens (not Hiroshima), Mon Amour

In the funeral speech that he delivered, according to Thucydides' version, Pericles urged all Athenians to demonstrate their desire for their city. In this case, the purpose of *eros* was not to link citizens to one another, but to unite them all, collectively, with their country, the object of all their attentions: "You must daily fix your gaze upon the power of Athens and become lovers [*erastai*] of her."[3] This is how the *stratēgos* transposed into the civic register the vocabulary associated with erotic masculine relationships. The fact is that, in the Greek world, ritualized pederastic links could connect an older citizen—the *erastēs*—with a young adolescent—the *erōmenos*—who was still in the flower of his youth. The importation of this vocabulary now used to describe the links between citizens and their city masked a number of implications. In the first place, this metaphor made it possible to set women radically apart; they were, of course, already excluded from the political scene. No symbolic compensation was offered to them in that speech, since what was proposed for the Athenians to meditate upon was a homoerotic model. Furthermore, that image presupposed the existence of a link of reciprocity between the two parties present: in a pederastic relationship, the *erastēs* was expected to educate and protect the *erōmenos* who, in return, offered him his company and favors. As Pericles saw it, the citizens should take the *erastēs'* role as guardian of the *city*, the *erōmenos* whom one contemplated with passion.

At first sight, this choice may seem surprising. The city appears to be relegated to a passive and subordinate role, leaving on the front of the stage the Athenians, who are described as a "vigorous elite" at the service of their country.[4] According to Sara Monoson, the metaphor may even conceal more disturbing implications. In their capacity as the *erastai*, the citizens may act in a shameful way and take advantage of the city, a naive and defenseless *erōmenos*.[5] That is, in fact, how the more or less declared opponents of democracy unhesitatingly interpreted the image, profoundly subverting its original meaning. In the first place, they applied the metaphor not to the links between the Athenians and their city, but to the relations that obtained between the citizens and their political leaders.[6] In the plays of Aristophanes, it is the demagogues who declare their love for the *dēmos*: "I love you, Demos, I am your *erastēs*,"[7] declares the Paphlagonian—a transparent caricature of Cleon,[8] in *The Knights*. Later, the comic poets portrayed those *erastai* as dangerous corrupters: with their self-interested love, the demagogues did nothing but debase the people, which, for its part, was portrayed as an aging *erōmenos*, at once capricious and depraved.[9] According to those ironical criticisms, Athens's leaders were guiding the city to its downfall, skillfully manipulating feelings and reactions.

However, that polemical view corresponded to a deliberately biased reading of the metaphor used by Pericles. When he resorted to that image, the orator had no intention of depicting a passive Athens, forced to accept whatever its citizens wanted; there is nothing to suggest that the metaphor had to be understood to the advantage of its citizens-*erastai*. As Mark Golden has shown, the supposed subordination of the *erōmenos* to the *erastēs* is not at all obvious if, without any preconceptions, one considers the texts and images that have come down to us.[10] In plenty of cases, the *erōmenos* seems to possess virtues characteristic of dominant personalities, while, in contrast, the *erastēs*, gripped by desire, frequently adopts a submissive or even miserable position. He finds himself at the mercy of his *erōmenos*, who is perfectly free to deny him his favors. Some authors even portray the youth as a tyrant, ruling harshly over his helpless lover.[11] Figurative codes repeatedly proclaim the paradoxical superiority of the *erōmenos*. On vases, instead of being represented as submissive, the adolescent is often facing up to his partner. He stands erect while the *erastēs* bends his knees and, in some cases, bows his head.[12] Sometimes, the latter is even presented in the traditional position of a suppliant, attempting to touch the youth's chin.[13]

In this context, the Periclean metaphor takes on a quite different meaning. By resorting to the language of pederastic love, the orator was in reality urging the citizens to offer their city extraordinary gifts, in the way that *erastai* were accustomed to shower their *erōmenos* with presents. Quite simply, instead of proffering hares or goblets, the citizens ought to offer the city their time, their money, even their lives, by performing many public services of both a financial and a military nature.

The role played by such a metaphor in Athenian democratic ideology no doubt needs to be qualified. This pederastic image is never directly repeated in the other funeral speeches that have come down to us. Generally, these mobilize a different if equally asymmetrical image, representing the city as the father of the citizens: the citizens are urged to sacrifice themselves for the "country," the land of their fathers.[14] So how should we explain why Pericles chose to resort to this erotic vocabulary? Perhaps it was because he wanted to become the object of desire of his fellow-citizens, so charmed were they by his rhetoric and his behavior.

In Love with Pericles

In his *Memorabilia*, Xenophon evokes the memory of Socrates, the master who taught him to think, by recording a number of dialogues that Socrates is said to have engaged in with his fellow-citizens. In one of these conversations, the philosopher produces a polemical rewriting of the image used by Pericles in his funeral oration. The philosopher is intrigued by the mechanisms by which one acquires friends.[15] He considers Pericles to have been a specialist in this domain, for he "knew many [spells] and put them on the city [*epaidon tēi polei*] and so made it love him."[16] By using the vocabulary of magical enchantment, Socrates ironically relates Periclean rhetoric to a kind of homosexual courtship.[17] At a deeper level, what he says constitutes an implicit response to the civic ideology expressed in the funeral speech. He turns Pericles' phrase inside out, like a glove: according to Socrates, it is the city that is in love with the famous *stratēgos*, rather than the other way round.

Xenophon's Socrates was not alone in drawing attention to the erotic dimension of Pericles' authority. The comic poets had already emphasized the power of attraction of his language: they considered that Pericles' speeches could sting his listeners, implanting in their ears their prick (*kentron*), the usual comic metaphor for a phallus.[18] The suggestion was that the orator wielded a veritable amorous constraint over those who heard him. The implication is clear: by arousing their desire, the leader obtained their consent and their vote. And this erotic seduction had lasting effects. It left its imprint on the souls of the Athenians to the point of arousing a nostalgic regret when Pericles was forced to step down from the political stage. After his deposition and condemnation in 430, the withdrawal of the *stratēgos* was believed to have aroused in his fellow-citizens the very same type of regret that haunted a lover once his beloved had disappeared—an emotion that the Greeks called *pothos.*[19] According to Plutarch, the city "missed him [*pothousēs d'ekeinōn*]"[20] and the Athenians decided to recall him to the tribune. When, a few months later, the *stratēgos* died, that emotion was exacerbated: "the progress of events wrought in the Athenians a swift appreciation of Pericles and a keen sense of his loss [*pothos*]."[21] The death of the *stratēgos* unleashed a love-struck grief that the Athenians never were able to surmount in a dignified fashion; according to Aristophanes, they abandoned themselves to the seduction of corrupting demagogues, dragging the city into a downward and catastrophic spiral.

If Pericles bewitched his fellow-citizens in the manner of a seductive *erōmenos*, it was not only on account of his words, but also because of his behavior, which bore the mark of *gravitas*, if not frigidity. It seems that Pericles was all the more attractive because, whatever the circumstances, he maintained a solemn distance and great self-control. Even as he invited the citizens to behave as lovers of their city, it was certainly not so that they could form real erotic relationships among themselves. On the contrary, military leaders were, as he saw it, supposed to observe the most absolute chastity while on duty: "Once, when Sophocles, who was general with him on a certain naval expedition, praised a lovely boy, he said: 'It is not his hands only, Sophocles, that a general must keep clean, but his eyes as well.' "[22] The message intended for the tragic poet is clear: a *stratēgos* must not be distracted from his duties either by money—and the bribes that one accepts with one's hands—or by erotic pleasures—and the boys that one desires with one's eyes.

If a leader must demonstrate his self-control in all circumstances, it is not only out of fear of seeming to be corrupt and ready to sell his country. By repressing his libido, he also acquires a certain charisma, as does a monk who owes his aura in part to his ostensible rejection of sexuality. As Socrates' disciples would theorize, a few years later, *eros* is the more intense the more it remains chaste, and erotic attraction is all the more powerful when it implies the impossibility of moving into action.[23]

All the same, this show of self-control had another purpose: by demonstrating his self-control, the *stratēgos* sought above all not to appear as a tyrant whose sexuality was uncheckable. For when one was in a position of power, any sexual act immediately took on a connotation of abuse. And Pericles was, indeed, reproached for being less virtuous than he appeared to be in public. His opponents ascribed to him sexual affairs as numerous as they were scandalous: Pericles was accused of perverting the wives of citizens, of cuckolding his own son, and of selling his own country in order to find himself in the beds of beautiful foreign women.

Pericles in Love

Contemporary sources were constantly criticizing Pericles' behavior in matters of *aphrodisia*, matters of sexual love. Far from being solely in love with the city, as he recommended his fellow-citizens to be, the *stratēgos* was said to have made many female conquests and to have been extremely lecherous.[24] Pericles was reputed to have lived a particularly dissolute life and even to have endangered the orderliness of families and city life.

In his *Life of Pericles*, Plutarch refers several times to his equivocal reputation. In the first place, the enemies of the *stratēgos* criticized him for using Phidias as a go-between or even as a pimp, providing him with sexual prey: "[It was said that] Phidias made assignations for Pericles with free-born women who would come ostensibly to see the works of art."[25] However, such accusations could have seemed quite harmless, as Pauline Schmitt Pantel has pointed out. There was nothing unusual about the type of relations mentioned; meetings with *hetairai* (these courtesans were free women) were considered perfectly acceptable in the city.[26] What was shocking, however, was the secrecy that surrounded such meetings: in a way, the dissimulation was more reprehensible than the act itself, because it was contrary to the transparency that the people demanded from their leaders.

But those were not the only reproaches that Pericles attracted regarding his sexual behavior. "The comic poets took up the story and bespattered Pericles with charges of abounding wantonness, connecting their slanders with the wife of Menippus, a man who was his friend and a colleague in generalship [*hupostratēgountos*], and with the aviculture [*ornithotrophia*] of Pyrilampes who, since he was a comrade of Pericles, was accused of using his peacocks and peahen to bribe the women [*gunaikes*] with whom Pericles consorted" (Plutarch, *Pericles*, 13.10). According to the rumors rife in the theater world, the *stratēgos* in this way betrayed the confidence of one of his closest friends, Menippus, and compromised the reputation of the latter's wife. Given the circumstances, we should try to gauge the scale of the outrage of which he was accused. Adultery was very severely punished by the Athenian laws because it cast doubt on the legitimacy of children born within the framework of marriage. Such an affair was considered so grave that a husband had the right to kill an adulterer caught *in flagrante delicto*;[27] and as for the wife, she had to be repudiated even if her husband did not wish for this. So, as an adulterer, Pericles technically deserved death without a trial.

The story of Pyrilampes completes the list of Pericles' depravities and adds a further touch. At first glance, Pyrilampes appears to fill exactly the same role as Phidias, for, like the sculptor, he acted as an intermediary of doubtful character for the *stratēgos*, secretly facilitating the satisfaction of the latter's pleasures. However, the services that he rendered had a very particular connotation. In fifth-century Athens, the breeding of birds, especially peacocks, was closely associated with Eastern luxury and, more particularly, with the Persian royalty.[28] A peacock, like a parasol, was a "Persian fad"—rather like eighteenth-century "Turkish fads"—that were imported into the Greek world to mark the particular distinction of members of the elite.[29] Besides, we know from Plato that Pyrilampes went on many embassies to the Great King,[30] so it was probably on one of those occasions that he brought back the precious birds as part of his luggage and took to breeding them—an extremely lucrative business given that, at the end of the fifth century, a pair of peafowl was worth about 1,000 drachmas, the price of a really good horse.[31] In these circumstances, the anecdote takes on a particularly political character: by having these gorgeous birds delivered to his favorites, Pericles became associated with the Great King and his pleasures and, more generally, with Eastern and despotic luxury (*truphē*). Sex, luxury, and dissimulation: this anecdote drew on a whole collection of connotations, all of which tended to portray Pericles as a tyrant.

There was one more rumor, of an even more serious nature, that circulated about the *stratēgos*. According to Stesimbrotus of Thasos, who was definitely hostile to Pericles, the *stratēgos* had even gone so far as to sleep with the wife of his son Xanthippus, committing what Françoise Héritier has called "indirect incest of the second type,"[32] so that the semen of both the father and the son mingled in the same womb. Plutarch refuses to believe this "odious and impious attack on the wife of his own son,"[33] and, following suit, most modern commentators have dismissed such anecdotes out of hand. However, over and above the question of their veracity, they do tell us a lot about popular expectations and the moral behavior expected of members of the elite.

It is hardly surprising, in this context, that Pericles was to be represented on the comic stage as the "king of the satyrs."[34] This was not just a way of referring to the Dionysiac universe and the *stratēgos*'s interest in the theater—for the satyrs were closely associated with Dionysus.[35] It was also a transparent allusion to his supposedly rampant sexuality. Given that satyrs were well known for their grotesque hypervirility,[36] the poets found it amusing to depict Pericles as the opposite of his well-advertised imperturbable and sober self. Worse still, they blamed him for indulging lasciviously in carnal pleasures just when he should have been leading his fellow-citizens into battle. These attacks on him reached a climax at the start of the Peloponnesian War, when they were targeting in particular his relationship with the lovely Aspasia.

PERICLES AND ASPASIA: THE RESURFACING OF WHAT WAS REPRESSED

Love-Stricken Pericles

"[Pericles] took Aspasia, and loved her exceedingly" (Plutarch, *Pericles*, 24.5). So here was our imperturbable *stratēgos* overcome by love for a foreign woman to the point of being accused of sacrificing the city's interests for her sake. In the fourth century B.C., the Socratic Heraclides Ponticus defined the meeting with Aspasia as one of the major turning points in Pericles' career. In his book *On Pleasure*, he declares that the great man "dismissed his wife from his house and preferred a life of pleasure [*hēdonē*]; and so he lived with Aspasia, the courtesan from Megara, and squandered the greater part of his property on her."[37] So, according to this fourth-century author, Pericles made two separate but symmetrical changes in his lifestyle: first, upon entering public life, he renounced the social life of the *sumposion* and all its extravagances; then, upon meeting Aspasia, he returned to an aristocratic mode of life that was ruled by expensive extravagance and luxury.

According to the Socratic philosophers, Pericles now abandoned his modest lifestyle and his proverbial imperturbability. In his *Aspasia*, the Socratic Antisthenes "claims that Pericles was in love with Aspasia and went into and out of her house twice a day just to say hello to her."[38] That anecdote was repeated by Plutarch: "Twice a day, . . . on going out and on coming in from the market-place, he would salute her with a loving kiss."[39] The reversion was total. Whereas, previously, he had been punctilious about avoiding banqueting and about treading only the path leading to the Agora and the Council Chamber, Pericles would now pay daily visits to a private house in order to embrace the lovely Aspasia. "To love a woman to the point where, even though she was a foreigner and a *hetaira*, one without compunction made a public show of it—that was a liberty and a nonconformist way of behaving that was found truly shocking."[40]

The Socratic Aeschines, whose testimony is repeated by Plutarch, tells us that Pericles' imperturbable stance was shattered when Aspasia was brought to trial by the Athenian lawcourts: "Aspasia he begged off, by shedding copious tears at the trial, as Aeschines says, and by entreating the jurors."[41] The trial of Aspasia kindled within the *stratēgos* feelings too long repressed, just as the death of his last remaining son, Paralus, caused him to succumb to an irrepressible torrent of tears.

This image of Pericles in tears over the fate of his companion should, however, be interpreted with a measure of reserve, for, contrary to Plutarch's claims (*Pericles*, 32.1–2), there is no evidence to confirm that Aspasia was in reality ever accused of impiety. Writing centuries after the event, the ancient authors may have mistaken for reality what was, in truth, just a collection of accusations made in the theater in order to raise a laugh from the Athenian audience. After all, Plutarch does suggest that Aspasia's accuser was none other than the comic poet Hermippus, "who alleged further against her that she received free-born women into a place of assignation for Pericles" (32.1). From there to believing that the biographer is confusing comedy accusations with legal procedures is only a small step and one that we are perfectly free to take.

Whether the trial was a reality or a fiction, Pericles seems to have lived for several years with Aspasia, who did at least bear him a son, Pericles the Younger. That liaison in itself was quite enough to scandalize some Athenians, who proceeded to accuse the *stratēgos* of succumbing to the manipulations of this beautiful foreigner.

The Warmonger: Aspasia, the New Helen

Socrates' followers belittled Pericles by portraying him as Aspasia's puppet. According to the Socratic Aeschines, this "wise, statesmanlike" woman turned the *stratēgos* into her disciple, even teaching him her rhetorical skills. That is likewise the ironical representation produced by Plato in his dialogue, the *Menexenus* (235e): according to Socrates, Aspasia coached plenty of orators, beginning with Pericles and himself. What is more, it was she who composed the funeral speech that the philosopher delivers in this dialogue, drawing on all the commonplaces of patriotic rhetoric. Plato's irony is at its most biting here: so it was a foreign woman who composed this praise of democratic Athens that was so proud of its masculine autochthonous roots! Implicitly, Plato even suggests that Aspasia could well have composed the funeral speech delivered by Pericles at the start of the Peloponnesian War.[42] Pericles schooled by Aspasia: that stereotype may well go back to the comic authors of the day, since the comic poet Callias was already repeating it in the second half of the fifth century.[43]

However, Aspasia is certainly not always represented in such a flattering manner. According to most of the *stratēgos*'s opponents, this lovely foreign woman charmed Pericles not so much with her words but with her body: in her company, the *stratēgos* was schooled in matters of the flesh rather than those of the mind, even if, as the Greeks saw it, the one did certainly not rule out the other.[44] Worse still, Pericles was said to have been obeying the whims of his beloved mistress when he embarked upon two wars: first the Samos campaign, then the Peloponnesian War.

Probably drawing his inspiration from Douris of Samos (ca. 300 B.C.),[45] Plutarch first evokes the role played by Aspasia in the unleashing of the war against Samos. Aspasia, who was a native of Miletus, with which the city of Samos was in conflict, is said to have persuaded Pericles to intervene in favor of her own country. In fact, the entire campaign was said to have been placed under the sign of eroticism run wild; another Samian author, the historian Alexis, claimed that Pericles' army included Athenian prostitutes who, in 439 B.C.,[46] at the end of the conflict, set up a cult to Aphrodite in Samos, by way of celebrating the victory! The anecdote is historically unreliable but it does reflect the hostile rumors that were circulating about the *stratēgos*, who was accused of having connived at the whims of his companion of ill-repute.[47]

According to the comic poets, Aspasia, not content with having sparked off that ferocious conflict, which was marked by cruel acts of revenge, was likewise accused of starting the Peloponnesian War. In his *Dionysalexandros* (Dionysus in the role of Paris/Alexander), Cratinus blamed Pericles for having started the war in order to please Aspasia, who was transformed for the occasion into a latter-day Helen of Troy. The play—which is now lost, although its plot is known to us[48]—was probably composed in 430–429 B.C., and, in the mode of an allegory, it likens Pericles to a latter-day Paris who prefers the gifts of Aphrodite to those of Athena and Hera:[49] the *stratēgos* is said to have provoked the war out of love for his companion, just as the Trojan hero, in his day, had done for the sake of Helen.[50]

In *The Acharnians*, Aristophanes spells out the accusation made against Aspasia, putting the following long tirade into the mouth of Dikaiopolis, the protagonist:

Members of the audience, my words are harsh but just . . .
Myself, I detest the Lacedaemonians, and how! . . .
But all the same, those were but trifles . . .
Some young tipsy cottabus-players went

And stole from Megara town the prostitute [*pornē*] Simaetha.
Then the Megarians, garlicked with the smart,
Stole, in return, two of Aspasia's hussies [*pornai*].
From these three Wantons o'er the Hellenic race
Burst forth the first beginnings of the War.
For then, in wrath, the Olympian Pericles
Thundered and lightened and confounded Hellas,
Enacting laws which ran like drinking songs,
"Let the Megarians presently depart
From earth and sea, the mainland and the mart."[51]

In these lines, Aspasia is portrayed as a brothel-keeper, a familiar enough figure in both Piraeus and Athens, leading by the nose a besotted Pericles who appears to be all-powerful but is in reality enslaved by the whims of his companion.

According to her enemies, Aspasia's seductive powers stemmed not only from her erotic expertise but also from her decadent, luxury-loving ways. When Pericles took her as his concubine, he surrendered not only to carnal pleasures but also to the sirens of Eastern luxury—what the Greeks called *truphē*. Aspasia, who was from Miletus, was seen as one of those Ionian women often characterized as "debauched and greedy for financial gain."[52] The comic writers called her the new Omphale, likening her to the eastern queen of Lydia at whose feet—according to myth—the powerful Heracles languished during a long period of servitude, spinning wool for her (*Pericles*, 24.6). The suggestion is that Pericles was groveling before his Eastern enchantress just as did the demi-god fascinated by the queen of Lydia. Certain modern historians have been so carried away by this image that they have turned Aspasia into a prefiguration of Mata Hari, Aspasia being the double agent working for the Persians and sent by malicious Ionian factions to plot on their behalf![53] In doing so, they picked up on particular accusations leveled at Pericles, even though no credible argument has ever been found to confirm them.

Aspasia, a Chiaroscuro Figure: Between Literary Fantasies and the Spotlight of Epigraphical Illumination

What is known for certain about the real Aspasia? The literary texts provide very little. Only her name and her patronymic seem to be cited with a degree of certainty: "That she was a Milesian by birth, daughter of one Axiochus, is generally agreed" (*Pericles*, 24.2). All the rest is largely a matter of fiction and fantasy; now a whore, now a mistress of rhetoric, she is an inexhaustible source of anecdotes that share but one feature in common: namely, their unverifiability. The name of Aspasia serves above all as a screen on to which all the masculine fantasies surrounding a woman from the East could be projected: she is lascivious, refined, and manipulative.[54]

The figure of Aspasia, a prisoner of history written by men, turns out to be totally indefinable.[55] This vagueness is conveyed by all the different descriptions in which the ancient authors have paraded her. The comic poet Cratinus calls her a concubine (*pallakē*) in the following, hardly flattering lines: "And Sodom [*Katapugosunē*] then fathered [for Cronos] this Hera-Aspasia, the bitch-eyed concubine [*pallakē*]."[56] Eupolis settles for "prostitute" (*pornē*),[57] while Plutarch reminds us that she "presided over a business that was anything but honest or even reputable, since she kept a house of young courtesans [*paidiskas hetairousas*]" (*Pericles*, 24.3).[58] Diodorus *Periegetes* claims, on the contrary, that she was Pericles' legitimate wife.[59] Now a concubine, now a prostitute, now a courtesan, now a procuress, now a wife: Aspasia oscillates between different statuses that are by no means all equivalent, as Apollodorus carefully points out in his speech *Against Neaera* (§ 122). How can we possibly decide? And besides, why should we decide between all these different views?

What we can at least do is try to establish a few objective facts upon which to reflect. Aspasia, a native of Miletus, must have met Pericles before 437, since their son, Pericles the Younger, was a *stratēgos* in 406 at the time of the battle of Arginusae; to be elected to such a magistracy a man had to be at least thirty years old. She was probably living in Athens even before the war against Samos broke out, if, that is, we can place any credit in Plutarch's account.

There is an inscription that may throw new light on this most shadowy file of documentation. Peter Bicknell has suggested connecting Aspasia's history with an Attic funerary inscription of the fourth century B.C. This mentions the names Aspasius and Axiochus—not to be found anywhere else in our documentation (*IG* II² 7349).[60] The text makes it possible to reconstruct Aspasia's family background in a manner that is, if not beyond question, at least plausible. According to Bicknell, Aspasia, although a foreigner, belonged to a powerful Athenian *oikos*. His theory is that it all started with the ostracism of the elder Alcibiades, in about 460. When banished from Athens, he went off to Miletus, in Ionia, where he married the daughter of a Milesian aristocrat by the name of Axiochus, by whom he had two children, Aspasius and Axiochus, before 451, and the law then passed on citizenship. When his ostracism at last ended, he finally returned to Athens, bringing with him, in his train, not only his wife and children but also his wife's sister, the beautiful Aspasia, whom Pericles met as a result of the close links that connected him to Alcibiades' family.

According to Bicknell's reconstruction then, Aspasia, when she first met Pericles, was a young unmarried woman, descended from the Milesian elite, who enjoyed the protection of a powerful Athenian household. Quite apart from its intrinsic interest, this reconstruction has the merit of underlining a fundamental feature of the figure of Aspasia: Pericles' beloved did not fall into any of the habitual preconceived categories by which Athenians identified the status of women. The figure of Aspasia confused them all: a foreigner in the city, she was nevertheless connected with an Athenian family very much in the public eye; so when she was taken for Pericles' concubine or even his legitimate wife, her very existence defied classification within the preestablished categories of Athenian males.

Perhaps it was precisely the uncertainty surrounding her status that explains the contradictory assessments of her position. As now a whore, now a teacher of rhetoric, she was impossible to categorize socially, in a precise manner. So, just as the Europeans were to do in the case of the "free women" of the nineteenth century, the Athenians tended to interpret that relative liberty as sexual license, as if (relative) social liberty was inevitably to be associated with moral libertinism.

That is what, ultimately, may lie at the root of the aggression that Aspasia attracted and concentrated upon herself and that, according to some ancient sources, found expression in an accusation of impiety in the lawcourts. Even if that supposed trial is just a fiction, it nevertheless, tellingly enough, raises the question of religious tolerance in Pericles' Athens.

CHAPTER 8

Pericles and the City Gods

Nothing was more alien to the Greeks than the notion of a separation between Church and State. In Athens, the community provided a tight framework for religious manifestations while, symmetrically, religion was deeply embedded in civic life.[1] Within this context, participation in the rituals was an action highly political—in the broadest sense of the term.

In the first place, religious practices shaped in the citizens a sense of belonging. When, at the end of the Peloponnesian War, the herald Cleocritus urged the Athenians to seek reconciliation after having torn one another apart, he appealed to the memory of that shared experience: "we have shared with you in the most solemn rites and sacrifices and the most splendid festivals, we have been companions in the dance and schoolmates and comrades in arms and we have braved many dangers with you both by land and by sea."[2] Every bit as much as warfare, religious festivals bonded the civic community together around practices and values shared in common.

Second, to manifest one's piety also had a more specific political meaning, one that, this time, played on individual distinction rather than collective solidarity. To celebrate a cult or to dedicate offerings was a way of distinguishing oneself personally—as politicians were well aware. However, to make a show of too great a proximity to the gods was risky: excessive piety, in the same way as a detachment that was too manifest, might be regarded by the Athenians as a lack of moderation. It was all a matter of balance.

To analyze Pericles' relations with the gods, one has to position oneself at the intersection of the general and the particular, where what was personal and what was shared by the whole community came together. On the one hand, the career of the *stratēgos* will illuminate the Athenians' collective relationship to all that was divine. As a reelected *stratēgos* and a persuasive orator, Pericles was the spokesman of a civic religion that was undergoing a mutation. He was implicated in a policy of making constant offerings and of launching huge architectural religious works not only on the Acropolis but also throughout Attica; and, furthermore, he was engaged in such activities at a time when the city was introducing profound changes into its religious account of its origins—that is, autochthony—within a context of strained diplomatic relations.

On the other hand, the ancient sources made it possible to glimpse the personal relations that Pericles had developed with the gods. These were relations of proximity in the first place: he was sometimes depicted as a protégé of Athena, but in Attic comedies he was also assimilated to Zeus, in an analogy that was in no way flattering. But then, there were also relations that emphasized distance: some philosophical accounts presented him as a man close to the sophists or even as a freethinker. And, finally, there were relations involving irreverence: some later—and untrustworthy—sources made much of several trials for impiety in which those close to him were involved, and this raises the question of religious tolerance in fifth-century Athens and, in particular, how far individuals enjoyed freedom of thought when faced with the civic community.

A Spokesman for the Civic Religion: Collective Relations with the Gods

In Athens, the city regulated religious expression down to the smallest details. The Assembly concerned itself with sacred affairs at regular intervals, and it was the Assembly that fixed the salaries of certain priests and priestesses and was also empowered to accept new cults.[3] Symptomatic of this overall civic control was the fact that the gods' money could sometimes spill over into the community coffers. Between 441 and 439 B.C., the city borrowed funds from the treasury of Athena in order to cope with the expenses incurred in the long conflict with Samos.[4] And in the speech that he delivered on the eve of the Peloponnesian War, Pericles himself presented, as a financial reserve, the heap of offerings that had accumulated on the Acropolis, at the same time accepting responsibility for restoring to the goddess the sum borrowed, once the hostilities came to an end.[5]

At the same time, though, religious rituals were ensconced at the very heart of the democratic institutional framework. When meetings took place in the Assembly, debates never began until the Pnyx had been purified by a sacrifice and the herald had pronounced blessings and curses too. On the tribunes, orators always had to wear a wreath, as did participants in a sacrifice. As for the juries in popular lawcourts, they pronounced a solemn oath, swearing by Zeus, Poseidon, and Demeter to give their verdict in accordance with the city laws.

Religion and Politics: A Festive Democracy

As a magistrate, Pericles participated fully in this rich and intense civic religion. The presence of Athenian magistrates was required at numerous rituals.

At the opening ceremony of the Great Dionysia, the ten *stratēgoi* all offered libations. They played a prominent part in the Panathenaea procession and were presented with the portions that were reserved for them from the first sacrifice in honour of Athena.[6] We even know that in the fourth century they were responsible for no fewer than eight sacrifices a year.

In his capacity as a *stratēgos*, Pericles was thus an actor in an intensely festive democracy. In his funeral speech of 431, he acknowledges this fact: "We have a succession of competitions and religious festivals throughout the year."[7] Although it delighted the democrats, this plethora of religious celebrations aroused hostility among the oligarchs. In a violent pamphlet composed between 430 and 415, the anonymous author of *The Constitution of the Athenians*—known as the Old Oligarch—regarded it all as specifically Athenian and typical of a debased mode of government. According to this author, the increasing number of festivals caused serious institutional problems, constantly interrupting the handling of important affairs:

> Objections are raised against the Athenians because it is sometimes not possible for a person, though he sit about for a year, to negotiate with the council or the assembly. This happens at Athens for no other reason than that, owing to the quantity of business, they are not able to deal with all persons before sending them away. For how could they do this? First of all *they have to hold more festivals than any other Greek city (and when these are going on it is even less possible for any of the city's affairs to be transacted).*[8]

Although it may be true that, placed end to end, the Athenian festivals occupied no less than one-third of the year, this was, to say the least, an exaggerated way of putting the matter. Only the major celebrations, such as the Great Dionysia and the Panathenaea involved the whole community and led to the suspension of institutional business.

More serious still, according to this ferocious opponent of democracy, these festivals were designed simply to redistribute public wealth to the most poverty-stricken of the citizens. "The Athenian populace realizes that it is impossible for each of the poor to offer sacrifices, to give lavish feasts, to set up shrines and to manage a city that will be beautiful and great, and yet the populace has discovered how to have sacrifices, shrines, banquets and temples. The city sacrifices at public expense many victims, but it is the people who enjoy the feasts and to whom the victims are allotted."[9]

In his view, the sole purpose of the religious festivals was to allow the people to indulge themselves whenever possible, at the expense of the city—that is to say, the wealthiest citizens.

According to his detractors, Pericles' actions simply aggravated this state of affairs. Plutarch tells us that the *stratēgos* increased the number of religious banquets and entertainments in order to curry favor with his fellow-citizens: "At this time, therefore, particularly, Pericles gave the reins to the people and made his policy one of pleasing them [*pros kharin*], ever devising some sort of a pageant in the town for the masses, or a public meal [*hestiasin*], or a procession 'amusing them like children with delights in which the Muses played their part.'"[10] Echoing a tradition hostile to the *stratēgos*, as it does, the preceding description is clearly much exaggerated if one bears in mind that no religious festival was created on Pericles' initiative except, possibly, the one in honor of Bendis, a deity of Thracian origin.[11]

The fact nevertheless remains that the *stratēgos* did reorganize certain celebrations. He is said to have introduced a music competition into the already extremely crammed festive ritual calendar, at the time of the Panathenaea, adding a whole day to this, the most important of all the Athenian festivals.[12] But even this addition should be viewed with circumspection; in all probability, Pericles simply reorganized an earlier musical competition, moving it into the Odeon and possibly giving it official status.[13] However, even if the action of the *stratēgos* was more limited than Plutarch suggests, it does testify to a real desire to democratize *mousikē*, the culture of the Muses that was in principle reserved for the Athenian elite.

However, the oligarchs' attacks focused less on the festivals supposedly instituted by Pericles than on the program of constructions in which they were to take place. On this score, they criticized him for acting in the manner of a munificent tyrant.

Great Works in the Service of the Gods

The architectural program of the "great works" is closely associated with the name of Pericles. The impetus for this ambitious policy of monumental building is well known: in 448, the *stratēgos* convened a congress of the Greek cities of Europe and Asia, to discuss the issues of the temples destroyed by the Persians, the sacrifices due to the gods, freedom of navigation, and peace. It was in the aftermath of the Persian Wars that they had vowed not to reconstruct those devastated sanctuaries, so as to preserve forever the memory of the impiety of the Persians.[14] In less than twenty years, numerous building sites were set up and, in many cases, completed. As well as a total remodeling of the Acropolis, a number of sanctuaries underwent more or less spectacular transformations: in eastern Attica, the sanctuary of Artemis at Brauron was given a double portico; and in the west, a new initiation hall (*telesterion*) was inaugurated at Eleusis.[15] Meanwhile, a number of medium-sized temples were constructed throughout the territory in honor of a variety of deities: Poseidon was honored at Sunium, in the south; Nemesis at Rhamnous and Ares at Acharnae, in the north; Athena at Pallene in central Attica; and, finally, Hephaestus in the town of Athens itself, on the hill overlooking the Agora. All these finely wrought buildings with clearly similar stylistic features were probably executed by the same architect.[16] In this way, in the space of twenty years the whole of Attica was affected by this epidemic of monuments.[17]

At this point, a historian is faced with two questions. First, what was Pericles' precise role in this transformation of the Athenian religious landscape? It is a question that calls for a nuanced reply. Far from acting as an all-powerful demiurge, the *stratēgos* was, in reality, simply one of many actors involved in this architectural metamorphosis. Strictly speaking, only the Parthenon, the statue of Athena Parthenos, the Propylaea, the Odeon, and the Telesterion at Eleusis can be credited to him.[18]

Next, did all this involve a radical break from earlier building practices? In those few operations of his, Pericles conformed to an already well-established tradition: a few years earlier, his rival, Cimon, had launched the construction of a great public sanctuary in the Agora, the Theseum, after having the bones of its founder brought back from the island of Skyros[19] with great pomp and ceremony. However, two major novelties characterized this Periclean moment. In the first place, the very scope of the operation was unmatched, with so many building sites being set up simultaneously throughout the territory; and furthermore, the new buildings testified as much to the city's domination over its allies as to the Athenians' piety toward their gods. Between 450–440, Athenian imperialism took to expressing itself in religious terms. As early as 450, Athens forced the cities belonging to the Delian League to take part, every four years, in the Great Panathenaea held in honor of Athena, bringing with them a heifer and a panoply as offerings to the goddess.[20] Then, in the 440s, the city confirmed its religious hold even beyond Attica, insisting on the construction of a number of sanctuaries of Athena on land seized from the allies, as is testified by several boundary markers discovered in Aegina, Chalcis, Cos, and Samos.[21]

Although Athena, the guardian goddess of the whole community, was the principal beneficiary of these grandiose building sites, marginal deities in the Greek pantheon were also honored. In this respect, Hephaestus was particularly favored, for he received a magnificent temple in the Agora, ensconced at the very heart of the Athenian democratic system. Nor was this choice at all fortuitous, for it should be understood in the light of the great story about autochthony and the origins of Athens, which was being reconstructed in this same period.

Reconstruction of the Myth of Autochthony

All the indications suggest that this great story of origins took shape in its definitive form between 450 and 430, at the very time when Pericles was in power and the religious building sites were springing up all over Attica.[22] It was at this point—not earlier, as is sometimes argued—that the Athenians began to proclaim themselves to be born from the earth, so that they were all, collectively, the descendants of the king Erechtheus, who was born from the very soil of Attica.[23]

To understand how this belief, central to Athenian imaginary representations, came to be elaborated, we must start with a comment on vocabulary. In the fifth century, the term *autokhthōn* did not mean people "born from the earth," but simply people who had lived on their territory from time immemorial, without ever migrating.[24] According to Herodotus, such were the cases of the Arcadians in the Peloponnese, the Carians in Ionia, and the Ethiopians and Libyans in Africa.[25] The Athenians also belonged to this category since, already by the time of the Second Persian War, they were claiming to have lived always in Attica.

Furthermore, the Athenians had long believed that one of their earliest kings was born from the earth (*gēgenēs*), as is attested by the following lines from the *Iliad*: "And they that held Athens, the well-built citadel, the land of great-hearted Erechtheus, whom of old Athene, daughter of Zeus, fostered, when the earth, the giver of grain, had borne him."[26] The story of Erechtheus is well-known to us thanks to the eponymous tragedy by Euripides, written in the late fifth century. Seized by a violent desire for Athena, the lame Hephaestus attempted, unsuccessfully, to rape her. His semen did spatter the goddess's thigh, however, and she grabbed a twist of wool (*eru*) to wipe her leg, and then dropped it on the Attic ground (*khthon*). From that fertilized earth, Erechtheus emerged and was received and raised by Athena.[27]

There is, however, nothing to prove that, as early as the Archaic period, the Athenians were considering themselves to be the descendants of Erechtheus. To believe in a king born from the soil is one thing; to believe yourselves, collectively, to be his descendants is quite another. It was not until the time of Pericles that the Athenians took to presenting themselves as the offspring of Erechtheus, thereby giving a new sense to the notion of autochthony. After a first fleeting appearance in the *Eumenides* of Aeschylus, the theme was developed by Sophocles in his *Ajax*, in the 440s. Here, the Athenians were presented as men born from the earth, the offspring of Erechtheus. It was at that point, and only then, that the various elements in the story of autochthony fused together, enabling the citizens to pride themselves on not only having always lived on the land of their fathers—their fatherland—but also being directly descended from their mother earth, their motherland.[28]

Autochthony, now part and parcel of the Athenian identity, functioned as a tale of collective ennoblement. This prestigious birth conferred upon the Athenians a very particular solidarity: since they all shared the same mother, they were all brothers; and on a social and ritual level, this was expressed by the *phratries* that united them all under the patronage of a common ancestor. Outside Athens, this belief justified them thinking that they were superior to other cities which, as Euripides put it, "were made up of elements imported from many origins, like counters set out on a chequer-board."[29]

It was this imaginary context that made sense of the construction, in the early 440s, in the Agora, of a building consecrated to Hephaestus and Athena. Even though the temple was completed only after the peace of Nicias in 421 and the cult statues were not installed until 416/415, the project and the early stages of the construction work were, if not Periclean, at least of the Periclean period.[30] This edifice, built entirely of marble, was by far the most luxurious in the Agora, and its sculpted ornaments spread over a larger area than any other Doric temple in the Greek world, except for the Parthenon. The splendor of the temple was matched by the munificence of the festival introduced in 421, when the great building was completed. It included a solemn procession, a torch-race between the tribes, imposing sacrifices and, possibly, a musical competition. The *Hephaesteia* celebrated the lame god with a lavishness unequaled anywhere in the Greek world.

While the celebration of Athena is perfectly explicable, should we not be astonished at such a sumptuous outlay being devoted to "a rather secondary god"?[31] We should indeed be somewhat surprised if, as a deeply rooted historiographical tradition has it, Hephaestus was celebrated in the Agora simply as the patron of craftsmen. The craftsmen, who were concentrated within the Ceramicus quarter, did certainly play a major role in the Athenian city, and it was probably by no means by chance that the decree relating to the organization of the *Hephaesteia* was proposed by an owner of craftsmen slaves who had made a fortune, Hyperbolus.[32] Nevertheless, it would be mistaken to reduce the significance of the festival and the edifice solely to a celebration of the craftsmanship of Athens. The celebrations did not give blacksmiths and potters pride of place, but mobilized the tribes of the entire city, without privileging any particular category. And even if the metics, of whom there were many among the craftsmen, did take part in the ceremony, they did so in a minor role: they received no more than a portion of raw meat and did not have access to the sacrificial feasts, which were reserved solely for citizens. The point is that, in the Agora, Hephaestus and Athena were honored not simply as the patrons of the craftsmen, but as the protagonists in the story of autochthony that had now been rearticulated. Significantly enough, the base upon which the statues of the cult of Hephaestus and Athena rested represented the birth of Erechtheus (figures 7 and 8).[33]

Admittedly, Pericles' personal involvement in the enterprise is not documented; even if the building site was set up in his lifetime, the festival in honor of Hephaestus was not established until eight years after his death.

FIGURE 7. Hephaisteion statue-group (ca. 421 B.C.), as reconstructed by Evelyn Harrison. Evelyn B. Harrison, "Alkamenes' Sculptures for the Hephaisteion: Part I, The Cult Statues." *American Journal of Archaeology*, 81, 2 (1977): 137–178. Courtesy of Archaeological Institute of America and *American Journal of Archaeology*.

FIGURE 8. Copy of the bas-relief sculpture of the Hephaisteion statue-group. Musée du Louvre; Galerie de la Melpomène (Aile Sully). Rez-de-chaussée—Section 15. No. d'inv. MR 710 (no. usuel Ma 579). Paris, Musée du Louvre. © RMN-Grand Palais (Musée du Louvre) / Hervé Lewandowski.

More troubling still, the *stratēgos* said not a word about the divine ancestry of the Athenians in the funeral oration that he delivered in 431, in which he went only so far as to mention the remarkable stability of the Athenian populace ever since its origins: "This land of ours, in which the same people have never ceased to dwell [*aei oikountes*] in an unbroken line of successive generations, [our ancestors] by their valor transmitted to our times as a free state."[34] Rather than put this down to a hypothetical memory lapse on the part of Thucydides, we should recognize that that lacuna could have been deliberately planned. For this speech, Pericles had decided to opt for an erotic vocabulary rather than an ancestral one, in order to describe the Athenians: he wanted his fellow-citizens to fight for the city as *erastai* would for their *erōmenoi*, not as sons defending their earth-mother.[35]

Nevertheless, one detail does show the *stratēgos*'s personal interest in the autochthony tale: the iconography of the statue of Athena Parthenos. Ensconced at the heart of the Parthenon, this immense effigy, over eleven meters high from top to toe, constituted "as it were a brief recapitulation of Periclean themes."[36] According to Pausanias (1.24.7), "Athena . . . holds a statue of Victory about four cubits high, and in the other hand a spear; at her feet lies a shield and near the spear is a serpent. This serpent would be Erichthonius." In this way, at the feet of the goddess there stood the first Athenian, born from the earth, for whom the city set up a cult on the Acropolis, in the Erechtheum, which was rebuilt shortly after the *stratēgos*'s death.

It turns out that Pericles was more the herald of civic religion than its hero. Even if he was actively involved in the ritual functioning of the community, his personal influence remained limited. He created no new festivals and was responsible for the construction of no sanctuary (for the Parthenon and the Odeon were not temples, in the ritualistic sense of the term). As for his direct involvement in the rehandling of the autochthony story, that cannot be confirmed. The *stratēgos* was thus a spokesman for the civic religion rather than its high priest.

But quite apart from this role as an intermediary, Pericles maintained with the gods personal relations that the sources take into account, allowing us to catch a glimpse of his religious convictions or, at least, of the beliefs ascribed to him, sometimes in order to glorify him, but often so as to denigrate him.

THE POSSESSOR OF AN EQUIVOCAL PIETY: A PERSONAL RELATIONSHIP WITH THE DEITY

The Divine Pericles

According to the ancient sources, Pericles had established privileged links with several deities in the pantheon. At the time of the construction of the Propylaea, the monumental entrance to the Acropolis (437–433 B.C.), the *stratēgos* benefited from the personal care of Athena, the poliadic, or City deity. During the construction work, the most zealous of the workmen slipped and fell from the top of the edifice. "He lay in a sorry plight, despaired of by the physicians. Pericles was much cast down by this, but the goddess appeared to him in a dream and prescribed a course of treatment for him to use, so that he speedily and easily healed the man. It was in commemoration of this that he set up the bronze statue of Athena Hygieia on the acropolis near the altar of that goddess, which was there before."[37]

At first sight, there is nothing exceptional about this dream. There was a well-known practice known as incubation that consisted in the sick receiving in their dreams a visit or revelations from the deity Asclepius. But such dreams came about only after the accomplishment of a well-established ritual: first, only the sick person could ask for a dream; then the god appeared in the sanctuary only after the appropriate rituals had been performed; and finally, the sick man never himself interpreted the signs that were sent to him, for that task fell to the deity's priests.[38] Nothing of the kind happened in the case of Pericles' dream: Athena visited the *stratēgos* outside any ritual frame-work, short-circuiting the traditional mediations and leaving the dreamer and the goddess face to face. The anecdote thus places Pericles in a privileged position vis-à-vis the goddess, "as a mediator and quasi-diviner between the goddess and the wounded man."[39]

That transaction operated, as was often the case, according to the logic of a gift and a counter-gift. The first gift—the monumental transformation of the Acropolis—elicited from Athena a response in the shape of a dream sent privately to the *stratēgos*. In return, Pericles offered her a new consecra-tion, which not only completed the exchange cycle, closing it upon itself, but also commemorated forever his special close relations with the goddess. It is quite clear that Plutarch was making the most of an embellished story: the dedication of the statue of Athena Hygieia discovered by the archaeologists makes no mention at all of the *stratēgos* and refers only to the Athenians; the individual is effaced when confronted by the collectivity which, in the fifth century, banned all excessive forms of personal distinction. The fact never-theless remains that the anecdote testifies to a tradition that is favorable to Pericles, since it draws attention to the divine protection that he enjoyed—as did Odysseus in the *Odyssey*.

To draw attention to such a proximity to the gods was nevertheless a risky business, for the Athenians might interpret it as a sign of concealed tyranni-cal ambitions. The Pisistratids had boasted of their privileged relations with the goddess and Pisistratus had seized power escorted by a false Athena, at the culmination of a ruse that was never to be forgotten.[40] Was Pericles too close to the gods? That was precisely the notion that his detractors sought to instill in the minds of the Athenians.

His opponents sometimes identified him with Dionysus, "king of the sa-tyrs,"[41] but it was to Zeus that the *stratēgos* was most frequently assimilated. This was a way of suggesting that Pericles had overstepped the boundaries of the human condition and had tipped over into overweening hubris. Plu-tarch was well aware of the accusation implied by such an association, and he endeavored explicitly to neutralize such attacks: "it seems to me that his otherwise puerile and pompous nickname [of "Olympian"] is rendered un-objectionable and becoming by this one circumstance, that it was so gracious a nature and a life so pure and undefiled in the exercise of sovereign power."[42] What could be more unsuitable, in a democracy, than a man who took him-self for a god—worse still, the king of the gods?

That identification was all the more problematic given that, in Athenian theater, Zeus was often portrayed as a despot who heeded nothing but his own desires: in *Prometheus Bound*, Aeschylus (or Pseudo-Aeschylus) even depicted Zeus as a tyrant usurping power in order to set up his own whims as laws (409), without any need for justification (324). So the poet Cratinus aimed to create alarm when he chose to identify Pericles with the most powerful of all the gods: "Faction [*stasis*] and Old Cronos were united in wedlock; their offspring was of all the tyrants the greatest and lo! he is called by the gods the head-compeller."[43] Such a comparison turned the *stratēgos* into an unscrupulous usurper, prepared to do anything in order to hang on to power.

Cratinus repeated that same accusation, making it more pointed, in his play titled *The Spirits of Wealth*, which was performed in 430–429, at the time when Pericles was under attack from all quarters for his handling of the war: "Here is Zeus, chasing Cronos from the kingship and binding the rebellious Titans in unbreakable bonds."[44] Through this analogy, the comic poet covertly evoked the ostracism of Cimon, in 462/1: confronting Zeus/Pericles, Cimon was identified with Cronos, a benevolent sovereign, ousted by his son. As it happened, the parallel was flattering to Pericles' fallen rival, for ever since Hesiod, the reign of Cronos had evoked the golden age when "the grain-giving field bore crops of its own accord, much and unstinting, and they themselves, willing, mild-mannered, shared out the fruits of their labours, together with many good things."[45] With this analogy, the comic poet recalled the proverbial generosity of Cimon, which Plutarch carefully assesses: "[Cimon] made his home in the city a general public residence for his fellow citizens, and on his estates in the country allowed even the stranger to take and use the choicest of the ripened fruits, with all the fair things that the seasons bring. Thus, in a certain fashion, he restored to human life the fabled communalism of the age of Cronos—the golden age."[46] In this game of masks, the comparison proved extremely disadvantageous to Zeus-Pericles, who, by getting rid of Cronos-Cimon is implied not only to have established an unjust tyranny but also to have brought about the end of the golden age.

There was another reason why this "pantheonization" was particularly unpleasant: by being assimilated to Zeus, Pericles was represented as a flighty lover who disrupted family life. In this respect, Zeus's reputation was by now certainly well established. Seducing both mortals and immortals as he pleased, he had engendered many bastards all over the world. So it was certainly not by chance that Aspasia was herself seen as Zeus's irascible wife Hera : "And Sodomy [*katapugosunē*] produced for Cronos this Hera-Aspasia, the bitch-eyed concubine."[47] Inevitably, the analogy rebounded against the *stratēgos*'s partner and also his bastard son, Pericles the Younger.

These often alarming and sometimes grotesque jokes cracked by the comic poets were intended to provoke laughter and alarm among the spectators and, as such, were inclined to reflect the fantasies of Pericles' opponents rather than Pericles' own religious thinking. In order to get some idea of his own deeper convictions, we need to turn to other sources that are, unfortunately, equally biased.

A Clear Head or a Weak Mind?

In the few accounts that bear upon his personal beliefs, Pericles appears to be torn between two diametrically opposed positions. At one moment, the *stratēgos* is presented as a defender of rationalist thinking, cursorily dismissing all supernatural interpretations; at other times, he is presented as a supporter of traditional religion or even a religion that never looked beyond superstition.[48] Choosing between these two alternatives, many contemporary historians have often seemed to favor the former, even going so far as to represent Pericles as an *aufklärer* (an enlightenment figure), the herald of a world moving toward secularization.[49]

It is true that several anecdotes portray the Athenian leader as an enlightened disciple of the sophists, stripping the world of its enchanted aspects, the better to mock all divine omens. In 430, when a fleet of vessels was about to set sail under his orders, "It chanced that the sun was eclipsed and darkness came on and all were thoroughly frightened, looking upon it as a great portent. Accordingly, seeing that his steersman was timorous and utterly perplexed, Pericles held up his cloak before the man's eyes, and, thus covering them, asked him if he thought it anything dreadful or portentous of anything dreadful. 'No,' said the steersman. 'How then,' said Pericles, 'is yonder event different from this, except that it is something rather larger than my cloak which has caused the obscurity?'"[50] It is a very nice story, but it has no historical basis since no eclipse of the sun is attested in that year.[51]

How should we interpret this cobbled-together anecdote? In order to understand it, we need to replace the story in the context in which it was circulated—that of the philosophical schools, according to Plutarch (*Pericles*, 35.2). The story was of a moral rather than a historical nature. The point was to set in contrast, term for term, the enlightened behavior of Pericles and the hidebound attitude of one of his unfortunate successors, Nicias. In late August 413, while in command of the Athenian troops massed against Syracuse, Nicias was confronted with a total eclipse of the moon. Faced with this omen, he dithered helplessly for several whole days, "spending his time making sacrifices and consulting diviners, right up until the moment when his enemies attacked."[52] That long delay had grave consequences, for it led to the rout of the Athenians at Syracuse and eventually decided the outcome of the war. So these two episodes reflected two leaders, two different attitudes, and two moments in Athenian history: the glorious start of the Peloponnesian War and the ignominious conclusion of the expedition to Sicily, and an implicit contrast was drawn between them.

Another account relayed by Plutarch tended to represent Pericles as, if not a sophist, at least a man close to them: "A certain athlete had hit Epitimus the Pharsalian with a javelin, accidentally, and killed him, and Pericles squandered an entire day discussing with Protagoras whether it was the javelin, or rather the one who hurled it, or the judges of the contests that 'in the strictest sense,' ought to be held responsible for the disaster."[53] Some historians believe that this passage confirms the *stratēgos*'s sympathy for the inflammatory ideas of the sophist Protagoras of Abdera. He had written a treatise titled *On the Gods*, in which he maintained that "man is the measure of all things" and even defended a number of agnostic ideas: "As to the gods, I have no means of knowing either that they exist or that they do not exist. For many are the obstacles that impede knowledge, both the obscurity of the question and the shortness of human life."[54]

However, this supposed complicity between Pericles and Protagoras remains unverifiable. First, no source from the classical period even mentions it. The fact that Protagoras may have played some role in the founding of Thurii—for which he may have drawn up laws—does not necessarily prove that he was an adviser to the *stratēgos*.[55] Besides, even if the anecdote recorded by Plutarch was true, the conversation was not about the gods but about irrelevant philosophico-juridical considerations. Finally, even Plutarch himself admits that he is recording biased or even untruthful words, for it was Xanthippus who was spreading this story, with the explicit intention of harming his father (36.4).

After examining the sources, we still have found nothing to suggest that Pericles was a visionary who rejected all forms of superstition. To be sure, the *stratēgos* did keep company with Anaxagoras and was in touch with other sophists who were living in Athens. But that does not mean to say that he accepted all their beliefs. On the contrary, Pericles was keen to show that he was not the captive of any doctrine and, besides, his close acquaintances also included men who held the most traditional of religious beliefs. Revealingly enough, it was the seer Lampon that the *stratēgos* chose as the founder of Thurii, not Protagoras, although the latter also took part in the expedition.

Plutarch tells us that the *stratēgos* did sometimes manifest superstitious beliefs. In 429, when struck down by the plague, he was assailed by "a kind of sluggish distemper that prolonged itself through various changes, used up his body slowly and undermined the loftiness of his spirit" (*Pericles*, 38.1). At this point, his clear head was supposedly taken over by a weak mind:

"Pericles, as he lay sick, showed one of his friends who was come to see him an amulet that the women had hung round his neck. [Theophrastus saw this as a sign] that he was very badly off to put up with such folly as that" (*Pericles*, 38.2). According to Aristotle's successor, Pericles forwent all control over his mores, abandoning himself to beliefs that were the more discredited for being associated with the world of women.[56] That demeaning story, which was doing the rounds in the philosophical schools, should be regarded with the utmost circumspection, since Plutarch, for his part, relates an alternative version of the death of the *stratēgos* that, on the contrary, transforms his death-throes into a most edifying scene. Although he missed out on a heroic death on the battlefield, the *stratēgos* is reported to have displayed an unshakeable lucidity right up to his dying breath, when he delivered one last calm message to his friends gathered about him.[57]

Pericles is portrayed now as a strong-minded man who pours ridicule on divine omens and is in communication with the sophists, now as a weak-minded individual abandoning himself to superstition. The fact is, though, that these contrasting pictures tell us more about the preoccupations of the philosophers than about Pericles' personal beliefs. Among the philosophical schools, Pericles became a stylized ideal type identified with one of the sharply defined caricatures of figures that Theophrastus sketched in so cleverly in his *Characters*.[58]

In *The Life of Pericles*, one passage conveys this tension particularly sharply:

A story is told that once on a time the head of a one-horned ram was brought to Pericles from his country-place, and that Lampon the seer, when he saw how the horn grew strong and solid from the middle of the forehead, declared that, whereas there were two powerful parties in the city, that of Thucydides and that of Pericles, the mastery would finally devolve upon one man—the man to whom this sign had been given. Anaxagoras, however, had the skull cut in two and showed that the brain had not filled out its position but had drawn together to a point, like an egg, at that particular spot in the entire cavity where the root of the horn began. At that time, the story says, it was Anaxagoras who won the plaudits of bystanders; but a little while after it was Lampon, for Thucydides was overthrown and Pericles was entrusted with the entire control of all the interests of the people.[59]

Here too, the story is unreliable, and its elegant symmetry may well arouse legitimate suspicion in the mind of a reader. All the same, one element in the account does ring true: Pericles does not himself choose between the two suggested interpretations. It is the others present who pronounce on the matter, initially inclining to favor Anaxagoras but then having second thoughts about the matter and swinging back to rally to Lampon. Throughout this process, the *stratēgos* himself remains obstinately out of view. Does this, once again, testify to the prudence of Pericles, who never commits himself unless it is absolutely necessary or unless it is in his precise interest to do so? That is perfectly possible, but there is another possible hypothesis. If the *stratēgos* refrained from expressing a preference, that may have been because he saw no obvious contradiction between the two explanations. Plutarch confirms this possibility in the conclusion to the anecdote: "There is nothing, in my opinion, to prevent both of them, the naturalist and the seer, from being in the right of the matter; the one correctly divined the cause, the other the object or purpose."

But, in truth, was Pericles a freethinker or of a traditionalist cast of mind? He may have been both, either alternately or simultaneously. The two attitudes were not as contradictory as is suggested by some of the public pronouncements made by either the sophists or the Hippocratic doctors; the latter were prone to emphasize such a contradiction the better to justify their own practices before an audience that they had to convince.[60] In reality, in the Greek world, there was no clear dividing line between rationality and "superstition"; in the fifth century, Hippocratic medicine and healing rituals functioned in parallel and for most of the time cohabited without clashing.[61] Making offerings, taking part in festivals, believing in prophetic dreams, trying out experimental remedies, and observing natural phenomena without any reference to any other world were all modes of behavior or interpretation that could coexist perfectly well, not only in Greek society generally but also within a single individual who, depending on the context, would turn to the experiences that seemed most appropriate in the prevailing circumstances.

However, even if Pericles did not see these different beliefs as contradictions, that was not necessarily the case for all his fellow-citizens. There is evidence to suggest a certain hardening in religious matters in the 430s, as the political and diplomatic climate became progressively more difficult. According to certain sources, this was when several of those close to the *stratēgos* were charged with impiety in the lawcourts.

The Problem of Impiety

The increase in the number of impiety trials in Pericles' time is a matter of historiographical debate. The fact is that this question involves adopting a definite position on the very nature of Athenian democracy. To accept their existence is to believe that this "Age of Enlightenment" was also a time of religious persecution, even before the Peloponnesian War brought about a hardening of attitudes. To reject it is to defend the irenic version of a tolerant and open democratic Athens. Depending on the view adopted, the trial of Socrates in 399 becomes either the climax of a series of attacks launched by the democracy against "freethinkers" or else an altogether exceptional case that can be explained by the philosopher's provocative behavior in a context of political tension.[62]

The documentation is fraught with pitfalls, but along with many question marks, some things are clear. The first certainty is that Pericles' reputation was murky on account of his maternal ancestors. As a member of the Alcmaeonid family, the *stratēgos* was sullied by the pollution of ancestors who had dared to massacre suppliants who had taken refuge on the Acropolis.[63] Shortly before the Peloponnesian War, the Spartans had seized the opportunity to re-activate the memory of this embarrassing episode:

> It was this "curse" that the Lacedaemonians now bade the Athenians drive out, principally, as they pretended, to avenge the honour of the gods, but in fact because they knew that Pericles, son of Xanthippus, was implicated in the curse on his mother's side, and thinking that, if he were banished, they would find it easier to get from the Athenians the concessions they hoped for. They did not, however, so much expect that he would suffer banishment, as that they would discredit him with his fellow-citizens, who would feel that to some extent his misfortune would be the cause of the war.[64]

That inherited pollution was clearly at the origin of all the accusations made in Athens against the *stratēgos*.

The second certainty: Spartan propaganda never succeeded in harming him directly. No lawsuit was ever brought against him and, according to the orator Lysias, Pericles was even passed down to posterity as a model of piety: "Pericles, they say, advised you once that in dealing with impious persons you should enforce against them not only the written but also the unwritten laws . . . which no-one has yet had the authority to abolish or the audacity to gainsay—laws whose very author is unknown; he judged that they would thus pay the penalty not merely to men, but also to the gods."[65] So Pericles was represented as promoting a strict, even intransigent view of piety, and urging his fellow-citizens to punish offenders even more severely than was prescribed by law. That astonishing excessiveness should probably be as-cribed to the very suspicion of impiety that surrounded him.

According to the ancient sources, his opponents, foiled in their attempts to damage Pericles in person, resorted to bringing charges of impiety (*asebeia*) against several of those close to him: the sculptor Phidias, Pericles' partner, Aspasia, and his teacher, Anaxagoras. It is at this point that a historian is obliged to abandon the solid ground of certainties and venture into the fogs of speculation and hypothesis.

Let us start with the misadventures of the sculptor Phidias. In *The Life of Pericles* (31.4), Plutarch reports that "when he wrought the battle of the Amazons on the shield of the goddess [belonging to the statue of Athena *Parthenos*], he carved out a figure that suggested himself as a bald old man lifting on high a stone with both hands, and also inserted a very fine likeness of Pericles fighting with an Amazon. And the attitude of the hand, which holds out a spear in front of the face of Pericles, is cunningly contrived as it were with a desire to conceal the resemblance, which is, however, plain to be seen from either side." Having discovered this subterfuge, citizens were apparently revolted by this transgressive action that "raised the memory of men to the level of the celebration of heroes and of gods."[66] Plutarch claims that the sculptor was thrown into prison, where he died, and meanwhile Meno, who had denounced him, was honored by the city.

However, there is no evidence to confirm the veracity of such an episode, which is related in this form only in the works of later authors.[67] Besides, Plutarch makes a factual error in his account: Phidias did not die in prison for, soon after 438, he went off to Elis to sculpt a gigantic statue of Zeus at Olympia.[68] From there, it is but a step to consign the entire anecdote to the gallery of Plutarchian fantasies. However, it is a step that we should forbear to take. Not only are the sculptor's misfortunes mentioned by several fifth-century and fourth-century sources,[69] but Plutarch does appear to be speaking from some experience. It is possible that during his stay in Athens, he had himself spotted the portraits sculpted on the goddess's shield.[70] Moreover, it seems that this was not the only misdemeanor of which the sculptor was accused: it was said that he had diverted for his own use some of the gold and ivory allotted for the construction of the statue of Athena Parthenos.[71]

Even if we accept that those accusations have some historical basis, it was certainly not impiety that fueled the Athenians' indignation. The statue of Athena was provided with no attested sacrifices, no altar, no priest, and it had no ritual role. Rather, it was a political monument erected to the glory of Athens. What Phidias was accused of was, first, of having ignored the ban on representations of individuals on public Athenian monuments—in effect, of manifest hubris, not impiety (*asebeia*)—and, second, of having embezzled public funds.

The legal attacks against Aspasia, Pericles' partner, are even more doubtful. According to Plutarch, the sole source to mention this affair, this Milesian woman was dragged before the courts on charges of impiety, prompting Pericles to abandon his usual reserve and to move the jurors' hearts with his tears. Far from being historically attested, the whole story is probably the fruit of a late reconstruction that misconstrues the accusations made on the comic stage as an actual lawsuit against impiety.[72]

Are we on any firmer ground with the lawsuit brought against Pericles' teacher, Anaxagoras? That is far from certain. He had been living in Athens for many years and is said to have been condemned for impiety at a date that is uncertain—possibly 432—and this prompted him to flee to Lampsacus, his home city, in northern Asia Minor, where he is said to have lived until his death.[73] However, the whole affair remains very unclear. The Hellenistic sources, recorded by Diogenes Laertius (2.12), in any case produce two different versions of the matter. In one, it is the demagogue Cleon who prosecuted him for impiety; in the other, it is Thucydides, Pericles' opponent, ostracized in 443, who accuses him of collaboration with the Persians.

Nor are these the only gray areas surrounding this supposed trial. On what legal basis could Anaxagoras have been found guilty? According to Plutarch, a certain Diopeithes proposed "a bill providing for the public impeachment of such as did not believe in gods [*ta theia*] or who taught doctrines regarding the heavens."[74] The suggestion, then, is that Diopeithes, an influential seer, was one of the zealous figures who clung to traditional piety and was shocked by Anaxagoras's studies on the heavenly bodies and phenomena. For did not Pericles' friend believe that the sun was an incandescent mass—not a deity—and did he not refuse to believe that eclipses were divine portents[75]?

Yet Plutarch is the only one to mention this strange decree, the authenticity of which is such a bone of contention for historians.[76] Without entering into this debate that is so full of pitfalls, we can perhaps try to rephrase the question. To be sure, attacks on "naturalists" (*phusikoi*) did make a comeback in the 430s,[77] for as the Spartan threat became more pressing, the Athenians were clearly keen to make sure that the gods were on their side. But does this imply that these critics resorted to a legal solution? There is no evidence to suggest that it does. What is certain, however, is that the comic poets were busy attacking not only the sophists and "nebulous chatterboxes" (*meteōroleskhai*), but any individuals who in some way drew attention to themselves in the city. In this respect, the seer Diopeithes was not spared any more than Anaxagoras was; the comic poets portrayed him as an oracular expert of doubtful repute, or even as a dangerous visionary.[78] Perhaps, after all, that is the main lesson to be learned here: in the 430s, all forms of individual distinction became suspect.

Thus, none of the trials for impiety involving those close to Pericles is attested with certainty. So it is hard to detect any symptoms of a democracy given to persecution let alone terrorism and bent on punishing the slightest religious deviation. If authoritarianism did become stricter, it probably did so after Pericles' death. The plague that carried off the *stratēgos* along with so many of his fellow-citizens did have a profound effect on the Athenians and their beliefs. According to Thucydides, the epidemic even drove men into nihilism and despair, as all their invocations to the gods remained unanswered: "The sanctuaries too, in which they had quartered themselves, were full of the corpses of those who had died in them; for the calamity which weighed upon them was so overpowering that men, not knowing what was to become of them, became careless of all law, sacred as well as profane. And the customs which they had hitherto observed regarding burial were all thrown into confusion, and they buried their dead, each one as he could."[79] Relations between men and the gods were lastingly undermined, as is testified by the mutilation of the Hermai and the profanation of the Mysteries of Eleusis, in 416/5. Readers of Thucydides will not be surprised to learn that the death of the *stratēgos* constituted a definite break; according to the historian, with the disappearance of the *stratēgos*, the life of the whole community underwent a change for the worse.

CHAPTER 9

After Pericles: The Decline of Athens?

In *The Peloponnesian War*, Thucydides treats the death of Pericles as a turning point in the history of Athens. He represents Pericles' "reign" as a clear dividing line between a community led by a virtuous elite and a democratic city abandoned to the hands of *kakoi*—the despicable demagogues. Once Plutarch had put the finishing touches to it, this Manichean vision was often readopted by modern historiography, without the slightest criticism.[1] Yet the ancient sources are by no means unanimous on the subject. Some ancient authors rejected the historiographical model that represents a rise up to Pericles, followed by a fall after the death of the *stratēgos*. The disciples of Socrates, for instance, had no hesitation in criticizing even Pericles' "reign." In Plato's view, Pericles was certainly no model. He proved himself incapable not only of raising his own children but also of educating the Athenian people. This showed that the *stratēgos* was at least partly responsible for the decadence which, according to the philosopher, had characterized the city right from the start. In Plato's view, democracy was a regime that was fundamentally vitiated and the personalities of its leaders were of little account; in the last analysis, it was the people, the true tyrant, who forced its leaders to do as it wished.

When stripped of their polemical thrust, Plato's analyses lead one to take a different view of the death of Pericles within the history of Athens. Rather than regarding it as a sudden break—whether for better or for worse—Plato's thinking encourages us to replace the life of Pericles within a great upheaval that encompasses and exceeds it—namely, the taming of the members of the elite at the hands of the Athenian people.

THE DEATH OF PERICLES AND THE RISE OF THE DEMAGOGUES

A Change in the Political Players?

Thucydides and Pseudo-Aristotle, each in his own way, detected a break in the political life of Athens. In the funerary appreciation of the dead leader that he composed, Thucydides drew a radical contrast between Pericles and his successors: "For so long as he presided over the affairs of the state in time of peace he pursued a moderate policy and kept the city in safety, and it was under him that Athens reached the height of her greatness . . . But the successors of Pericles, being more *on an equality* [*isoi*] *with one another* and yet striving each to be first, were ready to surrender to the people even the conduct of public affairs to suit their whims."[2] The author of the *Constitution of the Athenians* shares that view and interprets the history of the city in a fashion that unfolds in the same way: "So long, then, as Pericles held the leadership of the people [*dēmos*], the affairs of the state went better, but when Pericles was dead, they became much worse. For the people now, for the first time, adopted a head [*prostatēs*] who was not in good repute with the respectable men [*epieikeis*] whereas in former periods these always continued to lead the people [*dēmagōgein*]."[3]

Over and above differences in details,[4] the two authors are in agreement on a twofold diagnosis: first, structurally speaking, the leaders had dominated politics in Athens and the people were merely the puppets of those who led them; second, at a circumstantial level, both reckon that Pericles' death marked a decisive turning point. When the leaders of the *dēmos* came to resemble those whom they led and were no better than the latter, decadence was inevitable. The outcome of the Peloponnesian War—so terribly damaging to Athens—proved them right.

Let us make a detailed study of the argument set out in *The Constitution of the Athenians*. Up until the death of Pericles, the people's leaders belonged to the group of the "well-born" (*eupatrides*), the respectable men (*epieikeis*); the leaders of the *dēmos* all belonged to the traditional Athenian elite, whose fortunes were based on the possession and exploitation of land. The death of Pericles, it is claimed, opened the door to "demagogues," whose wealth was founded on craft activities: Cleon owned a tannery, Hyperbolus was a producer of lamps, and Cleophon made lyres. It was a switch from wealthy people to nobodies. This sociological evolution resulted in consequences that were catastrophic for the city. The new politicians corrupted the people not only symbolically, by their uncouth language and their undisciplined way of addressing the Assembly,[5] but also materially, by introducing new civic wages for the poorest citizens.[6]

If one believes Thucydides or the Aristotelian school, Pericles' death drew a line separating two distinct moments in Athenian political life: whereas the *stratēgos* had led the city to its greatest achievements, thanks to his wisdom and prudence (*phronēsis*),[7] the new loutish leaders had led Athens to disaster. There was a definite, even caricatural contrast between a carefully controlled *dēmos*, dominated by a Pericles who set a brake on the people's desires, and a *dēmos* beyond control, constantly flattered by Cleon and his successors.

That Manichean representation was not defended solely by the opponents of radical democracy, either writing in exile—as was Thucydides—or sheltered by the wall of the Lyceum—as was the author of the *Constitution of the Athenians*. It was reproduced in many of the comedies destined to be staged before the Athenians en masse. In the last third of the fifth century, the poet Eupolis was already contrasting the *stratēgoi* of the past to the current leaders in a striking mirror image: "And yet, despite the abundance of the subject-matter, I do not know what to say, so distressed am I by the spectacle of public life today. We, the older ones, used not to live like this. In the first place, in our day, the city had *stratēgoi* who came from the greatest houses [*oikion*] and were the first in both wealth and birth. We used to invoke them as though they were gods and indeed that is what they were. . . . But today, if we have to go to war, we elect as our *stratēgoi* polluted men [*katharmata*]."[8] This grandiloquent paean of praise for the past certainly testifies to the disarray that some citizens felt, faced with the eruption of "nouveaux riches," the *neoploutoi*,[9] onto the Athenian political stage.

A similar idealization of the past appears in Aristophanes. Although he treated Pericles badly in his *Peace*, staged in 422/1 B.C., this comic poet changed his tune in *The Frogs*, in 405 B.C., in which he had his character "Aeschylus" pronounce the following revealing tirade (1463–1465): "they [should] count the enemy's soil their own, / And theirs the enemy's: and know that ships /Are their true wealth, their so-called wealth delusion."

This passage, placed right at the end of the play in a particularly strategic position, reflects a new—and positive—view of the Periclean defensive system that consisted in placing all the city's hopes in the fleet, leaving the civic territory in the hands of the enemy. At this time, when the city was suffering one defeat after another both on land and at sea, Pericles was represented as the very embodiment of a past when Athens had been all-powerful.

The yawning gap between a rehabilitated Pericles and his despised successors seems immense, if not unbridgeable. Yet, upon closer inspection, the break was less definitive than the comic poets brutally depicted it to be and than the historians and philosophers theorized.

A Seeming but Misleading Break

In the first place, the "new politicians" were not unknown men of low birth. Cleainetus, the father of Cleon, had already been a *khorēgos* in 460/459 B.C.,[10] and around 440 his son made an advantageous marriage with the daughter of Dikaiogenes, an Athenian of particular distinction.[11] So his family had already been prosperous in the preceding generation. As for Cleophon's father, Cleippides, he had been elected *stratēgos* in 428 (Thucydides, 3.3.2). The "new" men were thus much less new than has been suggested by authors both ancient and modern.

Second, that claim was based on a presupposition that is far from universally accepted—namely, that in Athens only landed wealth was considered legitimate. To support that hypothesis, historians invoke the virulent criticisms aimed at demagogues whose fortunes were based on crafts. But those attacks, which emanated from certain specific circles, those of Athenian intellectuals, did not reflect the opinions of the majority of citizens. Besides, they were no more than relatively effective, since this new breed of demagogues were not only elected but frequently reelected by the *dēmos*. To be a wealthy craftsman was, at least after 430 B.C., by no means a handicap for anyone wishing to become one of the city's leaders. To be sure, such individuals were the butts of criticism and mockery, but no more so than a man such as Themistocles, who was called a "bugger" on an *ostrakon* found in the Agora, or one such as Cimon, who was accused of incest with his sister Elpinike.[12]

Finally, if indeed there was a break, it certainly did not date from the death of Pericles; the new politicians already held a definite influence in the city in the lifetime of the *stratēgos*. Without going right back to Ephialtes, about whom little is known, a number of pointers already suggest that the social origins of the Athenian political leaders were undergoing a gradual evolution. As early as the 440/430s, the *stratēgos* Hagnon, the founder of the colony of Amphipolis in 437, fitted the stereotype of a social climber suspected of having acquired his wealth by abusing his position in power. In a fragment from the *Ploutoi* (*The Spirits of Wealth*), a play by the comic poet Cratinus,[13] Hagnon was accused of having amassed his fortune by doubtful means: "—Prosecutor: 'This man is not wealthy in Athens in conformity with justice, so he should cook up some wealth for his city.' —Witness for the Defence: 'On the contrary, he has been wealthy for a long time [or 'he has grown rich from his magistracies (*arkhaioploutos*)'], he owns what he has had from the beginning [or 'by reason of his power (*ex archēs*)'].'"

Here, the poet was playing on the polysemy of the word *arkhē*, which meant now "origin" or "ancient beginnings," now "power" or "magistracies."[14] The double meaning made it possible for Cratinus to raise a laugh from the spectators by denigrating a *stratēgos* who had become suddenly rich; and this was well before Pericles' death and Cleon's arrival on the scene.

At a sociological level, it is thus not possible to detect any radical break between the period before Pericles' death and the period after it. The continuity of political practices was remarkable, contrary to the claims made by the author of the *Constitution of the Athenians*. Can one honestly, in good faith, set up a contrast between Pericles' policies and those of his successors, arguing that the latter corrupted the people by providing civic pay? Were not Cleon, Hyperbolus, and Cleophon simply imitating Pericles, who, as early as the 450s, had introduced *misthos* for jurors? Besides, even if Cleon was somewhat more aggressive than the *stratēgos* and opposed his rival's "wait-and-see" strategy, he and his fellows were, after all, essentially in agreement with Pericles' policy: keep on with the war against Sparta and, at all costs, maintain the empire.[15]

The comic poets were in no doubt at all about it; in his lifetime, Pericles was the victim of attacks just as violent as those later directed against Cleon. Accused, as he was, of aspiring to tyranny and having plotted Ephialtes' death, depicted as a corrupt demagogue and even an adulterer, Pericles was certainly not spared rumors, defamatory gossip, and innuendos. If chance had so had it that the earliest preserved comedy had been Cratinus's *Dionysalexandros*, in which Pericles was shamelessly criticized, and not Aristophanes' *Acharnians*, in which it is Cleon who is the prime target of the poet, we should probably have seen Pericles in a less favorable light.

Now, at the end of this analysis, Pericles no longer seems so different from Cleon. Both were skilful demagogues if, that is, the term is taken with its original meaning of "leader of the people," with no social or moral connotations. Initially, "demagogues" simply designated all those who, from the time of the Persian Wars down to 411, put themselves forward to lead the people. As Christian Mann has shown, the death of Pericles did not radically upset the functioning of the Athenian democracy.[16] To be sure, the fourth-century Athenians confusedly felt that they were living in a political world very different from that of the fifth century. However, most of them did not correlate the change with the disappearance of Pericles. As we have seen, at the end of the fifth century, Eupolis simply drew a contrast between the past and the present; he did not mention the *stratēgos* by name. As for Demosthenes, in the mid-fourth century he certainly did discern a change in Athenian political life, but he did not connect it with any particular moment or individual:

> I consider it right to set the welfare of the state above the popularity of an orator. Indeed, the orators of past generations, always praised but not always imitated by those who address you, adopted this very standard and principle of statesmanship [of putting the safety of the city before winning the favor of the people by flattering them]. I refer to the famous Aristides, to Nicias, to my own namesake and to Pericles. But

ever since this breed of orators appeared, who ply you with questions such as "What would you like? What shall I propose? How can I oblige you?" the interests of the state have frittered away for a momentary popularity.[17]

So this orator did not associate the end of the Golden Age with the death of Pericles, but extended that enchanted age to the time of Nicias, who died sixteen years after the *stratēgos*, in 413, during the expedition to Sicily.

However, it was Plato who most radically questioned any such break. According to him, it is completely pointless to try to separate the grain from the chaff and to set in contrast the period before Pericles and the period after him, quite simply because no leader, however virtuous, ever had any chance of controlling the Athenian people, given that it was so tyrannical and capricious.

THE SOCRATIC CRITIQUE: A *STRATĒGOS* WITHOUT INFLUENCE

The Periclean Moment: A General Pedagogical Failure

The Socratic authors—Plato, of course, but also Xenophon and Antisthenes—produced an extremely negative image of Pericles. Far from associating the *stratēgos* with a golden age, they portrayed him as a man who was certainly exceptional but was incapable of educating his contemporaries. Failing to dispense a suitable *paideia* for them, the *stratēgos* had no way of controlling the harmful desires of the masses.

To present that failure of Pericles, the Socratic authors chose to adopt one particular line of attack. In order to emphasize his fundamental inability to educate anyone at all, they concentrated their critiques on the *stratēgos*'s difficult relationship with his own children. It must be said that his children, in particular his elder son, Xanthippus, had not hesitated to criticize their father or even, according to Stesimbrotus of Thasos, to circulate the most appalling rumors about him.[18] The Socratics thus had a fine time opposing the discord (*stasis*) that reigned in the *stratēgos*'s family to the necessary unity that was believed to prevail in the city.[19]

Plato reproached Pericles in particular for not having taught his children the art of government. To the philosopher, this seemed truly scandalous, for he believed that politics stemmed from an overarching knowledge regime (*epistēmē*): "In private life, our best and wisest citizens are unable to transmit this excellence of theirs; for Pericles, the father of these young fellows here, gave them a first-rate training in the subjects for which he found teachers, but in those of which he is himself a master [the political art], he neither trains them personally nor commits them to another's guidance, and so they go about grazing at will like sacred oxen, on the chance of their picking up excellence here or there for themselves."[20]

Over and above the mediocre education provided for Pericles' own sons, Plato also complained about the *paideia*—or rather absence of any *paideia*—dispensed to Pericles' wards, Alcibiades and his brother, Cleinias II. As their official guardian, the *stratēgos* had failed to check the disorderly behavior of his young protégés—at least, that is the point of view that Plato's Socrates defends in his dialogue with the young Alcibiades. According to him, Pericles could not be considered a wise man since he had transmitted no wisdom either to his sons or to Cleinias. In the course of this conversation, Alcibiades himself actually acknowledges that the two sons of the *stratēgos* are stupid and that his own brother is crazy (*Alcibiades* I, 118d). Pressing his advantage, Socrates then asks the young man: "But tell me of any other Athenian or foreigner, slave or freeman, who is accounted to have become wiser through converse with Pericles?" (*Alcibiades* I, 119a). Unable to find an answer, Alcibiades is struck dumb, in his silence acknowledging the point made by the philosopher.

When he composed this exchange, Plato was clearly pursuing a number of objectives. In the first place, he wanted to lay the blame for the failure of the education of Alcibiades and his brother solely at Pericles' door. Alcibiades, involved as he was in a number of religious, political, and sexual scandals, became the symbol of the *stratēgos*'s failure as a teacher. Second, by launching this counter-assault, Plato aimed to exonerate Socrates of any responsibility in this pedagogic catastrophe, in reply to all those who were accusing his master of playing a harmful role in the young man's education.[21] And finally, Plato was widening his attack and denying Pericles the ability to educate anyone at all; his misdemeanors in the private sphere were prefigurations of his failure in the public sphere. Plato was so keen on this idea that he returned to the attack in the *Gorgias*: "Whether the Athenians are said to have become better because of Pericles, or quite the contrary, to have been corrupted by him? . . . what I, for my part, hear is that Pericles has made the Athenians idle, cowardly, talkative and avaricious, by starting the system of public payments" (*Gorgias*, 515d–e). Worse still, he even suggested that Pericles had made his fellow-citizens "even wilder than they were when he took them in hand" (*Gorgias*, 516c). Far from putting a break on the corruption inherent in the democratic system, the *stratēgos* had actually accelerated it.

In order to illustrate the decline of Athens, the Socratic authors sometimes even went so far as to use Pericles the Younger in their demonstration. Here again, it was a matter of using the son in order to criticize the father.

Aspasia's bastard did indeed, by his very existence, embody the blunders of Periclean policies: had not Pericles obtained his naturalization in flagrant contradiction to the law on citizenship that he himself had proposed in 451? Carried away by their enthusiastic demolition exercise, the Socratics carried irony to the point of making the son a ferocious critic of the radical democracy established by his parent. Pericles the Younger, having himself been appointed *stratēgos* (and destined to suffer an unjust death after the battle of Arginusae, in 406 B.C.), is thus represented in Xenophon's *Memorabilia* as lamenting the decadence of the city of Athens. Comparing the Athenians to athletes, formerly energetic but now lackadaisical, in order to reverse this doom-laden trend he proposes a return to the ancestral mores, just like those of . . . the Spartans.[22] Under the malicious pen of Xenophon, the son of Pericles was reduced to praising the sworn enemies of his father and celebrating their oligarchic political system.

As represented by the Socratics, Pericles thus appeared, at best, as an exceptional man who was nevertheless incapable of educating anyone at all, at worst as a despicable demagogue who flattered the base instincts of the people. So should we regard these acerbic criticisms simply as a form of an obsessional attack on the foremost leader of a despised regime? Maybe, but there is more to it. Over and above the case of the *stratēgos*, Plato aimed, in this work of his, to point the finger at the failure of the entire Athenian political personnel.

A Long-Term Evolution: The Establishment of "Tyranny" by the People

In the *Gorgias*, Plato targeted not just Pericles, but included in his critique all the leaders of Athens from Themistocles onward. According to him, not one of them had succeeded in the slightest degree in checking the desires of the people: "In persuading or compelling her people to what would help them to be better—*they were scarcely, if at all, superior to their successors*" (*Gorgias*, 517b). All things considered, Pericles was neither better nor worse than the rest of them: he behaved toward the Athenians "as to children, trying merely to gratify them, not caring a jot whether they would be better or worse in consequence."[23] In this respect, Plato agrees with the severe judgment passed on the Athenian politicians in this period by Theopompus of Chios. This pupil of Isocrates laid charges of demagogy against not only Pericles but also Cimon, despite the fact that the latter supported the aristocratic status quo.[24] According to Theopompus, the generosity of the former differed in no way at all from that of the latter. Both were nothing but sordid flatterers.

Unlike Theopompus, Plato did not stop at this bitter conclusion. Far from abusing the Athenian leaders, he exonerated them, with a certain degree of slyness, of all serious responsibility for the decline of the city. For even had they wished to do so, the leaders of the people were powerless when it came to opposing the whims of the masses. In Plato's view, it was always the people who held the whip-hand over the politicians, not the reverse. Contrary to the tradition favored by Aristotle and Xenophon, that proclaimed that the *dēmos* simply reflected its leaders, Plato held that the people were in truth responsible for the corruption of the Athenian elite groups: "What private teaching do you think will hold out and not rather be swept away by the torrent of censure and applause, and borne off on its current, so that he will affirm the same things that they [that is, the people] do to be honourable and base, and will adopt the same habits [*epitēdeusein*], and be even such as they?"[25]

According to Plato, the members of the elite were totally incapable of resisting the democratic "torrent" that swept away everything in its path. Unlike most of his fellows, this philosopher took the democracy that he so detested extremely seriously: far from the people being a mere puppet, it held terrifying power over its leaders, forcing them to align their behavior with the lowest common denominator. Faced with this tyrant-people, the leaders had to adjust their wishes to the expectations of the crowd or otherwise risk discredit, ostracism or even death. As Plato asserted in another context, in order to live in safety under the reign of a despot, it was best to agree with all that he said and resemble him as closely as possible.[26]

Within such an interpretative framework, Pericles' behavior takes on a new meaning. Despite his attempts at resistance, the life of the *stratēgos* testifies to the establishment of democratic conventions that became ever more intrusive. In the face of increasing public pressure, Pericles was obliged to show that his behavior was above suspicion and to reject all overostentatious forms of distinction. His rejection of sumptuary expenses, his avoidance of his friends (*philoi*), his manner of behavior in the Assembly, and his way of favoring the fleet's oarsmen, rather than the hoplite phalanx, all reflected the establishment of a new balance between the people and the Athenian elite. From this point onward, in both their public behavior and their private attitudes, the demagogues needed constantly to strive to diminish the social distance that separated them from ordinary citizens.

Once their polemical thrust is neutralized, the Platonic analyses make it possible to view relations between the "great man" and the democracy in a new light. Far from embodying a break, the Periclean moment fits into a long-term evolution that involved the people's taming of the Athenian elite. It was precisely the process of leveling that the Athenian oligarchs regarded as insupportable, being quick to interpret it as a sign of irremediable political and moral decline.

Pericles himself was at once an actor in and a witness to this progressive swing. Although a major player in it, he did not initiate the process nor did he bestow upon it its final form. At the time of his death, the people's ideological domination was still far from unchallenged, as the story of Alcibiades, the *stratēgos*'s ward, clearly shows. The munificence of this young Athenian and his disorderly behavior did not prevent him from fascinating the *dēmos* nor, despite all his transgressions, did it stop him being elected *stratēgos* several times in the 420s and 410s.[27] It was not until the fourth century and the lasting trauma created by the Peloponnesian War that the democratic system became stabilized and the compromise between the elite and the people found its definitive formulation.

CHAPTER 10

The Individual and Democracy:
The Place of the "Great Man"

Now, at the end of this biographical odyssey, let us return, if not to the shores of Ithaca, at least to the question that served as its starting point. Was Pericles an all-powerful figure or an evanescent one? How, exactly, did the actions of the *stratēgos* and the will of the people interact? Can we settle for the forthright conclusion expressed by Thucydides in his final panegyric for *stratēgos*: "Athens, though in name a democracy, gradually became in fact a government ruled by its foremost citizen" (2.65.9)? According to the ancient authors, there seemed to be no doubt about it. Pericles' monarchy, theorized by the historian of the Peloponnesian War, was also a favorite theme of the comic poets, who were always ready to represent the *stratēgos* as an unscrupulous tyrant. In truth, Pericles' admirers and detractors were all perfectly happy to agree on one point—namely, the predominance of the *stratēgos*'s position in the city of Athens. Some—Thucydides for one—depict him as a beneficent sovereign; others, as a dangerous and corrupting tyrant. Either way, the *dēmos* appears as a mere puppet manipulated by Pericles. Thanks to his establishing the *misthos* and launching his policy of major building works, the *stratēgos* is depicted as a monarch showering benefits upon his passive or even apathetic subjects.

Although that view is purveyed on every side by the ancient authors, it needs to be criticized and replaced in context. It fails to take into account the various control-mechanisms that surrounded the power of Athenian magistrates, Pericles first and foremost. Not only did he always have to negotiate with the other *stratēgoi*, which, de facto, limited his influence, but, like any other member of the elite, he was subject to many forms of supervision on the part of the people. At an institutional level, his authority was frequently the object of scrutiny; accounts had to be submitted, and there was always a real threat of ostracism or of an accusation of high treason. At the social and ritual level, Pericles was forced to withstand numerous attacks from the comic dramatists, justify himself in the face of insistent rumors about his behavior, both private and public, and suffer noisy abuse from the crowds in the Assembly. Although his influence over the city's destiny was undeniable, the *stratēgos* was obliged to take popular expectations into account and, accordingly, adopt an attitude in conformity with the democratic ethos. Far from ruling Athens as a monarch, Pericles lived constantly under tension in a context in which the power of the demos was relentlessly increasing.

"Pericles the Olympian": The Power of a Single Man?

Monarch and Tyrant

When addressing the Athenians right at the beginning of the fourth century, the orator Lysias, showing no concern for historical accuracy, declared "our ancestors chose as nomothetae [that is, lawgivers] Solon, Themistocles and Pericles."[1] There was no mention of Cleisthenes or Ephialtes in this idealized evocation of the ancestral constitution, the *patrios politeia*. That omission was in no way surprising. "The fact is that, in Athenian minds, there had been no institutional innovations except in great periods that could be identified with a single man known and recognized by the whole community."[2] In accordance with a mechanism well charted in the Greek world, as elsewhere, important changes were always associated with one great man in particular. As recollection of events faded, the collective memory effected a simplification and stylization that tended to associate the introduction of a variety of measures with certain leading figures. The Spartans thus attributed a whole collection of economic, social, and institutional reforms to one single semi-mythical lawgiver, Lycurgus, despite the fact that the Spartan *kosmos* was set in place only gradually; and in just the same way, the Athenians associated the creation of their city as a political community—the famous synoecism—solely with the name Theseus—even though the process had clearly taken place only gradually in the course of a considerable period of time.

The ancient authors tended to attribute to certain men far more than they had, in truth, accomplished, thereby eclipsing other historical actors who were just as important. Cleisthenes the lawgiver remained in the shadow of Solon, who was considered to be more consensual, just as Ephialtes was reduced to a mere puppet manipulated by Pericles:[3] that process of compression initiated in the fourth century found its fullest expression in Plutarch's *Life*, which turned Pericles into the man of providence for the entire *pentēkontaetia*.

Does this mean that we should submit to a radical revision the image of an all-powerful Pericles, on the grounds that it resulted from a biased functioning of the collective memory that had been further amplified by the preconceptions of the ancient authors? To do so would, to say the least, be overhasty. In truth, that personal cult was not a purely a posteriori recon- struction, but instead was a theme that had already been elaborated in the fifth century, as several sources of evidence show. Even then, Thucydides was presenting the *stratēgos* as "the first of the Athenians" (1.139), who, unchal- lenged, dominated the city's whole political life. According to this historian's account, Pericles seems hardly even to belong to the civic community, so outrageously does he dominate it: he alone confronts the anger of *all* the Athenians, who form a homogeneous block facing him, before obliging the *entire city* (*xumpasa tēn polin*), purely by the force of his oratory, to recognize his superiority, his *arkhē* (2.65.1–2). According to Thucydides, the *stratēgos* even managed to subjugate the people with its own consent: "he restrained the multitude while respecting their liberties [*kateikhe to plēthos eleutherōs*], and led them rather than was led by them" (2.65.8).[4]

Nor was the historian Thucydides alone in expressing that opinion. In Peri- cles' lifetime, already, the comic poets had delighted in setting the omnipo- tence of the *stratēgos* on stage, but in their case, did so in order to stigmatize it. They even went so far as to compare Pericles to the king of the gods, Zeus, although there was nothing complimentary about the assimilation, for, by calling him an Olympian, they were drawing attention to his hubris.[5] More- over, as well as describing him with that insolent label, the comic authors de- picted him as a man who held quasi-absolute power. According to Telekleides, a contemporary of Pericles, the Athenians had handed over to him "with the cities' assessments, the cities themselves, / to bind or release as he pleases, / their ramparts of stone to build up if he likes, and / then to pull down again straightway, / their treaties, their forces, their might, peace and / riches, and all the fair gifts of good fortune."[6] So it would seem that it was not just in for- eign policies that Pericles did as he pleased, but also within the city; according to this poet, the citizens had abdicated their own sovereignty in his favor.

More alarming still, one deeply rooted tradition linked Pericles with the tyrants of Athens, the Pisistratids. This dark legend can already be de- tected, reading between the lines, in the ambiguous account of the birth of the *stratēgos* recorded by Herodotus. Just before giving birth to Pericles, his mother was said to have dreamed that she produced a lion.[7] Although the analogy has certain heroic resonances,[8] in a democratic context it is, to say the least, equivocal. For it links Pericles with Cypselus, the tyrant of Corinth, whose mother had a similar dream. Above all, however, it linked him with Hipparchus, the son of the tyrant Pisistratus who, also in a dream, had been compared to a lion and was destined to suffer a dire fate.[9]

As his opponents saw it, that was not the only link that bound Pericles to the tyrants of Athens. The very features of his face rendered him suspect. According to Plutarch, "it was thought that in feature he was like the tyrant Pisistratus; and when men well on in years remarked also that his voice was sweet and his tongue glib and speedy in discourse, they were struck with amazement at the resemblance" (*Pericles*, 7.1). Moreover, quite apart from his physical appearance, his network of friends evoked the memory of tyrants and those close to him were described as "the new Pisistratids" (*Pericles*, 16.1).

The *stratēgos* may well also have been compared to those controversial figures on account of the policies that he pursued. Some aspects of his actions as leader of the city were certainly reminiscent of certain initiatives of the Athenian tyrants. When he reorganized the Great Panathenaea so as to secure a greater place for musical competitions, Pericles was following in the footsteps of Pisistratus, who had, if not created, at least lent new luster to this great Athenian festival.[10] Likewise, the construction policies of the *stratēgos* recalled Athens's tyrannical past. The gigantism of the Parthenon must have been regarded as an echo of the immense temple of Zeus Olympius, the construction of which, to the south east of the Acropolis, had been launched around 515 B.C. by the Pisistratids who, however, did not have time to complete it.[11] In suggesting that the embellishment of the city was, as Plutarch claimed, "manifestly subjecting it to tyranny" (*Pericles*, 12.2), Pericles' opponents no doubt hoped to associate the *stratēgos*'s monumental policies with the detested memory of the Pisistratids.

The monumental program launched by Pericles on the Acropolis played a crucial role in the process that led to Pericles being depicted as an all-powerful monarch. To some extent, the ancient sources did represent the *stratēgos*'s power as a reflection of the Parthenon, majestic, intimidating, even overwhelming, thereby transforming the magistrate into an emperor so intent on his building projects that he eluded all popular control.

The Builder-Emperor

If Plutarch so greatly admired Pericles, despite all his "demagogic" policies, it was primarily on account of the "great works" with which the biographer associated him so closely. In his final comparison between Pericles and Fabius Maximus, Plutarch expresses his boundless admiration for those buildings that, in a way, increased the prestige of the whole of Greece in comparison with the triumphant Rome of the early centuries of its empire: "By the side of the great public works, the temples and the stately edifices with which Pericles adorned Athens, all Rome's attempts at splendour down to the times of the Caesars, taken together, are not worthy to be considered."[12] In this way, Plutarch explicitly compares the action of the *stratēgos* to that of the Caesars. His monumental policies make him a prefiguration of the Roman emperors— in particular, Hadrian, who was a contemporary of the biographer and who, out of a sense of philhellenism, restored the edifices of Athens that were built under Pericles.[13]

Was this simply a later idea that emerged at the time when Plutarch was composing his *Lives*, as a result of a kind of contamination from the Roman imperial model? Not at all. In his own lifetime, the *stratēgos* was already associated with the monuments constructed at the peak of his career. The comic poets represented him as "carrying the Odeon on his head";[14] and one century later the orator Lycurgus of Athens, himself also a great builder who completed the construction of the theater of Dionysus, redesigned the Pnyx, and restored the temples of the Acropolis, wrote as follows: "Pericles, who had conquered Samos, Euboea, Aegina, *and had constructed the Propylaea, the Odeon, the Parthenon*, and had collected ten thousand talents for the Acropolis, was crowned with a simple crown of olive leaves."[15]

However, even if this vision of an architect-Pericles frequently recurs in the ancient sources, for a number of reasons it calls for qualification. In the first place, we should distinguish between the edifices that are "Periclean" because Pericles himself proposed them and the monuments that are called "Periclean" only because they were constructed at the time when the *stratēgos* wielded influence in the city.[16] If we credit the testimony of the orator Lycurgus, only the Odeon, the Parthenon, and the Propylaea—the last conceived by Mnesicles and all constructed in the five years between 437 and 433—should be attributed to the direct initiative of Pericles. To be sure, he also played a role in the construction of the Long Walls, which constituted a crucial element in his defense strategy. Nevertheless, he was not alone in taking part in their construction: Thucydides does not even mention his name in this connection,[17] and Plato's Socrates links him with only the construction of the inner wall that reinforced the northern wall that connected the city with Piraeus.[18]

Next, even Pericles' supposed control of the work sites in which he was directly involved needs qualification. So it is, to put it mildly, mistaken to speak of "the labors of Pericles" as if they were comparable to the "labors of Heracles." Pericles was no Hellenistic king, let alone a Roman emperor who, on his own, as an autocrat, decided upon the constructions to be undertaken. Every one of his projects was submitted to a vote of the Assembly that also decided how to finance it. Architects produced plans, models, and estimates, all of which were submitted for the approval of the Council. Magistrates then proceeded to adjudicate on the proposed works,[19] which, once started, were subject to the intrusive control of a college of ten *epistatai* elected by the Assembly.

Given this context, when Plutarch, on the subject of the Odeon, declares that Pericles "supervised" (*epistatountos*) the construction (*Pericles*, 13.9), the biographer was clearly misrepresenting the reality. Only two possibilities are plausible: either he was referring to the official post of an *epistatēs*, the supervisor of a construction site, elected by the people, in which case he forgets that the *stratēgos* was obliged to agree with the other nine members of the commission;[20] alternatively, he was assuming that someone held the power of general supervision over all such works, and that is something that is nowhere attested by the contemporary sources.

Plutarch's testimony also needs to be considered cautiously where he writes of the building sites on the Acropolis where, if we are to believe him, "everything was under Phidias's charge and all were under his superintendence, owing to his friendship with Pericles." For in the first place, strictly speaking only the construction of the statue of Athena Parthenos can be attributed to the hand of Phidias; and second because, in the case of every one of his projects, Pericles had to persuade the Assembly to vote in favor of them and was obliged then to submit to controlling procedures that were beyond his own official powers. The ancient authors tend to ascribe to the *stratēgos* monuments that were in fact constructed both by the people and in the name of the people. This conflicting information is laid bare whenever it is possible to compare literary sources to the epigraphical documentation. Whereas Plutarch presents Pericles as the one who dedicated the monumental statue of Athena Hygieia, the foundation stone discovered on the Acropolis mentions only the Athenian people; the name of the *stratēgos* does not appear at all.[21]

One thorny question nevertheless remains. How should we treat the claims of Lycurgus who, one century later, insisted on personalizing the great works produced between 450 and 430? That biased presentation makes sense once it is set in context. Clearly playing on the idea of a mirror image, by recalling memories of Pericles, Lycurgus was aiming to enhance his own actions as the builder who restored the Acropolis monuments. By magnifying the stature of the *stratēgos*, he hoped to increase his own.

So should we deny Pericles any role in the great building projects that, from the mid-fifth century onward, multiplied in Athens, on the Acropolis, and on Cape Sunium? To do so would be to go too far, redressing the balance in an excessive manner. Certain documents allow us to glimpse how, within the framework of this concerted monumental policy, the collective will and individual initiative interacted. To come to a clearer understanding, we need to turn away from the domain of great stone monuments and consider the construction of more modest structures: fountains. A fragment of a decree dating from 440–430 B.C. mentions the provision of a fountain at

Eleusis and explains how the project was financed: the Assembly decided to honor Pericles, Paralus, and Xanthippus, and his other sons, but to meet the costs by drawing on the money paid as tribute.[22] Although fragmentary (the name of the *stratēgos* has been restored by epigraphists), this inscription does make it possible, with a certain degree of likelihood, to trace the process that led to the fountain's construction. Initially, Pericles and his sons proposed to use their own resources to pay for either the whole or at least part of the monument. In doing so, they were acting as men keen to earn the favor of the people, for the provision of water was a matter of crucial importance in a Mediterranean land blasted by the sun and with insufficient supplies of water,[23] not only for physical survival but also for performing numerous rituals both civic and private, such as lustrations and sacrifices, nuptial baths, and the washing of corpses. The people thanked them for this proposal but nevertheless declined the offer and eventually financed the project using funds received as tribute from the allies.[24]

This interaction between individual initiative and popular control echoes an episode recorded by Plutarch that likewise involves polemics sparked off by the financing of major architectural works:

> Thucydides and his faction kept denouncing Pericles for playing fast and loose with the public moneys and annihilating the revenues. Pericles therefore asked the people in assembly whether they thought he had expended too much, and on their declaring that it was altogether too much, "Well then," said he, "let it not have been spent on your account, but mine, and I will make the inscriptions of dedication in my own name [*tōn anathēmatōn idian emautou poiēsomai tēn epigraphēn*]." When Pericles had said this, whether it was that they admired his magnanimity or *vied with his ambition to get the glory of his works*, they cried out with a loud voice and bade him take freely from the public funds for his outlays and to spare naught whatsoever (*Pericles*, 14.1–2).

As in the case of the Eleusis fountain, the Athenian people were definitely keen to preserve their own major responsibility for great works; these had to redound to the glory of the whole community, not distinguish private individuals (*idiōtai*). All the same, Pericles' influence was by no means minimal in the process of decision-taking, for he seems to have acted as the spur or even the initiator for the decisions taken by the community. The great works thus appear to have been the product of close negotiation between the people and the members of the Athenian elite.

However crucial Pericles' influence on monumental policy may really have been, his name rapidly became associated with these grandiose constructions and this helped to confer upon him exceptional political stature in the eyes of the western world. And there was another element that supported this impression of Periclean domination: namely, the introduction, for the first time, of pay for civic services. In the ancient sources, the creation of the *misthoi* was certainly interpreted as a symbol of the patronage that Pericles exercised over the Athenian people, reducing it to a passive recipient of the great man's benefactions.

The Beneficent Patron

In the second half of the fourth century, already, the author of the *Constitution of the Athenians* was defending such an analysis, and Plutarch later concurred with his account:

> Pericles first made service in the jury-courts a paid office, as a popular measure against Cimon's wealth. For as Cimon had an estate large enough for a tyrant, in the first place he discharged the general public services in a brilliant manner, and moreover he supplied maintenance to a number of members of his deme; for anyone of the Laciadae who liked could come to his house every day and have a moderate supply, and also all his farms were unfenced, to enable anyone who liked to avail himself of the harvest. So as Pericles' means were insufficient for this lavishness, he took the advice of Damonides of Oea . . . , since he was getting the worst of it with his private resources, to give the multitude what was their own; and he instituted payment for the jury-courts; the result of which according to some critics was their deterioration, because ordinary persons always took more care than the respectable to cast lots for the duty.[25]

Within this framework of Aristotelian analysis, the *misthos* was represented as a means for Pericles to rival the wealth of Cimon and become the patron of the people, which this collective gift had the effect of infantilizing. However, that version of the situation needs to be considered with circumspection. By the late 450s, Cimon no longer held any real political power. He had been ostracized ten years earlier and, although he was recalled to Athens in 451, his influence must by then have been limited.[26] It is above all the interpretation given by the *Constitution of the Athenians* that needs to be reexamined. Its author analyzes the pay given to jurors from a typically anti-democratic point of view (later emulated by Plutarch[27]), regarding it simply as a way of buying the people and, for Pericles, a means by which to turn himself into the patron of the poorest of the Athenians. According to that author, the introduction of the *misthos* was simply the fruit of a rivalry between aristocrats before which the people were mere spectators mechanically tending to support whichever side seemed the more generous.

As Pauline Schmitt Pantel has shown, that polemical interpretation deserves radical revision. With the creation of the *misthos*, Pericles was not establishing a new form of patronage—community patronage—to take over from private patronage, which Cimon embodied, as is clear for two reasons. In the first place, the *misthos* was not distributed by any identifiable individual, but by the community itself. So its assignation created no personal dependence between donor and recipient. Instead, it was the community that redistributed to a particular fraction of itself (the judges) wealth that it considered them to deserve. Second, its aim was radically different from that of private patronage: far from being a form of assistance, as was claimed by the detractors of radical democracy, this payment was awarded for active participation in the city institutions and so in no sense had an infantilizing effect.[28]

Instead of being a measure reminiscent of the Roman client-system, the introduction of the first *misthoi* diminished the influence that members of the Athenian elite could acquire through patronage. However, it never quite ousted the latter phenomenon, if only on account of the size of the sum of money paid, which was relatively small, certainly not enough to satisfy the needs of the poorest citizens.[29] However that may be, the payments did not turn Pericles into the unchallenged patron of the Athenian community.

By now, at the end of our investigation, that supposed Periclean monarchy seems no more than a myth. The great construction works and the establishment of the *misthos* testify to the growing sovereignty of the *dēmos* just as much as to the domination of the *stratēgos*. Not only was Pericles obliged constantly to work with the other magistrates, but, both institutionally and socially, he was placed under the strict control of the Athenian people.

PERICLES UNDER CONTROL: THE POWER OF THE ENTIRE COMMUNITY!

One of Many Magistrates

Pericles never held military power on his own. The *stratēgoi* always acted in a collegial fashion, never individually:[30] a single magistrate could never impose his will upon his colleagues, unless, that is, they wished him to do so.

So his influence has probably been overestimated, partly as a result of the point of view adopted by the literary sources and the context in which they were produced. The comic writers based their craft on personal attacks and always set particular individuals on stage, often enough exaggerating their influence the better subsequently to demolish them. It was as if one were to pass judgment on the British political scene, gauging it solely in relation to the TV series *Spitting Image*, a satirical puppet show. As for Plutarch, his biographical viewpoint inevitably focused excessively on his particular hero, and it did so the more emphatically given that he was writing within a political framework—the Roman Empire—in which personal power had become the norm.[31]

An attentive rereading of the texts suggests that we should adopt a more circumspect attitude. Although Thucydides is always quick to ascribe unequaled domination to Pericles, he also mentions plenty of other important actors in the period between 450 and 440,[32] at both the military and the diplomatic levels. First, at the military level it is the *stratēgos* Leocrates who is in command in the war against the people of Aegina in the early 450s (1.105.2); Myronides distinguished himself at Megara (1.105.3), as did the spirited Tolmides both at Chalcis and against the Sicyonians in 456/5 (1.108.5), before suffering a bitter defeat at Coronea in Boeotia in around 447 (1.113.2). In the years between 440 and 430, the *stratēgos* Hagnon seems to have held all the key roles. He was *stratēgos* alongside Pericles in the second year of the campaign against Samos (440–439),[33] and was then, in 437/6,[34] sent to found the colony of Amphipolis in Thrace, which was a great honor for him. In fact, Hagnon was judged by the Athenian people to be sufficiently powerful to deserve ostracism,[35] although, in the event, not enough votes favored his banishment. Second, at the diplomatic level, Pericles clearly remained in the background—whether or not deliberately is not known—in the negotiations with the Spartans. The Thirty Years' Peace was negotiated by Callias, Chares, and Andocides in 446, and Pericles was not even present at the negotiations.[36] Similarly, at the time when the plague was ravaging the city and the Athenians sent ambassadors to parley with the Spartans (Thucydides, 2.59), this was clearly against the advice of the *stratēgos*.[37]

It is true that the posthumous aura of Pericles eclipsed many actors of the time, but they too shaped the destiny of the Athenian city in the course of those troubled decades. Throughout his career, the *stratēgos* inevitably had to share power, as was the custom in Athens, and above all had to submit to popular control. In the final analysis, it was the people who remained sovereign. However persuasive Pericles may have been, his influence was only temporary and could at any point be challenged by a change of heart on the part of the *dēmos*. As there were no political parties in Athens, nor any stable majority, every decision was the subject of negotiation between the orator and the people. The balance was precarious, and the situation of orators was often uncomfortable, for the popular assembly could change its mind and sometimes did so very rapidly, retracting its earlier commitments. Not long after Pericles' death, Thucydides mentions two successive assemblies, the second of which reversed the decisions made a few days earlier on the fate of the Mytilenaeans who had revolted in 427 B.C. Even an orator with a huge majority of votes in favor of his advice on one day could find himself totally rejected on the next.[38]

In a wider sense too, the people exercised strict control over the orators and *stratēgoi*, maintaining them in a perpetual state of tension by resorting to more or less formalized supervision.

Multiform Institutional Supervision

In Athens, the *stratēgoi* and, more generally, all incumbents of magistracies were submitted to frequent and persnickety controls. These checks involved, in the first place, a rendering of accounts at the end of a magistrate's mandate, necessitating a double examination. In the fourth century—and probably as early as the fifth—*stratēgoi* had to face a commission of controller-magistrates, the *logistai*, who verified all financial aspects of their management. In cases of proven irregularities the *logistai*, who were selected by lot from among all the citizens, could refer the affair to the courts. Furthermore, the *stratēgoi* could be prosecuted by any citizen before the members of yet another committee, an offshoot of the council. These were the *euthunoi*. If they judged the complaint to be well founded, they passed the case on to the competent magistrates (*thesmothetai*), who then organized a trial.[39]

Historians have for many years maintained that, in cases where a *stratēgos* was reelected, this procedure was omitted for practical reasons—for instance, the magistrates might be on a mission far from the city, rendering the examination impossible. In that case, Pericles would not have had to render any accounts during the fourteen years in which he had, without fail, been reelected; and this would have greatly diminished the control exercised over him. But in reality this hypothesis has to be abandoned. In the first place, expeditions of long duration were rare in the fifth century; Pericles was never away from Athens for more than a year, except at the time of the war against Samos, which lasted from 441 to 439. Second, Pericles did render his accounts after the Euboean revolt, in 447/6, despite the fact that he was reelected as *stratēgos* for the following year. "When Pericles, in rendering his accounts for this campaign, recorded an expenditure of ten talents as 'for sundry needs,' the people approved it without officious meddling and without even investigating the mystery" (Plutarch, *Pericles*, 23.1). So it is clear that *stratēgoi* did render their accounts even when they were reappointed to their posts.[40]

One anecdote recounted by Plutarch conveys just how stressful the procedure was for Athenian magistrates, even the most influential of them: "[Alcibiades] once wished to see Pericles and went to his house. But he was told that Pericles could not see him; he was studying how to render his accounts to the Athenians. "Were it not better for him," said Alcibiades, as he went away, "to study how not to render his accounts to the Athenians?" (*Alcibiades*, 7.2). Alcibiades was Pericles' evil genius, but this remarkable role-reversal turns the undisciplined youth's tutor, Pericles, now no longer Alcibiades' teacher, into his pupil in the school of crime!

Over and above that exercise of control, at the end of a magistrate's duties, the Athenians had the power to depose the city's principal magistrates even while they were still carrying out their official mandate: each month the Athenians voted, with a show of hands, on whether or not they confirmed their magistrates in their positions, *epikheirotonia tōn arkhōn*.[41] In the event of a negative vote (*apokheirotonia*), the magistrate was forthwith deposed. This was probably the procedure of which Pericles was a victim in 430/429, when he was dismissed from his duties as a *stratēgos*.[42] Following that first sanction, the *stratēgoi* could be arraigned for high treason (*eisangelia*). Treason was a fairly vague notion to the Athenians; losing a battle or being suspected of corruption was sometimes enough to set the procedure in motion. Pericles himself probably suffered this bitter experience in 430/429, when, after being deposed, he was judged and sentenced to pay a very large fine.[43] According to Ephorus, the source for Diodorus Siculus,[44] his accusers blamed him for being corrupt, and this probably explains why Thucydides, in contrast, goes to such pains to emphasize the incorruptibility of Pericles in his final panegyric for the *stratēgos* (2.65.8).

Last, the Athenians also had at their disposal a more general mode of control over members of the city's elite: the procedure of ostracism. This was instituted following Cleisthenes' reforms; it consisted of exiling for a period of time any figure considered to wield too much influence. This limited the risks of a return to tyranny. The decision did not need to be justified—a fact that many ancient authors considered to be scandalous. It was applied for the first time in 488/7 B.C. against a certain Hipparchus, son of Charmus, who was probably related to the family of the former tyrants of Athens. In 485 B.C., Pericles' father was a victim of the procedure of ostracism, but he was recalled at the time of the Persian Wars. According to Plutarch, it was because Pericles feared that he, in his turn, might be ostracized that he sided with the *dēmos*. Ostracism thus constituted a permanent threat that hung over the heads of the most influential Athenians and encouraged them to conform to popular expectations.

Ostracism, which was voted upon every year, took place in two stages. In the sixth month of the year, a preliminary vote that took the form of a show of hands decided whether or not to initiate the procedure. If this was in principle accepted, a second (secret) vote took place to decide who was to be condemned. This vote was conducted using potsherds (*ostraka*) upon which the citizens wrote the name of the man they wished to ostracize—a process that provides a good indication of the relative literacy of Athenian society. The individual with the most votes was then exiled, provided that a *quorum* of at least 6,000 voters had taken part. Those graffiti did not always stop at naming a victim but in some cases also mentioned the reasons that motivated the vote. It sometimes happened that the sexual reputation or even sexual behavior of men involved in politics was invoked to justify their exile. While some were blamed for their excessive wealth—such as one "horse breeder"— others were accused of adultery (*moikhos*). As for Cimon, Pericles' first opponent, on one of the ostracism shards bearing his name (figure 9), he was even accused of maintaining an incestuous relationship with his sister, Elpinike: "Cimon [son of] Miltiades, get out of here and take Elpinike with you!"[45] Because a vote of ostracism did not need to be justified by any particular offence that was penally reprehensible, it rested partly on the accusations laid against politicians for their personal behavior.[46]

FIGURE 9. *Ostraka* of Cimon (ca. 462 B.C.). From S. Brenne, 1994, "*Ostraka* and the Process of *Ostrakophoria*," in W.D.E. Coulson et al., eds., *The Archaeology of Athens and Attica under Democracy*. Oxford, UK: Oxbow Books, 13–24, here fig. 3-4, p. 14.

The fact was that the Athenians not only set controls upon the Athenian elite by imposing numerous laws that affected them. They also did so by circulating rumors about their behavior that were first given expression in the theater and from there spread throughout the city. In this way, they exerted strong moral and ideological pressure upon those responsible for important duties.

Omnipresent Social Controls

The Invectives of the Comic Poets: Pericles on Stage

Comic poetry, which was full of allusions to contemporary political life, fulfilled a function of social control over the members of the Athenian elite. In the orchestra of the theater of Dionysus, at the time of the Great Dionysia or the Lenaea, the poets often directed personal attacks—*onomasti kōmōidein*—against the individuals most deeply involved in civic life. Politicians were directly named by the actors performing before the entire assembled people. Gibed at or even ridiculed, they were attacked as much for their public actions as for their lifestyles and their behavior in private.

Pericles was a particular target of such personal attacks. His relationship with Aspasia and his supposed sympathies for tyranny were frequently mocked on stage.[47] Such accusations peaked at the beginning of the Peloponnesian War. Plutarch certainly testifies to the growing hostility then surrounding the *stratēgos*: "Many of his enemies [beset him] with threats and denunciations and *choruses sang songs of scurrilous mockery, designed to humiliate* [*ephubrizontes*] *him*, railing at his generalship for its cowardice and its abandonment of everything to the enemy" (*Pericles*, 33.6). In view of all this, it might seem but a small step to assuming that comedy—and, more generally, simply rumors—played a part in the *stratēgos*'s removal from power in 430/429. But that is a step that should not be taken.

In the first place, there were limits imposed upon the freedom of speech (*parrhēsia*) of the comic poets. The ancient sources even record certain episodes of censure in which Aristophanes and other comic writers were targeted, at particularly delicate moments in the history of Athens.[48] Although the cases brought against comic poets are by no means all confirmed,[49] a decree aiming to ban personal attacks in the theater does appear to have been passed in 440/439 at the instigation of Pericles; no doubt, the *stratēgos* hoped in this way to put a stop to the most virulent attacks launched against him while the city was engaged in the lengthy siege of Samos. However, this measure that had been approved within the context of a crisis was waived less than three years later;[50] in the fifth century, no law restrained the freedom of speech of the comic poets for very long.[51]

Second, those gibes did not necessarily directly influence the Athenians' voting in the Assembly. Even as he was being subjected to constant fire from his critics, Pericles was reelected without interruption from 443 to 429, and, similarly, Cleon retained the people's confidence despite the success, in 424 B.C., of Aristophanes' *Knights*, in which the demagogue was dragged through the mud in the person of an uncouth Paphlagonian.[52] So such invectives seem not to have had much direct effect politically. There was a strong ritual dimension to those insults and outrageous claims, and their function was mainly cathartic. The violence of comic language stemmed more from a ritualized process of verbal abuse than from any clearly articulated political program.[53]

All the same, that is not to say that such attacks had no impact at all. They affected Pericles significantly, leading him to modify his behavior. The reason he decided, upon entering political life, to adopt a totally transparent way of life was precisely so as to try to avoid such verbal attacks.[54] In order to avoid being attacked on the comic stage, politicians thus had good reason to keep a check on their own behavior and to adjust it to satisfy popular expectations. Comedy certainly did affect Athenian political life, not directly—by influencing the citizens' votes—but rather indirectly, by reflecting in a magnifying mirror the "ethico-political" norms with which members of the elite were invited to conform.

The Strength of Rumors: The Goddess with a Thousand Mouths

The criticisms that were amplified in the theater, which acted as a sounding-board, started off in the Agora, where they circulated in a diffuse manner. As they passed from mouth to mouth and from ear to ear, rumors swiftly grew into an anomalous and sometimes disquieting collective phenomenon.[55] Pericles was himself a victim of this gossip and these whispers that grew mysteriously without being associated with anyone in particular. *Legetai* or *legousin*, as the Greek texts put it: "it is said" or "they say." This is the formula to which Plutarch resorts in order to convey the rumors surrounding the *stratēgos*, who was said to be transfixed with love for Aspasia, corrupting the wives of other citizens, and mixing with enemies of the city.[56]

Through what channels were these rumors spread? The poets would sometimes lend them their voices, but initially the rumors circulated in informal spaces, as murmurings in the shops or even in the meetings of phratries and other associations.[57] The workplaces of certain craftsmen—barbers, cobblers, and fullers—constituted important meeting places,[58] where information would gather to the point where it would even turn into veritable waves of opinion.[59] Even before rumors became rife in public places, they would sometimes emerge in private ones. According to Plutarch, Pericles was the target of slander started by members of his own family, who were indignant at his intransigent attitude where financial matters were concerned: "Xanthippus, incensed at this, fell to abusing his father and, to make men laugh, publishing abroad his conduct of affairs at home, and the discourses that he held with the sophists" (*Pericles*, 36.2). It seems that, later, Pericles' elder son even increased his attacks to the point of starting a rumor that his father was sleeping with his own (Xanthippus's) wife (*Pericles*, 36.3)!

Even if these rumors were groundless, they were certainly not harmless. They forged collective beliefs that could not simply be swept aside by their victims. The fourth-century orators were even ready to recognize a degree of truth in them. According to Aeschines, "In the case of the life and conduct of men, a common rumor which is unerring does of itself spread abroad throughout the city,"[60] which was why, probably at the time of Cimon and Pericles, the Athenians had devoted a cult to it, "as the most powerful of goddesses" (*hōs theou megistēs*).[61] The philosopher Plato was likewise astonished at the amazing power of rumor[62] that, praising some and denigrating others, defined norms of behavior that were all the more influential because they were not formalized. *Phēmē* thus acted upon the very heart of reality, as "a great subterranean power, an essential part of what is held to be true."[63] It oriented the actions of the Athenian leaders, who were often enough obliged to dance to the tune of slander, in order to save their very lives: rumor, "the eternal accuser" (*katēgoron athanaton*),[64] dogged the steps of the politicians who, as a result, were forced to adjust their behavior.[65]

Chatter and malicious gossip formalized the fears and expectations of the *dēmos*, structured public opinion, and surreptitiously defined the behavior that the people expected from the Athenian elite. Rumors, although informal, undeniably affected the behavior of the political actors just as much as or even more than legal procedures did. We should not regard social pressure and institutional controls as radically opposite. The fact was that the people exercised a kind of informal control at the very heart of the city institutions: speaking in the Assembly, orators had to cope with reactions from the *dēmos* that were sometimes brutal and unpredictable, as Pericles well knew, often in glorious circumstances, but sometimes in bitter ones.

Heckling in the Assembly: Orators under Pressure

Even in the *Ekklēsia*, which is where the ancient authors ascribe the most influence to him, Pericles' speeches were always controlled by the crowd. The people did not hesitate to express their disapproval noisily or even to heckle the orators despite—or because of—all their rhetorical skills.[66] Even though most citizens did not, themselves, dare to speak, that does not mean that they remained passive, silently gaping as they listened to the speeches delivered from the tribune. Time and again, the orators had to contend with great bursts of noisy applause, protests, whistles. and laughter and were even faced with heckling (*thorubos*), as many speeches of the Attic orators testify.[67] "Vocal interruptions and heckling in court and Assembly undermined the speaker's structural advantage as the focus of the group's attention and reminded him that his right to speak depended on the audience's power and patience."[68] The heckling stemmed from the normal Athenian exercise of freedom of speech, and its effect was to regulate the functioning of collective institutions while, in contrast, religious silence on the part of the masses was characteristic of peoples that were subjected to authoritarian regimes.[69]

Pericles was on several occasions forced to confront a restless, even hostile, crowd that was perfectly prepared to interrupt him in the Assembly. According to Plutarch, the *stratēgos* was initially the target of violent criticism at the time when his ambitious building projects were discussed. Led by his political opponent Thucydides and his followers, the revolt broke out right in the middle of the discussions held on the Pnyx: "They slandered him [*dieballon*] in the assemblies, 'The people has lost its fair fame and is in ill repute because it has removed the public moneys of the Hellenes from Delos into its own keeping.'" (*Pericles*, 12.1). Nor did the hostility aroused by the great construction works abate. In the course of another *Ekklēsia* meeting, Pericles had to render an account of the money provided for this vast building program. Faced with the people's violent recriminations, right there in the Assembly, the *stratēgos* offered to complete the constructions using his own funds, on condition that all the merit would then go solely to him. But the Athenians rejected that solution and even "cried out with a loud voice [*anekragon*] and bade him take freely from the public funds for his outlays and to spare naught whatsoever."[70] While this episode certainly draws attention to Pericles' persuasive powers, it also indicates the limits of his influence. Placed in danger on the tribune, the *stratēgos* could defuse the hostility of the people only by persuading it of how useful his project would be for the whole community; it was because these constructions increased the prestige of their city that the Athenians now noisily approved of the *stratēgos* and his building policy.

When the conflict against the Peloponnesians began, that public pressure became more alarming. In 430, the *stratēgos* needed all his skills to calm down the anger of the people that now found itself enclosed within the city walls and infected by the plague: "After the second invasion of the Peloponnesians the Athenians underwent a change of feeling, now that their land had been ravaged a second time while the plague and the war combined lay heavily upon them. They blamed Pericles for having persuaded them to go to war and held him responsible for the misfortunes which had befallen them, and were eager to come to an agreement with the Lacedaemonians. They even sent envoys to them, but accomplished nothing. And now, being altogether at their wits' end, they assailed Pericles" (Thucydides, 2.59.1–2). It was, according to Thucydides, only with great difficulty that he eventually managed to swing his audience round in his favor.[71] As Arnold Gomme remarks: "Perhaps nothing makes more clear the reality of democracy in Athens, of the control of policy by the ekklesia, than this incident: the ekklesia rejects the advice of its most powerful statesman and most persuasive orator, but the latter remains in office, subordinate to the people's will, till the people choose to get rid of him."[72]

A few months later, even the magic of his oratory was no longer enough. Thucydides does not dwell on this episode, which does not reflect well on his hero, but he does record that Pericles was relieved of his responsibilities as *stratēgos* at an Assembly session, probably following an *epikheirotonia tōn arkhōn* procedure. "They did not give over their resentment against him until they had imposed a fine upon him" (Thucydides, 2.65.3). Dismissed from the tribune and brutally stripped of his magistracy, Pericles retired to his *oikos* until a little later, when the remorseful Athenians summoned him back.

Without doubt, heckling from the people had the power to counterbalance the rhetoric of even the most distinguished orators: these inarticulate murmurs could neutralize any *logos*, however persuasive it might be. It was in this way that the people tamed its elite leaders: far from dominating their audience, the Athenian leaders found themselves controlled by the *dēmos*, at the mercy of its more or less spontaneous reactions. Faced with ever possible dissent, it was very difficult for the orators to propose points of view that were too much at odds with popular expectations.

Persnickety institutional procedures, tumultuous popular interventions in the Assembly, outrageous comic insults, and obsessive rumors: in the course of the fifth century, all these progressively combined to promote the political and ideological dominance of the Athenian *dēmos*. Plato, in the next century, was the writer who best described the powers by which the elite groups were tamed by the people—a process that the philosopher considered to be seriously pathological.[73] Democracy was, in other words, for him a leveling downward. Plato developed an eminently polemical point of view toward the Athenian city, but he was fundamentally right, for in the fourth century, orators could no longer openly distinguish themselves from the common crowd on the basis of their supposed superiority.

Yet this evolution was by no means always interpreted as a crippling defect in Athenian democracy. All that Plato denounced was, on the contrary, celebrated by Demosthenes in his speech *On the Crown* (§ 280): "But it is not the diction of an orator, Aeschines, or the vigour of his voice that has any value: *it is supporting the policy of the people [hoi polloi]* and having the same friends and the same enemies as your country." Demosthenes recognized the imperious need for the *rhētores* to fall into line with popular norms, which in effect, in the fourth century, meant with the demagogues (in the neutral sense of that term) and to strive constantly to diminish the social distance that separated them from the ordinary citizens.[74]

Was this conclusion reached by the fourth-century orators and philosophers something that was already sensed by Pericles and the age in which he lived? Not entirely. The life of the *stratēgos* testifies to the fragile balance maintained between, on the one hand, the persistent prestige of members of the Athenian elite and, on the other, the growing power of the people. But even if Pericles still stood out from the majority of the Athenians by virtue of both his wealth and his charisma as an orator, his behavior also reflected a desire to conform with the aspirations of the people. It was a provisional compromise that continued to evolve in the decades that followed. In this respect, Pericles' career symbolizes a point of equilibrium just as much as a moment of rupture: to the Athenians, his death seemed to mark the end of an era. To be sure, it was far from being a total reversal, for the demagogues who succeeded him were by no means newcomers who had emerged from the gutter and now proceeded to turn the city upside down![75] Nevertheless, they were the first leaders who explicitly paraded their close social and cultural ties with the people, thereby incurring the wrath of members of the traditional elite, who still clung on to their own distinction. Indeed, the death of the *stratēgos* brought about not so much a revolution, but rather a revelation. Once Pericles had gone, it was no longer possible to deny the plain fact: *pace* Thucydides, Athens certainly was now, in fact as well as in name, a democracy.

So, in order to speak dispassionately of Pericles, should we put aside Thucydides and his biased judgements? It would be impossible to do so, if only for historiographical reasons. However much of a caricature it may have been, the historian's view has, ever since Antiquity and right down to the present day, lastingly influenced the way that the Periclean moment is interpreted. The fact is that, transmitted as it was by Plutarch, that view soon became a commonplace that was for the most part accepted totally uncritically by the Moderns. However, Pericles did need to recover his status as a "great man," and this proved no easy matter. For a long time, the *stratēgos* occupied no more than a marginal place in references to Greek and Roman Antiquity: the "Age of Pericles" was a very long time coming.

CHAPTER 11

Pericles in Disgrace: A Long Spell
in Purgatory (15th to 18th Centuries)

The *Oeuvres Complètes* (Complete Works) of Voltaire, published in 1771, contain an intriguing conversation between Pericles, a Russian, and an eighteenth-century Greek.[1] After such a long time in the Underworld, the *stratēgos* is keen to find out what modern men think of him. Addressing his compatriot, he naively asks, "But tell me, is not my memory still venerated in Athens, the town where I introduced magnificence and good taste?" To his great disappointment, his Greek companion has never heard either of him or even of Athens: "So you are as little acquainted with the famous and superb town of Athens as with the names of Themistocles and Pericles? You must have lived in some underground place, in an unknown part of Greece." The Russian, who is less ignorant than his companion, intervenes to explain to the *stratēgos* how much the world has changed since his death: the Greeks, now subjects of the Ottomans, no longer know even the name of Athens. The opulent city has been replaced by "a wretched, squalid little town called Setines." Contemplating the ravages of time with horror, the disillusioned *stratēgos* concludes, "I hoped to have rendered my name immortal, yet I see that it is already forgotten in my own land."

This conversation from beyond the tomb strikingly condenses Pericles' uneven trajectory in the Western world. Having suffered a long eclipse up until the eighteenth century (this chapter), the *stratēgos* progressively made a comeback. Even as he confirmed the fact that Pericles had been forgotten, Voltaire contributed toward his rehabilitation, and helped to forge the expression "the age of Pericles" (chapter 12).

A disgraced, even forgotten Pericles: the very idea will come as a surprise to readers accustomed to identify Athens with the prestigious figure of the *stratēgos*. One of the primary virtues of a historiographical inquiry is certainly its ability to dispel automatic assumptions and show that traditions do themselves have a history. No, Pericles was not always an admired icon.

In the accounts of Athens from Antiquity right down to the eighteenth century, the *stratēgos*, ignored and sometimes discredited, became no more than a marginal figure.

How can one understand that journey across a desert without memories? By way of explanation, a number of factors may be considered. In the first place, there is the crushing influence on Western culture of Plutarch's *Parallel Lives*: the success of this work played a major role in the relative marginalization of the *stratēgos*. Second, a particular kind of relationship to the past: Pericles was the victim of a kind of history that was designed as "a lesson for life" and that above all looked to Antiquity to provide moral and aesthetic models. The moderns found Pericles too slippery a character and preferred more straightforward types. Moreover, last but not least, Pericles was a victim of the anti-democratic prejudice that pervaded the monarchical Europe of the modern period. In such a context, this Athenian leader certainly did not constitute an attractive model for those in power or for their cultural representatives.

So, after receiving an early, rather timid burst of acclaim in the Renaissance, Pericles was totally ignored by the Moderns. If his figure ever was evoked, it was as a foil—now as an embodiment of democratic instability (Machiavelli and Jean Bodin), now as a model of misleading eloquence (Montaigne). And in the great quarrel between the Ancients and the Moderns that gathered momentum at the end of the seventeenth century, the *stratēgos* remained for the most part sidelined, being considered unworthy of comparison to Louis XIV. Tellingly enough, his rare appearances were limited to "dialogues of the dead"—as if Pericles could be imagined only in the Underworld, relegated to the kingdom of ghosts and oblivion.

The Enlightenment tempered this representation no more than marginally. Up until the end of the French Revolution, the *stratēgos* remained in the shadow of an Antiquity that was, to be sure, glorified, but that resolutely remained either Spartan or Roman. Amid the chorus of authors fascinated by Lycurgus or the Gracchi, a few dissenting voices nevertheless began to be heard, preparing the way for Pericles' return to favor, in the nineteenth century, in totally different historiographical circumstances.

An inquiry such as the present one must clearly be based on no more than a drastic selection from the vast body of documentation that is available. So it will above all be a matter of sketching in the main guiding lines in a quite exceptional historiographical itinerary, sometimes proceeding in a series of "skips and jumps" (*à sauts et à gambades*), as Montaigne famously put it.

Pericles in the Renaissance

A False Start: An Isolated Eulogy from Leonardo Bruni

Yet it had all started well. In the fifteenth-century Italian republics—in particular, Florence—the humanists drew directly upon Greek works in which, among the Ancients, they found models that they could follow. They lived on an equal footing with Antiquity, using it as a means to break away from their own past (which was to become known as the Middle Ages). In this way, there emerged "a vision of a new world reconstructed from the words of Antiquity."[2] It was in this civic context that, in the West, the figure of Pericles was first mobilized.

Leonardo Bruni was one of the main vectors of this early acclimatization. He was born in Arezzo and was one of the brilliant generation of humanists grouped around Coluccio Salutati, whom he later succeeded as head of the chancellery of Florence. Immersed in Greek literature, as he was, he translated Aristotle, Plutarch, Demosthenes, and Plato and even produced a theoretical account of his experience of translation in a treatise titled *De interpretatione recta*. He used his intimate knowledge of the ancient sources in his *Laudatio Florentinae urbis* (In praise of the city of Florence), composed in 1404.[3] At the turn of the fourteenth and fifteenth centuries, the Florentines had just expelled the Visconti and adopted a republican form of government. Leonardo Bruni, the humanist, composed his *Laudatio* in order to legitimate this development and, naturally enough, it was the Athenian model to which he turned. He drew his inspiration from Thucydides' *Peloponnesian War* and the *Panathenaic Oration* of Aelius Aristides—two texts that unambiguously exalted the institutions of Athens. In a clear imitation of the funeral speech, Bruni celebrated the geographical position of Florence, the crucial role that it had played against the foreign autocrats (the struggle against Milan was then raging), the superiority of the political institutions of Florence and its cultural supremacy.[4] The humanist Leonardo Bruni was treading in the footsteps of the *stratēgos*.

Two decades later, in 1428, it was again to the Periclean model that Bruni turned when he composed the funeral oration for Nanni degli Strozzi.[5] Taking advantage of this funeral in order to celebrate the city of Florence as a whole, in this speech Bruni extolled the liberty and equality of citizens ruled by an exemplary government that offered opportunities to every good man who deserved them. Even if Pericles was not explicitly mentioned, it was certainly his thinking and heritage that Leonardo Bruni used to promote his own political project.

Not long after this, the thinking of Pericles received more publicity. Around 1450, at the request of Pope Nicholas V, the great humanist Lorenzo Valla completed the first translation of Thucydides into Latin, thereby making the text more accessible. This Latin version was diffused in printed form. It was published in Treviso in 1483, and several more editions appeared in the course of the sixteenth century, incorporating the corrections made by Henri Estienne in 1564. The stage thus seemed set for the promotion of a positive view of Athens and its leader.

It all came to nothing, however. As a result of a number of structural factors, the memory of Pericles remained in limbo in the Western imagination. The first of those factors was the incredible success of Plutarch: traditions favorable to the *stratēgos* for a long time remained overshadowed by *The Parallel Lives*. The second was the prevalence of a particular attitude toward the past that was fueled by a perpetual quest for exemplary heroes; in the perspective of *historia magistra vitae*, the figure of Pericles was widely judged to be too lackluster or even repulsive.

The Reasons for a Long Eclipse

Lost in Translation: The Distorting Filter of Ancient Translations

In order to understand Pericles' failure to engage with modern Europe, we need to recognize a somewhat shocking fact: even when the ancient texts were translated, they were not necessarily read. Out of all the formidable efforts that were devoted to publishing and translating in the Renaissance, only a limited number of works eventually rose to the surface and were selected as required reading in the education of a gentleman. The works of Plutarch in particular must be picked out, along with those of Livy on the Roman side. For whole centuries, *The Parallel Lives*, more or less on their own, provided all that members of the cultivated elite knew about Greece and its successive leaders.

The rediscovery of Plutarch dated from the early sixteenth century, when the humanist Guillaume Budé, "the prince of Hellenists," who was close to Francis I of France, published a series of *Apophtegmes* (precepts), borrowed from Plutarch's works. But his popularity really took off in 1559, when Jacques Amyot translated the *Parallel Lives*. Amyot was the Grand Chaplain of France and the Bishop of Auxerre and he gave the work a new title, *Vies des hommes illustres Grecs et Romains comparées l'une avec l'autre* (The lives of illustrious Greeks and Romans compared to one another), dedicating it to Henri II, who had appointed him tutor to the royal children. This was the launching point of Plutarch's incredible popularity both in France and beyond—in fact, throughout the West. As early as 1572, Henri Estienne, in Geneva, produced the first complete edition of the work. It was divided into two great tomes—on the one hand the *Vies Parallèles* and on the other the *Oeuvres morales* (the *Moralia*), taking over a division that dated back to the work of the Byzantine monk, Maximus Planudes.

The impact of Amyot's translation was long-lasting. At the end of the sixteenth century, Montaigne was writing, "We ignorant fellows had been lost had not this book raised us out of the dirt; . . . 'tis our breviary."[6] Montaigne even went so far as to turn Plutarch into a close friend, almost a brother: "Plutarch is the man for me,"[7] he exclaimed, to some extent setting him up as a rival to La Boétie! Far from being an isolated view, Montaigne's admiration was shared across the board, from Machiavelli to Jean Bodin. It was thus through the prism of the *Parallel Lives* that the members of the elite groups of the modern age saw the figure of Pericles.[8] But however much Plutarch admired Pericles' great works, he denigrated the democrat and was only too happy to record the traditions that were the most hostile to the *stratēgos*.[9]

Should not a reading of Thucydides have somewhat redressed the balance? The Athenian historian had been translated into Latin very early on by Lorenzo Valla and subsequently into French by Claude de Seyssel (in a volume published posthumously, in 1527, under the aegis of King Francis I). However, up until the late eighteenth century *The Peloponnesian War* reached no more than a limited readership. In the first place, the translations of it left quite a lot to be desired. According to the scholar and publisher Henri Estienne, Valla and Seyssel had "distorted" the historian (Seyssel did not even read Greek).[10] But above all, the work was out of step with the taste of the period. Occasionally, it was judged to be sublime and full of majesty, but the general opinion was that Thucydides' style was austere and inelegant, and his dry, spare prose offended the aesthetics of classicism which, in contrast, praised to the skies the elegant expansiveness of Plutarch, which was even magnified by Amyot's translation. Completed by a reading of Plato and of Aristotle (the *Politics*), the education of a man of the modern age paid no attention to any texts that might have corrected the detestable reputation of the *stratēgos*.

All this resulted in the creation of a filter that lastingly warped the reception of Antiquity in general and of Pericles in particular. Plutarch held first place and was followed by Plato and Aristotle. Clearly democracy and its leaders did not emerge flatteringly from the selective process applied to the ancient texts.

Pericles, a Man without Merit: Not an Exemplary Figure

Plutarch's great popularity was accompanied by another factor that was equally negative for Pericles. This was a particular attitude to history that

FIGURE 10. *Pericles*, detail from the fresco *Strength and Temperance* (ca. 1497), by Perugino. Perugia, Collegio del Cambio. Image courtesy of the Collegio del Cambio. Photo by Sandro Bellu.

can be traced back to Cicero. Up until the eighteenth century, history was regarded primarily as a "teacher of life" (*magistra vitae*), as that Roman orator famously put it. It could be summed up as a collation of examples which, when picked out (*ex-empla*) elicited either imitation or, on the contrary, execration.[11] All that men remembered from history were characters and images, great tableaux, and symbolic scenes that painters delighted in reproducing.[12]

As an exemplary figure, Pericles did not seem an attractive model. He was not among the colorful figures around whom analogies and comparisons crystallized. When the *stratēgos* was mentioned, it was seldom on his own account. Often enough he was cited in passing among the rest of the politicians who embodied Athenian democracy: Themistocles, Aristides, Cimon, and Alcibiades.[13] Neither a glorious conqueror such as Alexander the Great, nor a brave warrior such as Themistocles or his own rival Cimon; neither a wise lawgiver such as the consensual Solon nor a heroic martyr such as Socrates; not even as scandalous a *stratēgos* as his pupil Alcibiades—nothing about Pericles really caught the eyes and attention of members of the modern elite. Even his death left them indifferent: how boring, to die in one's bed, consumed by disease! That is why there were so few pictorial representations of the *stratēgos*. Apart from one timid appearance in Perugia, in the strange guise of a bearded old man painted by Perugino (ca. 1497; figure 10) in the reception hall of a guild of money-changers,[14] Pericles was ignored by both the Renaissance painters and those of modern times. In Raphael's famous painting, *The School of Athens* (ca. 1509–1510), he is conspicuous by his absence despite the fact that he might logically have found a place there since it was, after all, he who turned Athens into "a living lesson."

Shunned by painters and poets, Pericles remained in the shadow of other ancients who were deemed more presentable. The glorification of those few figures affected the image of Pericles himself disastrously. What the readers of Plutarch remembered was that the great men of Athens were all dragged through the mud: Themistocles, Aristides, and Cimon had all been ostracized; Socrates and Phocion were executed. It was hard to cherish their memory without condemning the form of governance that had set them aside or put them to death. The role of the anti-hero was therefore assigned to democracy and to Pericles himself, who was more or less strongly associated with it.

Those who did deign to take an interest in him dwelt on his disturbing aspects; only the most equivocal events in his life were selected, all with a view to criticizing him. Presented as he was, now as a war-monger, now as a corrupter of the people, he seemed the very embodiment of both democratic instability and deceptive eloquence.

Pericles, or the Democratic Anti-model

Even in the small Italian city-states of the Renaissance, Pericles never became a positive model; in this respect, Leonardo Bruni was far more of an exception than a general rule. Moreover, even he did not explicitly praise the *stratēgos*, but drew his inspiration solely from his funeral speech. The fact was that the political thinkers of the Italian Renaissance displayed a marked preference for the Roman Republic and the government of Sparta. In view of the constant revolutions of Athenian democracy, they loudly and strongly proclaimed their admiration for the stability of the Spartan regime and its well-balanced constitution. In the writings of Machiavelli (1469–1527), the armed camp on the banks of the Eurotas River was presented as an ideal to imitate, while the city of Athena was an example to be avoided.[15]

Pericles in Italy: A Bad Counselor or a Virtuous Citizen?

In his *Discourses on the First Ten Books of Titus Livius*, published between 1512 and 1517, the great political thinker Machiavelli set up the following striking parallel:

> Amongst those justly celebrated for having established such a constitution, Lycurgus beyond doubt merits the highest praise. He organized the government of Sparta in such manner that, in giving to the king, the nobles and the people each their portion of authority and duties, he created a government which maintained itself for over eight hundred years in the most perfect tranquillity, and reflected infinite glory upon this legislator. On the other hand, the constitution given by Solon to the Athenians, by which he established only a popular government, was of such short duration that before his death he saw the tyranny of Pisistratus arise (1.2).[16]

According to Machiavelli, Solon was the sole inventor of democracy: so *exit* Pericles, along with all the other Athenian leaders. But, as it happened, that mattered little since, according to the Florentine writer, the Athenian regime was vitiated right from top to bottom.

When Machiavelli cites Pericles by name (the only time in his entire work), it is, moreover, to mock his views. He criticizes his military ideas, declaring them to be totally misconceived: "History proves in a thousand cases what I maintain, notwithstanding that Pericles counselled the Athenians to make war with the entire Peloponnesus, demonstrating to them that by perseverance and the power of money they would be successful. And although it is true that the Athenians obtained some successes in that war, yet they succumbed in the end; and good counsels and the good soldiers of Sparta prevailed over the perseverance and money of the Athenians."[17] He claims that the *stratēgos* proved himself incapable of correctly evaluating the balance of power on the eve of the Peloponnesian War. Overconfident in the financial resources of his country, he forced it into a conflict that it was bound to lose.

In the writings of Guicciardini (1485–1540), a friend of Machiavelli's and a Florentine politician, blame gave way to praise. Pericles makes no more than a discreet appearance in his writings, but he does so to his advantage. The author draws attention to the incorruptibility of the *stratēgos*, thereby justifying his view that there was "no citizen more worthy and glorious" than Pericles, who governed Athens for thirty years "thanks solely to his authority and his reputation for virtue."[18] Did this amount to an exception to the doubtful reputation of the *stratēgos*? Not altogether. His praise was somewhat qualified: even if he gladly acknowledged Pericles' virtue, Guicciardini criticized his demagogic views and maintained that to come to power thanks to the Senate was preferable to depending on the people in order to do so.[19]

One generation later, Carlo Sigonio (1523–1584), a native of Modena, returned to a negative view of the *stratēgos*, in the very first monograph to be devoted to the city of Athens, the *De Republica Atheniensium* (1564).[20] Having been a teacher in Venice, where its powerful fleet reminded him of Athens, Sigonio was very well informed about the ancient sources and stuffed his text with Greek, citing not only philosophers but also the Athenian historians and orators. However, this scholar remained extremely reserved on the subject of Pericles, whom he accused of having ruined Solon's admirable constitution: "As for Aristides, who acquired great authority through these [Persian] wars and, after him, Pericles, a man adept at speaking and action, both amplified the constitution of this popular republic and granted to the *plebs* and the incompetence of the multitude all that Solon's laws had denied them."[21] A few pages later, Sigonio made his criticisms more explicit: "Pericles made the people more insolent and arrogant by assigning to the *plebs* the financial means to set up courts and to construct theatres for their entertainment, thereby toppling the power of the Areopagus through the intermediary of Ephialtes."[22] Despite Sigonio's admiration for the democratic city, which was very rare in his day, he remained captivated by Plato's vision, which spared neither Pericles nor even Aristides.[23]

"The Ruination of the Republic": The Disenchanted View of Jean Bodin

In France, at the end of the sixteenth century, Jean Bodin (1530–1596) seized upon Pericles, making him the execrated emblem of all republican regimes. This remarkable jurist endowed with an encyclopedic mind was writing in a France rent apart by the religious quarrels between the Catholics and the Huguenots. Faced with the Religious Wars, Bodin chose to exalt the royal State that alone was capable of bringing those internecine struggles to an end. It was he who set out the bases of the first real doctrine of sovereignty, having engaged in an in-depth historical inquiry in the course of which he investigated the political regimes of the past.

Bodin began his investigations with a book that was published in 1566, titled *Methodus ad Facilem Historiarum Cognitionem* (*Method for the Easy Comprehension of History*). In chapter 6, devoted to the constitution of republics, Bodin set out to "compare the empires of the Ancients with our own" in order, by establishing historical parallels, to discover the best possible form of government. The Athenian system was scrutinized in a demonstration in which Pericles played a key role by reason of his actions against the aristocratic Areopagus and his introduction of payment for public services: "At length Pericles changed a popular state into a turbulent ochlocracy by eliminating, or at least greatly diminishing, the power of the Areopagites, by which the safety and dignity of the state had been upheld. He transferred to the lowest *plebs* all judgments, counsel, and direction of the entire state by offering payments and gratuities as a bait for dominion."[24] No good could come from this action of the *stratēgos*, whom Bodin found guilty of having put an end to the "constitutional and just" regime that preceded the evil government by the *plebs*.

In his great work, *The Six Books of the Commonwealth* (1576), which was published in French a few years later, Bodin continued in the same political vein, adding a number of new touches to his picture. As in the *Method*, Pericles was judged to be responsible for the decline of Athens: "As Pericles, to gain the favor of the common sort, had taken away the authority from the Areopagites and translated the fame to the people . . . shortly after, the state of that Commonwealth, sore shaken both with foreign and domestic wars, began forthwith to decline and decay."[25] Worse still, the *stratēgos* was said to have dragged his city into warfare so as to avoid having to present his accounts: "Pericles . . . , rather than he would hazard the account that [the people] demanded of him for the treasure of Athens, which he had managed, and so generally of his actions, raised the Peloponnesian war, which never after took end until it had ruined divers Commonwealths, and wholly changed the state of all the cities of Greece."[26]

This was certainly a dark picture, but Bodin did introduce one shaft of light into it. He suggested that Pericles did nevertheless manifest a degree of genius in his management of the people:

> So the wise Pericles, to draw the people of Athens into reason, fed them with feasts, with plays, with comedies, with songs and dances; and in time of dearth caused some distribution of corn or money to be made amongst them; and having by these means tamed this beast with many heads, one while by the eyes, another while by the ears, and sometimes

by the belly, he then caused wholesome edicts and laws to be published, declaring into them the grave and wise reasons thereof: which the people in mutiny, or in hunger, would never have hearkened unto.[27]

Bodin, adapting a passage from Plutarch's *Life of Pericles* (11.4), the tone of which was extremely critical, nevertheless turned it into praise for the *stratēgos*. What can be the explanation for this paradoxical praise? The fact is that, between *The Method for the Easy Comprehension of History* (1566) and *The Six Books of the Commonwealth* (1576), the massacre of Saint Bartholomew had taken place (1572). Horrified by the spectacle of those popular "emotions," Bodin was forced to admire the way that Pericles had managed to tame the people, "this beast with many heads" that was always ready to launch into unbridled violence.

But despite that late correction of a detail, the picture as a whole was still a sinister one: as described by Bodin, the *stratēgos* remained the symbol of an eminently detestable regime in which the monarchist jurist could find nothing good.

Pericles the Flatterer: Montaigne's Critique

Michel de Montaigne (1533–1592) was equally critical of Pericles but adopted a different angle of attack in order to denigrate the *stratēgos*—not that he was systematically hostile to Athens, for, influenced by Plutarch, he was quite prepared to admire Aristides and Phocion. However, he regarded Pericles as the archetype of rhetoricians and grammarians who were adept at "the science of the gift of the gab." In the *Essays*, the first two books of which were published in Bordeaux in 1580, Pericles thus found himself accused of having used language to corrupt "the very essence of things":

> A rhetorician of times past said that to make little things appear great was his profession. . . . They would in Sparta have sent such a fellow to be whipped for making profession of a tricky and deceitful act; and I fancy that Archidamus, who was king of that country, was a little surprised at the answer of Thucydides, the son of Melesias, when inquiring of him which was the better wrestler, Pericles or he, he replied that it was hard to affirm; for when I have thrown him, said he, he always persuades the spectators that he had no fall and carries away the prize.[28]

Now Pericles was reduced to one single outstanding characteristic: he was expert in "the art of flattery and deception" and was represented as a sophist who misled his listeners by the sole power of his speech.

Montaigne's critique conveyed a political point: according to him, rhetoric was "an engine invented to manage and govern a disorderly and tumultuous rabble," and it was primarily a feature of "discomposed States," "such as that of Athens."[29] Montaigne contrasted this anti-model to Sparta, the virtue of which lay precisely in a sparing use of speech: "the republics that have maintained themselves in a regular and well-modelled government, such as those of Lacedaemon and Crete, had orators in no very great esteem."[30] The laconic Spartans, who refused to indulge themselves with words, emerged all the greater from being compared to the *stratēgos*.

Pericles the flatterer: By assimilating the *stratēgos* to a fast talker, Montaigne set up a stereotype that was lastingly to haunt the imagination of members of the European elite, when, that is, they deigned even to consider the case of the *stratēgos*. For he now interested hardly anyone; at the threshold of the seventeenth century, the name of Pericles evoked above all the hero of a tragicomedy by Shakespeare. In this play, written around 1608, William Shakespeare set on stage the ups and downs of Pericles, prince of Tyre, who, like a latter-day Odysseus, traveled around the Mediterranean, meeting with extraordinary adventures, before returning home to reign over his country. The fact that the name "Pericles" could be given to an Eastern prince in this way testifies to the oblivion into which Pericles had sunk in the imaginary representations of the western world.

Pericles, Forgotten in the Great Classical Age

Pericles Nowhere to Be Found: The Quarrel between the Ancients and the Moderns

At the turn of the seventeenth century, relations with the Ancients imperceptibly changed. With the advent of the Classical age—the age of princes, the national interest, and absolutism—the great figures of Antiquity were considered no longer as political models but rather as a collection of admirable modes of behavior and incarnations of moral virtues such as heroism, self-control, and a sense of honor and obedience.[31]

In this new situation, Pericles was seldom mentioned. Even the most erudite of authors tended to pass over his actions in silence, one of them being Jacob Spon, the great Protestant scholar who produced one of the very first collections of Latin inscriptions, the *Miscellanea eruditae antiquitatis*. In his *Voyage d'Italie, de Dalmatie, de Grèce et du Levant fait aux années 1675 & 1676*, which he wrote in collaboration with George Wheler, the *stratēgos* appeared nowhere except where the Parthenon was described as "a temple built by Pericles."[32]

Among the Greeks, it was now Alexander the Great who was the center of attention. In France, the great Condé and Turenne were both likened to the Macedonian king as, after the siege of La Rochelle (1627–1628), was Richelieu, who was called "the French Alexander." But of course it was chiefly the French monarch who was compared to Alexander. Louis XIV even assigned him a key role in royal propaganda: in the 1660s, the painter Charles Le Brun, at the king's request, produced a great cycle of paintings depicting the achievements of Alexander; and in 1665, the tragedian Racine played explicitly on the analogy when he dedicated his play, *Alexandre le Grand,* to the king.[33]

In the early 1670s, the wind of history suddenly veered. Parallels with the ancients were abandoned. Now Louis XIV would advance alone in all his majesty, refusing to be compared to anyone else, even Alexander. The court rapidly fell into line. In 1674, Jean Desmarets de Saint-Sorlin, in his *Triomphe de Louis et de son siècle* thus berated the Ancients, accusing them of not having displayed "the love and respect that they owed their country." In 1687, the quarrel between the Ancients and the Moderns took off. In a session at the Académie Française, Charles Perrault had his poem *Le Siècle de Louis le Grand* read out, to celebrate the recovery of the convalescent king. Its opening lines became famous:

> La belle antiquité fut toujours vénérable
> Mais je ne crus jamais qu'elle fût adorable.
> Je vois les anciens, sans plier les genoux;
> Ils sont grands, il est vrai, mais hommes comme nous
> Et l'on peut comparer, sans craindre d'être injuste,
> Le siècle de Louis au beau siècle d'Auguste.

> (Fine antiquity was always venerable
> But I never considered it adorable
> At the sight of the ancients I do not bend the knee;
> True, they are great but just men as are we;
> And we may, with no fear of seeming unjust,
> Compare our age of Louis to that fine age of Augustus.)

In 1688, one year later, Perrault's first dialogue on the *Parallel between the Ancients and the Moderns*, which underpinned and justified that poem, was published. It was followed by three further dialogues that appeared, respectively, in 1690, 1692, and 1697. Perrault did not attack Antiquity as such, but denied it his allegiance. Convinced that there is "nothing that is not improved by time," the courtier-poet proclaimed the Moderns' superiority over the Ancients. The present became the supreme yardstick that had to be considered as both a reference and the pattern to be followed.[34] Meanwhile Boileau and La Bruyère, as partisans of the Ancients, on the contrary continued to regard Antiquity as an essential resource and, above all, a model that encouraged Moderns not to be carried away by an excess of self-satisfaction.

It was, of course, not the first time that Greek Antiquity had come under attack.[35] As early as the Renaissance, the Greek language had been accused by a Catholic and Latin Europe of being the vehicle of ancient paganism, the Byzantine schism, and, later, Lutheran heresy. Despite the eventual success of the humanists, in the Europe of the Counter-Reformation, Greek literature remained lastingly suspect. Criticism of Greek literature now again became fashionable, thanks to Charles Perrault, who lambasted Homer and the corrupt religion of the Greeks.[36] However, what was new was that now the prestige of Rome too was being, if not questioned, at least challenged. Sometimes the discredit of the Ancients reached a ridiculous level: Father Hardouin, prompted by a radical skepticism, even suggested that most of the Greek and Roman texts were in truth the work of fourteenth-century Dominican forgers![37]

In this long drawn-out quarrel, the figure of Pericles played an extremely marginal role. He was seldom targeted by the moderns but nor was he enrolled by the defenders of the Ancients. Attracting so little interest, the *stratēgos* remained in the shadows, or even in Hades, and he made no more than a few fleeting appearances in the Quarrel.

In his great poem on *Le Siècle de Louis le Grand*, Charles Perrault never even mentioned Pericles, whereas he did refer, each in turn, to Plato, Aristotle, Demosthenes, and Menander. More significantly still, in his works as a whole, which accumulate so many references to the Ancients, allusions to the *stratēgos* can be counted on the fingers of one hand, and, even then, he is never cited on his own. In the *Parallèle entre les Anciens et les Modernes*, Pericles is merely one of the many ancient orators that, according to Perrault, pedants use quite irrelevantly: "They make an appalling din and with the grandiose words of Demosthenes, Cicero, Isocrates and Pericles that are constantly on their lips and that they emit with an altogether unnatural pronunciation, they astonish even the cleverest people and sweep along the common folk to whom these kinds of ghosts always seem grander than the real scholars who possess both minds and life."[38] In this way, Perrault belittled Pericles even without targeting him in particular, along with other representatives of a hoary old rhetorical culture.

The same goes for a letter addressed to a friend, in which Perrault derides the pompous eloquence of the Ancients:

As for Prose, you complain that one no longer dares to mention the names of Cambyses or Epaminondas in a speech. Such a great shame!… Have not those two names, *along with those of Themistocles, Alcibiades, and Pericles, sufficiently tired the ears of all our Princes, in the speeches that are addressed to them*? Do you expect the King, when the good of the State obliges him to travel here and there in his kingdom, to suffer the same persecution in every town with a mayor or dignitary who fancies himself as an eloquent speaker? Just imagine how exhausting it must be to be assailed twice a day by Themistocles or Epaminondas or even both of them at once![39]

For Perrault, Pericles was no more than a pompous name among others, a symbol worn threadbare by provincial dignitaries lacking all distinction.[40]

Charles Perrault's niece, Marie-Jeanne l'Héritier de Villandon made the very same point in her *Enchantements de l'éloquence* (*The Enchantments of Eloquence*), a collection of stories dating from 1695. One of these, titled "The Fairies," ends with a parallel that disparages the *stratēgos*:

I do not know, Madame, what you think of this story, but it seems to me no more incredible than many of the tales that ancient Greece brings us; and when describing the effects of Blanche's eloquence, I am as happy to say that pearls and rubies fall from her lips as I am to say that flashes of lightning came from the mouth of Pericles. Story for story, it seems to me that those of ancient Gaul are worth roughly the same as those from Greek antiquity; and the fairies have just as much right to produce wonders as do the gods of fable.

As a worthy heir to Perrault, Madame de Villandon wished to tell French stories, unburdened by weighty ancient references, especially those involving heroes of Greece from a bygone age, such as Pericles.

Nor were the Ancients' defenders any keener on the figure of Pericles than the supporters of the Moderns were. And on the rare occasions when they used it, they drowned him in a list in which the *stratēgos* was hard put to make his mark. That was the case, for example, in the speech that Jean Racine delivered to the Académie Française in honor of Pierre Corneille, who died in 1648: "This was a figure truly born for the glory of his country, comparable (I will not say to all Rome's excellent tragedians, since Rome admits that she was not very successful in that genre) but at least to the likes of Aeschylus, Sophocles and Euripides of whom Athens was as proud as she was of figures such as Themistocles, Pericles and Alcibiades, who lived in that same period."

Although the citation is undeniably appreciative, Pericles is reduced to the role of a mere foil for the Athenian tragic poets and, on the rebound, for the deceased Corneille.

When the *stratēgos* does appear in the seventeenth century, it is in a very particular genre, that of Dialogues of the Dead, which flourished in the reign of Louis XIV. In these, we find a pensive or even saddened Pericles, meditating on his descent to the Underworld.

A Pericles in Torment: The *Stratēgos* in Dialogues of the Dead

Dialogues of the Dead were all the rage at the end of the seventeenth century. This narrative technique, inspired by Lucian of Samosata (A.D. 120–180) accommodated all kinds of encounters. Here, Ancients and Moderns could meet freely and talk together after their deaths. For those who adopted this format, imagining improbable postmortem encounters from which the heroes did not always emerge enhanced, it seemed an amusing way to undermine great figures of the past.

In 1685, Fontenelle (1657–1757), a well-established partisan of the Moderns, produced a series of Dialogues of the Dead in which, in the Elysian Fields of the Greek Underworld, figures from Antiquity met with more contemporary characters. For him, this was an ideal opportunity to confront ancient thought with modern ideas, rejecting the primacy so often accorded to the Ancients. In his third dialogue, Socrates and Montaigne are chatting in the Underworld and, ironically enough, it is the Greek philosopher who takes it upon himself to deflate the prestige of the great figures from Antiquity:

> SOCRATES.—Take care you are not deceived; Antiquity is an Object
> of a peculiar kind; its distance magnifies it. Had you but known
> Aristides, Phocion, Pericles and myself (since you are pleased to
> place me among their number), you would certainly have found
> some to match us in your own Age. That which commonly pos-
> sesses people so in favour of Antiquity is their being out of humour
> with their own times, and Antiquity takes advantage of their
> spleen. They cry up the Ancients in spite to their contemporaries.
> Thus, when we lived, we esteemed our ancestors more than they
> deserved; and, in requital, our posterity esteem us at present more
> than we deserve.[41]

However, the appearance of Pericles here is still very discreet. Although mentioned in passing, the *stratēgos* is not characterized at all, as if Fontenelle did not consider him worthy of being a major character in a dialogue of the dead. Five years later, in his *Digression sur les Anciens et les Modernes*, he did not even mention the *stratēgos*, but cited only Homer, Plato, and Demosthenes in support of his thesis.

It was not until the Dialogues of the Dead composed by Fénelon (1651–1715) that Pericles at last landed a leading role, even if this did not necessarily redound to his advantage. Fénelon, a latecomer to the Quarrel of the Ancients and the Moderns, presented himself as a conciliator, refusing to take sides. He was appointed tutor to Louis XIV's grandson (between 1689 and 1695), and during this period wrote his *Dialogues des morts*, which were, however, not published until after his disgrace.[42] The purpose of this work, designed for the edification of the *dauphin*, was educational. The *dauphin* was presented with models either to emulate or, on the contrary, to shun. Freely inspired by an anecdote told by Plutarch,[43] the eighteenth dialogue was entirely unambiguous in this respect. In it, Pericles held the role of a counterexample.

The *stratēgos*, here greeting his pupil Alcibiades upon the latter's arrival in the Underworld, was depicted as a tormented man, bewailing his fate and his lost authority:

> PERICLES.—You know very well, that could eloquence prevail (and this I may say without vanity) I should come off as well as any other: but talking to them is in vain. Those flatteries by which the Athenians were won, those subtle turns in discourse, those insinuating ways by which men are taken, by falling in with their humours and passions, are of no service here. Their ears are stopped, and their hearts of brass cannot be moved. Though I died in the unhappy Peloponnesian war, yet am I punished for it here below. They ought to have forgiven me such fault, in the commission of which I lost my life; and which I was led into by your persuasions.
>
> ALCIBIADES.—True, I advised you to undertake this war, rather than be obliged to make up your accounts. . . . Can your judges here below be angry at such maxims?
>
> PERICLES.—Yes, so very angry, that though in that cursed war I lost the confidence of the people, and died of the plague, *yet have I suffered terrible punishments here, for having unseasonably disturbed the public quiet. By this you may judge, cousin, how well you are like to come off.*[44]

Confessing himself guilty of unleashing the Peloponnesian War, Pericles thus ended up suffering in the Underworld, where his formidable rhetorical skills were of no avail to him and could not mollify his judges who remained deaf to all his fine words and judged only his actions.[45] For once, he attracted attention at centerstage, but he was depicted as an unscrupulous politician, now punished for his reprehensible actions.

However, despite these timid appearances in the Underworld, for most of the time Pericles remained confined to the margins of Western imaginary representations.

A Flash of Lightning in the Darkness: Hobbes's Pericles

The work of Thomas Hobbes (1588–1679) presents an exception in this gloomy panorama. Before becoming the now famous great philosopher, the author of *Leviathan* made his name with a translation of *The History of the Peloponnesian War*, which was published in 1629 (figure 11). To translate this work by Thucydides was by no means an obvious thing to do, for the Greek historian aroused scant interest in Tudor England except among a few scholars, such as Francis Bacon. To be sure, the work had already been translated almost a century earlier, in 1550, by Thomas Nicoll. However, that translation was not at all trustworthy insofar as it was based on the faulty French translation by Seyssel, which was itself derived from the "faithless beauty" in Latin by Lorenzo Valla. "No doubt Hobbes was right in saying that Thucydides had been traduced rather than translated into English."[46]

Hobbes, who came from a modest family, with neither fortune nor reputation, undertook this vast enterprise while employed as a tutor in the noble Cavendish family. In the humanist manner, he regarded history as a determining element in the education of the young aristocrat in his charge. Pericles, depicted as an honest man, motivated solely by virtue, emerged enhanced from a reading of this work. In contrast to Hobbes's pessimistic diagnosis of human nature, Pericles did not appear as a bloodthirsty wolf but rather as an attentive shepherd, struggling against the impulses of his flock, with no concern for his own egoistic interests.[47]

Hobbes explained the mainsprings for his admiration for the *stratēgos* in a short text devoted to the life of Thucydides that accompanied the translation.[48] According to him, the Athenian historian harbored no sympathy for democracy: "From his opinion touching the government of the state, it is manifest that he least of all liked the democracy."[49] According to Hobbes, Thucydides instead favored not only oligarchy but, even more, monarchy. In his view, Athens reached the peak of its glory when ruled by sovereigns, first Pisistratus, then Pericles: "He praiseth the government of Athens when it was mixed of the few and the many, but more he commendeth it

FIGURE 11. Detail of the title page to Thomas Hobbes's translation of Thucydides' *Eight Bookes of the Peloponnesian Warre*, 1634 [first edition 1629]. Engraving by Thomas Cecill, 1634. Photo © Victoria and Albert Museum, London.

both when Peisistratus reigned (saving that it was a usurped power) and when, in the beginning of this war, it was democratical in name, but in effect monarchical under Pericles. So that it seemeth that as he was of regal descent, so he best approved of the regal government."[50] Hobbes's approval of the *stratēgos* was thus based on a particular reading of Thucydides, whom he considered to be a fervent supporter of monarchy. On those grounds, he interpreted the famous formula of book II—"It was in name a state democratical; but in fact a government of the principal man"—as a barely veiled monarchist slogan.[51]

In his old age, in 1672, Thomas Hobbes's opinion remained unchanged. Looking back over his career, he claimed in his autobiography written in Latin verse that Thucydides pleased him "more than all the other" historians, because "he has shown that democracy was bad and [that] a single man was far wiser than the crowd."[52] The rehabilitation of Pericles thus took place to the detriment of democracy, which was depicted as a pure simulacrum that concealed an acceptance of royalty or, at any rate, of personal power: "This was to be not only the position of Thucydides, but a great political discovery that was to make it possible, throughout history, for conservatives in all countries and all ages, to admire the greatness of Athens without approving of the popular regime."[53]

By inventing this elegant solution (praising Pericles and at the same time stigmatizing the popular regime), Hobbes established the bases for the rehabilitation of the *stratēgos* in a Europe dominated by monarchist culture and ideals. So, a priori, the period seemed ready for Pericles' return to grace, given that, in the years that followed, the ancient models made a triumphant return. But, alas, the chance was yet again missed, and anti-Periclean clichés even enjoyed a rejuvenation.

PERICLES AS JUDGED BY THE ENLIGHTENMENT

After the Moderns' victory over the Ancients in the last years of the seventeenth century, the century that followed was marked by a sudden "return to Antiquity." Europe was seized by a veritable mania for the ancient world, which was sharpened by the discovery of the towns buried beneath the lava from Vesuvius: Herculaneum in 1738 and Pompeii ten years later: "for the first time, people penetrated, as if committing a burglary, *right into* Antiquity."[54] And this was not simply a return to the *status quo ante*. The eighteenth century helped to "repoliticize" the relationship to the Ancients and, in particular, to focus on Greece. However, this "repoliticization" process took place through the intermediary of the Sparta of Lycurgus, not the Athens of Pericles.

Pericles Eclipsed: Overshadowed by Lycurgus

After 1720, the return to Antiquity took place in a selective manner, drawing a dividing line within ancient history. Lycurgus's Sparta and Republican Rome, both praised wholeheartedly, were set in opposition to the Athenian democracy, threatened by anarchy, and imperial Rome, "subjected to the bloodthirsty despotism of half-mad Caesars."[55] As a result of this great division, the Spartans found themselves credited with every virtue, leaving the Athenians very pallid by comparison.

A number of factors combine to explain the incredible success of Sparta in the Europe of the Enlightenment. First, the persistent popularity of the same texts (with the same lacunas) continued to produce the same effects. Thucydides remained the least appreciated of all the ancient historians, so much so that he was even considered—somewhat exaggeratedly—as "the major victim of the Enlightenment"[56]: *The Peloponnesian War* was treated to no French translation between the "faithless beauty" by Nicolas Perrot d'Ablancourt in 1662 and the version produced by Pierre Charles Lévesque in 1795. Plutarch, in contrast, continued to enjoy the same prestige among cultivated elite groups. Better still, it became easier to access his "Spartan works," for in 1721 André Dacier offered a new translation of the *Life of Lycurgus*, in which the language was more accessible than that of Amyot's 1559 translation.

In the *Parallel Lives*, Sparta also benefited from another advantage over Athens. The entire history of Sparta was covered by the *Life of Lycurgus* and, more marginally, that of Lysander, whereas the image of Athens was spread over eight different *Lives*, ranging from Solon to Demosthenes. Reduced to a single survey, the Spartan city was able to accommodate philosophical generalizations more easily than Athens, embroiled as it was in complex constitutional developments. The Spartan system, established all at once and fixed forever, offered the philosophers of the Enlightenment a fascinating model.

For the Athens of Pericles likewise to become "good to think with" required a quite different attitude to erudition in order to escape from so caricatural a representation. But the *philosophes*, on the contrary, developed a marked aversion to erudite scholars, accusing them of accumulating knowledge without the ability to discriminate between what was valuable and what was not. In the *Discours préliminaire* (preface) to the *Encyclopédie*, D'Alembert described an erudite scholar as "a kind of miser . . . who picks up the most worthless metals along with the most precious of them" and, in order to do so, needs nothing but a good memory, the faculty that is the first to be cultivated because it is the easiest to satisfy."[57] In France, the *philosophes* in no way sought to expand the available range of ancient sources, preferring to bask in the vision of a stylized Antiquity that was provided by Plutarch, with a little Plato and Aristotle mixed in.

Sparta held a final trump card that made its attraction almost irresistible to the *philosophes* of the Enlightenment: its austere mores. Lycurgus's city fueled the critique of luxury that developed in reaction to the excesses of the Regency (1715–1723). Rousseau, among many others, referred constantly to the Spartan model in order to defend an ideal of frugality and to oppose the corruption of his day.[58]

The Greece of the eighteenth century was therefore primarily Spartan. Rousseau, Mably, Helvétius, Turpin, and the Encyclopédistes were all admirers of Sparta, ready to revile fifth-century Athens by contrast. To be sure, a number of discordant voices were raised and, in the Europe of the Enlightenment, Pericles' fatherland was not solely denigrated by detractors; Rollin and Voltaire presented a definitely positive view of this member of the Alcmaeonid family, as we shall see in the next chapter. All the same, it was not necessarily the *stratēgos* who caught the attention of the few intellectuals sympathetic to the democratic city.

The case of Montesquieu is the most telling in this respect. In his *Esprit des lois* (1748), Athens, along with Rome, was presented as the model for "good democracies."[59] But we should be clear about the meaning of those words—in this case, what Montesquieu had in mind was not Pericles' city but the voting qualifications established by Solon. This was the "democracy" that was close to his heart. In it, only the wealthy could become magistrates, the Council of the Areopagus supervised the regime's stability, and commerce flourished without obstruction.[60] In this entire work of his, there was no mention of Pericles either at this point or, indeed, later! For the author of *L'Esprit des lois* the *stratēgos* was the very embodiment of an excessive liberty that leads to decadence. In book VIII, chapter 4, Montesquieu considered that "the victory over the Persians at Salamis corrupted the republic of Athens" by engendering "the spirit of extreme equality, which leads to the despotism of one alone."[61] Even among the rare defenders of Athens, Pericles thus found himself eclipsed by more irenic figures such as the wise lawgiver Solon.[62]

Turgot proposed an equally ambivalent view. Before famously becoming Louis XVI's great reformist minister, in about 1750 he had favored an on the whole positive view of Athens in his fragmentary universal historical sketch of the progress of science and the arts.[63] All the same, that praise did not extend to the democratic regime as such: "Athens, governed by the decrees of the multitude, whose tumultuous excesses the orators calmed or encouraged as they saw fit, Athens where Pericles had taught its leaders to buy the State at the expense of the State itself and to dissipate its treasures so as not to have to render accounts; Athens, where the art of governing the people was the art of amusing it and feeding its ears, eyes and curiosity, always greedy for novelties, festivals, pleasures and constant spectacles: Athens owed to the very vices of its government that led to its defeat by the Spartans all the eloquence, taste, magnificence and the splendour in all the arts that made it the model of all nations."[64] This was, to put it mildly, an ambiguous paean of praise: even if, through its dazzling cultural achievements Athens had risen to the rank of "the model of all nations," it owed that success to a vitiated culture that ineluctably condemned it to decadence and destruction. This was how Turgot contributed to the famous "quarrel about luxury" that led many other *philosophes* of the Enlightenment to mock the splendors of Periclean Athens in the name of the sacrosanct frugality of Sparta.[65]

Pericles under Attack: The Critique of the Sparta-Loving *Philosophes*

Rousseau and Mably: Pericles and the Corrupting Effects of Luxury

Jean-Jacques Rousseau admired Sparta so much that, in his *Discourse on the Sciences and the Arts*, he described the city of Lycurgus as "a Republic of demi-gods rather than of men."[66] In the view of the *philosophe* of Geneva, the city of Sparta had managed to combine austere mores with well-balanced institutions. It had seized a fortunate initiative and had "expelled the Arts and Artists, the Sciences and Scientists from [its] walls," making itself "equally famed for its happy ignorance and for the wisdom of its Laws."[67] Athens was seen as an absolute foil to this model of austerity and sobriety. Rousseau, influenced by Montaigne's *Essays*, could see Athens only as a land of "vices" and "fine arts." This *philosophe* did not even deign to consider it a true democracy: "Athens was, in fact, not a democracy, but a most tyrannical aristocracy governed by learned men and orators."[68]

In this dark picture, Pericles occupied a special position, as an orator in love with the fine arts rather than with virtue. "Pericles had great talents, much eloquence, grandeur and taste; he embellished Athens with excellent sculptures, lavish buildings and masterpieces in all the arts. And God knows how much he has been extolled as a result by the writing crowd! Yet it still remains to be seen whether Pericles was a good magistrate, for in the management of leading States, what matters is not to erect statues but to govern men well."[69] Echoing Plato's attacks in the *Gorgias* and the *Alcibiades*, Rousseau deplored the *stratēgos*'s fundamental inability to improve his fellow-citizens in any way at all.

Rousseau's reflections, in their turn, inspired the ferocious attack of Abbé Mably, who was Condillac's brother. In his writings, this *philosophe* railed against the inequality of conditions and fortunes and yearned for a more egalitarian and virtuous society. Seen from this critical point of view, Pericles' splendid Athens operated as an anti-model: it was nothing but a place of vice; the citizens of which clearly cared nothing for the common good. In his *Observations sur l'histoire de la Grèce ou Des causes de la prospérité et des malheurs des Grecs* (*Observations on the history of Greece or On the causes of the prosperity and misfortunes of the Greeks*), which appeared in 1766, this *philosophe* accused the arts and letters, in particular, of having encouraged debauchery and sensuality.[70]

In this process of accelerated decadence, Pericles was given a crucial role: "Elevated to the sublime views of Themistocles, [Athens] falls a dupe to Pericles, who leads her to the brink of her ruin."[71] Because he was extraordinarily talented, Xanthippus's son was all the more effective as a corrupter: "A great captain, a great statesman and a still greater orator, Athens had never yet had a citizen who re-united in himself so many talents; but all these accomplishments employed to serve his ambition proved fatal to his country."[72] Mably then pinpointed his attack, accusing the *stratēgos* of having persuaded his fellow-citizens to replace their concern for republican virtue by a love of servile politeness: "[Pericles] foresaw with pleasure that Athens, in the midst of festivals, entertaining spectacles and pleasures, would abandon the customs suitable for a free State and that arts that were useless soon would become those most respected; the Athenians, distracted from their duties, would eventually aspire only to the puerile and dangerous glory of being the most polished and amiable people in Greece."[73] Mably thus added a Rousseauist touch to the generally accepted traditional picture derived from Plutarch, for, as Rousseau saw it, nothing could be worse than "this uniform and treacherous veil of politeness" that smothered republican liberty.

Mably even regarded Pericles as a veritable despot who sought the people's support only the better to crush his own opponents: "This talented tyrant of Athens was too skilful to rely on the stability of their affections if he did not continually labour to fix them upon an immovable basis . . . He held the Great in subjection through the abasement wherein he had thrown the Areopagus and all the Magistracies so that no question was decided but conformably to his own will."[74] Having dispelled all competition, according to Mably, Pericles surrounded himself with insignificant and fawning courtiers: "Pericles had always banished merit from high places and employed only such persons in the Administration as were incapable of exciting his jealousy."[75]

Pericles, "the scourge of his country and of Greece," "the adroit tyrant of Athens," a corrupt and corrupting *stratēgos*: there could be no appeal against such a verdict. In contrast to this terrible ogre, Abbé Mably sang the praises of an austere fourth-century Athenian, Phocion. It was a by no means fortuitous choice. Phocion, an ally of the Macedonians, possessed what Mably considered to be two inestimable qualities. In the first place, before being sentenced by the people to die by drinking hemlock, he had put a stop to democratic disorders by establishing a voting system based on tax qualifications. But above all, he had manifested Spartan virtues: "even in corrupt Athens, he retained the simple and frugal ways of ancient Sparta."[76] In this respect, Phocion constituted an exception in an Athens that had been corrupted by its orators. Mably represented him as heralding his own indictment of the *stratēgos*: "Pericles, whose superior genius might have made not only Athens but all Greece happy, did not stick at corrupting our morals, to cajole and gain the commonality; he made us the tyrants of our allies to make himself be thought necessary; and lastly kindled the fatal Peloponnesian War to shore up his tottering interest, and save himself from being called to an account for his maladministration."[77] Mably thus bestowed a whole new dimension upon the critique sketched in by Rousseau.

However, it was another Abbé (and another Jean-Jacques too) who, on the eve of the revolution, put the finishing touches to this dark portrait of the Pericles of the Enlightenment.

Abbé Barthélemy: Pericles, the Father of All Vices

In 1788, Abbé Jean-Jacques Barthélemy published his *Voyage du jeune Anacharsis en Grèce*. This work caused a great stir and attracted widespread attention throughout Europe.[78] Instead of producing a conventional historical treatise, the author chose to approach Antiquity in a quite original manner. Readers discovered the world of Greek cities—its places, inhabitants, customs, and way of life—through the innocent eyes of a young Scythian traveling through Greece in the mid-fourth century. The work was also noticeably unusual in another respect. It was the result of thirty years of research and was based on first-hand knowledge that the author had acquired from work in the medallions section of the King's Library in Paris.

But that intimate knowledge of Antiquity did Pericles no favors.[79] While Abbé Barthélemy showered praise upon Solon, he poured bitter criticism upon the *stratēgos*, blaming him for being largely responsible for the decadence of Athens. In the long introduction designed to establish the background to his account, the abbé spelled out his reproaches in a separate section devoted to "the age of Pericles."[80]

Admittedly, the portrait begins on a positive note, for Barthélemy ascribes a number of altogether exceptional virtues to the son of Xanthippus: he manifested "in his domestic life the simplicity and frugality of ancient times; in the administration of public affairs an unalterable disinterestedness and probity; in the command of armies a careful attention to leave nothing to chance and to risk his reputation rather than the safety of the state."[81] But all this was nothing but an "illusion," as Barthélemy put it, for his personal qualities were not accompanied by any care for the public good.

On the contrary, Barthélemy alleges that Pericles acted as an unscrupulous demagogue. Predictably enough, the Abbé contrasted his pernicious behavior to the noble attitude of Cimon. While this rival of Pericles used his own fortune "in embellishing the city and relieving the wretched," Pericles used the public treasury of the Athenians and that of the allies, with the sole aim of flattering the multitude: "The people, seeing only the hand that gave, shut their eyes to the source from whence it drew. They became more and more united to Pericles who, to attach them still more strongly to himself, rendered them the accomplices of the repeated acts of injustice of which he was guilty."[82] This was doubly unjust, for, as a result of Pericles' demagogic maneuvers, Cimon was ostracized and the Areopagus was marginalized. "Under frivolous pretexts, [Pericles] destroyed the authority of the Areopagus, which vigorously opposed its influence to his innovations and the growing licentiousness of the times."[83]

After driving away the aristocrat Thucydides, his last major opponent, the *stratēgos* is represented as having exercised his power without restraint and all the more effectively given that he never made a show of it. Like a skillful illusionist, Pericles governed hidden in the shadows, so that the people did not notice that he was manipulating it: "Everything was governed by his will, though everything was apparently transacted according to the established laws and customs; and liberty, lulled into security by the observance of the republican forms, imperceptibly expired under the weight of genius."[84]

Beyond the city, Pericles' behavior is represented as equally deplorable. Admittedly, Barthélemy recognizes his wise decision not to increase the conquests of Athens. "When he saw the Athenian power attain to a certain point of elevation, he deemed it disgraceful to suffer it to decline and a misfortune any farther to augment it. All his operations were governed by this consideration and it was the triumph of his politics so long to have retained the Athenians in inaction while he held their allies in dependence and kept Lacedaemon in awe."[85] Yet that strategic prudence was counterbalanced by his extreme rigor where the allies were concerned; all their revolts were crushed in bloodbaths of violence. Where the other nations of Greece were concerned, "Pericles was odious to some and formidable to all."[86] As an all-powerful demagogue within the city and a pitiless oppressor beyond it, Barthélemy's Pericles had no saving graces at all.

The account of the Peloponnesian War does nothing to dispel this negative impression. On the contrary, according to Abbé Barthélemy, the conflict even dissipated the illusion that the *stratēgos*, with his genius, had created, for it brought to light the true extent of the corruption in the city:
"At the commencement of the Peloponnesian war, the Athenians must
have been greatly surprised to find themselves so different from their ancestors. A few years had sufficed to destroy the authority of all the laws,
institutions, maxims and examples accumulated by preceding ages for the
conservation of manners."[87] It seemed that in the space of three decades,
Pericles had stripped the city of all the virtues painstakingly acquired by
previous generations.

Barthélemy considered the increasing numbers of courtesans in Attica to
be the very symbol of the general dissoluteness. In his view, Pericles was, if not
the promoter of this fashion imported from Ionia, at least a passive accom-
plice in its development: "Pericles, a witness to the abuse, did not attempt to
correct it. The more severe he was in his own manners, the more studious was
he to corrupt those of the Athenians, which he relaxed by a rapid succession
of festivals and games."[88] Inevitably, the Abbé made the most of the chance
to remind his readers of the evil influence of Aspasia, whom he accused of
having brought about the war "to avenge her personal quarrels."[89] And his
conclusion fell with all the force of a guillotine blade: "Pericles authorized
the licentiousness; Aspasia extended it."[90]

As if the cup were not by now full, in his summing up Barthélemy blamed
Pericles' Athens for yet another reason. As a man of the Enlightenment, he
ranted against the sectarian behavior of Athenians under the reign of the
stratēgos: "Under Pericles, philosophical researches were rigorously proscribed by the Athenians and, whilst soothsayers frequently received an honourable public maintenance in the prytaneum, the philosophers scarcely ven-
tured to confide their opinions to their most faithful disciples."[91] By the end
of this exercise in character-assassination, the Periclean edifice was shattered
from top to bottom: as an illusionist, a demagogue, a tyrant, and an intoler-
ant and corrupting oppressor, the *stratēgos* was reduced to the anti-hero of a
city adrift.

In this historiographical journey of ours, *The Travels of the Young Anacharsis*
deserved, if not such a long detour, at least a pause. For, in the first place, this
work presents the most extreme expression of the anti-Periclean tradition,
amassing a vast collection of reproaches and gearing them up to a climac-
tic paroxysm. Second, this work's influence on the cultivated elite groups of
the late eighteenth and early nineteenth centuries should not be underesti-
mated,[92] for it ran into many editions and was widely diffused. It was this

degenerate image of Pericles, produced by a combined reading of Plutarch and Barthélemy, that was particularly prevalent in revolutionary France.

The Opponent of Liberty: Pericles in the Revolutionary Era

The men of the revolution were not sparing in their references to Antiquity. Although the French Revolution regarded itself as a new era, it constantly reverted to the past in order to legitimate itself. This new world presented itself as a return to the Ancients. In the course of the Convention (21 September 1792–26 October 1795), certain ancient heroes became "the saints of the new revolutionary cult."[93]

"Everything Had to Be Spartan or Roman": The Revolution and Antiquity

But which Antiquity? As Volney, the orientalist, observed as early as 1795 in his *Lectures on History*, "Names, surnames, dress, manners, laws seem all about to become Spartan or Roman."[94] Mainly Roman, it should be said: Jacques Bouineau's study of the *Archives parlementaires* and the *Moniteur*— roughly thirty thousand pages between 1789 and 1799—shows that, in the speeches of the revolutionaries, there are almost twice as many references to Latin culture as there are to that of Greece.[95]

What is the explanation for this prevalence of Rome? The revolutionaries, steeped in the Latin rhetoric that was taught by the Jesuits and teachers of oratory had, for the most part, received a solid grounding in law (for example, Danton, Desmoulins, Robespierre, Barnave, Pétion, Vergniaud, Barère, Barbaroux, and Saint-Just), and the law taught in the French faculties of the eighteenth century was, essentially, Roman. All that the men of the Revolution knew about Greece was what they had read in the works of Plutarch or Abbé Barthélemy; and, compared to their lengthy exposure to Latin culture, that was very little.[96]

When the revolutionaries did refer to the Greek world, they usually favored Sparta. Among the Montagnards, this was perfectly clear; according to Robespierre, the city of Sparta "blazed like a streak of lightning through the immense darkness,"[97] illuminating humanity and revealing the path to follow. This fascination with the Spartans was often expressed to the detriment of Athens, which was disparaged for its lax manners and the corruption of its morals.[98] Not even the sage Solon always escaped their criticisms. Billaud-Varenne crudely contrasted the two rival cities and their respective lawgivers as follows: "Citizens, the inflexible austerity of Lycurgus, in Sparta, became the unshakeable basis of the republic; the weak and trusting character of Solon plunged Athens back into slavery. This is a parallel that reflects the entire science of government."[99] As for Saint-Just, he was equally harsh with ancient democracy, expressing nothing but scorn for a system in which "everything proceeded as the orators directed."[100]

Was the image of Athens presented by the Girondins any different?

On this point, we should not be misled by the nineteenth-century historiography, which sets the "Spartan" Montagnards in opposition to the "Athenian" Girondins.[101] The Girondins rejected the Spartan mirage, regarding it as nothing but "a dreadful equality of poverty," but that did not mean that they favored the city of Pericles. For example, on 11 May 1793, the Girondin Verniaud dismissed both regimes, declaring, "I conclude that you do not wish to turn the French into a purely military [that is, Spartan] people, with praetorian guards that hold all the power . . . nor into a people so beguiled by the soft ways of peace that, like the Athenians, it fears kings that attack it for being enemies of its pleasures rather than enemies of its liberty."[102] So Athens gained nothing from the political divisions that were tearing France apart in the period prior to Thermidor.

Among the revolutionaries, Sparta was often exalted while Athens was frequently reviled. So did the revolutionaries simply take over the clichés that had been elaborated in earlier centuries? That would be too hasty a conclusion to draw, for in truth a number of differences are detectable. In the first place, the revolutionaries invoked the patronage of the great ancient lawgivers with singular acuity. This was a way for them, by analogy, to think through the rupture that they were themselves introducing. The figure of Lycurgus could certainly not be ignored, and his memory was indeed constantly invoked. A bust of the Spartan lawgiver was set up, alongside that of Solon, in the meeting hall of the Convention, when it took over the Tuileries on 10 May 1793.[103]

Besides, the revolutionaries drew upon a number of other episodes from the Greek past, exalting in particular the occasions when the Greeks had put up a heroic resistance to invaders. Of course, this was hardly surprising at a time when France itself was facing attack from the European powers that were in league against the young Republic. For instance, the *Marseillaise* (1792) was freely adapted from the paean sung by the Athenians at Salamis, and, in the summer of 1794, three plays relating to the Persian Wars were staged in Paris in less than one month: *Miltiades at Marathon*, *The Battle of Thermopylae*, and *The Marathon Chorus*.[104]

Following Thermidor and the end of the Terror, other moments from Greek history also came to the fore. Under the *Directoire* (1795–1799), the Athenians came to be celebrated for their ability to achieve reconciliation after such deep political divisions. In this respect, the action of Solon and the amnesty decreed by Thrasybulus attracted considerable attention: "Thrasybulus was surrounded by a certain aura in post-Thermidor France, owing to the fact that he had helped to impose the unity of the city upon the victorious Democrats of 403. In a France rent asunder, he was regarded as the model of a conciliator and French orators did not fail to mention his name."[105]

The Warmonger: The Pericles of the French and American Revolutionaries

In these troubled circumstances, Pericles was mostly conspicuous by his absence. Just as well, probably, for when his memory was invoked, he was portrayed, among the Montagnards and the Girondins alike, as a corrupt aristocrat or even as a liberty-killing tyrant.[106]

His example was cited in May 1790 already when, in the Constituent Assembly, a question of burning importance prompted intense debate: should the king be stripped of the right to declare war? While the orator Barnave pleaded the cause of the patriotic party, recalling all the unjust and calamitous wars that kings had undertaken, Mirabeau defended the interests of the sovereign, whose secret adviser he then was.

According to Barnave, the right of war should be entrusted to the legislative body, not to the executive power, for a very simple and excellent reason: the National Assembly was less prone to corruption than the king's ministers. In support of his argument, Barnave cited the case of Pericles, "a skilful minister" who was prepared to spark off the Peloponnesian War "so as to bury his own crimes": "Pericles embarked upon the Peloponnesian War when he realized that he was unable to justify his accounts."[107]

Mirabeau's reply to him in the Assembly came the very next day, pointing out the inadequacy of that ancient analogy: "He [Barnave] has cited Pericles waging war so as not to have to present his accounts. According to what he says, does it not seem that Pericles was a king or some despotic minister? Pericles was a man who, knowing how to flatter the passions of the populace and win its applause as he left the tribune, by reason of his largesse and that of his friends, dragged Athens into the Peloponnesian War. . . . Who did? The national Assembly of Athens."[108] In this way, Mirabeau put his opponent straight: in the first place, Pericles was not the king of the Athenians; and second, it was the Athenian Assembly that voted for this disastrous war—not some kind of sovereign. So Barnave's reference to Pericles did nothing to advance his own cause![109] All the same, over and above their differences, the two orators were in agreement on one point: Pericles was indeed a corrupt and corrupting warmonger.

On the other side of the Atlantic, criticism was equally ferocious. The American republicans, influenced as they were by their readings of Plutarch and Plato, had no sympathy at all for fifth-century Athenian democracy, which they judged to be unstable and anarchical. They far preferred that of Solon.[110] But it was the Romans who fascinated them the most. Significantly enough, when the founding fathers of the American nation met in Philadelphia in 1787, they set up, not a Council of the Areopagus, but a Senate that was to meet in the "Capitol."

Even when not totally ignored, Pericles became a target of virulent attacks. Alexander Hamilton (1757–1802), who founded the Federalist party and was an influential delegate to the 1787 Constitutional Convention, launched a direct attack on the *stratēgos* in an article in the *Federalist Papers* on 14 November 1787. At this point, we should note the importance of this collection of papers. It was designed to interpret the new American Constitution and promote it. Using the pen-name "Publius," a pseudonym chosen in honor of the Roman consul Publius Valerius Publicola, Hamilton confirmed all the anti-Periclean clichés: "The celebrated Pericles, in compliance with the resentments of a prostitute, at the expense of much of the blood and treasure of his countrymen, attacked, vanquished and destroyed the city of the Samians. The same man . . . was the primitive author of that famous and fatal war which, after various vicissitudes, intermissions and renewals, terminated in the ruin of the Athenian commonwealth."[111] On both sides of the Atlantic, Pericles was thus presented as an unscrupulous warmonger.[112]

A Liberty-Killing Tyrant: The Pericles of the Terror

In France, the nature of the attacks against Pericles underwent a change in the Convention period (1792–1795). After the king was deposed, Pericles came to embody not a corrupt orator, but a liberty-killing tyrant. Abbé Grégoire was the first to make this accusation, in his report to the Convention dated 8 August 1793. What was at stake at this point was the justification of the suppression of all scholarly academies and societies, on the pretext that they had placed themselves at the service of despotism: "Tyrants have always adopted the policy of assuring themselves of vociferous fame; and so it was in the case of Pericles who, after ravaging Acarnania in order to please his mistress, through his example corrupted an Athens that was cowed by his skill and persuaded historians to tell lies in his favor."[113] According to Grégoire, Pericles in this way concealed his tyrannical power, thanks to the scholars who served him and were prepared to misrepresent reality in their works, just as did so many Academicians of the Ancien Régime.

Under the Terror, the *stratēgos* was yet again represented as a manipulating tyrant. However, he was invoked not as a figure who encouraged a break with the monarchical past, but rather as one who anticipated eventual tyrannical consequences. That was, indeed, the purpose of Billaud-Varenne, a Montagnard and member of the Committee of Public Safety, in his report dated 1 Floreal, Year II (20 April 1794): "The wily Pericles clothed himself in popular colours in order to conceal the chains that he was forging for the Athenians. For a long time, he made the people believe that he never ascended to the tribune without telling himself, 'Remember that you will be speaking to men who are free.' And then that same Pericles, having managed to seize absolute power, became the most bloodthirsty of despots."[114] This was a transparent allusion to Robespierre, who was accused of pretending to love the people, the better to obtain undivided power for himself. A few months later, Billaud-Varenne broke off relations with "the Incorruptible Robespierre," thereby hastening the latter's downfall.

After Thermidor and the execution of Robespierre, Abbé Grégoire turned that implicit analogy into an explicit comparison: on 17 Vendémiaire, year III (8 October 1794), in his *Rapport sur les encouragements, récompenses et pensions à accorder aux gens de lettres et aux artistes* (*Report on the encouragement, rewards and pensions to be granted to scholars, literary men and artists*), he associated the Athenian *stratēgos* and the French Revolutionary in a common condemnation: "And in what century have talents been more atrociously persecuted than under Robespierre's tyranny? Pericles drew the line at just ejecting the philosophers."[115] Abbé Grégoire thus added intolerance to the long list of Pericles' vices, thereby following in the footsteps of that other abbé, Jean-Jacques Barthélemy.

At this point, Pericles vanished from the revolutionary scene. The fact was that, under the Directoire, a few scholars occasionally challenged the use that had so copiously been made of ancient references ever since 1789. In his *Lectures on History*, delivered in the Ecole normale supérieure in 1795, Volney launched into a violent attack against "the new sect [who] swear by Sparta, Athens and Titus Livy."[116] This orientalist sought to correct the ideas of his listeners and readers by presenting a more realistic picture of Antiquity: "Eternal wars, the murder of prisoners, massacres of women and children, breaches of faith, internal factions, domestic tyranny and foreign oppression are the most striking features of the pictures of Greece and Italy during five hundred years, as it has been portrayed to us by Thucydides, Polybius and Titus Livy."[117] Pericles' Athens was by no means exonerated in this depressing judgment. According to Volney, the masterpieces of Athenian art were "the primary cause" of Athens's downfall "because, being the fruit of a system of extortion and plunder, they provoked both the resentment and defection of its allies and the jealousy and cupidity of its enemies, and because those masses of stones, although well cut, everywhere represented a sterile use of labour and a ruinous drain on wealth."[118] Periclean Athens, denigrated both before and after Thermidor, certainly was a major victim of the Revolution.

An Alternative Tradition? Camille Desmoulins's Liberal Pericles

Even though it was hard for them to emerge from such an ocean of criticisms, a few rare signs do suggest the existence of an alternative tradition that was more favorable to the Athenian *stratēgos*. At the pictorial level, the painter Augustin-Louis Belle (1757–1841) exhibited an *Anaxagoras and Pericles* (today in the Louvre) in the 1796 Salon (figure 12). The painting illustrated the scene in which the old philosopher, believing that his friend has forgotten him, allows himself to starve to death (Plutarch, *Pericles*, 16.7). Although the choice of this episode testified to a certain interest in the *stratēgos*, it was nevertheless ambiguous, for it tended to underline the shortcomings of

FIGURE 12. *Anaxagore et Périclès* (1796), by Augustin-Louis Belle (1757–1841). Oil on canvas. The Matthiesen Gallery, London. © RMN-Grand Palais (Musée du Louvre) / image RMN / © Direction des Musées de France. Photo courtesy of The Matthiesen Gallery, London.

Pericles. Anaxagoras's extended arm was highly symbolic; it was as if the philosopher was bidding the *stratēgos* to exit from the scene.

It is definitely in the writings of Camille Desmoulins that the only positive view of Pericles is to be found. When elected to the National Convention, Desmoulins took his seat amid the Montagnards, but he felt nothing but disdain for Sparta. In truth, he was one of the rare revolutionaries who possessed a solid knowledge of Greek culture.[119] Having progressively distanced himself from his great friend Robespierre, he founded a new newspaper *Le Vieux Cordelier* (The Old Friar) in which he attacked the *Enragés* ("the Angry Ones") and, in particular, their unbridled enthusiasm for Sparta: "What do you mean with your black broth and your Spartan freedom? What a fine lawgiver Lycurgus was, possessing knowledgeable skill that consisted solely in imposing privations upon his fellow-citizens and who made them all equal just as a storm renders all who are shipwrecked equal?"[120] In opposition to the mirage of Sparta, Desmoulins set up an idealized Athenian city. According to him, only the Athenians had been "true republicans, lasting democrats by both principle and instinct."[121]

However, it was not until the seventh and last number of *Le Vieux Cordelier*, dated Pluviose, Year II (early February 1794) that Desmoulins celebrated Pericles openly, praising his steadfast opposition to all forms of censorship. In particular, he admired his ability to accept criticism instead of wiping it out: "So rare, in both Rome and Athens, were men like Pericles. When attacked by insults as he left the assembly, he was accompanied home by a Father Duschesne-figure endlessly screeching that Pericles was an imbecile, a man who had sold himself to the Spartans. Even in these circumstances, Pericles summoned up sufficient self-control and calm to say coldly to his servants, 'Take a torch and accompany this citizen back to his home.'"[122]

We should, however, assess this praise correctly. In the first place, Desmoulins praised Pericles only insofar as he protected freedom of expression, not as a promoter of direct democracy. What he liked about Athens was, above all, "the freedom for each man to live as he wished to and for poets and singers to laugh at contemporary politicians."[123] Second, the impact of his writings was minimal, for this last issue of *Le Vieux Cordelier* circulated only in proof-form and was published only posthumously. One month later, on 5 April 1794, Camille Desmoulins was guillotined, and his praise of Pericles resounded hardly at all and remained without parallel.

Really without parallel? Perhaps not. Another member of the Convention, Marc-Antoine Baudot (1765–1837), also seems to have swum against the anti-Periclean tide. Trained as a doctor and a staunch Montagnard, he nevertheless had leanings toward the "Indulgent" group, and after Robespierre's fall he was forced into exile, from which he returned only with the advent of Louis-Philippe, in 1830. In one of his plans for an epitaph for his tomb, Baudot described himself as *republicanus Periclidis more*, a republican in the manner of Pericles.[124] So was this a second revolutionary who was declaring loud and strong his preference for a Periclean Athens? To believe so would be mistaken. That epitaph dated from the 1830s, not from the revolution itself. Baudot was probably kidding even himself when, in his *Notes historiques*, he declared "I wanted a Republic in the manner of Pericles, that is to say one with luxury, the sciences, the arts and trade. Poverty, in my opinion, is good for nothing at all and I would join with Dufrêne in declaring it to be not a vice but even worse."[125] In his youth, Baudot was in truth by no means a lover of Athenian luxury but on the contrary poured anathema upon the wealthy. His exaltation of a bourgeois Pericles does not date from the Revolutionary period. Rather, it reflects the tempered ideals of Baudot in his twilight years. The fact is that, between 1789 and the July Revolution (1830), there had been a radical change in paradigms: the nineteenth century saw the construction of a bourgeois Athens, and here, Pericles once more headed the field.

Pericles Rediscovered: The Fabrication of the Periclean Myth (18th to 21st Centuries)

From the Renaissance right down until the beginning of the nineteenth century, Pericles was seldom raised to the rank of a model. For most of the time, he was arrogantly ignored and remained in the shadow of the great men of Sparta and Rome. When his memory was recalled, it was mainly to his disadvantage; depicted, as he was, now as a corrupting demagogue, now as a corrupt warmonger, for the elite groups of the modern era his role was that of a scarecrow. That critical approach, inspired by Plutarch, became even more entrenched in the eighteenth century and peaked at the time of the French Revolution.

Yet it was at the point when those attacks became most virulent that a more favorable view of the *stratēgos* was quietly taking shape. For not all the men of the Enlightenment were particularly keen on austere Sparta or the moderate democracy of Solon. Although Charles Perrault sought to compare "the age of Louis XIV" solely to that of Augustus, Voltaire insisted that "the age of Pericles" would not be at all shamed by such a comparison. The famous formula "the age of Pericles," which was to enjoy a fine future, now made its appearance.

However, it was only in Germany that, as early as the eighteenth century, Pericles became an undisputed icon. In the relationship to Antiquity, the Germans were already following a *Sonderweg*, or path of their own, in that they preferred not only Greece to Rome, but also Athens to Sparta, and it was, moreover, Classical—not Archaic—Athens that won all their attention. As early as 1755, Winckelmann was presenting an enchanted view of the Athenian art of the mid-fifth century, a view with which Pericles was closely associated.

Elsewhere in Europe, it was not until the following century that there appeared a magnified image of Pericles in the guise of a great bourgeois parliamentarian. The monumental *History of Greece* written by the liberal historian George Grote and published in the mid-nineteenth century played a crucial role in this change of view. This work, which was rapidly translated into French, in its turn inspired the reflections of European historians such as Victor Duruy and Ernst Curtius. Within a few decades, Pericles became the very embodiment of the Greek miracle, to the point of being celebrated as the genius who had bequeathed to posterity two imperishable monuments: the marble creation of the Parthenon and the verbal creation of the funeral oration.

For the Periclean myth to become rooted, it was necessary for two parallel developments to come together. In the first place, a change in political practices and ideas: the progress made by parliamentary democracy in the nineteenth century did much to boost the new popularity of the *stratēgos*. Second, a new perception of historical time was needed: just as the model of a *historia magistra vitae* was receding, there emerged a mode of history that was, if not scientific, at the least attentive to the succession of different ages and civilizations—their births, their peaks, and their declines. In this new regime of historicity, Pericles found a place of importance, as an essential player in the constitution of this Classical age that presented Antiquity with its most beautiful monuments.

But the nineteenth century was also marked by the matter of nationalisms. This impassioned interest in identities affected relations with Antiquity in a lasting fashion. Through a strange kind of osmosis between interconnecting vessels, just as the French and the English were rediscovering Pericles, the Germans seemed to be turning away from him. Within the framework of Bismarck's new State, the Athenian *stratēgos* was no longer surrounded by an aura of sanctity; the landowning and military elite groups of Prussia, the Junkers, were now identifying with the Spartans, while the Hohenzollern dynasty took its models from Alexander and the Hellenistic kings.

These divergent historiographical trajectories appeared in the full light of day in the twentieth century. In World War I, for example, the British invoked the memory of Pericles when faced with the Germans, who were converted to Spartans. But the allocation of roles was not always so clearcut. Even as the memory of the *stratēgos* was cherished by European democrats, Pericles also elicited a certain fascination among Nazi intellectuals, who were won over by his oratorical charisma, his great architectural works, and his intransigent imperialism.

After the end of World War II, attitudes toward Pericles changed again. Once he had been converted to an innocuous icon for school classrooms, within popular culture the *stratēgos* came to arouse nothing but indifference.

Meanwhile, among historians, his image was deteriorating as decolonization speeded up and the ideology of the rights of man—and woman—was increasingly forcefully affirmed. Now, Pericles was sometimes presented as the promoter of an imperialist, slave-based, and macho system in a mirror held up to a Western world that was now assailed by doubt as to its founding values. Having for centuries been criticized for being too democratic, now he was attacked for not being democratic enough.

THE ROOTS OF THE PERICLEAN MYTH

The Genealogy of a Formula: "The Age of Pericles"

Even today, "the age of Pericles" formula is a cliché.[1] That expression, along with the milder "Athens in Pericles' day," until recently appeared in school syllabuses for sixth-grade students in France to indicate the study of Athenian democracy as a whole. But, far from being neutral, it is a formula that implies a particular way of thinking about time and historical developments; it is, in itself, already an interpretation that suggests that one individual can model the face of a whole period to the point of coming to embody it entirely.

To trace the genealogy of the expression, we need to go back to the early centuries of the Christian era, when Eusebius, Jerome, and Augustine were proposing that historical development should be envisaged as an immutable sequence of four "ages" or "centuries":[2] the Assyrians (or Babylonians); the Persians (or Medes/Persians); the Macedonians; and, finally, the Romans. The concept was based on an interpretation of the vision of Daniel, in the Old Testament (*Daniel* 7.2–8)—a vision that introduced four beasts that symbolized four future kings or kingdoms.

In the sixteenth century, Jean Bodin recalled that ancient image, the better to dismiss it. In chapter 7 of his *Méthode de l'histoire* (*Historical Method*), he tried to refute "the theory of the four monarchies and the four golden ages [*aurea secula*],"[3] which, according to him, was based on a mistaken interpretation of the sacred texts. However, the notion of an "age" was not abandoned, even if, at this point, it was profoundly rearranged. Instead of serving to suggest a succession of empires leading up to the second coming of Christ, the formula came to characterize particular periods, regardless of any concern to insert them into some historical continuum. For instance, at the time of the quarrel between the Ancients and the Moderns (ca. 1680–1720), the royal historiographers constructed "the age of Louis XIV" as a mirror of "the age of Augustus,"[4] as if those two high points in human history reflected one another timelessly across the intervening centuries.

The formula was applied to Pericles only quite late in the day, for it did not appear until the mid-eighteenth century, when it was used for the first time—to my knowledge—by the future Frederick II of Prussia. In 1739, the young prince had the idea of writing a refutation of Machiavelli, underlining the need for a monarch to serve the State, govern according to reason and reject all wars of conquest. Voltaire, won over by this enlightened concept of power, showered endless praises upon the manuscript and even found himself entrusted with the task of editing it. After many ups and downs, that task was completed in 1741,[5] just as Frederick came to the throne. In his *Anti-Machiavelli*, the new sovereign tried to define an ambitious artistic policy, taking Athens as his model: "Nothing makes a Reign more illustrious than the Arts that flourish under its protection. *The age of Pericles is as famous for the great men of genius who lived in Athens as for the Battles that the Athenians were then fighting.*"[6] In its first appearance, "the age of Pericles" thus found its unity in the flourishing of its arts, not in the birth of politics—for democracy was certainly by no means compatible with the ideals, however enlightened, of Frederick II. Several years before Winckelmann and shortly after the publication of the *Ancient History* composed by Rollin (1731–1738), the *Anti-Machiavelli* thus heralded the pro-Periclean turning point reached by the members of the German elite in the eighteenth century.[7]

In France, this positive view was relayed ten years later by Voltaire in his *Le siècle de Louis XIV* (*The Age of Louis XIV*). Right at the beginning of this work, the *philosophe* resuscitated the theory of the four ages of humanity, although he subverted the original meaning: "Whosoever thinks, or what is still more rare, whosoever has taste, will find but four ages in the history of the world. These four happy ages are those in which the arts were carried to perfection and which, by serving as an era of the greatness of the human mind, are examples for posterity."[8] Voltaire allotted ancient Greece a place of honor, mixing together politicians, philosophers, and artists in exuberant chronological disorder: "The first of these ages to which true glory is annexed is that of Philip and Alexander or that of a Pericles, a Demosthenes, an Aristotle, a Plato, an Apelles, a Phidias, and a Praxiteles."[9] So the writer did not, strictly speaking, isolate an "age of Pericles," since this list of names amalgamated not only different periods—the fifth and the fourth centuries B.C.—but also antagonistic political regimes—the monarchy of Macedon and the democracy of Athens. In truth, Voltaire had no sympathy for Periclean democracy, as such, as he explained to Frederick the Great at the end of 1772: "When I begged you to restore the fine arts of Greece, my request did not go so far as to ask you to reestablish Athenian democracy; I have no liking for government by the mob."[10] If the *philosophe* valued Athens so highly, it was not so much for its political liberty but for its trade and opulence, in which he detected fertile ground that favored a blossoming of the arts and letters.[11]

In France, the expression "the age of Pericles" did not become common currency until the eve of the revolution; and when it did, it was not in a positive sense. Condillac, influenced by his brother, Mably, used the formula negatively in his *Histoire ancienne*, composed in 1775 for Louis XV's grandson, the prince of Parma. In opposition to Voltaire's paean of praise, Condillac declared, "The excesses to which luxury leads are always harbingers of the fall of empires. The ages in which it holds sway are those that come to be called fine ages and *the age of Pericles was the first of those prized centuries. They would be valued more accurately if the clamour of those celebrating them allowed the groans of the people to be heard.*"[12]

In 1788, Abbé Barthélemy, in his turn, employed the expression in his *Voyage du jeune Anacharsis*, using it as the title of a section of the introduction that preceded the story. Before tackling the book's actual subject, the author reflected upon "the age of Solon" (630–490); "the age of Themistocles and Aristides" (490–444); and, finally, "the age of Pericles" (444–404), indicating the dates of each period in a note. This chronological arrangement was by no means favorable to the *stratēgos*. The short "age of Pericles," which lasted no more than forty years, did not include the glorious Persian Wars but only the shameful Peloponnesian War. Barthélemy thus chose to link together what Thucydides had deliberately set apart—the time before and the time after Pericles and the glorious reign of the *stratēgos* that was followed by the sordid domination of the demagogues, which led to Athens's undoing.

So it was not until the following century that the expression acquired a definitely positive connotation, with the elaboration of a representation of a bourgeois and liberal Athens that was in step with the political developments of the period. All the same, in the eighteenth century, Voltaire was neither the only one nor the first to sketch in a more favorable portrait of the *stratēgos*. Influenced by Thucydides, a number of the Enlightenment historians did likewise, without, however, jettisoning a number of prejudices that had resulted from the reading of Plutarch.

A Two-Faced Pericles: The Ambivalence of Enlightenment Historians

Although the partisans of Athens were certainly less numerous than Sparta's admirers, their voices did not go unheeded. Montesquieu, Voltaire, and Condorcet all contrasted the frugality of Sparta to an Athens whose power rested not on weapons but on trade and luxury.[13] Nevertheless, this alternative tradition does not necessarily redound to the credit of Pericles himself. The article titled "Luxury" composed by Saint-Lambert for the *Encyclopédie* is altogether symptomatic in this respect: while he rejected Rousseau's idea that Athens was corrupted by the theater, it was certainly not so as to rehabilitate the *stratēgos*, for he went on to explain, "It was by bringing down the Areopagus, not by constructing theatres, that Pericles destroyed Athens."[14] Even in the eyes of the *philosophes* who were fascinated by Athenian elegance, the reputation of Pericles remained lastingly tarnished.

However, the Enlightenment historians were kinder to the *stratēgos*. One of them was Charles Rollin (1661–1741). In his monumental *Histoire ancienne* in thirteen volumes,[15] which was read throughout scholarly Europe and was immediately translated into English, Athens was presented as an enlightened city, open to both arts and letters.[16] In particular, Rollin admired its well-balanced political regime in which popular government was harmoniously combined with the influence of great men. The reign of Pericles naturally occupied a major place in his account, even though blame was still mixed in with praise for Pericles.

In the section devoted to the "character of Pericles," Rollin started off by considering all the clichés produced about Pericles' supposed demagogy. He noted that, in order to discomfit his rival Cimon, the *stratēgos* had distributed plots of land, multiplied entertainments, and distributed pay to the people. His opinion, which was influenced by Plutarch, was by no means flattering to Pericles: "It is impossible to say how fatal these unhappy politics were to the republic and the many evils by which they were attended. For these new regulations, besides their draining the public treasury, gave the people a luxurious and dissolute turn of mind; whereas before they were sober and modest, and contented themselves with getting a livelihood by their sweat and labour."[17] More surprisingly, Rollin even cast doubt on the advisability of the great construction works launched by Pericles: "Was it just in him to expend in superfluous buildings and vain decorations the immense sums intended for carrying on the war?"[18] Following the example of Plato, the historian even declared "that Pericles, with all his grand edifices and other works, had not improved the mind of one of the citizens in virtue, but rather corrupted the purity and simplicity of their ancient manners."[19]

However, criticism then gave way to praise. We are told that, having rid himself of his last great rival in 443, Pericles began "to change his behavior. He now was not so mild and tractable as before, nor did he submit or abandon himself any longer to the whims and caprices of the people, as so many winds."[20] In marking this change, Rollin was clearly following the account that Plutarch gives in his *Life of Pericles*;[21] but he was also drawing upon other sources and, in particular, based his remarks upon a close reading of Thucydides: "It must nevertheless be confessed that the circumstance that gave Pericles this great authority was, not only the force of his eloquence but, *as Thucydides observes*, the reputation of his life and great probity."[22] Having exalted the incorruptibility of the *stratēgos*, Rollin again referred to the Athenian historian in order to exonerate Pericles from any responsibility in starting the Peloponnesian War: "But Thucydides, a contemporary author, and who was very well acquainted with all the transactions of Athens, . . . is much more worthy of belief than a poet who was a professed slanderer and satirist."[23] And it was again Thucydides who inspired Rollin's final eulogy after he had described Pericles' death—at precisely the same point as in the Athenian author's account:

> In him were united almost all the qualities which constitute the great man; as those of admiral, by his great skill in naval affairs; of the great captain, by his conquests and victories; of the high-treasurer, by the excellent order in which he put the finances; of the great politician, by the extent and justness of his views, by his eloquence in public deliberations, and by the dexterity and address with which he transacted the affairs; of a minister of state, by the methods that he employed to increase trade and promote the arts in general; *in fine*, of father of his country, by the happiness that he procured to every individual and which he always had in view as the true scope and end of his administration. But I must not omit another characteristic which was peculiar to him. He acted with so much wisdom, moderation, disinterestedness and zeal for the public good; he discovered in all things, so great a superiority of talents, and gave so exalted an idea of his experience, capacity and integrity, that he acquired the confidence of all the Athenians; and fixed, in his own favour, during the forty years that he governed the Athenians, their natural fickleness and inconstancy.[24]

It was one of the first times since the rediscovery of Greek writings that Pericles benefited from a panegyric so full and well argued. By paying unprecedented attention to Thucydides, Rollin's *Histoire ancienne* paved the way for the rehabilitation of the *stratēgos*.

At the end of the eighteenth century, another historian succeeded in engineering a decisive rehabilitation of Thucydides and, along with him, Pericles. Pierre Charles Lévesque, who was a professor at the Collège de France and a member of the Académie des inscriptions et belles-lettres, published a new translation of the *Peloponnesian War* in 1795—more than a century after the "faithless beauty" by Nicolas Perrot d'Ablancourt that had appeared in 1662; and it was in Lévesque's version, in the following century, that Thucydides, "of all the ancient historians the one who deserves most to be trusted,"[25] was read and reread. Even so, in his *Etudes d'histoire ancienne* Lévesque did not manifest unconditional admiration for the Athenian leader: "The Greece of Pierre-Charles Lévesque is a composite construction in which the heritage of Isocrates and Plutarch, that is to say Abbé Barthélemy, coexists, not without a number of glaring contradictions, alongside his readings of Thucydides. Thus, on the very same page in the *Etudes*, Lévesque describes Pericles both as the demagogue who changed the democracy of Theseus and Solon into a 'violently conflict-ridden regime' and also as an irreplaceable statesman, whose death delivered up the Athenians to 'upstart wretches such as Cleon.'"[26] Despite his real admiration of Thucydides, the historian still remained partly dependent on the clichés produced by Plutarch. Scorched as he was by the Terror, Lévesque was doubtless wary of the excesses of direct democracy and rejected any servile imitation of Antiquity in the manner of his colleague Volney.

To find an unalloyed paean of praise for Pericles in the eighteenth century, one must leave France and cross the Rhine. It was, in fact, in the German world that, for the first time, the *stratēgos* became an indisputable model in the writings of Winckelmann.

Pericles in the Germanic World: Selective Similarities

At the start of the eighteenth century, there were no visible signs of the phil-hellenic vogue that was about to seize Germany. What is the explanation for this fascination that took hold around 1750 and peaked at the turn of the century? It was a craze that cries out for an explanation all the more because it ran counter to all the uses to which Antiquity was currently being put.

First, why choose Greece rather than Rome? Precisely so as to be original and different: in the great European interplay of affiliations to Antiquity, Rome had already been taken over by Italy and, worse still, by the imperialistic and universalist France of Louis XIV, the revolution and, finally, the empire.[27] Greece, on the other hand, seemed a model that was available to Germans in quest of an identity. But a mere desire to be different cannot explain everything. More positively, Greece represented a model of non-state-based civilization that was united by its language and culture—in short, a plausible ancestor for a German nation that was divided into several hundred states that were virtually independent but shared a common linguistic and cultural horizon.[28]

But why did German authors prefer Athens to Sparta? Here too, it was a matter of distancing themselves from the dominant cultural model, the better to affirm Germanic originality. But this preference for the city of Athens did not result solely from a choice by default. It was also based on a specific relationship to Antiquity that was founded, not on literature, but on the visual arts. German authors focused not on a purely literary Greece—that of Homer or of Plutarch—but on a tangible Greece, above all that of sculpture and architecture. In this particular respect, Sparta clearly could not compete with Athens.

If Frederick II of Prussia was the first to sing the praises of the fine "age of Pericles," it nevertheless fell to a young librarian, Johann Joachim Winckelmann (1717–1768), to provide a historical and scientific basis for German philhellenism. In less than ten years, Winckelmann published two works that produced an immense effect throughout scholarly Europe: in 1755, the *Reflections on the Imitation of Greek Works of Painting and Sculpture*, and, in 1764, the monumental *History of Ancient Art in Antiquity*, which was very promptly translated into French. In it, Winckelmann, inspired by "an obsessive quest for origins,"[29] exalted Greek art to the point of turning it into a source [*Quelle*] and model [*Urbild*] for his German readership.[30]

And in Winckelmann's eyes, it was the Athens of Pericles that constituted the pinnacle of Greek art and, consequently, of the human spirit.

> The happiest time for art in Greece, and especially in Athens, were the forty years in which Pericles ruled the republic—if I may so express myself—and during the obstinate war that preceded the Peloponnesian War, which had its beginning in the eighty-seventh Olympiad. . . . [Pericles] sought to introduce wealth and superfluity into Athens by giving employment to all sorts of men. He built temples, theatres, aqueducts, and harbours and was even extravagant in ornamenting them. The Parthenon, the Odeon and many other buildings are known to the whole world. At that time art began to receive life, as it were, and Pliny says that sculpture as well as painting now began.[31]

Winckelmann's study closely associated "beauty (natural and artistic), well-being (individual and collective) and liberty (personal and political)."[32] Athenian art was thus certainly not set apart from the fertile political terrain that had favored its blossoming.

A few decades later, this "politicization of aesthetics" peaked in the work of Johann Gottfried von Herder. In 1791, this German philosopher published his *Outlines of a Philosophy of the History of Man* (*Ideen zur Philosophie der Geschichte der Menschheit*), in which he proclaimed an equal dignity of all the civilizations that had appeared on Earth. This display of relativism did not, however, prevent him from paying emphatic homage to Greece "whose monuments speak to us with a philosophic spirit."[33] Referring explicitly to Winckelmann, Herder stressed the degree to which, in Athens, the artistic flowering and the democratic regime were linked: "But the republican constitutions, which in time were diffused throughout all Greece, gave a wider scope to the arts. In a commonwealth, edifices for the assembly of the people, for the public treasure, for general exercise and amusement were necessary . . . , as Winckelmann no doubt considered when he esteemed the liberty of the Grecian republics was the golden age of the arts."[34]

In support of his argument, following a remarkable change of attitude, Herder cited the precise case of Pericles. Instead of criticizing the *stratēgos*'s demagogy, he represented it as the very motor that produced the artistic climax of Athens: "Pericles flattered the people with these notions of fame, and did more for the arts, than ten kings of Athens would have done."[35] It was in order to please his fellow-citizens that the *stratēgos* had launched his policy of great architectural works: without his frantic pursuit of popularity, there would have been no Parthenon, no Odeon, no Propylaea! Even the oppression of the allies met with Herder's approval, given that "even these grievances were subservient to the public arts."[36]

Throughout the late eighteenth and early nineteenth centuries, the German fascination with Pericles' city never flagged. Through the voices of writers such as Schiller and Hölderlin, the German bourgeoisie set about "speaking Greek," since it was too weak to "speak German" (that is, to constitute its own national State).[37] Meanwhile, over and above philosophy and poetry, this enthusiasm also found expression in architecture. German builders adopted a neoclassical style of openly Greek inspiration, in particular in Berlin and Munich. The Brandenburg Gate, set up in 1788 and 1791, today still testifies to this, for its architect Carl Gotthard Langhans took the Propylaea as the model for his project (figure 13).

In Germany, the flattering reputation of Pericles lived on into the first decades of the nineteenth century. Hegel, for instance, praised the *stratēgos* unhesitatingly in his lectures on *The Philosophy of History*, which he delivered between 1822 and 1830. Won over by the Athenian spirit—which he admired more than Spartan rigidity—the philosopher sang the praises of the democratic leader, even straying into hyperbole: "Pericles is the Zeus of the human pantheon of Athens," "the most profoundly accomplished, genuine, noble statesman."[38] All the same, Hegel no longer regarded Periclean Athens as a model for Germany to follow. Unlike Winckelmann and Herder, this philosopher did not believe that such an imitation would be possible or

FIGURE 13. *Napoleon passing through the Brandenburg Gate after the battle of Jena-Auersted* (1806), by Charles Meynier. Oil on canvas. The Brandenburg Gate was inspired by the Propylae of Mnesicles. Versailles, châteaux de Versailles et de Trianon. © RMN-Grand Palais (Château de Versailles) / rights reserved.

even desirable. The Greek cities, which embodied the adolescence of Reason, could offer no political perspective for the future.[39] So Hegel's praises had all the characteristics of an embalming; Pericles was certainly canonized but was turned into a relic from the past that was definitely now beyond reach. At this point, a distance developed between the Germans and the *stratēgos*, at the very point when English and French historians were rehabilitating him and turning him into the patron saint of parliamentary democracy.

The Periclean Myth at Its Peak

After the French Revolution, the status of Greek Antiquity changed in Europe. At this point, a different relationship to history developed, involving not so much imitation as distancing, an accurate assessment of which was provided by Benjamin Constant's 1819 lecture on "The Liberty of the Ancients Compared to That of the Moderns." From now on, Greece was approached as a period and a civilization within the history of the world rather than a reservoir of *exempla* from which one could take one's pick. This distancing was accompanied by an increasing professionalization of historical writing, based on the development of philology and a critical study of sources. Within this new historiographical framework, Thucydides had his revenge on Plutarch to the point of becoming the archetype of a scientific historian, passionate about truth and rigor. Periclean Athens profited from these developments and was now recognized in Europe and the United States as the major model of an ancient city. Two liberal historians played a crucial role in this great transformation—George Grote in England and Victor Duruy, who introduced Grote's theses into France.

The Birth of a Great Bourgeois Parliamentarian: The Pericles of the English Nineteenth-Century Historians

The British Anti-Periclean Tradition

In the early nineteenth century, Periclean democracy still had a detestable reputation among British elite groups raised on readings of Plutarch. The work of Sir George Lyttleton is typical in this respect.

When he retired from political life, this former First Lord of the Treasury and Chancellor of the Exchequer wrote a collection of *Dialogues of the Dead* (1760), imitating Fontenelle and Fénelon, in which Pericles did not appear to advantage. In dialogue XXIII, Pericles conversed with Cosimo dei Medici and passed severe judgement on his own government:

> We are now in the regions where Truth presides, and I dare not offend her by playing the orator in defence of my conduct. I must therefore acknowledge that, by weakening the power of the court of the Areopagus, I tore up that anchor which Solon had wisely fixed to keep his republic firm against the storms and fluctuations of popular factions. This alteration which fundamentally injured the whole State, I made with a view to serve my own ambition, the only passion in my nature which I could not contain within the limits of virtue. For I knew that my eloquence would subject the people to me, and make them the willing instruments of all my desires.[40]

In the Underworld imagined by Lord Lyttleton, Pericles was condemned to wander like a soul in pain, mocked by wise Athenians who accused him of having cast Athens into irremediable corruption.[41]

It is true that, in the same period, a few British scholars had tried to present a more flattering vision of Athenian democracy.[42] But that rehabilitation did not extend to Pericles himself, as can be seen from the work of the Irish historian John Gast. *The Rudiments of the Grecian History*, published in Dublin in 1753, is presented as a series of thirteen dialogues between three people: a master, a scholar who has made some progress as an ancient historian, and, last, a novice. This unusual arrangement allows the author to present a critical evaluation of Greek history from which Pericles does not emerge at all enhanced. In dialogue XI, the government of the *stratēgos* is riddled with criticisms. The first remarks are laudatory: the Athenian is described as "an accomplished statesman and a powerful speaker, beyond all that ever were in Athens before him."[43] But the praises soon dry up: the *stratēgos*, spurred on by his all-consuming ambition, is said to have used his formidable powers for the worse rather than for the better—in particular, manipulating the people in order to obtain the condemnation of the noble Cimon, even at the risk of endangering his own country. "He was a man, tho' in arms as great as Cimon, and as to brightness of parts and fine improvements of mind far greater, yet in most other respects the reverse of him; sacrificing his country to his ambition, lavishing away the riches of the State to obtain the suffrages of the multitude, seeking to establish his power even on the ruins of the Public Wealth, and scheming destructive Wars."[44] And his speech for the prosecution continues in the same vein. Although himself a man of frugal habits, Pericles is accused of giving the people corrupt habits, the better to dominate it: "He sought to govern Athens; for this purpose he opened the Exchequer to the craving multitude, he gratified their passions, he fed their voluptuousness, he multiplied their wants.... The very virtues which he had, undid his country."[45]

As for William Young (1749–1815), although he favored the Athenian democratic regime, his description of the *stratēgos* was no kinder. In his *History of Athens*, published in 1777,[46] Young accused Pericles of having unleashed the Peloponnesian War "to screen some past malversation or to make his abilities necessary for the future, or even for meaner motives."[47] The *stratēgos* is said to have been a master of intrigue who introduced "licentiousness in the State."[48] The only shaft of light in this somber picture is that Young does recognize Pericles' genius in managing, through cunning and corruption, to hold together "the heterogeneous and uncemented mass" that the Athenian people then was.

Similar but even greater prejudice prevails in the two great syntheses that appeared at the end of the eighteenth century: John Gillies's *The History of Ancient Greece*, which appeared in 1786, and William Mitford's *The History*

of Greece, a vast fresco in multiple volumes, published in various editions between 1784 and 1829. These two works shared the common hostility toward
the city of Athens. Gillies, the official historiographer of the Royal House
of Scotland, was appalled by the "democratical licentiousness and tyranny
introduced by Pericles"[49] and even accused the *stratēgos* of having initiated
the decadence of the entire Hellenic world: "In one word, the vices and extravagances, which are supposed to characterise the declining ages of Greece
and Rome, took root in Athens during the administration of Pericles, the
most splendid and most prosperous in the Grecian annals."[50] As for William
Mitford, he professed a greater scorn for the democratic regime, criticizing
"the inherent weakness and the indelible barbarism," although he did also
confess to a sneaking admiration for the Athenian leader.[51]

A Change of View: George Grote's Moment

In his monumental publication, *A History of Greece*, which appeared between
1846 and 1856, George Grote (1794–1871) attacked those widespread attitudes. This work by an erudite ex-banker opens with a predictable attack
on Mitford and goes on to defend a liberal and democratic view of the Greek
city, following the example set by Connop Thirlwall.[52] Grote, a former member of the English parliament, was close to utilitarian philosophers such as
John Stuart Mill, and he admired Pericles without reserve. His eulogy was
founded on close scrutiny of the ancient texts, and, as far as possible, he favored the judgments of Thucydides, "our best witness in every conceivable
respect,"[53] above all other ancient sources. This led him not only to reject
the generally accepted distinction, drawn originally by Plutarch, between the
first and the second parts of the *stratēgos*'s political career, but also to exonerate Pericles of all responsibility for the outbreak of the Peloponnesian War,
sweeping aside all the accusations of the comic poets.[54] And while Grote did
criticize the Athenians' treatment of their allies, he considered that "it was
beyond the power of Pericles seriously to amend," even maintaining that
"practically, the allies were not badly treated during his administration."[55] In
conclusion, the historian, in one lengthy sentence, gathered together the essence of the praises showered upon Pericles in the course of his book:

> Taking him altogether, with his powers of thought, speech and action—
> his competence civil and military, in the council as well as in the field—
> his vigorous and cultivated intellect, and his comprehensive ideas of
> a community in pacific and many-sided development—his incorrupt-
> ible public morality, caution, and firmness, in a country where all those
> qualities were rare, and the union of them in the same individual of

course much rarer—we shall find him without parallel throughout the whole course of Grecian history.[56]

This enchanted view of Periclean Athens was supported by John Stuart Mill, who produced an enthusiastic review of the work, carrying in his wake the flower of the British intelligentsia.[57] The fact is that George Grote was by no means a scholar without influence. This British historian had been the leader of the "Philosophic Radicals" Party in the House of Commons, and, even though he wrote his work after his retirement from politics in 1841, he retained many supporters willing to spread his theories.

In any case, his success was such that the English of the second half of the nineteenth century sometimes saw themselves as Athenians dressed in frock coats and top hats. This trend to draw comparisons peaked in George Cox's *History of Greece*, published in 1874, in which Periclean Athens was presented as a blueprint for Victorian England and its maritime empire. On the basis of the Thucydidean funeral oration, Cox declared, somewhat sanctimoniously,

> All the special characteristics of English policy—its freedom of speech, the right of people to govern themselves . . . may be seen in equal development in the policy of Athens.[58]

The Liberal and Republican Pericles of the French: From Duruy to Gambetta

In France, Grote's work was a resounding success. As early as 1848, Prosper Mérimée was spreading the word and relating the book's major message to the current political situation. "For us, who live under a government founded upon universal suffrage, the study of Greek history is of particular interest and the example of the little republic of Athens may well be profitable for the great republic of France."[59] Mérimée found in the theses developed by Grote a means of breaking away from a deeply rooted French orthodoxy: "M. Rollin and many others have accustomed us to regard the Athenians as the most flighty people in the world, frivolous, cruel, careless and bent solely on pleasure. Yet this flighty and frivolous people elected Pericles as their *stratēgos* or president year after year. This great man laughed good-naturedly at the comedies that mocked him but, upon leaving the theatre, he still found his power respected."[60] With Mérimée, the rehabilitation of democratic Athens—and its leader—took off.

This turn of events is the more remarkable given that, up until 1850, the French had shown scant interest in Pericles, as can be seen from their pictorial art. Although Aspasia was the object of a certain vogue in the early nineteenth century, painters never showed her in the company of the *stratēgos*, but always at the side of the handsome Alcibiades or the wise Socrates.[61]

It is true that Pericles did appear in the famous *Apotheosis of Homer* that Ingres painted in 1827, to decorate one of the ceilings of the Charles X Museum in the Louvre (figure 14). But his portrait was only roughly sketched in and was lost among the crowd of figures to the left of the poets, where he was almost entirely blocked out by Phidias. It was not until 1851 that François Nicolas Chifflart did him the honor of placing him in the foreground of his painting titled *Pericles at the Deathbed of His Son*," exhibited at the

FIGURE 14. *The Apotheosis of Homer* (1827), by Jean-Auguste-Dominique Ingres. Oil on canvas. Pericles is hardly visible, a sign that he is less important than Homer and Phidias, who almost entirely hide him. The tableau is imagined at the same moment as George Grote was preparing to put the *stratēgos* back center-stage in the West. Paris, Musée du Louvre. © RMN-Grand Palais (Musée du Louvre) / Thierry Le Mage.

Ecole Nationale des Beaux-Arts (figure 15).[62] The fact that this oil painting won the Grand Prix de Rome for a historical painting seems symbolic, for in that same year, Hachette published the first edition of the *Histoire grecque* by Victor Duruy (1811–1894), which devoted particular attention to Pericles.

Declaring his disdain for Sparta, which was reduced to "a mere war-machine," this French historian celebrated bourgeois Athens and its incomparable leader, with unprecedented enthusiasm: "Never before, in Athens, had any man held such power . . . and never was power acquired and preserved by such pure means. Pericles, with no particular title and no special post of command and through the sole authority of his genius and virtues, became the master of Athens, a post that he filled with more nobility than

FIGURE 15. *Périclès au lit de mort de son fils* (1851), by François Nicolas Chifflart (1825–1901), Saint-Omer, Musée de l'Hôtel Sandelin, inv. 975.001. © Musées de Saint-Omer, D. Adams.

Augustus in Rome."[63] The idealization of Pericles now reached its peak, for Duruy even went so far as to justify the city's imperialistic policy: "Of all the regimes that were destroyed, only one was to be regretted, that of Athens and Pericles. As long as it existed, there were fewer instances of cruelty and injustice and greater glory and prosperity than Greece had ever known."[64]

However, this eulogy did not go so far as to celebrate the democratic system as such, as, for the author, those Athenians all belonged to an elite group, "an aristocracy raised by its taste, its elegance, its intellectual culture and its habit of command, far above the ordinary condition of other peoples."[65] So it was not the "ignoble populace" that governed the city, but an aristocracy of 15,000 citizens. From this point of view, Duruy's argument was perfectly compatible with the authoritarian regime that, in the very same year as that of the first edition of his work, had been established by Louis-Napoléon Bonaparte.

This idealized representation of Periclean Athens did not triumph without encountering a degree of resistance in French intellectual circles. The philologist Charles Nisard, a devoted supporter of Sparta, produced an acerbic review of Duruy's work, accusing its author of devoting a "juvenile admiration" to Athens.[66] However, the situation evolved rapidly in the years that followed, when Duruy obtained uncontested power in the educational world.[67] Having risen through every level of the educational system, he was in a position to spread his ideas in textbooks such as his *Abrégé d'histoire grecque pour la classe de cinquième* (*Abridged history of Greece for fifth-year pupils*), which appeared in 1858 and ran into many further editions. Having become the general inspector of secondary education (1862–1863) and subsequently the Minister for Public Instruction (1863–1869), under the Second Empire, he found himself in an unchallengeable position to impose his view of Greece throughout the colleges and secondary schools of France.

The advent of the Third Republic put the finishing touches to this slow conversion of attitudes. While Napoleon III remained fascinated by Julius Caesar—to whom he devoted a biography in 1865—Gambetta regarded Periclean Athens as a model for the new Republican regime. He explicitly referred to the analogy in the funeral speech he delivered on 24 May 1874, in the Montparnasse cemetery, at the tomb of Alton Shée: "If it has the intelligence to rally to the new France, the France of work and science, [the nobility], through proud patriotism and noble delicacy, will contribute to providing the French republic with the flower of elegance and distinction that will make it, in the modern world, into what the Athenian republic was in Antiquity."[68] Modeling his speech on Pericles' funeral oration,

Gambetta looked forward to the establishment of a moderate Republic that brought together the work of the populace, the knowledge of scholars, and the elegance of aristocrats.

Pericles in the *Altertumswissenschaft*: The History of a Disenchantment

Beyond the Rhine, Pericles benefited from the popularity of Thucydides that was then sweeping through Europe. The founders of *Altertumswissenschaft*, the "science of Antiquity," shared a boundless admiration for the author of *The Peloponnesian War*. They included Barthold Georg Niebuhr, Leopold von Ranke, and Wilhelm Roscher—whom Marx even went so far as to call Wilhelm *Thucydides* Roscher.[69] The author of *The Peloponnesian War* underwent a veritable historiographical apotheosis.[70] His history was regarded as an "extraordinary work";[71] and Niebuhr even considered Thucydides to be "the most perfect historian among all those that have ever written,"[72] while Ranke, for his part, confessed that Thucydides was the writer "before whom he fell to his knees."[73]

This admiration was reflected in opinions of Pericles, as is clear from the *Griechische Geschichte* by Ernst Curtius (1814–1896), which appeared between 1857 and 1867.[74] Following in the neohumanist steps of Winckelmann, Curtius extolled Athenian prosperity and launched into a "defence and illustration" of Pericles. Like Grote, he based his eulogy on the rehabilitation of Thucydides, "the only man who makes it possible for us to rediscover the original features of this image [that of Pericles] that has been so disfigured."[75] He claimed that the *stratēgos*, who was a statesman as well as a philosopher, exerted upon the people a "consistent and firm government," thereby creating a perfect "combination of democracy and monocracy."[76] No major fault could be attributed to him, including where the members of the Delian League were concerned: "as to the treatment of allies, the sagacity as well as the sense of justice of Pericles led him to object to the imposition of any undue burdens upon them, and to any measure tending to irritate their feelings."[77] Even his private life was praiseworthy: Curtius found no fault with his love of Aspasia, a woman who possessed "a lofty and richly endowed nature, with a perfect sense of all that is beautiful." According to Curtius, "the possession of this woman was in many respects invaluable for Pericles. Not only were her accomplishments the delight of the leisure hours which he allowed himself, and the recreation of his mind from its cares, but she also kept him in intercourse with the daily life around him." Better still, he declared, she initiated him into Sicilian eloquence and "was of use to him through her various connexions at home and abroad, as well as by the keen glance of her sagacity and by her knowledge of men."[78]

All the same, Curtius had no admiration for Athenian democracy as such—which is hardly surprising in the man who was the tutor of Frederick III, the heir to the throne of Prussia. The reason he so admired Pericles was precisely because the Athenian leader had removed all substance from the power of the people; under his leadership, "all the principles of democracy were virtually abolished, viz the constant change and the distribution of official power, and even the responsibility attaching to it and forming the strongest guarantee of the sovereignty of the people. . . . Pericles, alone invested with a continuous official authority which commanded all the various branches of public life, stood in solitary grandeur firm and calm above the surging State."[79] Curtius, who was both a liberal and a monarchist, thus constructed the image of an Athens without democracy, the popular institutions of which were tempered or even neutralized by an aristocracy of the virtue that was embodied by Pericles.

The vision defended by Curtius soon entered general circulation. His work was rapidly translated into English and French and was certainly the Greek history that was most widely read in the nineteenth century and that, in its turn, influenced a number of great German historians. One was Wilhelm Adolf Schmidt, who described Pericles as "the zenith of the entire ancient and classical world" and the cultural peak of human history.[80]

However, this idealized image soon faded away in the Germanic world. Two developments combined to marginalize or even discredit Pericles in Germany. In the first place, Athens was no longer alone in attracting the attention of historians, many of whom now turned to Rome or to the history of the Hellenistic kingdoms; and second, the progress made by the new "science of Antiquity" led to disenchantment with Pericles' city, revealing hitherto unrecognized shortcomings.[81]

Following the Napoleonic occupation, one of the priorities of the Prussian government was to organize *Altertumswissenschaft* around subjects previously left aside in the Germanic world. Rome, for a long time the preserve of the French, now attracted the attention of German scholars. After Barthold Georg Niebuhr's seminal study, published between 1811 and 1832, Theodor Mommsen flung himself into composing his *Roman History* in eight volumes, publication of which was spread over more than thirty years, from 1854 to 1886. Now that Germany assumed as its objective the constitution of a national state or even a unified empire, there could no longer be any question of ignoring Roman history.

That same quest for unity steered Germanic historians toward the study of Alexander the Great's empire and the states that emerged from it. As early as the 1830s, Johann Gustav Droysen paved the way for this new "Hellenistic" history. In his *Hellenistic History* (*Geschichte des Hellenismus*), written between 1836 and 1843, this historian, who had sat in on the lectures given by Hegel, exalted the political work of Philip II, praising him for having unified all Macedonia into a homogeneous "nation" while, on the contrary, he had nothing but scorn for the *Kleinstaaterei*, the political fragmentation of the Greek world.[82] In his *Alexander*, which appeared in 1833, he cast Pericles in a villainous role. Although he recognized that his reign had marked the peak of Athens's glory, he accused him of having handed over all decisions to the people, "the people among which Pericles constantly encouraged a taste for democratic ideologies."[83] According to Droysen, that excessive liberty led to the establishment of a veritable tyranny over the allies, which eventually rebounded against itself, propelling the city into ruination.[84] Seen from this teleological point of view, in which a unified State constituted the vanishing point, the figure of Pericles symbolized the Greek cities' inability to achieve political unity and put an end to their internal quarrels.

This rejection of Athens was further emphasized by the evolution of *Altertumswissenschaft* scholarship. As early as the start of the nineteenth century, Pericles had been a target of criticism, breaking with Winckelmann's kind of admiration. In 1817, Augustus Böckh, in his scholarly treatise on *The Public Economy of Athens* (*Die Staatshaushaltung der Athener*), was declaring that "depravity and moral corruption were rife throughout the Athenian community."[85] And Pericles was certainly not excepted from this bitter observation. On the one hand, Böckh recalled the various accusations of corruption leveled at him, reassessing their credibility but not wholly rejecting them;[86] on the other, he criticized the *stratēgos* for his sumptuary expenditure on the people, even though, backed up by his sources, he did recognize that Pericles never offered pay for attending the Assembly.[87]

From 1870 onward, criticism increased, as knowledge about Athens became more detailed thanks to the acquisition of a large epigraphic corpus and, above all, the discovery of the *Constitution of the Athenians* in 1891. As early as 1884, Karl Julius Beloch was distancing himself from "the unilateral views of Grote's school" and "the cult of radical democracy" that had become fashionable.[88] Moreover, in Beloch's *Greek History*, which appeared in 1893, Pericles was even subjected to an all-out attack. The German historian, who was skeptical about the real power possessed by "great men," considered that the son of Xanthippus was even inferior to his predecessors, Themistocles and Cimon. He was no more than "a great parliamentarian" (*ein großer Parlamentarier*),[89] lacking any military talent. In the new Germany of Wilhelm II, disdain for representative democracy was now expressed openly. But Beloch did not limit his attack to this, for he went on to accuse Pericles of plunging Greece into a fatal internal war; even if sentencing the *stratēgos* to pay a hefty fine in 430 was legally unjust, it was nevertheless basically justified in that it was aimed at the politician "who had unleashed the fratricidal Hellenic conflict for personal reasons and *had thereby been guilty of the greatest crime ever known in the whole of Greek history*."[90] Pericles was the destroyer of the unity of the Hellenic world; in the recently unified Germany, this was the gravest of accusations.

In 1898, the Swiss German Jacob Burckhardt, for his part, returned to a more traditional vein, accusing the Athenians of having used their power in an unjust manner both inside the city and beyond it. He claimed that slavery and various handouts of pay gave rise to laziness, depravity, and excessive luxury: "The most demoralizing tax was the *theorikon*, doled out to the poorer citizens for theatre tickets, for celebrating festivals and games, and for sacrifices and public meals. The waste caused by this tax was relatively as great as that at the most sumptuous courts, and later wars were lost for lack of money because this sacrosanct tradition could not be abolished."[91] Pericles, "responsible for most of the taxes just mentioned," was powerless to oppose such deadly tendencies. Far from being an educator of the people, "he was also forced to humour their greed with pleasures of all sorts—not to satisfy it would have been impossible."[92] The outbreak of the Peloponnesian War may even have seemed to him desirable, for it offered him an opportunity to avoid the anger that the people felt against him.

At the turn of the century, the elective similarities formerly detected between Pericles and the Germans had had their day. Now transformed purely into a parliamentarian and reviled for having stirred up ill-feeling in the Greek world, his image was repudiated and other models more in tune with the ideology of the Second Reich took its place. By the time of the outbreak of World War I, the divorce was complete: clearly rejected by the Germans, the *stratēgos* was now enrolled in the service of British propaganda. This prompted a renewed use of the figure of Pericles that sometimes took unexpected turns, not only in England, but once again in Germany when that conflict came to an end.

The Deterioration of the Periclean Myth

The Exploitation of the Periclean Myth: Pericles amid the Turmoil of the Two World Wars

During World War I, the Germans showed scant interest in Pericles. If ever they did evoke the democratic city, it was, rather, in order to denigrate fourth-century Athens and its loquacious orators. In 1916, Engelbert Drerup published a book that attacked Demosthenes and the ancient "Republic of lawyers" (*Advokaten-republik*) in which the most inflammatory of modern issues rose to the surface. By means of an analogy, Drerup explicitly targeted the Entente leaders, first and foremost "the lawyer, Lloyd George," who was then Minister for War in Great Britain.[93] It was also a way of countering Clemenceau, who was devoting a veritable cult to Demosthenes, whom he presented as championing the resistance to Philip II of Macedon.[94]

Pericles remained mostly uninvolved in this battle between great men. Significantly enough, it was not until the day after the armistice, on 12 November 1918, that the *stratēgos* made a timid appearance on the Parisian stage, in an operetta by Henri Christiné titled *Phi-Phi*. Although it was an instant success, Pericles did not emerge favorably from this lighthearted comedy that enjoyed a three-year run in the "Bouffes parisiens" theater. His role was no more than that of a foil, which was eclipsed by that of Phidias (alias Phi-Phi), the play's real hero. The latter mocked the *stratēgos*, who was prepared to dye his hair in order to marry the "charming young" Aspasia. And this new "arch-countess" of Athens then proceeded to cheat on her husband with the sculptor, who teased her, saying, "You need so many men that our statesman does not satisfy you!"[95] Pericles was thus mobilized, not as a figure of resistance and heroism, but as one that represented loose moral behavior. This play founded the genre of musical comedies and started off the "Flapper Years."

Pericles in an England at War: A Call to Arms

Only in England was Pericles truly honored during World War I. One year after the start of the conflict, in the autumn of 1915, all the London buses carried an advertisement bearing an extract from the funeral oration in which the *stratēgos* called upon his fellow-citizens to imitate the bravery of the soldiers who had fallen in defense of their city (figure 16): "For you now it remains to rival what they have done and, knowing the secret of happiness to be freedom, and the secret of freedom a brave heart, not idly to stand aside from the enemy's onset."[96]

Cited in the fine translation by the British historian Alfred Zimmern,[97] this passage rested on a set of implicit references that suggested that the English were identified with the Athenians, the Germans with the Spartans. The analogy was the more apposite given that a number of Germanic historians had rehabilitated the Spartans in the course of the nineteenth century, even going so far as to represent those harsh warriors as "the Prussians of Antiquity," as Karl Otfried Müller put it.[98]

What can be the explanation for the remarkable interplay of roles between the French, fascinated by Demosthenes, and the English, committed to

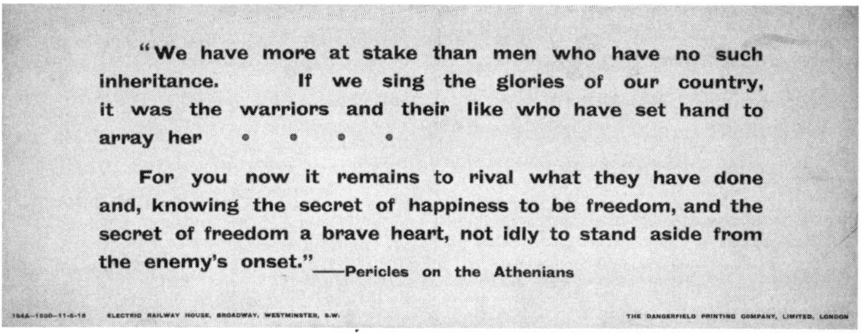
"We have more at stake than men who have no such inheritance. If we sing the glories of our country, it was the warriors and their like who have set hand to array her • • • •
For you now it remains to rival what they have done and, knowing the secret of happiness to be freedom, and the secret of freedom a brave heart, not idly to stand aside from the enemy's onset."
—Pericles on the Athenians
ELECTRIC RAILWAY HOUSE, BROADWAY, WESTMINSTER, S.W.
THE DANGERFIELD PRINTING COMPANY, LIMITED, LONDON

FIGURE 16. "Pericles on the Athenians" (1915), by unknown artist. Published by Underground Electric Railway Company Ltd, 1915. Printed by the Dangerfield Printing Company Ltd, 1915. Panel poster. Reference number: 1983/4/8159. © TfL from the London Transport Museum collection.

Pericles? Or, to put that another way, why did Clemenceau, after retiring from political life, write a life of Demosthenes rather than a biography of Pericles? The explanation is easy enough to find when one reflects upon the identities of Athens's enemies. For the French, the struggle against the Macedonian kings provided a more attractive parallel than the struggle against the Spartan oligarchy. As a reflection of French resistance to Kaiser Wilhelm II, the war against Macedonia could be likened to a republican crusade against the despotism of Philip II. The English, however, had nothing against royalty as such; the Peloponnesian War offered them a chance to play upon a different register—not the opposition between a republic and a monarchy, but the confrontation between a liberal sea-power and an aggressive continental power.[99]

Periclean Athens remained a model for English politicians right up to 1945. In his *Memoirs*, Winston Churchill showered praise upon Lord Beaverbrook (then minister for food supplies), who, in one of his letters, had quoted the last sentence from Pericles' last speech: "Open no more negotiations with Sparta. Show them plainly that you are not crushed by your present afflictions. They who face calamity without wincing and who offer the most energetic resistance, these, be they States or individuals, are the truest heroes."[100] Impossible not catch an echo of the famous "We shall never surrender" pronounced by the English prime minister in June 1940. In that same speech, Churchill too promised to continue the battle, whatever the cost, with the help of "our Empire beyond the seas," in the same way as Pericles did in the Peloponnesian War.[101] English historians were quick to set the two situations in parallel. At the end of World War II, the Greek scholar Gilbert Murray wrote of the outbreak of hostilities between Sparta and Athens as follows:

"Just as in 1914 or 1939, a rich democratic sea-power with a naval empire, full of interest in all forms of social, artistic and intellectual life, was pitted against a reactionary militarist land power, which had sacrificed most of its earlier culture to stark efficiency in war."[102]

Yet we should not exaggerate the relevance of such comparisons. In the first place, those "Anglo-Periclean" affinities were by no means exclusive, for Gilbert Murray also quoted Demosthenes in support of his thesis.[103] Furthermore, not all British leaders felt the same admiration for the *stratēgos*. In 1940, the future director of the Intelligence Service cited the funeral oration in an official report, with a view to stigmatizing the dangers of open democracy in times of war: "Athens lost the war," he reminded his correspondent, so Pericles' city could surely not constitute a model to be followed.[104] Finally, the English were not alone in referring to the Athenian leader. Ever since the second half of the nineteenth century, the Americans too had claimed the figure of the *stratēgos*, with a view to turning him into one of the guardian-heroes of American democracy. President Abraham Lincoln has been shown to have been inspired by the funeral oration when composing the famous "Gettysburg Address" in honor of the dead who fell in battle in July 1863.[105]

Paradoxically, however, it was in Germany that the exploitation of the Periclean myth was carried furthest, in particular after Hitler's accession to power. The upshot of a strange alliance between *Altertumswissenschaft* and Nazi propaganda was that the *stratēgos* became the archetype of the charismatic Führer, stamping his imprint upon both time and space with his monumental constructions.

Pericles in Defeated Germany: The Quest for a Führer

In the immediate postwar years, a humiliated Germany again turned to Athens in order to think through its own present situation. As Anthony Andurand has shown, Germanic historians identified the situation of their vanquished country with the fate of the Athenian city in 404: in both cases, the military defeat was accompanied by a change of political regime.[106] In September 1919, in a lecture titled "Thucydides and Ourselves," the historian Max Pohlenz drew a contrast between the glorious Athens of 430 and the broken city of 404, in a bid to find lessons for the Germany of his own day. He was a supporter of the conservative Right, who regarded Periclean democracy as the archetype of a *Volkstadt*, a state in which the sovereignty of the *dēmos* was limited by all the citizens' blind obedience to the law. According to Pohlenz, this "democracy of duty" implied a Führer in whom the people could believe. Whereas Pericles had ideally filled that role, his successors had turned out to be incapable of carrying on his work: "There was no longer any statesman who possessed the qualities necessary to be the people's leader [*Führer des Volkes*]. Now there were only Party leaders [*Parteiführer*]," "purely professional politicians [*reine Berufsparlamentarier*],"[107] all fighting one another with no thought for the interests of the community as a whole (*des ganzen*). As Pohlenz presented Pericles, the latter was the embodiment of a glorious but bygone period. However, the evocation of his memory indicated a path to follow, even a political solution: reading between the lines, the historian's compatriots were invited to elect a new Führer, one capable of breaking with the Weimar Republic and all its useless partisan squabbles.

A similar quest inspired Werner Jaeger, then a professor at the University of Berlin, in the first volume of his *Paideia*, which appeared in 1934. Calling for the birth of a "third humanism," this Greek scholar proposed a return to the Greeks, which he envisaged as a cure for the German decline—for the parliamentary Republic with all its "vulgarity" failed to win his approval. Faced with such a depressing present, he exalted "the genius of Athens," whose funeral oration seemed to him to encapsulate its quintessence.[108] But that was not all: according to Jaeger, Pericles' speech pleaded for the emergence of a charismatic Führer. "In Athens, says he, every man is alike before the law, but in politics the aristocracy of talent is supreme. Logically, *that implies the principle that if one man is supremely valuable and important he will be recognized as the ruler of the State.*"[109] Jaeger suggested that the *stratēgos* was just such an exceptional man who, by combining power (*Macht*) and spirit (*Geist*), Dorian discipline and Ionian creativity, turned Athens into an unsurpassable model. Such was the political lesson provided by the case of Pericles: "History has shown that this solution depends on the appearance of a genius to lead the state [*des genialen Führers*]—an accident as uncommon in a democracy as in other types of state."[110] This proposal, advanced at the very moment when Hitler was democratically elected to power, inevitably took on a particular resonance. Jaeger himself certainly had no respect for the Nazis, whose popularism he detested. Nevertheless, he did share their fascination with charismatic heroes and leaders; and the reason why this Greek scholar eventually, in 1936, exiled himself to the United States was in order to protect his Jewish wife from persecution, not for any ideological reasons.[111]

Pericles, a Mirror-Image of Hitler: The Builder-Leader

The advent of the Third Reich increased the glorification of Pericles. At first sight, this may seem strange or even grotesque. Clearly, the Nazis both used and abused Antiquity: the arts, costumes, architecture, and sport all now took on an antique veneer. However, Athenian democracy was, for the most part, eclipsed by imperial Rome and, above all, by Dorian Sparta. Whereas Humboldt, Hegel, Nietzsche, and Burckhardt harbored nothing but scorn for Sparta, which they considered to be a backward state, resistant to any refined culture, the Nazis rehabilitated the Spartans, radicalizing the theses developed in the nineteenth century by Karl-Otfried Müller. The Dorians were now assimilated to a superior race, set up as ancestor to the Aryans. Their essentially Nordic vitality was represented as even regenerating the Greek race, which had been bastardized as a result of the long contact with Asia.[112] For the Nazis, the exaltation of Sparta was doubly gratifying politically: the city was "for them, the archetype of an elitist, racist, and eugenicist Nordic State, pretotalitarian in its concept and practice of education, but at the same time the finest illustration of the virtues of military obedience and self-denial."[113] So it was in no way surprising that Hitler himself made Sparta the model for the future Third Reich and even went so far as to regard it as "the first racist State in history."[114]

All the same, Pericles was not neglected by Hitlerian propaganda, for the fact is that it had no respect for the principle of noncontradiction: just as the Nazis celebrated both Augustan imperial Rome and Arminius's heroic resistance to the legions of Augustus in the forest of Teutoburg,[115] they venerated the Spartan city even as they continued to sing the praises of the Athenian *stratēgos*.

However, their admiration for Pericles was selective, focusing on two characteristic features, to the exclusion of all others. First, in the wake of Pohlenz and Jaeger, Nazi scholars celebrated the charismatic leader, drawing a direct parallel with Hitler. As early as 1933, in a collective volume sponsored by the new National-Socialist State, Fritz Schachermeyr maintained that the Athenian leader had arisen at a time of crisis for the democracy, a crisis "exactly similar to that which we experienced before Adolf Hitler came upon the scene."[116] According to this Austrian historian, the reforming will manifested by Pericles had nevertheless hit a snag in the form of the "Mediterranean substratum that was foreign to the Nordic race," represented by Pericles and the Indo-Germanic elite groups of Athens. The implication was clear: if Athens had had the courage to rid itself of its parasitic elements—as Germany was doing—it would never have lost the Peloponnesian War.

Another Nazi Hellenist, Hermannhans Brauer, developed a similar line of argument in 1943. But the wind had changed and now it was a matter of exonerating Hitler from any responsibility for the defeat at Stalingrad. With such apologetic aims, this historian claimed that if Athens had been defeated, it was no fault of Pericles but, rather, in spite of him: for "he had embodied the 'Nordic values: courage, honour, fidelity and patriotism' that the

Athenians had not managed to honour when the moment of truth came."[117] Slipping from enthusiasm into open resentment, the Athenian people, it was claimed, was guilty of a great mistake: "In a life-and-death struggle, it rejected its support of its leader and denied him its loyalty because it placed too much value on temporal things and neglected the eternal values to which the country subscribed."[118] The analogy was clumsy but effective. In this way, it suggested that the Stalingrad defeat could be imputed to the weakness of the troops and betrayal on the part of the German General Staff, which was incapable of rising to the level of its genius of a Führer.

Quite apart from the charismatic leader, the Nazis above all admired Pericles, the man of great architectural works. In his *Memoirs*, Albert Speer recalled that Hitler himself liked to be seen as a latter-day Pericles: the Athenians had erected the Parthenon and the Long Walls, just as he had constructed the *Autobahnen*.[119] The fact was that architecture was an essential element in Hitlerian policy and, in *Mein Kampf*, the Nazi leader was already declaring that "a strong state should leave its imprint upon space and not allow private edifices to proliferate."[120] In this respect, Antiquity provided a model to imitate or even to surpass. Although Hitler was, above all, intent on outdoing the monumental policy of the Roman Empire—the great Berlin Stadium was designed to outdo the Colosseum—he was nevertheless impressed by the classical Greek style and, in particular, the Doric order, for Hitler "believed that in the Dorian people he had discovered a number of points in common with the Germanic world."[121] He was full of admiration for the Parthenon, which he regretted never having visited; the monument was even reproduced on the tableware used for meals in his Austrian retreat, the *Berghof*.[122] It was therefore perfectly logical that certain historians of art, as good courtiers, should bring the two monument-builders together so as to have two artistic moments of unequaled artistic flourishing mirror one another.[123]

In his inaugural lecture as rector of the University of Leipzig, in February 1940, Helmut Berve pushed the parallel between Pericles and Hitler even further.[124] This historian, the author of a work on Thucydides, held an eminent position in the Nazi hierarchy. He had been a member of the Nazi Party (NSDAP) ever since 1933 and, in 1940, was appointed "war minister of the German science of Antiquity [*Kriegsbeauftrager der deutschen Altertumswissenschaft*]."[125] In his speech devoted to Pericles, Berve began by justifying the subject, taking care to represent the *stratēgos* as a good Aryan: his government, he claimed, constituted "the unique *acme* of Indo-Germanic humanity." There then followed a dense interplay of implicit analogies between the Nazi Führer and the Athenian *stratēgos*. First, Pericles' democratic policy was said to be to get every Athenian to participate in the life of the city, the aim being to provide work and subsistence for one and all. Between the lines, everyone recognized this as an allusion to Hitler's *Arbeit und Brot*. This policy of economic revival depended on the great architectural works into which Pericles flung himself, body and soul. As Johann Chapoutot has rightly stressed, "the parallel between the Pericles-Phidias relationship and the Hitler-Speer duo is very striking, as is the assimilation of the new Athens project and that of Germania."[126]

According to Berve, this ambitious monumental policy depended on a pitiless exercise of violence: "So it was the brutal force of Athens and the iron will of its *Führer* that made it possible to erect these marvels, the Parthenon and the Propylaea on the Acropolis, which, still today, and even in their ruined state, represent the most sublime evidence of the creative force of man."[127] For Pericles was not only a captivating orator but also a warrior who fought until his last breath: "He had hardened himself throughout fifteen years spent in a bath of steel, so that he possessed a strength of resistance that was hard to overcome despite internal oppositions and external difficulties."[128] Like all Nordic leaders, Pericles had experienced all the trials of warfare, even "looking into the eyes of death in the course of battles." Those lines were written during the Phoney War and they were intended to be prophetic: which, indeed, they were, although not in the way that Berve had hoped. Like Periclean Athens, Hitlerian Germany was eventually completely vanquished.

The Myth Destroyed? Pericles and the End of the Greek Miracle

By the end of World War II, the reference to Sparta as a model, having been overmanipulated by the Nazis, was definitively disqualified. In contrast, Athenian democracy emerged enhanced from the conflict; the association between Hitler and Pericles had not been established firmly enough to blemish the reputation of the *stratēgos*, particularly given that the allies—led by Churchill—had likewise enrolled Pericles in their struggle against the Axis forces.[129] In France, for example, Pericles continued to benefit from the persistent influence of the *Histoire grecque* published by Gustave Glotz (1862–1935) in 1931. For this historian, who was close to Durkheim and had long been a professor at the Sorbonne, Pericles' governance was laudable in all its aspects. Not only did Glotz praise Pericles' "pacific imperialism"—a most revealing combination of words—but he also celebrated the "State Socialism" set in place by the Athenian leader and ended by concluding that Pericles "was the soul of the city at a time when that city was the very soul of Greece."[130]

In Italy, the work of Gaetano De Sanctis (1870–1957) took a similar idealizing line.[131] Abandoning Roman history, which had become the preserve of Mussolinian historians, De Sanctis—one of the rare university professors who had refused to swear allegiance to the Fascist regime—devoted a flattering biography to Pericles, which appeared in 1944. In it, the *stratēgos* was described as a man devoted to the interests of his city, a friend of the philosophers and possessed of "great spiritual audacity," who had led Athens into a veritable Golden Age.[132] On many points, his analysis agreed with that of Gustave Glotz, particularly on the great works that, according to De Sanctis, were designed not only to render the city more beautiful, but also "to wipe out unemployment among the working classes"[133] and to "establish greater social justice."[134] That closeness to Glotz is also evident in his celebration of Pericles' "pacific imperialism"—an expression that De Sanctis took over.[135] This irenic view of Athenian domination is not surprising, for, although anti-Fascist, De Santis adhered to the myth of a "civilizing" Italian colonialism, and it is by this yardstick that we should judge his praise of Periclean policy toward the allies.[136]

Such idealization persisted in the postwar years, particularly in the *Pericles* written by Léon Homo (1872–1957) in his twilight years.[137] Abandoning the domain in which he had specialized—Roman history—this French historian now represented the Athenian *stratēgos* as a hero possessed of every virtue: as a great general, a great admiral, an intelligent economist, and an honest man through and through, Pericles was "one of the most luminous spirits ever produced by the Greek race."[138] According to Homo's analyses, Pericles was the leader of a "directed democracy" in which the citizens enjoyed an "illusion of liberty" even as they were subjected to a "legal dictatorship."[139] For this politically conservative historian, admiration for Pericles was thus accompanied by a devaluation of the democratic regime. And, like his predecessors, Homo was careful to justify Periclean imperialism, for which he found 'serious excuses."[140]

In 1960, François Châtelet (1925–1985) adopted a similar line in the biography that he devoted to the *stratēgos*. In this youthful work of his, this French philosopher portrayed Pericles as a Hegelian hero, shining in the firmament of human history as did the "blazing light of Greece."[141] Even a Marxist historian such as Pierre Lévêque confessed to huge admiration for the Athenian leader, as is testified by the vast fresco that he devoted to *L'Aventure grecque*, published in 1964. Although he deplored Athenian imperialism and the exploitation of slaves, he nevertheless praised the *stratēgos* for his great architectural works, saying, "after all, should we not salute this first experiment in 'State Socialism' (G. Glotz)?"[142] For this generation of leftist intellectuals, "State Socialism" in the Periclean mode exercised an irresistible attraction, for it testified to "the great hope that for the first time illuminated Greece."[143]

In the field of historical studies, enthusiasm for Pericles was nevertheless tempered by a double fundamental movement. In the first place, the intellectual hegemony of the *Annales* school tended to marginalize or even discredit the study of great men. Instead of taking an interest in the lives of State leaders, it was now a matter of assessing long-term developments, those of the *longue durée*, without being distracted by the froth produced by individual actions. Revealingly enough, in France no specialist in Greek history saw fit to devote a biography to Pericles in the second half of the twentieth century; the only writers to undertake such a task were a historian of Rome (Léon Homo) and a philosopher (François Châtelet).[144] From the 1960s onward, the development of historical anthropology further accentuated the lack of interest in the *stratēgos*. Turning its back on political and institutional history, this new way of tackling the Greek world focused on rituals rather than individual events, and on mental representations rather than the history of battles. And even when it did turn to politicians, it was in order to rehabilitate figures that had been forgotten—such as the enigmatic Cleisthenes, of Athens, or the obscure Ephialtes—and, taking them as its starting point, to reflect on the mental structures of classical Athens: space and time, in the case of Cleisthenes; memory and forgetting, in that of Ephialtes.[145] The Greece of great men was done for. Besides, historical anthropology rejected idealization of Athens in any form and set out to study "the Greeks without miracles" (to use Gernet's expression), denying them any ontological privileges over other peoples.

Pericles' democracy was now regarded as a mirage rather than a miracle. From the 1970s onward, attacks multiplied on a democracy that, like a magnifying mirror, reflected all the shortcomings of an imperialist and male-chauvinist West. Quite apart from slavery, which had already for some time been arousing indignation,[146] the treatment of women now attracted criticism. And Pericles was accused of having encouraged the enslavement of half of humanity given that, in his funeral oration, he had invited women to be neither seen nor heard, "thereby reducing them to a state of non-being."[147]

However, it was on the score of imperialism that the Athenian leader was chiefly taken to task. The Belgian historian Marie Delcourt (1891–1979) had, as an enlightened pioneer, already sharply criticized Periclean imperialistic policy in the biography that she devoted to the *stratēgos* in 1939.[148] This great Greek scholar, a professor at the University of Liège, attacked in particular the cleruchies, which were condemned simply as a means of seizing land with no regard for its existing occupants, just like "the Europeans in Africa and the New World": "It is strange that Pericles never noticed that the spread of cleruchies was both dangerous and ineffective. It generated hatred for Athens and gave it the reputation of treating the States of the Delian League like conquered countries."[149] In Marie Delcourt's works, the criticism of Western colonialism (Belgium itself was a colonial power) spread to affect Periclean foreign policy as a whole.

Tormented by the memory of Nazism, German historians too cast doubt upon Pericles' supposed moderation in his management of the Delian League.[150] And elsewhere attacks increased as decolonization proceeded and the Cold War conflicts developed. At this point, some Anglo-Saxon historians questioned the opposition that Thucydides identified between, on the one hand, the moderate imperialism of Pericles and, on the other, the radical imperialism of his successors. At the end of the 1960s, Victor Ehrenberg—who had left Nazi Germany via Prague and settled in England—argued that the central element in the Periclean legacy had been, quite simply, imperialism.[151] One year after the end of the Vietnam War, the American historian Chester Starr expressed the following disenchanted opinion that was not unaffected by the political failures of Nixon's policies: "In view of Pericles' promotion of arrogant imperialism and his serious mistakes in foreign policy, which in the end ruined Athenian power, his reputation may well be overrated."[152] The same conclusion, albeit expressed less polemically, was reached by Simon Hornblower in the work that he devoted to Thucydides in the late 1980s: "The real mistakes [that led to the defeat of Athens] were after all mistakes of the 430s and earlier. That means that they were Periclean mistakes."[153] Hornblower suggests that Thucydides, so fascinated by the *stratēgos*, misjudged the real moment when Athens lurched into the delirium of omnipotence and the *pleonexia* that caused its downfall.

This critical tradition has lost none of its rigor. Indeed, Loren Samons has recently carried it to a climax, echoing an anti-Periclean tone unheard since the late eighteenth century. In his indictment, titled *What's Wrong with Democracy?*, this American historian targets the two major pillars upon which admiration for Pericles rests: the Parthenon and the funeral oration. The Parthenon, which was partly financed by the allies, serves simply as an ode to the imperial excesses of Athens. The colossal statue of Athena sums this up in striking fashion: the winged Victory (*nikē*) placed in her right hand, symbolizes the city's imperialism, while the representation of Pandora, engraved on the soles of her sandals, recalls the despised nature of women, the better to justify their political relegation. As for the funeral oration, it is nothing but a militant or even militarist propagandist speech expressing "a fervent nationalism designed to underpin Athenian power."[154] Samons's verdict allows for no appeal: Pericles, responsible as he was, through his intransigence, for the unleashing of the war, is "one of the most charismatic—and dangerous—leaders in Western history."[155]

This vein of anti-Periclean literature, still very much alive, is often accompanied by virulent attacks against Thucydides, who is accused of misrepresenting historical truth the better to praise the *stratēgos*. For instance, in a book published in 2011, Robert Luginbill declares that the main purpose of *The History of the Peloponnesian War* was to exonerate Pericles of any responsibility for Athens's defeat. Following up this theme, the American historian defends an extremely dark picture of the *stratēgos*, whom he accuses not only of having unleashed the Peloponnesian War for ill-founded reasons, but above all for having pursued it, committing Athens to a path leading to ineluctable defeat: "in fact, Pericles doomed Athens."[156]

The Myth Sterilized: A Pericles for the Classroom

Despite the preceding citations, it would be mistaken to conclude that Pericles is now somewhat discredited in the Western world, for, on the contrary, the idealization of the *stratēgos* still continues today, sometimes quite openly—as in the case of the biography by Donald Kagan, for example[157]—sometimes in a covert manner, if one thinks of Harold Mattingly's attempt to redate Athenian decrees, which tends to exonerate Pericles from all responsibility for the extreme development of Athens's imperialism.[158] Today still, very few historians fail to bend a knee before the icon of Pericles, following the example of Hermann Bengtson: "Without the initiative of Pericles, Athens would have remained as it had been: a typical provincial town which, under Pericles, became not only the wealthiest but also the most beautiful town in the whole of Greece."[159] And in French school textbooks, Pericles still occupies a prime place, eclipsing all the other Athenian political leaders of the classical period. A bust of the *stratēgos*, an image of the Parthenon, and a passage from the funeral speech: few textbooks sidestep that stereotypical triptych.[160]

The *stratēgos* thus continues to enjoy a brilliant career in occidental schools and universities, while regularly being mobilized in arguments about the European identity and its supposed Greek origins.[161] But there is another side to this gleaming medallion; this "official" Pericles now arouses only indifference in popular culture worldwide. As a result of being used as a mouthpiece for democratic values, the *stratēgos* has become a mere symbolic sketch, a silhouette possessing neither substance nor charm, a symbol that, although, to be sure, admirable, is insipid. One might apply to him Marguerite Yourcenar's remark about Greek studies in general: "We have no use for this all too perfect statue sculpted from marble that is all too white."[162]

Transformed into a didactic implement, Pericles is, in effect, conspicuous by his absence from contemporary imaginary representations: no costume drama, no video game, virtually no comic strip is devoted to him. In the cinema, it is the Romans, the Spartans, and mythical heroes who are favored by the public.[163] A list of recent Hollywood productions speaks for itself: *Gladiator*, *Troy*, *Alexander*, *The Three Hundred*; nothing that deals, even remotely, with Pericles or even Athens.[164] The fact is that what seems to be fascinating about Antiquity is above all its violence and its urge to acquire power: by this yardstick, the *stratēgos* seems rather a dim subject. How can one get excited about an orator who died in his bed and was famous for his prudence rather than as a heroic warrior? And although we find a character named Pericles in a recent film made by Tim Burton, it is no more than a derisory name given to a primate trained to be an astronaut, in *The Planet of the Apes* (2001)!

Nor are the creators of video games any more charitable to the *stratēgos*. In this cultural industry, the budget of which now exceeds that of the cinema and music, there is no trace of Pericles; in the 157 titles that relate either closely or distantly to Antiquity, Alexander and ancient Rome take the lion's share, leaving no more than a few crumbs to the rest.[165] The same disappointing tally relates to comic strips, with but one exception: the *Orion* series launched by Jacques Martin, the creator of *Alix*. However, Pericles is no more than a secondary character in the plot and is, moreover, not a sympathetic figure, for he betrays the confidence of the young hero, in the name of national interests; he is left out of the latest volume.[166]

Although embalmed or even canonized by official culture, Pericles elicits boredom rather than fantasy. Indeed, it is only in bureaucratic imaginary representations that the *stratēgos* still arouses some interest, albeit in an unexpected manner. His name has become one of the favorite acronyms used by national and European administrations. In Wallonia, there is a Partenariat Economique pour le Redéploiement Industriel et les Clusters par l'Economie Sociale (PERICLES); the European Union has launched a Programme Européen de Renforcement des Institutions des Collectivités Locales et de leurs Services (likewise PERICLES); and as for UNESCO, it has set up a Programme Expérimental pour Relancer l'Intérêt de la jeunesse en faveur des Cultures et des Langues limitrophes à partir de l'Environnement naturel et des Sites patrimoniaux (PERICLES again)! More disturbing is the fact that the name of the Athenian leader has also been given to a number of repressive projects, such as the *programme de lutte contre le faux monnayage ou le futur fichier informatisé* (the European program to counteract counterfeit coinage and the future computerized database envisaged by the law of "internal security") adopted in January 2010. Transformed into a name devoid of content, Pericles has become the symbol of an Antiquity that hardly makes any sense today beyond a close circle of specialists—except as a jokey wink or a decontextualized citation.

Faced with such a diagnosis, what room for maneuver remains for a historian? Should one launch into an apology for Pericles or, on the contrary, expose him to public contempt in the hope of provoking some debate? To limit oneself to such an alternative would be intellectually questionable and, in any case, be doomed to failure. Rather than attempt by any means to reconnect Pericles to the present world and establish him as our great ancestor, perhaps it would be better first to accept his radical strangeness so as to restore to his "all too white statue" the vivid colors that it has lost and, above all, accept that he has no useful lessons for our times. Only if we recognize all these differences will Pericles be able to return to the present day, liberated from the problems surrounding the whole question of the Greek origins of Western democracies.

NOTES

Foreword: Introducing Azoulay's *Pericles*

1. For his *Périclès. La Démocratie athénienne à l'épreuve du grand homme* (Paris: Armand Colin, 2010), Dr. Azoulay was awarded the Prix du Sénat du Livre d'histoire. This was not his first monograph; that was *Xénophon et les grâces du pouvoir: De la charis au charisme* (Paris: Publications de la Sorbonne, 2004), the book of his 2002 Sorbonne *thèse* directed by Professeure Pauline Schmitt Pantel, for which—I declare an interest—I was one of the examining "jury" that granted him the degree of Doctor with highest distinction. Dr. Azoulay is currently Maître de conférences en histoire grecque at l'Université Paris-Est Marne-la-Vallée and a leading member of the research "Equipe Anhima," which devotes itself to studying "Anthropologie et histoire des mondes antiques."
2. In his bibliography, Dr. Azoulay lists several works addressed to a supposed "Periclean Age" or to "Periclean Athens"—for example, Châtelet 1982; Cloché 1949; Flacelière 1966; Hurwit 2004; and Samons II ed. 2007. I myself have contributed ("Pericles-Zeus: a study in tyranny") to a fairly recent such collection titled (in Greek) *The Democracy of Pericles in the 21st Century*, edited by Ch. Giallourides (Athens: I. Sideres, 2006). The publication of a "sourcebook and reader" titled just *Pericles* by a leading U.S. press (University of California Press, 2009, ed. S. V. Tracy) is symptomatic.
3. Anglophone readers may wish to consult Louise Bruit Zaidman and P. Schmitt Pantel, *Religion in the Ancient Greek City*, ed. and trans. P. Cartledge (Cambridge, UK: Cambridge University Press, 1992 and repr.).
4. Helen Roche, *Hitler's German Children: The Ideal of Ancient Sparta in the Royal Prussian Cadet-Corps, 1818–1920, and in National Socialist Elite Schools (the Napolas), 1933–1945* (Swansea: Classical Press of Wales, 2013).

Introduction

1. "Prayer on the Acropolis," in Renan 1929, 50.
2. See later, chapter 12.
3. Loraux 1993a.
4. See, for example, Cloché 1949; Flacelière 1966; and Châtelet 1982. In the Anglo-Saxon world, Robinson 1959; and Samons II ed. 2007. In the Germanic world, Filleul 1874–1875; and Schmidt 1877–1879.
5. See Loraux 2011.
6. See the remarks of Schmitt Pantel 2009, 204.
7. Lahire 1999, 121–152.
8. The date is probable but not certain. See the remarks of Lehmann 2008, 30 and 273.
9. See later, chapter 10.
10. See Keesling 2003, 193–195; Hölscher 1975, 191.
11. See later, chapter 2.

12. See Pelling 2002 and Schmitt Pantel 2009, 175–196 ("Plutarque, biographe et historien").
13. See Strasburger 1955, 1–25, here p. 3, who traces the idea to Eduard Meyer, Ulrich von Wilamowitz, and Victor Ehrenberg.
14. *Histories*, 6.131. On this ambiguous dream, see later, chapter 1.
15. See later, chapter 1 and chapter 4. On Herodotus's nuanced opinion of Pericles, see Schwartz 1969, 367–370, according to whom the historian's remark about illegitimate children among the Lycians incorporates a slur against Pericles and Aspasia (at 1.173); cf. also Thomas 1989, 265–272.
16. On Cratinus and Pericles, see McGlew 2002, 42–56, and Bakola 2010, 181–208.
17. See later, chapters 6 and 7, and, more generally, Vickers 1997.
18. Saetta Cottone 2005.
19. See Geddes 2007, 110–138. Although his work is ostensibly apolitical, in truth it reflects the social position of its author, Ion, who lived under an oligarchic government in Chios and himself belonged to the elite, was critical of the democratic and patriotic politics promoted by Pericles, and preferred Cimon, who was more in step with his own pan-Hellenic political ideals.
20. Banfi 2003, 46 ff.
21. See Schmitt Pantel 2009, 12–13 and 197–205.
22. That admiration of his was by no means without reservations, according to Foster 2010, 210–220. She suggests that Thucydides did indeed admire the *stratēgos*, but implicitly criticized his imperialist policy and his overconfidence in Athenian military power. It is a view that is shared by Taylor 2010. She radicalizes that analysis to the point of maintaining that Thucydides "implicitly censures Pericles" and the Athenian imperial project itself (p. 1). But this "reading between the lines" is not convincing: given that Thucydides openly criticizes democracy and the way that it functions, there seems to be no reason for him to praise Pericles but at the same time to slip in a covert negative message intended to be picked up by the "happy few" capable of detecting it.
23. See the remarks of Gribble 2006, 439.
24. See Dodds 1959, 325–326, for references to "great men" by orators. See, in particular, Isocrates, *Antidosis*, 111 and 234–235, and Lysias, *Against Nicomachus* (30), 28.
25. Aubenque 1986, 53–60.
26. *Pericles*, 12.1. Cf. Plutarch, *Were the Athenians More Famous in War or in Peace?*, 348C and 351A.
27. Aelius Aristides, *To Plato, In Defence of the Four* (3), 11–127, and, in particular, 20 (see also *Panathenaica*, 383–392). The speech was composed between 161 and 165 A.D. See Behr 1986, 460.
28. Pausanias, 8.52.3. See the remarks of Pébarthe 2010a, 273–290.
29. See later, chapter 11.

Chapter 1. An Ordinary Young Athenian Aristocrat?

1. Aristotle, *Politics*, 4.4.1291b14–30.
2. Callias I, who was a priest of Eleusis, is the only notable exception, for he also promoted several decrees in the mid-fifth century and negotiated the peace

that bears his name, in 449. It was not until the defeat at Chaeronea in 338 B.C. and the rise of the orator Lycurgus, a member of the Eteoboutadae (who held the priesthood of Poseidon Erechtheus) that a member of a *genos* played an important political role. There is also another historiographical myth that needs to be refuted: there is no attested link between the Philaid *genos*—which may or may not have existed—and the Cimonid family, the origin of which is said to go back to Philaius (Herodotus, 6.35.1). On this subject, see Parker 1996, 316–317.

3. Ps.-Aristotle, *Constitution of the Athenians*, 28.2.

4. Historians of Greek religion do not agree about the roles of the Bouzygae: were they a true priestly family (*genos*) or did they just exercise a religious function in the city? See Parker 1996, 287–288. Whatever the case may be, their function concerned the earth's fertility and the ritual purity of the soil.

5. Eupolis, fr. 103 K.-A., probably from his play, *The Demes*. On this subject, see Storey 2003, 135.

6. See Bourriot 1976, 1270–1275.

7. In Athens, the kinship system was bilateral, with a patrilinear bias. The importance of the maternal branch was strengthened by the law that Pericles himself promoted in 451. See later, chapter 5.

8. Isocrates, *Concerning the Team of Horses* (16), 25.

9. Plutarch is mistaken when he claims that Agariste was the legislator's granddaughter (*Pericles*, 3.1). It is a mistake that is sometimes repeated in certain modern works, such as that of Kagan 1991, 68.

10. According to Thucydides (1.126.10–11), Cylon himself escaped and only his followers took up the position of suppliants at the altar on the Acropolis.

11. See later, chapter 8.

12. Herodotus, 5.59–61.

13. See Gernet 1981, 289–302.

14. Herodotus, 5.131. The historian furthermore suggests that Cleisthenes the Athenian introduced his reforms modeling himself on his grandfather, Cleisthenes of Sicyon, as if his action resembled that of a tyrant (5.65).

15. *IG* I³ 1031 = ML 6C = Fornara 23C. See Pébarthe 2005. Was it in order to wipe out the memory of his ancestor's collaboration that Pericles stressed the action of the tyrannicides in 514, rather than the reforms introduced by Cleisthenes? He certainly seems to be the one who proposed that the descendants of Harmodius and Aristogeiton should thenceforth live at the expense of the city in the Prytaneum, to commemorate the liberating act of their ancestors. Cf. *IG* I³ 131 (between 440 and 432 B.C.), where the proposal is made by a certain "...ikles" (unfortunately, the inscription is mutilated), which many historians believe to be part of the *stratēgos*'s name, on the strength of Wade-Gery 1932–1933, 123–125.

16. Herodotus, 6.115.

17. On this matter, see Williams 1980.

18. Herodotus, 5.92.3.

19. The fact that Pericles physically resembled Pisistratus, the founder of tyranny in Athens, cannot have favored the young man's reputation (Plutarch, *Pericles*, 7.1). On this matter, see later, chapter 10.

20. Plutarch, *Pericles*, 16.2–3.
21. See *Pericles*, 6.2 and 16.5. See later, chapter 5.
22. Plutarch, *Pericles*, 33.2. See later, chapter 6.
23. Thucydides, 2.13.1.
24. See, for example, Kagan 1991, 39.
25. On the number of *liturgists* in Athens, see Gabrielsen 1994. The group of men liable for liturgies numbered around 1,000 to 1,200 individuals. Demosthenes' law of 340 was not designed to reduce their number to 300, but simply to make sure that most of the burden fell upon the 300 Athenians who were the most wealthy.
26. Balot 2001a, 125–126.
27. Herodotus, 6.125.5.
28. Author unknown [*adespota*], fr. 403 Edmonds.
29. Plutarch, *Pericles*, 8.4. On this, see Banfi 2003, 57–58.
30. See for example, Aristophanes, *Clouds*, 1015–1019.
31. Isocrates, *Antidosis* (15), 235: in defense of the role of the sophists, the orator pointed out that "Pericles was the pupil of two sophists, Anaxagoras of Clazomenae and Damon, who was considered the wisest of the citizens in his day."
32. *Phaedrus*, 269e–270a. See later, chapter 6.
33. The same goes for the relations between Pericles and Zeno of Elea, who is mentioned only by Plutarch, *Pericles*, 4.3. See later, chapter 6.
34. According to Plato (*Republic*, 400c), he also had Socrates as a pupil.
35. Plato the comic poet, fr. 207 K.-A.
36. Wallace 2004a.
37. *Pericles*, 4.2. See the doubts expressed by Raaflaub 2003, 317–331, and later, chapter 6.
38. Plutarch, *Cimon*, 4.4.
39. See Lysias, *The Defence of an Anonymous Man Accused of Corruption* (21), 1 (3,000 drachmas for a tragic *khorēgia* in 410), and Lysias, *On the Goods of Aristophanes* (19), 29 and 42 (5,000 drachmas for a tragic *khorēgia* in 392).
40. Wilson 2000, 133–134.
41. Other spectacular liturgies were undertaken by very young citizens: see Demosthenes, *On the Crown* (18), 256–267; Lysias, *The Defence of an Anonymous Man Accused of Corruption* (21), 1 (a tragic *khorēgia* at the age of 18).
42. *Constitution of the Athenians*, 56.2. On the matching of poets to *khorēgoi*, see Antiphon, *On the Choreutes* (6), 11, for the Thargelia (but the procedure was probably similar for the Dionysia).
43. After that first success, Aeschylus won five victories in as many competitions. See Podlecki 1966, 1–7, on Aeschylus's career.
44. *Pericles*, 7.1. Schmitt Pantel 2009, 35.
45. See the doubts expressed by Fornara and Samons II 1991, 158–159.
46. Plutarch, *Cimon*, 14.3–4, recording the testimony of Stesimbrotus of Thasos.
47. This means not that more experienced politicians never attacked their enemies, but rather that they divided their energies between attack and defense. Lycurgus of Athens, who remained an accuser throughout his career, was in this respect a notable exception. On this subject, see Azoulay 2011, 192–204.
48. See Osborne 1990, 83–102; and Christ 1998.

49. Herodotus, 6.104.
50. Herodotus, 6.136. One *ostrakon* describes Xanthippus as *alitērios*, "accursed," a term that probably alludes to the curse laid upon his family-in-law: see Duplouy 2006, 93. However, for a different view, see Valdes Guia 2009, 313–314 (who regards Xanthippus as a member of the Bouzygae *genos*).
51. See Loraux 2001, 71–75.
52. Diodorus Siculus, *Library of History*, 11.77.6. See also Antiphon, *On the Murder of Herodes*, 68; Ps.-Aristotle, *Constitution of the Athenians*, 25.4; Plutarch, *Pericles*, 10.8. On the murder of Ephialtes as an aborted "great cause," see the remarks of Payen 2007a, 30–31.
53. Idomeneus of Lampsacus, *On the Demagogues, FGrHist* 338 F 8 (= Plutarch, *Pericles*, 10.6).
54. On this matter, see Fornara and Samons II 1991, 27–28.

Chapter 2. The Bases of Periclean Power: The *Stratēgos*

1. Thucydides, 1.139.4.
2. Contra, for example, Jouanna 2007, 17 or 31. According to one circular argument, the fact that he served as a *stratēgos* proved that Sophocles, the son of a craftsman, "came from a census class that allowed him to serve as a *stratēgos*" (p. 31). But this involves accepting, without criticism, the a priori assumptions of the late biography, *The Life of Sophocles*, 1: "For it is unlikely that a man born from a modest father should be judged worthy of the office of *stratēgos* alongside Pericles and Thucydides, the foremost leaders of the city." But this in no way proves the existence of any kind of census-barrier denying access to the post of a *stratēgos*.
3. Ps.-Aristotle, *Constitution of the Athenians*, 58. *Stratēgoi* also presided over the people's tribunal for affairs concerning military law and conflicts between trierarchs.
4. This idea, already present in Grote 1870 (vol. 5), 429, stems from an initial reading of Thucydides, 2.59.3, in which Pericles seems, on his own initiative, to convene an assembly. On this matter, see Hansen 1991, 133 and 229.
5. Perlman 1963; and Hamel 1995, 29–31.
6. See Ps.-Aristotle, *Constitution of the Athenians*, 61.1. Five *stratēgoi* were assigned very precise tasks: defending the territory, leading the hoplites, and overseeing the symmories or guarding the Piraeus. Furthermore, the board of *stratēgoi* as a whole could no longer be sent off on expeditions, as used to happen in the fifth century.
7. However, this break should not be exaggerated. As is pointed out by Ober 1989, 91–93 and 120, orators (*rhētores*) and *stratēgoi* were considered to be a coherent group of powerful men who stood out from the mass of ordinary citizens—the *idiōtai*. See, for example, Demosthenes, *On the Crown* (18), 171; Hyperides, *Against Dēmosthenes* (5), fr. 6, col. 24; Dinarchus, *Against Philocles* (3), 19.
8. See Androtion, *FGrHist* 324 F 38 (= Strabo, 14.1.18). He was a member of the office of *Hellēnotamiai*—federal treasurers—in 443/2 (*IG* I³ 269). See Develin 1989, 90; and Jouanna 2007, 23–27.

9. Ion of Chios, *FGrHist* 392 F 6 (= Athenaeus, 13.603E–604F).
10. See later, chapter 6. See also Jouanna 2007, 35–36, who emphasizes Pericles' distrust of the poet's military competence at the time of the war against Samos.
11. Pericles was also elected *stratēgos* three times in succession between 448/7 and 446/5.
12. Androtion, *FGrHist* 324 F 38. In his history of Athens, written in the mid-fourth century, Androtion provides eleven names. But this passage appears to be corrupt and one of those names should probably be suppressed, as almost all commentators agree—for example, Develin 1989, 89; and Harding 1994, 143–148. Only Brulé 1994, 85, claims that the people elected eleven *stratēgoi*: first ten ordinary *stratēgoi*, elected within each tribe, and then Pericles, voted by the whole people to be an exceptional supernumerary *stratēgos*. But there is no proof to support this.
13. On this matter, see Ehrenberg 1945.
14. See Hamel 1998, 86, following Fornara 1971, 71.
15. See Gomme 1956, 183 (ad loc.).
16. *Pericles*, 13.10. See also Plutarch, *Precepts of Statecraft*, 812C: "Pericles used Menippus to command his armies."
17. Lycurgus, [*Against Kephisodotos on the honours allotted to Demades*], fr. 8.2. On these various successes, see later, chapter 4.
18. *Pericles*, 8.6; and Aristotle, *Rhetoric*, 1.7.1365a32–33. In this speech, Pericles resorted to hyperbole, for he evoked those who died in Samos not only by associating them with cosmic cycles ("The year has lost its spring") but also by comparing them to the immortal gods.
19. See, for example, Lycurgus, *Against Leocrates*, 5. On this subject, see Azoulay 2009, 325.
20. Actually, he simply copied a strategy for glorification introduced by Cimon, following the victory over the Persians at Eurymedon: see Aeschines, *Against Ctesiphon* (3), 183; and Demosthenes, *Against Leptines* (20), 112.
21. Pausanias, 1.28.2.
22. Plutarch alludes to a physical abnormality in Pericles' skull, which the *stratēgos* apparently concealed by his helmet (*Pericles*, 3.2): this is a late "medical" explanation for a type of statue that was no longer understood.
23. *Comparison of Pericles and Fabius Maximus*, 1.2.
24. On the careers of these *stratēgoi* who surrounded Pericles, see Podlecki 1998, 55–76.
25. Banfi 2003, 69.
26. *Pericles*, 28.4.
27. Thucydides, 2.41.4.
28. *Pericles*, 10.2.
29. *Pericles*, 29.1–3.
30. See Thucydides, 1.45.2, and *IG* I³ 364 (= ML 61 = Fornara 126 = Brun 116), which cites the names of three *stratēgoi* dispatched on the mission: Lakedaimonius from the Lakiadai deme, Proteas from the Erchia deme, and Diotimus from the Euonymon deme. The Corcyraeans, threatened by a naval expedition of Corinthians, had contracted a defensive military alliance (*epimakhia*) with Athens in 433 B.C.

31. *Pericles*, 18.1.
32. Pericles may have been inspired by the strategy of Themistocles, at the time of the Persian Wars: see Krentz 1997, 62.
33. Thucydides, 1.113.
34. See later, chapter 4.
35. Thucydides, 1.127.3 (author's italics).
36. Aristophanes, *Peace*, 605 ff.: "What started [the war] in the first place was Phidias getting into trouble. Then Pericles became frightened that he might share Phidias's fate—for he was afraid of your character and your hard-biting temper—and before anything terrible could happen to him, he set the city ablaze by dropping in a tiny spark of a Megarian decree: and he fanned up so great a war that all the Greeks were in tears, in the smoke, both those over there and those over here" (trans. Sommerstein 1990).
37. See Rhodes 2006, 88.
38. Plutarch, *Cimon*, 13.6–7. The Phaleron wall had been constructed earlier: see Thucydides, 1.107.1.
39. On this phase of the construction (known as 1b), see Conwell 2008, 77.
40. These different elements are stressed in Thucydides' account (1.143.4–1.144.1). See Conwell 2008, 81.
41. See later, chapter 8.
42. The "plague" that struck Athens at the beginning of the war was apparently a form of typhus, although this is still a subject of debate among specialists.
43. Hermippus, *Moirai*, fr. 47 K.-A. (= Plutarch, *Pericles*, 33.7). The poet Cratinus launched into similar attacks in this same period. See Tatti 1986, 325–332, and the nuances introduced by Bakola 2010, 181–208.
44. On these various area sizes, see Bresson 2007, 150.
45. Ps.-Xenophon, *Constitution of the Athenians*, 2.14.
46. Thucydides, 2.62.3.
47. See Ober 1985, 171–188.
48. See Thucydides, 2.65.

Chapter 3. The Bases of Periclean Power: The Orator

1. Thucydides, 2.40.2.
2. Aeschines, *Against Ctesiphon* (3), 2.
3. Aeschines, ibid. For an analysis of this democratic tumult, see later, chapter 10.
4. The fact that two men proposed the same decree in no way implied that they agreed on the city's policies as a whole—as was the case, for example, of Demades and Lycurgus, in the fourth century. See Brun 2000, 135–136.
5. *Gorgias*, 452e. This dialogue, composed in the fourth century by Plato, describes a clash between Socrates and Gorgias in the late 410s. Although the term "rhetoric," for a specific *tekhnē*, was probably invented by Plato, as early as the mid-fifth century the arts of discourse were not unknown to the Athenians: Schiappa 1990, 457–470.
6. Euripides, *Suppliant Women*, 425.
7. These speeches, constructed with great care, contain numerous allusions to the works of the sophists and the tragic authors. To mention but one example,

Pericles, in one of the speeches ascribed to him by Thucydides (2.61.2), uses a metric trimeter that probably came from a tragedy well-known to the Athenians. See Haslam 1990, 33.

8. Thucydides, 1.22.1.

9. See, for example, Thucydides, 2.61.2: "For my part, I stand where I stood before and do not recede from my position; but it is you who have changed. For it has happened, now you are suffering, that you repent of the consent that you gave me when you were still unscathed, and in your infirmity of purpose my advice to you now appears wrong."

10. "By instruction and reason, Pericles tries to discourage all mistaken popular action and to transform the crowd into a collection of responsible individuals": Tsakmakis 2006, 168.

11. Plutarch, *Pericles*, 8.5. See earlier, chapter 1.

12. *Kentron* often denotes the masculine phallus. See Henderson 1975, 122. See also Xenophon, *Memorabilia*, 1.3.12, where Socrates compares a kiss to the sting of a spider: "Don't you know that the scorpion, though smaller than a farthing, if it but fasten on the tongue, inflicts excruciating and maddening pain?" Speech, like beauty, can produce a sting from a distance.

13. *Pericles*, 8.3. See also Aristophanes, *Acharnians*, 530–531.

14. See Detienne and Vernant 1991, 75–79.

15. Cratinus, fr. 171 K.-A., I, 18–22. See Bakola 2010, 49–53 and 317 (the passage is unfortunately very mutilated and the sense is not certain). On the implications of this identification with Zeus, see later, chapter 8.

16. In Athens, this way of distinguishing oneself was very ambivalent: although the Athenians were fascinated by the power of language, they also deeply distrusted it. In the fourth century, the speeches of Attic orators even testify to the existence of "an anti-rhetoric rhetoric," the aim of which was to criticize the excessive skill of their opponents in such a way as to make the people mistrust them. See Hesk 1999, 208–218.

17. *Pericles*, 5.1.

18. Ps.-Aristotle, *Constitution of the Athenians*, 28.3.

19. Respectively, Thucydides, 3.36.6, and Aristophanes, *Knights*, 137.

20. Aeschines, *Against Timarchus* (1), 25–26.

21. Plutarch, *Pericles*, 34.1. See earlier, Thucydides, 2.60.1.

22. Plutarch, *Pericles*, 5.2–3. It was this singular ability to tolerate insults that prompted Plutarch to compare Pericles to Fabius Maximus, who was himself expert at doing this: see Plutarch, *Pericles*, 2.4. See Bloomer 2005, 224.

23. Demosthenes, *Against Midias* (21), 32–33.

24. As Aristotle states, in *Nicomachean Ethics*, 1126a6–8, "it is considered servile [*andrapodōdes*] to put up with an insult or to suffer one's friends to be insulted."

25. Tanner 2006, 128–129.

26. Ion of Chios, *FGrHist* 392 F 15 (= Plutarch, *Pericles*, 5.3).

27. In *Hippolytus*, 91–96, Euripides explicitly underlines the risks of a solemnity that may soon be taken for arrogance.

28. Cratinus, fr. 348 K.-A.: *anelktais ophrusi semnon*. See Banfi 2003, 41.

29. Demosthenes, *On the Embassy* (19), 314 (author's italics). See Tanner 2006, 129–130.

30. Frowning brows such as these characterize both tragic kings in South Italian fourth-century painting and the effigy of Philip of Macedon, exhibited in the Copenhagen Glyptotek (a Roman bust, a copy of an original of the late-fourth century).
31. *Precepts of Statecraft*, 812C–D. See also *Pericles*, 7.7: "the rest of his policy, he carried out by commissioning his friends and other public speakers."
32. Ps.-Demosthenes, *Against Neaera* (59), 43. See Ps.-Aristotle, *The Constitution of the Athenians*, 29.1–3 for an example that goes back to the fifth century: at the time of the establishment of the regime of the Four Hundred, in 411, Melobius addressed the people, but it was Pythodorus who made the proposal. On this, see Hansen 1991, 145–146.
33. Metiochus may have been the brother-in-law of Cimon, Pericles' great opponent, which shows that hostile relations between great families were by no means definitive in Athens (Herodotus, 6.41.2).
34. *Adespota* [author unknown], fr. 741 K.-A.
35. See Plutarch, *Pericles*, 6.2–3.
36. Cratinus, *Drapetides* (*The Runaway Female Slaves*), fr. 57–58 and 62 K.-A.
37. See later, chapter 4.
38. Aeschines, *Against Ctesiphon* (3), 220.
39. *Precepts of Statecraft*, 811C–D.
40. See later, chapter 8.

CHAPTER 4. PERICLES AND ATHENIAN IMPERIALISM

1. Diodorus Siculus, 12.4.4–6. Even if the existence of such a treaty is not entirely certain—since Thucydides makes no mention of it—the fact is that from 449 B.C. onward the Persians and the Greeks were no longer de facto at war.
2. See Lewis 1992, 121–146.
3. *IG* I^3 34 = ML 46 = Fornara 98 = Brun 9.
4. See later, chapter 5.
5. The term is used for the first time by Thucydides (1.117.3) in connection with Byzantium. See Raaflaub 2004, 118–122.
6. See, for example, Mattingly 1992.
7. Brun 2003, 24. On this thorny question, see the helpful assessment by Papazarkadas 2009.
8. This is, in particular, the position adopted by Mattingly 1996, 147–179 ("Periclean imperialism"): "None of the inscriptional evidence for fully organized Athenian imperialism can be dated before 431 B.C. Even the very language of imperialism does not seem to have been current until the last years of Pericles' ascendancy" (p. 178).
9. See Banfi 2003, 64.
10. Thucydides, 1.100.2–101.3.
11. *IG* I^3 14 = ML 40 (ca. 453/2 B.C.?).
12. Gauthier 1973, 163–178.
13. That is the hypothesis of Briant 1995, 51–52.
14. See Kagan 1991, 141, on Samos: "There must have been some sentiment in Athens for a harsher punishment, but Pericles was able to convince the Athenians

to restrain their anger. This moderation was characteristic of Pericles' management of the empire in the remaining years before the Peloponnesian War. By
the standards of the time, and sharply in contrast with Athenian practice after
Pericles' death, his was a firm but reasonable policy." The American historian
joins a long tradition going back to George Grote and Victor Duruy in the
mid-nineteenth century, analyzed later, in chapter 12.

15. See also Romilly 2000.

16. Thucydides, 1.114.1. See Diodorus, 12.22.2.

17. Plutarch, *Pericles*, 23.2.

18. See *IG* I³ 39–40 (decrees for the Euboean cities of Eretria and Chalcis).

19. *Clouds*, 211–213. See Aristophanes, *Wasps*, 715, and the anonymous comic
author [*adespota*], fr. 700 K.-A. (= Plutarch, *Pericles*, 7.8): after Ephialtes, "the
people were rendered unruly, just like a horse, and, as the comic poets say, 'no
longer had the patience to obey the rein, but nabbed Euboea and trampled on
the islands.'"

20. See Meritt 1984, 123–133.

21. *IG* I³ 363 (= ML 55). On this repayment, see Thucydides, 1.117.3. The Samians subsequently became a model of fidelity up until the end of the Peloponnesian War, for they remained committed to the Athenians despite the progressive dislocation of the Delian League.

22. *Pericles*, 26.3–4. The lexicographer Photius (*s.v. Samiōn ho dēmos*) tells the
story, attributing it to Douris of Samos (*FGrHist* 76 F 66). In the *Babylonians*
(fr. 71 K.-A.), Aristophanes also alludes to this episode: "This people of Samos,
how rich in letters [*polugrammatos*] it is!" This remark probably refers to the
coinage of the island, for there was a Samian monetary series (class VII, identified by Barron 1966), marked with different letters of the alphabet, possibly
indicating the year of coinage. These coins were minted either by the aristocrats
before 440, or else by the democrats after that date, possibly for paying the in-
demnities of war. See Shipley 1987, 114 (and n. 12).

23. Jones 1987, 149.

24. See Suda, *s.v. Samiōn ho dēmos*. We know of a Samian currency, dated 493–
489, representing the prow of a Samian ship, with a ram that is an extension of
the keel. The prow of this vessel is particularly wide and the ram is very large.
See Basch 1987, no. 520. See also von Reden 1997, 174.

25. Douris of Samos, *FGrHist* 76 F 67 (= Plutarch, *Pericles, 28.1–2*). Significantly
enough, Donald Kagan chooses not to mention this episode that is so inconve-
nient for his exposition.

26. See Allen 2000, 199–200. This punishment is marked by a series of distinct
stages: exposure in a public place (the Agora); attachment to a piece of wood;
torture and death; and finally the abandonment of the corpses without any
funerary rituals.

27. Herodotus, 9.120.4. See also 7.33.

28. See Tracy 2002, 315–319 and Balot 2001a, 126.

29. *Pericles*, 34.1. In his description of this episode, Thucydides (2.27.1–2) does
not mention Pericles by name, perhaps out of respect for the *stratēgos*, whom
he admires.

30. The reason why, in 483 B.C., Themistocles managed to persuade his fellow-citizens to use the money discovered in the Laurium mines to construct a fleet of triremes, was not in order to face up to a hypothetical Persian invasion, a notion at that point still in limbo, but rather in order to go and subdue the Aeginetans; see Herodotus, 7.7.
31. Plutarch, *Pericles*, 8.5.
32. See earlier, Bloedow 2000.
33. This argument may seem strange. According to Pericles, the least sign of submission represents a form of slavery. He cannot conceive of anything in between *arkhē* and *douleia*, domination and dependence: either one dominates or else one is dominated.
34. See Thucydides, 3.47; Aristophanes, *Knights*, 1111 (424 B.C.), who presents the people, adorned by splendors worthy of the Great King and "feared by all as if it were a tyrant." See Tuplin 1985, and Balot 2001a, 172–175.
35. Cratinus, *The Women of Thrace*, fr. 73 K.-A. (= *Pericles*, 13.6). The *ostrakon* refers to the exile of his opponent Thucydides of Alopeke in 443 B.C.
36. Some historians even believe that the royal tent served as scenery in the performance of Aeschylus's *Persians*, of which Pericles was the *khorēgos*. From there to detecting an interplay of influences is but a step that nothing, however, authorizes one to take.
37. Briant 2002, 256–258.
38. Miller 1997, 218–242.
39. Ibid., 242.
40. See Raaflaub 2009, 111.
41. See later, chapter 5.
42. At first, the monument itself was simply called "the great temple" or "the temple." It was only at the end of the fourth century, from the time of Demosthenes onward, that the expression was used to refer to the temple as a whole.
43. We should remember that the cult-statue of Athena was to be found, not in the Parthenon, but in the Erechtheion. The colossal statue by Phidias was an offering, not a cult-statue. See Holtzmann 2003, 106.

Chapter 5. A Periclean Economy?

1. Saller 2005, 233.
2. See Bresson 2007, 150–151.
3. See earlier, chapter 1.
4. See Kurke 1999. On this peculiarly Periclean way of managing an *oikos*, see Burn 1948, 125.
5. *Pericles*, 16.5.
6. Bresson 2000.
7. Descat 1995, 969.
8. *Pericles*, 16.4.
9. These boundary markers came in various types. The most common model consisted of a mortgage guaranteeing a loan of money: it took the form of a sale "on the condition of a liberating repurchase" (*prasis epi lusei*). The borrower "sold" his property to a creditor, promising to buy it back within an agreed

period, by repaying the borrowed sum plus interest (12 to 18 percent per year). In the meantime, the debtor owner retained the usufruct (right of use) of his property.

10. Finley 1981, 62–76. However, returning to the evidence, Shipton 2000 has shown that wealthy Athenians were also deeply involved in nonagricultural sectors.

11. See earlier, *Pericles*, 16.4. In Aristophanes' *Clouds*, the character Pheidippides closely resembles the young Xanthippus.

12. Ps.-Aristotle, *Oeconomica*, I.6.1344b32.

13. The ancient authors suggest three names, Aristides, Cimon, and Pericles, but there is no way of knowing for certain. See Pritchett 1971, 7–14 for the sources and commentary.

14. The Mediterranean Sea was "closed" to navigation during the winter, from November to February, because of the winds and storms that blew up and the fragility of military vessels; soldiers usually slept on land, rather than on their ships, at sea.

15. Ps.-Aristotle, *Constitution of the Athenians*, 24–25.1.

16. Ibid., 24.2–3.

17. The earliest example even dates from before the creation of the alliance: in 506, the Athenians confiscated the land of the Chalcidian aristocrats and divided them into 4,000 *klēroi* that were assigned to citizens who, having become cleruchs, obtained part of the harvest without having to cultivate the land themselves.

18. Plutarch, *Pericles*, 11.5.

19. Tolmides had already taken some to the island, as Diodorus Siculus reports (11.88.3).

20. Moreno 2009, 213–214.

21. *IG* I³ 46, 43–46 = ML 49, 39–42: "Let the colonists for Brea be taken from among the thetes and the *zeugitae*." See Figueira 1991, 59–60.

22. See Moreno 2009, 213–214.

23. See Foxhall and Forbes 1982.

24. Moreno 2007, 32–33, has recently indicated Athens's heavy dependence on grain by increasing (to 75 percent) the calculations of Garnsey 1989, 89–164 (50 percent). Whatever the figure accepted, one thing is certain: Athens depended largely on the outside world in order to feed its population.

25. These calculations are based on the figures provided by Demosthenes, *Against Leptines* (20), 31–33 (ca. 355 B.C.), who mentions a total of 800,000 *medimnoi* of cereals imported by Athens every year.

26. *Pericles*, 11.5. This may possibly be the expedition to which the inscription *IG* I³ 1162 refers.

27. *IG* I³ 61 = ML 65 = Fornara 128 = Brun 15.

28. However, we should not anticipate the law of Agyrrhius, dated 374/3, which stipulates that Athenian merchants do not have the right to unload wheat from the Pontus anywhere apart from Piraeus. Concern about supplies of wheat remained constant throughout the whole classical period, peaking in the 330s on account of the food shortages that affected the Aegean world at that time. See Oliver 2007.

29. Thucydides, 2.38.2.
30. These inscriptions, published by American scholars, are generally known as the Athenian Tribute Lists (ATL). According to calculations based on the ATL, whereas the number of allies is much higher than in 478, the total sum is much lower than the 460 talents mentioned by Thucydides, for it amounts only to about 400 talents. Instead of doubting the figure given by Thucydides, we should perhaps consider two alternative solutions: either the figure given by the historian also includes the value of the triremes and the pay for the troops—that is to say, the estimated value of the *phoros* in kind—or the figures given by the ATL refer only to the *surplus* of the tribute brought to Athens, with the expenses for military operations already deducted.
31. See earlier, chapter 4.
32. Thucydides, 2.13.3–5.
33. Of course, it might have been a way of safeguarding appearances where the accounts were concerned: even today, after all, in the state budget there are many "slippages" between different categories of expenses.
34. See later, chapter 8.
35. Kallet-Marx 1989, 252–266; Giovannini 1990 and Giovannini 1997; but see Samons 1993. It is true that the use of the *aparkhē* for the great works is attested by the Propylaea accounts.
36. Plutarch, *Pericles*, 12.5–7.
37. See Descat 1995, 978.
38. Austin and Vidal-Naquet 1977, 276–282, no. 73. See Feyel 2006, 322–325.
39. Wages were sometimes paid, not by the day, but for particular piecework. That was the case for the cutters of flutes for the columns or for the sculptors of the figurines for the outside frieze of the building, made from Eleusis marble. These tasks, which were far better paid, could be accomplished by citizens or by metics, but not by slaves, who were never employed for work that required such skills.
40. Glotz 1931, 178–184. See later, chapter 12.
41. Plutarch, *Pericles*, 11.4. See later, chapter 8.
42. Ulpian, *Ad Demosthenem, Olynthian I*. See Wilson 2000, 167 and 265–266. In the fourth century, the *theorikōn* coffer received all the surpluses from the revenues (*prosodoi*). The allocation from the theoric fund appears to have been two obols (Demosthenes, *On the Crown* (18), 28)—one to pay for a seat, the other to cover the spectator's needs during the day.
43. See Stadter 1989, 116–117.
44. *Gorgias*, 515e.
45. Plutarch, *Pericles*, 9.3.
46. The courts judged public and private affairs on three hundred days of the year (Aristophanes, *Wasps*, 661–663). Remuneration was always paid not annually but daily, so this varied according to the judges who sat.
47. Ps.-Aristotle, *Constitution of the Athenians*, 27.3; and Plutarch, *Pericles*, 9.2.
48. See Verilhac and Vial 1998; and Patterson 1981.
49. *Pericles*, 37.3–4. The date of the reform is deduced from a passage in Ps.-Aristotle, *Constitution of the Athenians*, 26.3: "three years after Lysicrates in the year of [the archonship of] Antidotus, owing to the large number of the

citizens, an enactment was passed on the proposal of Pericles confining citizenship to persons of citizen birth on both sides [*astoin*]."

50. See later, chapter 8. But this agreement is paradoxical when one considers that autochthony was primarily a way of conceiving of birth in the community without the need of any woman's womb: after 451, a woman became necessary to transmit a citizenship that she herself did not actively possess.

51. Furthermore, by means of this endogamous measure, the city discouraged matrimonial alliances that members of the elite contracted outside the Athenian world. It is worth noting that no marriage of this type is recorded between 508 and 451, as if Athenian matrimonial practices had anticipated this reform. See Wilgaux 2010.

52. See French 1994; and Patterson 1981.

53. See Thucydides, 2.13.6–7: in the first year of the Peloponnesian War, the expedition against Megara included, as well as 10,000 Athenian hoplites, 3,000 metics, to whom should be added 3,000 metics sent at the same time to Potidaea (II, 31, 2). See Rhodes 1988, 271–277.

54. See Isaac 2004, 116–124.

55. See Noiriel 2001.

CHAPTER 6. PERICLES AND HIS CIRCLE: FAMILY AND FRIENDS

1. See *Alcibiades*, 1.1. See the convincing reconstruction by Brulé 2003, 115–116; and Schmitt Pantel 2007, 202–204.

2. Leduc 2003, 279.

3. See, for example, Plato, *Alcibiades* I, 121a; Plutarch, *Alcibiades*, 1.1; and the remarks of Parker 1996, 323 (and n. 94).

4. See Cox 1989: Matrimonial alliances did not automatically lead to political support. On the contrary, it was within the family, often, that attacks on one another were the most ferocious, even leading to the dissemination of dreadful rumors about one's relatives.

5. See earlier, chapter 5.

6. However, this name could be analyzed in a different manner. By choosing to name his younger son in this way, Pericles may also have been referring to the faction of coastal citizens (the "Paralians") led by his great-grandfather, Megacles, one century earlier. The name "Paralus" therefore made it possible to play upon two registers: allegiance to the people and family fame. See Burn 1948, 60.

7. Hippocleides, one of the suitors of Agariste, the daughter of the tyrant of Sicyon, set to dancing on the table in the course of one banquet in which too much wine was flowing, thereby covering himself in ridicule in the eyes of the future bride's father (Herodotus, 6.129–130). In the end, it was the Alcmaeonid Megacles, Pericles' ancestor, who won the hand of Agariste.

8. In Iasos, "it was forbidden to entertain more than ten men and ten women as wedding-guests" and the festivities were not allowed to last for more than two days: see Heraclides of Lembos, *Excerpta Politiarum*, fr. 66 Gigon (= Dilts 1971, 38–39). See also Plutarch, *Solon*, 20.4 (on the value of dowries). The fourth-century philosophers continued to reflect upon the need to regulate marriage celebrations: Plato, *Laws*, 6.775a–b; Aristotle, *Nicomachean Ethics*, 9.2.1169b.

9. The number of women in a funeral procession was limited so as not to encourage excessive manifestations of grief: see Ps.-Demosthenes, *Against Macartatus* (43), 62; Cicero, *De Legibus*, 2.65.

10. This custom is reflected in, for example, Aeschylus's *Choephoroi* (l. 8–9), when Orestes bitterly regrets not having been able to join the funeral procession of his father, Agamemnon.

11. See later, chapter 8.

12. See Loraux 1986, 180–202; and Loraux 1993b, 37–71 and 111–143.

13. Ober 1989, 259–266; and earlier, chapter 5.

14. Murray 1990. The association of oligarchic revolutions and the *sumposion* is well attested by the fourth-century Attic orators: see Ps.-Demosthenes, *Against Stephanus* 2 (46), 26; Hyperides, *For Euxenippus* (4), 7–8.

15. Connor, 1992.

16. See Aelian, *Miscellany*, 2.12.

17. That is true in particular in the case of Cleon, as W. R. Connor remarks in passing (Connor 1992, 104, n. 26). Yet, like Pericles, Cleon had made a show of cutting himself off from his former circle of friends when he entered political life. He hoped, by this means, to show that his sole concern was the well-being of the *dēmos* (Connor 1992, 129–131) and that he was following the example set by Pericles.

18. Xenophon, *Hellenica*, 1.4.18–20.

19. For an analytical study of the sources and historiography of this question, see Podlecki 1998.

20. See Stadter 1991. On Protagoras and Pericles, see later, chapter 8.

21. Lysias, *Against Eratosthenes* (12), 4. The same applies to Herodotus, "the father of history": see earlier, introduction.

22. Plutarch, *Pericles*, 32.1. The date of the trial suggested by Ephorus is probably without foundation. Philochorus, in his *Atthis* (*FGrHist* 328 F 121), claims that the sentence was passed seven or eight years (*hepta etesin*) before the outbreak of the war. See Banfi 1999.

23. Plutarch, *Pericles*, 13.9. See later, chapter 7.

24. Aristophanes, *Peace*, 604–609 (referring to "the setbacks of Phidias"). Phidias was probably accused of appropriating public funds at the time of the construction of the statue of Athena Parthenos. See Diodorus Siculus, 12.39.1–2, who repeats Ephorus's version.

25. Ps.-Aristotle, *Constitution of the Athenians*, 27.4. The Greek text gives the name of his father, Damonides, but that is probably an error. See the discussion in Rhodes 1993, 341–342 (ad loc.). See earlier, chapter 5.

26. Plutarch, *Pericles*, 4.1. See earlier, chapter 1.

27. See Siewert 2002, 50: *Damon Damonidou (Oathen)*. On the ostracism of Damon, however, see the doubts expressed by Raaflaub 2003.

28. Cratinus, fr. 118 K.-A.; and Bakola 2010, 222–223. On the meaning of this assimilation to Zeus, see later, chapter 8.

29. Thucydides, 2.13.1 (repeated by Plutarch, *Pericles*, 33.2). On the *xenia* linking the two men and its consequences in the early days of the war, see Herman 1987, 142–145.

30. It is not the case that links of *xenia* were totally proscribed in Athens, but aristocratic networks were becoming increasingly controlled both within the *polis* and beyond it: they were no longer recognized in the city unless they served the interests of Athens. See Mitchell 1998, 106, which opposes in particular the overstated view of Herman 1987, 156–161.

CHAPTER 7. PERICLES AND *EROS*: CAUGHT BETWEEN CIVIC UNITY AND POLITICAL SUBVERSION

1. Scholtz 2007, 13–17; Wohl 2002, 30–72; Ludwig 2002, 7–14.
2. Aristotle, fr. 98 Rose (= Plutarch, *Dialogue on Love [Erotikos]*, 760E–761B). See Calame 1999, 108–109.
3. Thucydides, 2.43.1. See Aeschylus, *Eumenides*, 851–853. For an analysis of this passage, see Monoson 2000, 64–87 (chapter 3: "Citizen as *Erastēs* [lover]: erotic imagery and the idea of reciprocity in the Periclean funeral oration").
4. Winkler 1990, 47.
5. Monoson 2000, 83. See also Balot 2001b, 511–512.
6. Lévy 1976, 141.
7. *Knights*, 732. See also *Knights*, 783–789, 871–872, 1163, 1340; *Wasps*, 699.
8. On this traditional identification, see Connor 1992, 96.
9. Far from giving themselves to honest citizens, the people surrender only to lamp-lighters, cobblers, or leather merchants, "just like pretty boys [*paides*], those lover-tormenters [*erōmenoi*]": *Knights*, 736–740 (based on the modified French translation by Debidour).
10. Golden 1984. Contra Dover 1978, 84, according to whom "homosexual relationships in Greek society are regarded as the product not of the reciprocal sentiment of equals but of the pursuit of those of lower status [that is, *erōmenoi*] by those of higher status [that is, *erastai*]."
11. Plato, *Meno*, 76b. However old he may be, the *erastēs* may become the slave of the *erōmenos*: see Xenophon, *Memorabilia*, 1.3.11, *Symposium*, 4.14, *Oeconomicus*, 1.22; Plato, *Symposium*, 183a, and *Phaedrus*, 252a.
12. Golden 1984, 314–315 (examples cited in nn. 34–35).
13. Golden 1984, 315 (with many examples in n. 37). According to this author, these conventions are designed to set aside the *real* subordination of the *erōmenos*. The fact is the latter is usually a young Athenian close to adulthood whom it would be embarrassing to represent in a subjected position, let alone a degraded one.
14. See Monoson 2000, 81–82; and, more generally, Sebillotte Cuchet 2006.
15. "There are spells [*epoidas*], they say, wherewith those who know charm whom they will and make friends of them and drugs which those who know give to whom they choose and win their love" (*Memorabilia*, 2.6.10).
16. Ibid., 2.6.13.
17. See Winkler 1990, 76–77.
18. Eupolis, *The Demes*, fr. 102 K.-A. See earlier, chapter 3.
19. Vernant 1990, 40, describes the way that a lover is haunted by the image of the loved one as follows: "A vision of him, instead of delighting him as would the sight of the real person, produces, not pleasure but, precisely, *pothos*, a nostalgic regret that he is absent."

20. *Pericles*, 37.1. According to Aristophanes, *Frogs* (1425), *pothos* is also the word for what the people feel about the handsome Alcibiades: "[The people] long for him [*pothei men*], detest him, and yet desire him."
21. *Pericles*, 39.4.
22. Plutarch, *Pericles*, 8.5. This anecdote echoes a tradition that can be traced back to Ion of Chios, according to whom the tragic poet was a better *stratēgos* in the domain of love than in that of warfare: see Ion of Chios, *FGrHist* 392 F 6 (= Athenaeus, 13.603E–604F).
23. See Azoulay 2004, 375 f.
24. Schwarze 1971, 111–112.
25. Plutarch, *Pericles*, 13.9. See earlier, chapter 6.
26. Schmitt Pantel 2007, 205.
27. Lysias, *On the Murder of Eratosthenes* (1), 33, with the commentary of Patterson 1998, 166–174. In the Athenian attempt at suppressing adultery, the question of the child's legitimacy is central. That is why a rape is less grave than adultery: better a one-off criminal act than a slow process of corruption that may cast doubt on the legitimacy of the marriage's already existing children. On this subject, see Harris 1990.
28. At the end of the fifth century, the comic poet Strattis (fr. 28 K.-A. = Athenaeus, 14.654F) was linking the breeding of peacocks with frivolity and luxury.
29. Cartledge 1990, 52–54; Miller 1997, 189–192.
30. Plato, *Charmides*, 158a. Pyrilampes, a friend of Pericles and married to Plato's mother, was wounded and captured at Delion in 424 (Plutarch, *The Genius of Socrates*, 581D). Although extremely wealthy, he had named his son Demos, which shows his desire to conform with the democratic ideology (see Plato, *Gorgias*, 481d, for a pun on his name). See the family tree in Cartledge 1990, 45–46.
31. Antiphon, fr. 58 Thalheim. See Cartledge 1990, 53 n. 52; and Miller 1997, 191. *Ornithotrophia*, the breeding of birds, was an activity even more distinctive than the breeding of horses, *hippotrophia*, which itself also aroused suspicions among the people. A number of discovered *ostraka* testify to how people reacted to this in the way they voted: horse breeding suggested that one was too wealthy to be honest.
32. Héritier, Cyrulnik, and Naouri 1994. However, see Bonnard 2002.
33. *Pericles*, 13.11. See also 36.3.
34. Hermippus, *Moirai*, fr. 47 K.-A. (= *Pericles*, 33.7); and Cratinus, *Dionysalexandros* (K.-A., p. 140).
35. See earlier, chapter 2.
36. On satyrs as highly sexed creatures, see Lissarrague 1990.
37. Heraclides Ponticus, fr. 59 Wehrli (= Athenaeus, 12.533C). Heraclides Ponticus (or Athenaeus, who cites him) here confuses Miletus and Megara. The confusion is probably linked to a faulty reading of Aristophanes' *Acharnians*, 524–531, where the comic poet mentions the Megarians' seizure of two courtesans trained by Aspasia.
38. Athenaeus, 13.589E.
39. Antisthenes, *SSR* Va 143 (= Plutarch, *Pericles*, 24.6). Antisthenes is probably Plutarch's source, for Athenaeus attributes exactly the same story to him in his *Deipnosophistae* (13.589E).

40. Brulé 2003, 196. See Loraux 2003, 161–162.
41. *Pericles*, 32.1. Loraux 2003, 159.
42. Loraux 2003, 140.
43. Callias, *Pedetai*, fr. 21 K.-A.: in this play, dated, according to the authors, either to the late 430s or else to soon after the peace of 421 B.C., Pericles learns from Aspasia how to speak in public.
44. Schmitt Pantel 2007, 213: "But, in any case, the two statuses—whore and teacher of rhetoric—are perhaps not really all that opposed: both refer to the register of seduction; among the Greeks, *peithō* was as much a matter of rhetoric as of sexual attraction." Rhetoric, like love, can establish one's control over others.
45. See Lenfant 2003a, 402.
46. Alexis of Samos, *FGrHist* 539 F 1 = Athenaeus, 13.572F.
47. See D'Hautcourt 2006, according to whom the sanctuary was founded after a naval victory, as thanks to Aphrodite, the goddess of sea navigation—not by prostitutes.
48. Text: Kassel and Austin 1983, 140, col. I (1–25) and II (26–48); text and translation, Edmonds 1957, 32–33; and now also Bakola 2010, 320–321 (appendix 4).
49. See Tatti 1986; and McGlew 2002, 46–56. The three gifts offered to Paris are supposed to symbolize the main resources of the Periclean government: Aphrodite offers him beauty and love, Athena courage in warfare, and Hera tyranny. Bakola 2010, 180–208, nevertheless refuses to analyze the play purely as an allegory and insists upon what she calls "the multi-layered composition of the play"; in the play, "Dionysus acts sometimes as the god familiar from satyr plays and comedies, sometimes as the Paris/Alexandros of the *Iliad*, sometimes as 'Pericles', and sometimes as an initiand" (p. 207).
50. Mattingly 1977, 231–245, nevertheless emphasizes that the *Dionysalexandros* could just as well date from the early 430s and refer to the campaign against Samos—which involved Miletus, Aspasia's birthplace. The poet doubtless presented Pericles in the guise of Dionysus-Paris, carrying a *thyrsus* and a drinking vessel and surrounded by a chorus of satyrs.
51. Aristophanes, *Acharnians*, 524–531.
52. Aeschines Socraticus, *SSR*, VIa III, 61 (in which the philosopher, bent on his task of rehabilitation, tries to dissociate Aspasia from the detestable image of her Ionian sisters).
53. Montuori 1981, 87–109; the argument is based on a passage in which Plutarch describes the beautiful Thargelia, who "stealthily sowed the seeds of Persian sympathy" and who, it is suggested, Aspasia took as her model (*Pericles*, 24.2).
54. On Aspasia as a *hetaira*, see for example Keuls 1993, 198 ("the best known hetaira of the Classical age"). On Aspasia as an intellectual, see Stadter 1991, 123.
55. See Henry 1995.
56. Cratinus, fr. 241 K.-A. (= Plutarch, *Pericles*, 24.6).
57. Eupolis, *Demes*, fr. 110 K.-A.
58. On all these names, see Halperin 1990, 111.
59. *FGrHist* 372 F 40 (fourth century B.C.). There was no reason why Pericles and Aspasia should not have been married: the law of 451 affected only the status

of any children they might have and did not imply any illegality of the marriage itself. Marriage was a private affair that was none of the city's business.

60. Bicknell 1982.

Chapter 8. Pericles and the City Gods

1. Sourvinou-Inwood 1990, 295–322.
2. Xenophon, *Hellenica*, 2.4.20–21.
3. Ps.-Aristotle, *Constitution of the Athenians*, 47.1 (Treasurers of Athena) and 54.6–7 (*hieropoioi*).
4. *IG* I³ 363 = ML 55 = Fornara 113. See Boedeker 2007, 57–58.
5. Thucydides 2.13.4.
6. See *IG* II² 134 (around 335 B.C.).
7. Thucydides, 2.38.1.
8. *Constitution of the Athenians*, 3.1–2 (author's italics).
9. Ibid., 2.9.
10. Plutarch, *Pericles*, 11.4 (trans. Perrin, modified).
11. See the discussion in Planeaux (2000–2001).
12. *Pericles*, 13.6. In the early fourth century, the first day of the Panathenaea—which lasted for over a week—was devoted to musical and rhapsodic competitions: See *IG* II² 2311.
13. Many vases dating from the late Archaic period already carry scenes of musical performances in a Panathenaic framework, so such competitions must already have taken place before the time of Pericles. See Neils 1992, 57.
14. See also Etienne 2004, 67, which mentions that in Phocis, at Kalapodi, a memorial was erected in the sanctuary ruined in the Persian wars.
15. This hall, which was begun in 450, was not completed until the 420s.
16. Parker 1996, 154.
17. See earlier, chapter 5.
18. *Pericles*, 13.4–7. But even this statement needs to be qualified: see later, chapter 10.
19. Cimon had even begun work on the Acropolis, constructing a surrounding wall; this contained the sacred space where the remains of the old temple of Athena that the Persians had destroyed stood on the northern side that faced the Agora, so that "it showed to all who saw it that the divinity of the Acropolis was not neglected even if the ban on reconstructing the sanctuary was respected"; see Etienne 2004, 69.
20. *IG* I³ 34 = ML 46 = Brun 9.
21. See Shapiro 1996.
22. See Blok 2009 (which clarifies the chronology adopted by Loraux 1993b, 37–71, esp. 41, which mentioned only "a myth of the fifth century").
23. See, for example, Plato, *Menexenus*, 237B (in an ironic mode); Lycurgus, *Against Leocrates*, 100; Demosthenes, *Funeral Oration*, 4; Hyperides, *Funeral Oration*, 4.
24. Rosivach 1987.
25. See Herodotus, 8.73 (Arcadians), 1.171 (Carians), 4.197 (Libyans and Ethiopians).

26. *Iliad*, 2.546–549.
27. Gantz 1993, 235–236. Before the date of the testimony of Euripides, Athenian painters of images were already representing the birth of Erechtheus (from 490 B.C. onward). The scene chosen is nearly always the same: Gaia, half-buried in the earth that she symbolizes, entrusts Erechtheus to Athena, who picks him up and clasps him in her arms, copying the gesture made by a father to his son in the Amphidromia ritual.
28. Blok 2009, 153.
29. Euripides, *Erechtheus*, fr. 14, lines 8–10, Jouan-Van Looy.
30. On the question of dates, see Camp 1986, 87, who suggests a range of possible dates, between 460–450/448, for the start of the project.
31. Brun 2005a, 249.
32. *IG* I³ 82 = Brun 129.
33. Rolley 1999, 144–145. This makes it easier to understand why the exploits of Theseus were represented on the metopes surrounding the temple, causing interpreters for a long time to believe that the edifice was dedicated to him. In fact, though, the Athenians were representing the exploits of the founder of the Athenian political community, who in this way mirrored the figure of Erechtheus, who was himself placed in the position of founding father.
34. Thucydides, 2.36.1.
35. See earlier, chapter 7.
36. Etienne 2004, 88–89.
37. *Pericles*, 13.8.
38. See Bruit 2005, 85–103. At the supposed time of the dream, there did not yet exist any sanctuary of Asclepius in Athens; it was only after the great plague of 432–427 that Asclepius was introduced into the city, probably in 420/419, and it was not until the fourth century that a civic priest was attached to his cult.
39. Schmitt Pantel 2009, 96.
40. Herodotus, 1.60 (see Ps.-Aristotle, *Constitution of the Athenians*, 14.4; and Cleidemus, *FGrHist* 323 F 15). See Sinos 1993, 73–91.
41. See earlier, chapter 7.
42. *Pericles*, 39.2.
43. Cratinus, *Chirons*, fr. 258 K.-A. (= Plutarch, *Pericles*, 3.3). The poet was playing on a comic association with one of the traditional epithets for Zeus used by Homer, who calls him "The Assembler of Clouds." According to Plutarch, it was Pericles' squill-shaped head that explained the variation chosen by Cratinus ("The Assembler of Heads").
44. Pack² 253 = K.-A. On the dating and themes of the play, see Ceccarelli 1996, 112.
45. Hesiod, *Works and Days*, 111 ff. See Cratinus, *The Spirits of Wealth* [*Ploutoi*], fr. 176 K.-A. (= Athenaeus, 6.267E).
46. *Cimon*, 10.6. According to Ceccarelli 1996, 142, Plutarch may have been inspired by a passage in Cratinus, *The Spirits of Wealth* (fr. 175 K.-A.), in which foreigners partake of a Laconian banquet (Cimon is well known for his philo-laconianism), grabbing sausages from doorways where they were hanging.

47. Cratinus, fr. 241 K.-A. (= Plutarch, *Pericles*, 24.6). See earlier, chapter 7.
48. Schachermeyr 1968.
49. See, among others, Beloch 1914, 295; and Châtelet 1982, 137–138.
50. Plutarch, *Pericles*, 35.1–2.
51. See Parker 1996, 214.
52. Plutarch, *Nicias*, 24.1.
53. *Pericles*, 36.3.
54. Diogenes Laertius, 9.51 (third century A.D.); and Eusebius of Caesarea, *Preparation for the Gospel*, 14.3.7 (fourth century A.D.). See Plato, *Cratylus*, 385e–386a: "man is the measure of all things [*khrēmata*], of the existence of those that exist, and of the nonexistence of those that do not." According to Diogenes Laertius (9.51), he was forced to leave Athens on account of his impiety, while his books were publicly burned. But Plato's testimony refutes this (*Meno*, 91e).
55. Heraclides Ponticus (fourth century B.C.), fr. 150 Wehrli (= Diogenes Laertius, 9.50). See Stadter 1991; and earlier, chapter 7.
56. Schmitt Pantel 2009, 166.
57. *Pericles*, 38.3–4.
58. See Theophrastus, *Characters*, 16 (the superstitious man).
59. *Pericles*, 6.2.
60. See, for example, Ildefonse 2005, 232.
61. Bruit 2005, 86–87.
62. See, above all, Dover 1988b, 146–147.
63. See earlier, chapter 1.
64. Thucydides, 1.127.1–2.
65. Lysias, *Against Andocides* (6), 10.
66. Schmitt Pantel 2009, 102–104.
67. See Dio of Prusa, *Olympikos*, 6. According to the pseudo-Aristotelian *Peri kosmou* (first century A.D.), Phidias positioned his portrait at the center of the shield, linking it to the statue by an invisible mechanism in such a way that if any attempt was made to remove it, the entire construction fell to pieces.
68. Donnay 1968, 19–36; and Rolley 1999, 128.
69. Aristophanes, *Peace*, 605; and Philochorus, *FGrHist* 328 F 121.
70. See Rolley 1999, 64; and Holtzmann 2003, 113.
71. Scholia to Aristophanes, *Peace*, 605a and b. See now Bakola 2010, 305–312, according to whom the trial probably took place in 434/3.
72. Plutarch, *Pericles*, 32.1–2. See earlier, chapter 7.
73. Banfi 1999.
74. *Pericles*, 32.1. See Connor 1963, 115–118; and, earlier, Derenne 1930, and Rudhardt 1960.
75. See, respectively, Plato, *Apology*, 26d; and Plutarch, *Nicias*, XXIII, 3.
76. Lenfant 2002.
77. Ibid., 146.
78. On the critique of Diopeithes, see Aristophanes, *Knights*, 1085, *Wasps*, 380, Ameipsias, fr. 10 K.-A.
79. Thucydides, 2.52.3–4.

CHAPTER 9. AFTER PERICLES: THE DECLINE OF ATHENS?

1. See for example Connor 1992, who, however, does not himself adopt the moral and "decadentist" views of the ancient sources.
2. Thucydides, 2.65.5 and 10.
3. *Constitution of the Athenians*, 28.1. This dividing line is later, in the second century B.C., also recognized by Polybius: "At Athens at least we find that during the government of Aristides and Pericles the state was the author of few cruel actions, but of many kind and praiseworthy ones, while under Cleon and Chares it was quite the reverse" (*Histories*, 9.23.6).
4. Whereas Thucydides contrasts Pericles to all his successors, Ps.-Aristotle sets out a double opposition: on the one hand, between the leaders of the *dēmos* and the leaders of the elite, on the other, between the leaders of the people down to Pericles and those who succeeded him.
5. See earlier, chapter 3.
6. Ps.-Aristotle, *Constitution of the Athenians*, 28.3, mentions the "two-obol dole" introduced by Cleophon. This grant given to a citizen to enable him to take part in festivals (*IG* I^3 188, l. 10 f.) was established right after the fall of the oligarchy of 411 and was abolished in 404, though it was reestablished not long after.
7. In the *Nicomachean Ethics*, 6.5.1140b4 f., Pericles appears as an emblem of *phronēsis*, the practical ability to deliberate accompanied by reason, and knowing how to adapt to the constant movements of the world. See Aubenque 1986, 53–60.
8. Eupolis, fr. 384 K.-A., possibly from his play titled *The Demes*.
9. The term is attested for the first time in Aristophanes in 422 B.C. in *Wasps* (1309). See Connor 1992, 155–156, n. 40. In 428 B.C., just after the death of Pericles, Cratinus had coined the composite name *neoploutoponeroi*, the "new rich criminals," which implies the earlier existence of a shorter word (fr. 223 K.-A.).
10. *IG* II^2 2318, l. 34.
11. Davies 1971, no. 8674 (Cleon) and no. 3773 (Dikaiogenes).
12. Brenne 1994.
13. Cratinus, fr. 73, l. 69–71 K.-A.
14. Podlecki 1998, 129.
15. See Bloedow 2000, 295–309, which shows to what extent the opposition between Pericles and his successors on the subject of imperialistic behavior needs to be relativized. See earlier, chapter 4.
16. Mann 2007.
17. Demosthenes, *Third Olynthiac* (3), 21–22.
18. *FGrHist* 107 F 11 (= Plutarch, *Pericles*, 36.3). See earlier, chapter 6.
19. See Plutarch, *Pericles*, 36.1. This pedagogic failure is also noted by Antisthenes, according to Athenaeus (5.220D): The *Aspasia* [of Antisthenes] slanders Xanthippus and Paralus, the sons of Pericles. One of them, he says, lived with Archestratus, who plied a trade similar to that of women in the cheaper brothels; the other was the boon companion of Euphemus, who used to make vulgar and heartless jokes at the expense of all whom he met."

20. *Protagoras*, 319e–320a. See also *Meno*, 93b–e: "The great Pericles himself did not succeed in teaching his sons virtue, nor did he provide them with a teacher in that discipline."
21. See Xenophon, *Memorabilia*, 1.2.12–13.
22. Ibid., 3.5.13.
23. *Gorgias*, 502d–503b.
24. *FGrHist* 115 F 90 (= Athenaeus, 12, 533A–C).
25. *Republic*, VI, 492c.
26. Plato, *Gorgias*, 510b–e.
27. See Schmitt Pantel 2009, 72.

Chapter 10. The Individual and Democracy: The Place of the "Great Man"

1. Lysias, *Against Nicomachus* (30), 28.
2. Brun 2005b, 197.
3. Tackling the Plutarchian tradition, Gustave Glotz 1931, 133, thus referred to Ephialtes as "Pericles' lieutenant." Will 1972, 172, on the contrary does not even mention Pericles in connection with this affair.
4. See Wohl 2009, 172–173.
5. See earlier, chapter 8.
6. Telekleides, fr. 45 K.-A. (= Plutarch, *Pericles*, 16.2).
7. Herodotus, 6.131. See earlier, chapter 1.
8. Heracles and Achilles both possess lion's hearts: see Homer, *Iliad*, 5.639, *Odyssey*, 11.267; Hesiod, *Theogony*, 1007.
9. Herodotus, 5.56.1. Some man was said to have spoken the following enigmatic words to Hipparchus: "Lion, with an enduring heart, endure the unendurable trials that strike you."
10. In 566, the ancient festival of Athena was reorganized and turned into the Great Panathenaea. See Neils 1992, 20, on the supposed role played by Pisistratus in this reorganization. See also Nagy 1996, 111 and nn. 23–24. On Pericles and the Panathenaea, see earlier, chapter 8.
11. Aristotle, *Politics*, 5.11.1313b23.
12. Plutarch, *Comparison between Pericles and Fabius Maximus*, 3.5.
13. See Etienne 2004, 190–205 ("La nouvelle Athènes d'Hadrien").
14. Cratinus, *The Women of Thrace*, fr. 73 K.-A.
15. Lycurgus ["Against Cephisodotus, on the honours given to Demades"], fr. VIII, 2.
16. See Hurwit 2004, 98 [chapter 3, "Pericles, Athens and the building program"].
17. Thucydides, 1.107.1: "The Athenians began the construction of the Long Walls."
18. Plato, *Gorgias*, 455e: "You know, I suppose, that these great arsenals and walls of Athens and the construction of your harbours are due to the advice of Themistocles and in part to that of Pericles, not to your craftsmen . . . and, as to Pericles, I heard him myself when he was advising us about the middle wall." See earlier, chapter 2.
19. See the enlightening remarks of Brulé 1994, 97.

20. See Brulé 1994, 97.
21. See *Pericles*, 3.8 and *IG* I³ 506 (= *Syll.*³ 1001): *Athenaioi tei Athenaiai tei Hugieiai. Purros epoiesen Athenaios.* See earlier, chapter 8; and Leventi 2003, T 4.
22. *IG* I³ 49, l. 13–14 (= ATL II, D 19). See Mattingly 1961, 164–165.
23. We should remember that the population of Piraeus, the port of Athens, depended entirely on cisterns for its water supply. This project was part of a more extensive policy designed to safeguard the welfare of the Athenians in times of war. See Woodhead 1973–1974, 751–761.
24. From the mid-fourth century onward, acts of euergetism were accepted more readily by the Athenian people. In 333/2, Pytheas was elected as the city superintendent of works connected with the supply of water (*epimeletēs tōn krēnōn*). When he had completed his term of office, the city honored him with a golden crown worth 1,000 drachmas for having used his own resources to cover certain expenses and, in particular, for having repaired a fountain in the sanctuary of Amphiaraus and for having constructed another one in the sanctuary of Ammon. See *IG* II² 338, l. 11–17 (= *Syll.*³ 281). See Dillon 1996.
25. Ps.-Aristotle, *Constitution of the Athenians*, 27.3–5 and 18.1. See also Theopompus, *FGrHist* 115 F 89 (= Athenaeus, 12.532f–533c).
26. He died soon after his return, during the siege of Citium on Cyprus, in 449 B.C.
27. See Plutarch, *Pericles*, 9.2–3 and also Plutarch, *Cimon*, 10.1–3.
28. Deniaux and Schmitt Pantel 1987–1989, 153.
29. On this question, see Schmitt Pantel 1992, 180–196; followed by Pébarthe 2007.
30. See earlier, chapter 2; and Dover 1960, 76.
31. See earlier, introduction.
32. See Ehrenberg 1945, 113–134.
33. Thucydides, 1.117.2. Socrates of Anagyrous was also *stratēgos* during the Samos war in 441/0. He was sufficiently influential to risk ostracism in 443, having possibly been *khorēgos* for the poet Euripides in 442. In the 430s, he dedicated a *khorēgos*'s monument celebrating a victory in the rural Dionysia, the first known monument of this kind: see *IG* I³ 969; and Csapo 2010, 91 and 94.
34. Thucydides, 4.102. At this point, Hagnon may have again been elected *stratēgos*. See Podlecki 1998, 129.
35. Four *ostraka* bearing the name Hagnon are listed in Siewert 2002, 53. See, more generally, Pesely 1989, 191–209.
36. See Andocides, *On Peace*, 6; and Diodorus Siculus, 12.7.1. There were ten negotiators, but Pericles was clearly not among them.
37. See Kallet 2009, 56.
38. Thucydides, 3.36.2–3.49.1. On the *dēmos*'s power over the orators: Sinclair 1988, 136–162; Ober 1996, 132–135.
39. Fröhlich 2000, 83–86.
40. Pericles was a *stratēgos* at least three times in succession between 448/7 and 446/5. See Fornara 1971, 47.
41. Ps.-Aristotle, *Constitution of the Athenians*, 61.1 and 43.4.
42. See MacDowell 1978, 169.
43. Plutarch, *Pericles*, 35.4, mentions a fine of 15 or 50 talents; Diodorus Siculus, 12.45.4, for his part, records a sum of 80 talents. See Podlecki 1998, 51. While

the nature of the charges indicates a rendering of accounts (theft, misappropriation of funds), the timing—in mid-mandate—suggests, rather, a trial for high treason.

44. Ephorus, *FGrHist* 70 F 196 (= Diodorus, 12.38.3–4): "As he had used for his own personal purposes [*idiai*] quite a large part of the sum [from the treasury of the Delian League that had been transferred to Athens] he was asked to explain this, but he fell ill and was incapable of providing a justification."

45. Brenne 1994, 13–24. See Plutarch, *Cimon*, 4.7.

46. Hall 2006, 388.

47. See earlier, chapter 7, the section titled "Pericles and Aspasia" (for the critics of his relationship with Aspasia).

48. Information relating to these censure issues has been collected and examined by Halliwell 1991.

49. See Sommerstein 2004, 145–174.

50. See Scholium to Aristophanes, *Acharnians*, 67; and Suda, *s.v. Euthumenēs*: it was during the archonship of Euthymenes (437/6 B.C.) that "the decree forbidding comic personal attacks [*to psēphisma to peri tou mē kōmōidein*], passed under Morychides [440/439 B.C.] was abrogated."

51. See Lenfant 2003b.

52. The fact that the demagogue Cleon was mocked by Aristophanes in the *Knights* did not prevent him being elected *stratēgos* a few weeks later by the very same Athenians who had vociferously applauded Aristophanes' play. See Dover 1989, LVI.

53. See Saetta Cottone 2005; and Stark 2004.

54. See earlier, chapter 3.

55. See Dover 1988a; Hunter 1993, 96–119 ("The politics of reputation: gossip as a social construct").

56. See, for example, *Pericles*, 6.2, 8.3, 13.5, 16.7, 24.3, 24.6, 28.5, 30.1, and 31.2.

57. Demosthenes, *On the Embassy* (19), 122: "because the situation was not yet stable and the future was uncertain, the Agora was full of groups and gossip of every kind."

58. See, for example, Xenophon, *Memorabilia*, I.2.1.

59. See, for example, Demosthenes, *Against Callimachus* (18), 9; Lysias, *Against Pancleon* (23), 2. See Ober 1989, 148.

60. See Aeschines, *Against Timarchus* (1), 128–129; Demosthenes, *On the Embassy* (19), 253. Their disagreement concerned, not the status of rumor, but the people incriminated by it.

61. *Against Timarchus* (1), 127–128. Rumor was the object of a cult in Athens, possibly ever since Cimon's victory at Eurymedon, in the early 460s. See Parker 1996, 155–156 and 233–234.

62. Plato, *Laws*, 838c. See Bertrand 1999, 329–336, esp. p. 329.

63. Detienne 2003, 70–77 (citation, p. 77).

64. Aeschines, *Against Timarchus* (1), 129.

65. Accept rumor, even when unfounded: that is precisely what Aristides does when he writes his own name on an an ostracism potsherd, in response to a request made by a fellow who does not know him but says he is irritated by his reputation as a just man who is "royal and divine" (Plutarch, *Aristides*, 7.1–7).

66. See, for example, Plato, *Protagoras*, 319c.
67. Applause: Demosthenes, *Against Midias* (21), 14; and Aristophanes, *Assembly of Women*, 427–436. Protests: Aeschines, *Against Ctesiphon* (3), 224. Whistles: Xenophon, *Hellenica*, 6.5.49. Laughter: Aeschines, *Against Timarchus* (1), 80–84; Thucydides, 4.27.5. See Bers 1985; and Wallace 2004b, 223–227.
68. Roisman 2004, 265.
69. Villacèque 2013, 268-276.
70. *Pericles*, 14.2. See Tacon 2001, 183.
71. Thucydides, 2.60.1–5. See Ostwald 1986, 200–201.
72. Gomme 1956 (ad loc.).
73. Plato, *Republic*, VI, 492c. See earlier, chapter 9.
74. Ober 1998, 190.
75. See earlier, chapter 9.

CHAPTER 11. PERICLES IN DISGRACE: A LONG SPELL IN PURGATORY (15TH TO 18TH CENTURIES)

1. Voltaire 1765, 270–276 ("Périclès, un Grec moderne, un Russe")—even though the editors doubted the authenticity of the dialogue and instead attributed it to François Arnaud Jean Baptiste Antoine Suard (1732–1817), a publicist and the son-in-law of the publisher Panckouche, who was a royal censor and a member of the Académie Française.
2. Rico 2002, 19.
3. The date is certain, as S. Baldassarri has shown in his edition of the work (Bruni 2000, xv–xvii).
4. Roberts 1994, 122–123.
5. See Rawson 1969, 138.
6. Montaigne 1877, vol. 2, 42–43 (*Essays*, II, 4).
7. Ibid., vol. 2, 111 (*Essays*, II, 10: *On Books*).
8. In 1566, Jean Bodin, in *La méthode de l'histoire* (Bodin 1941, 49) referring to Plutarch, exclaimed admiringly, "What could elude such wisdom?"
9. See earlier, introduction.
10. Thucydides was translated again (badly) into French by Jean-Louis de Jassaud in 1600, before becoming the object of the "faithless beauty" by Nicolas Perrot d'Ablancourt, in 1662, which was an extremely free translation with numerous omissions.
11. See Starobinski 1985, 14–17.
12. Grell 1993, 138.
13. See later in chapter 12, the section titled "The Periclean Myth at Its Peak."
14. See Castellaneta and Camesasca 1969, plate LI. Here, Pericles is the very embodiment of temperance, urging these men who handle money to be as incorruptible as the *stratēgos* himself.
15. See, for example, Machiavelli, preface to *The History of Florence* [1525], in Machiavelli 1965. See Roberts 1994, 129.
16. *Discourses on the First Ten Books of Titus Livius* [1512–1517], in Machiavelli 1882, vol. 2, 102.
17. Ibid., vol. 2, 258.

18. *Consolatoria, Accusatoria, Difensoria* (1527), in Guicciardini 1867, 111 and 222 (author's translation).
19. See Roberts 1994, 125–126.
20. On Carlo Sigonio, see Ampolo 1997, 16–19; and Cambiano 2003, 168–169.
21. Sigonio 1593, 480: "tum vero Aristides, qui plurimum ex iis bellis auctoritatis erat adeptus, et post eum, vir manu et lingua promptus, Pericles popularem hunc reip. statum amplificarunt, cum omnia plebi et imperitae multitudini tradiderunt, quibus Solonis legibus ei fuerat interdictum" (author's translation).
22. Ibid., 483: "Pericles populum mercede plebi ad iudicandum, et ad locos in theatris ludorum causa emendos assignata insolentiorem, atq; arrogantiorem effecerit, & per Ephialtem summam illam Areopagi potentiam labefecit" (author's translation).
23. See Baron 1968, 117–118.
24. Bodin 1945, 237–238.
25. Bodin 1606, 261 (book III, chap. 1).
26. Ibid., 430 (book IV, chap. 1 ; modernized spelling).
27. Ibid., 531–532 (book IV, chap. 7).
28. Montaigne 1877, 405 (book I, chap. 51 : "Of the vanity of words").
29. Ibid.
30. Ibid.
31. Hartog 2005, 172.
32. Spon 1678, vol. 2, 147. See Pébarthe 2010b, 464–465.
33. See Grell and Michel 1988.
34. Hartog 2005, 203–204.
35. See Saladin 2000.
36. Grell 1995, 379–380.
37. *Chronologiae ex nummis antiquis restitutae* and *Prolegomena ad censuram veterum scriptorum* (1696). See Grell 1995, 409.
38. Perrault 1693, vol. 1, part II, 206 (modernized spelling).
39. Perrault 1697, vol. 4, 319–320.
40. In the *Parallèle des anciens et des modernes*, in justification of the Quarrel, Perrault chose to cite Pericles' funeral oration in the translation produced by Nicolas Perrot d'Ablancourt, in order that readers could pass judgment as objectively as possible.
41. Fontenelle 1730, 93–94.
42. The *Dialogues des morts* by Fénelon appeared in successive waves. The first four were published as early as 1700, but it was not until 1712 (the year of the death of the duke of Burgundy) that a collection of forty-five further dialogues appeared. After Fénelon's death, the corpus of dialogues progressively grew until its definitive form was reached with the publication of the *Oeuvres complètes de Fénelon* in the so-called Versailles edition, in 1823. It contained seventy-nine dialogues, of which fifty-one were between ancient characters and twenty-eight were between modern ones.
43. *Alcibiades*, 7.3. See Diodorus Siculus, 12.38.
44. Fénelon 1760, 80–81.
45. The following dialogue picks up the same theme, again presenting Pericles as a warmonger encouraged by Alcibiades. Pericles makes a more discreet

appearance in dialogue LV, which sets Louis XI, the symbol of a scheming tyrant, against Cardinal Bessarion, the embodiment of a clerical scholar buried in his books. The Athenian Pericles is once again the emblem of bombastic and, above all, outdated rhetoric.

46. See Schlatter 1945, 351.
47. Johnson 1993, 214.
48. Hobbes 1989, 569–586: "On the life and history of Thucydides."
49. Ibid., 572.
50. Ibid., 572–573.
51. See Schlatter 1975, 14. Hobbes returns to a similar argument in the dedication that he had written for his patron, Sir William Cavendish: "To Sir William Cavendish" in Hobbes 1989, xx: he recommends reading Thucydides "for that he had in his veins the blood of kings."
52. Hobbes 1839, LXXXVIII, l. 80–83 (*Thomas Hobbes Malmesburiensis Vita Carmine Expressa*).
53. Dabdab Trabulsi 2006, 169.
54. Hartog 2005, 78.
55. Grell 1995, vol. 1, 498.
56. Grell 1993, 136–137. However, Thucydides was restored to the taste of the time by Charles Rollin, as P. Payen has shown. See later, chapter 12.
57. D'Alembert 1893, 77 and 85.
58. Johnson 1992, 149–157.
59. Montesquieu 1989, 43 (*The Spirit of the Laws*, V, 3). See Cambiano 1974; and Nelson 2004, 155–194.
60. Montesquieu 1989, 10–15 (*The Spirit of the Laws*, II, 2). See Mossé 1989, 56–58.
61. Montesquieu 1989, 115 (VIII, 4) and 113 (VIII, 2).
62. See, for example, Montesquieu 1989, 363 (XXI, 7): "The fine institutions of Solon." Similarly, in the article devoted to "Athens" in the *Encyclopédie*, Jaucourt has eyes only for the Athens of Solon: he suggests that the decline of the city began almost immediately after the Persian Wars. See also his article, "Démocratie" (*Encyclopédie, ou Dictionnaire Raisonné des Sciences, des Arts et des Métiers*, V [1754], 816–818) and the remarks of Roberts 1994, 169–170.
63. See Nippel 2010, 94; and Pébarthe 2010b, 465.
64. Turgot, *Tableau philosophique des progrès successifs de l'esprit humain*, 11 December 1750, in Turgot 1913, 214–235, citations p. 225.
65. On the quarrel about luxury, see for example Johnson 1992; and Ross 1975.
66. *Discourse on the Arts and Sciences* [1761], in Rousseau 1997a, 11.
67. Ibid.
68. *A Discourse on Political Economy* [1761], in Rousseau 1997b, 8.
69. *Last Reply*, in Rousseau 1997a, 75 and note.
70. See Guerci 1979, 182–183.
71. Mably 1784, 80.
72. Ibid., 88.
73. Ibid., 89–90 (a passage not translated in the English version). Only in a short note at the bottom of the page does Mably deign to recognize a degree of virtue in the *stratēgos*: "It must be acknowledged to the honour of Pericles that whatever works of Greece either in architecture, sculpture or painting have commanded

the admiration of after ages were the fruit of his Government and of the attention bestowed by him upon the most elegant subjects" (p. 92 and note).

74. Ibid., 90. The English version considerably weakens and waters down the expression used by Mably, when it translates "Cet adroit tyran d'Athènes" (this adroit tyrant of Athens) as "This Leader of the people."

75. Ibid., 103.

76. Mably 1769, preface, "Life of Phocion." See also Roberts 1994, 162–165.

77. Mably 1769, 117–118.

78. Barthélemy 1806.

79. Vidal-Naquet 2000, 214.

80. On the genealogy of this formula, see later, chapter 12.

81. Barthélemy 1806, 268–269.

82. Ibid., 269–270.

83. Ibid.

84. Ibid., 271. "In proportion as Pericles augmented his power, he was less lavish of his influence and his presence. Confining himself to a small circle of relations and friends, he was supposed to be solely occupied with plans for the pacification or disturbance of Greece" (ibid.).

85. Ibid., 272.

86. Ibid., 274.

87. Ibid., 329.

88. Ibid., 330.

89. Barthélemy 1806, 153.

90. Ibid., 331.

91. Ibid., 161.

92. See Vidal-Naquet 1995, 90.

93. See Mossé 1989, 88.

94. Volney 1800, 169.

95. See the remarks of Dubuisson 1989, 38, based on the study by Bouineau 1986: 2,597 explicit mentions of Rome as against 1,575 for Greece, while the implicit allusions show an even greater imbalance.

96. Dubuisson 1989, 33.

97. Robespierre 1967, 444.

98. See Mossé 1989, 92–93 and 124–125.

99. Billaud-Varennes, "Rapport du 1 floréal an II (20 avril 1794)," in *Le Moniteur*, II, no. 212: 860.

100. Saint-Just 1791, II, 5.

101. That was how P. Buonarroti saw it (Buonarroti 1828, 5): "The former [the Girondins and the 'Indulgents'] sighed for the riches, superfluities and splendour of Athens; the latter desired the frugality, simplicity and modesty of the glory days of Sparta."

102. Buchez and Roux 1836, 394.

103. Mossé 1989, 136.

104. Ibid., 139.

105. Ibid., 147. Already in Year II, Camille Desmoulins was singing the praises of Thrasybulus, calling him "the restorer of peace": Desmoulins 1825, 72 [*Le Vieux Cordelier*, no. 4]; and Desmoulins 1825, 90–91 [*Le Vieux Cordelier*, no. 5].

106. Bouineau 1986, 106.
107. Buchez and Roux 1834, 108.
108. Ibid., 118.
109. In the end, the Assembly passed a motion of compromise: "The right of peace and of war belongs to the Nation. War will be decided only by a decree from the Legislative Body following a formal and necessary proposal from the king, which must then be sanctioned by His Majesty."
110. Hansen 1992, 18.
111. *Federalist Papers*, no. 6.
112. This association between Pericles and warfare persisted in the decades that followed. So, in 1803, when Hamilton wanted to proclaim that, for the French party of Louisiana, war was ineluctable, he, logically enough, chose the pseudonym Pericles. See Adair 1955, 285–287.
113. Grégoire 1977, 45. See Mossé 1989, 113.
114. *Moniteur*, Year II, no. 20, 860.
115. Grégoire 1977, 182.
116. Volney 1800, 171.
117. Ibid., 174–175.
118. Ibid., 178 (cited by Vidal-Naquet 1995, 99).
119. Vidal-Naquet 2000, 229.
120. Desmoulins 1825, 124 [*Le Vieux Cordelier*, no. 6 Nivôse an II, December 1793].
121. Ibid., 148.
122. Ibid., 157 [*Le Vieux Cordelier*, no. 7, February–March 1794].
123. Ibid., 153–154 [*Le Vieux Cordelier*, no. 7, February–March 1794].
124. Baudot 1893, 210. As Rawson 1969, 297, points out, Baudot's Latin is altogether revolutionary!
125. Baudot 1893, 311.

Chapter 12. Pericles Rediscovered: The Fabrication of the Periclean Myth (18th to 21st Centuries)

1. See, for example, the titles of Cloché 1949; Flacelière 1966; Mossé 1971, 43–66; and Maffre 1994. English-language scholarship speaks of "The Age of Pericles": Watkiss Lloyd 1875; Robinson 1959; and Samons II ed. 2007. The Germans, for their part, evoke the "Perikleische Zeitalter": see, in particular, Schmidt 1877.
2. Arnaud-Lindet 2001, 130–131.
3. Bodin 1945, 287.
4. See earlier, chapter 11.
5. Frederick had wanted his text to appear anonymously. Having entrusted his text to Voltaire, he changed his mind when Frederick Wilhelm I of Prussia died, on 31 May 1740. Then, once on the throne, Frederick decided to prevent the appearance of his book, which nevertheless did appear after numerous corrections and rewritings. See Aizpurua 1994.
6. Frederick II of Prussia 1846–1856, book VIII, 304 (author's italics).
7. On the importance of the work of Rollin, see later in this section.
8. Voltaire, *Age of Louis XIV* [1751], in Voltaire 1901 (vol. 12), 5.

9. Voltaire 1901 (vol. 12), 1–2. See Mortgat-Longuet 2006.
10. Voltaire 1784–1789 (vol. 66), lettre XLV, 108 (letter dated 28 October 1772).
11. See Mat-Hasquin 1981, 148. Unlike Rousseau, Voltaire had nothing but disdain for frugal Sparta and, in *A Philosophical Dictionary* (1764), in the article on "Luxury" (in Voltaire 1901 [vol. 6], 157), he exclaimed, "What benefit did Sparta confer on Greece? Had she ever a Demosthenes, a Sophocles, an Apelles or a Phidias? The luxury of Athens formed great men of every description. Sparta had certainly some great captains, but even these in a smaller number than other cities. But allowing that a small republic like Lacedaemon may maintain its poverty, men uniformly die, whether they are in want of everything or enjoying the various means of rendering life agreeable."
12. Condillac, *Cours d'études pour l'instruction du prince de Parme* [1775], cited in Condillac 1798, 283 [*Histoire ancienne*, II, 5].
13. See Guerci 1979, 219.
14. Saint-Lambert 1765, 765.
15. Rollin 1790.
16. See Payen 2007b, 191; and Payen 2010.
17. Rollin 1790, vol. III, book 7, chap. 1, section 7, 204.
18. Ibid., section 10, 217.
19. Ibid. A few chapters further on, Rollin also deplores the detachment shown by Pericles at the deaths of those close to him: "Exceeding error! Childish illusion! Which either makes heroism consist in wild and savage cruelty; or, leaving the same grief and confusion in the mind, assumes a vain exterior of constancy and resolution, merely to be admired. But does martial bravery extinguish nature?" (Rollin 1790, vol. III, book 7, chap. 3, section 2, 279).
20. Rollin 1790, vol. III, book 7, chap. 1, section 11, 217–218.
21. See earlier, introduction.
22. Rollin 1790, vol. III, book 7, chap. 1, section 11, 218 (author's italics).
23. Ibid., chap. 1, section 11, 230, n. 1.
24. Ibid., chap. 3, 283. See Thucydides, II, 65.
25. Lévesque 1811, preface, xx.
26. See Vidal-Naquet 1995, 108, citing Lévesque 1811 (vol. 3), 25.
27. See Hartog 2005, 85; and Chapoutot 2008, 168–175. In Germany, French culture was fundamentally perceived as Roman—to the point of French language and literature studies being, still today, classed as *Romanistik*.
28. See Bruhns 2005, 23.
29. Decultot 2000, 123.
30. For the purposes of his demonstration, Winckelmann revolutionized the history of art by defining "artistic styles" according to a chronological sequence linked with the history of civilizations. Winckelmann thereby initiated a classification still used today, with different titles ("archaic style," "early classicism of the fifth century," then "late classicism of the fourth century," then "Hellenistic style").
31. Winckelmann 2005 (vol. 3), 191–193.
32. Calvié 1999, 473.
33. Herder 1800, 354. See Tolbert Roberts 1994, 210–211.
34. Herder 1800, book XIII, chap. 3, "The arts of the Greeks," 367–368 (author's italics).

35. Herder 1800, 368.
36. Ibid., 368.
37. See Calvié 1999: in 1788, Schiller wrote *The Gods of Greece*, and ten years later Hölderlin's great poem, *Hyperion*, was published (1797–1799), setting the seal on the success of a form of Hellenizing paganism.
38. Hegel 1902 (citations p. 343 and p. 45).
39. Roberts 1994, 219.
40. Lyttleton 1760, 254–255.
41. Ibid., 256.
42. See Murray 2010, which questions the thesis of a unanimously negative view of Athens in the eighteenth century.
43. Gast 1753, 471.
44. Ibid., 484.
45. Ibid., 488.
46. Young 1786. On the context in which the work was written, see Murray 2010, 144 and 149.
47. Young 1786, 155.
48. Ibid., 152–153.
49. Gillies 1820 (vol. 2), chap. XIII, 108, n. 10.
50. Ibid., 126.
51. Mitford 1814, 100. On pages 127–130, Mitford gives a guarded appreciation of Pericles: he recognizes his role as a corruptor and his detestable political behavior, but also takes into account the great respect shown him by Thucydides, Xenophon, and Isocrates.
52. Thirlwall 1835–1844. On the differences between Thirlwall, who remained close to Germanic historiography (he translated Niebuhr as soon as his work appeared), and Grote, see Momigliano 1966, 61–62.
53. Grote 1869–1870 (vol. 5), 440.
54. Ibid., 437–439 and 441–442.
55. Ibid., 442.
56. Ibid., 443.
57. See Momigliano 1966, 60.
58. Cox 1874, 184.
59. Mérimée 1868, 185. See Pontier 2010, 635–648.
60. Mérimée 1868, 186.
61. Jouanna 2005, 311–321.
62. See Grunchec 1983, 27. The most that can be done is to add a *Pericles*—in the form of a mere bust—painted by Antoine-Jean Gros on a ceiling in the Louvre Museum in 1827, and a statue of Pericles handing out crowns to artists, sculpted by Jean-Baptiste Debay and installed in the Tuileries in 1833. In 1852, Philipp von Foltz, a German painter, depicted Pericles addressing the people from the *bema*, with the Acropolis in the background.
63. Duruy 1867, 155.
64. Ibid., 333.
65. Ibid., 156.
66. Nisard 1851. See Avlami 2001, 77.
67. See Hansen 1992, 21.

68. See Chauvelon 1902, 97–99.
69. Mazzarino 1990, 359–370; and Montepaone, Imbruglia, Catarzi, and Silvestre 1994.
70. Murari Pires 2006, 811.
71. Niebuhr 1852a (vol. 2), 54 and 391, and (vol. 1), 54; and Niebuhr 1852b (vol. 2), 352.
72. Niebuhr 1852a (vol. 1), 211. See also von Ranke 1975, 256–257.
73. Von Ranke 1867–1890 (vol. 53/54), 26–31 and 58–59.
74. Curtius 1857–1867; French trans.: Curtius 1880–1883; English trans.: Curtius 1868–1873.
75. Curtius 1883, 80, which states: "even more rewarding is the task of whoever, led by Thucydides, follows, with pious admiration, the traces that this great spirit [Pericles] has left on the history of his people." The English translation does not include this important passage.
76. Curtius 1871, 459 and 442 (book III, chap. 3).
77. Ibid., 468–469.
78. Ibid., 461–462.
79. Ibid., 459.
80. Schmidt 1877, 3. See Will 1995, 8.
81. See Bruhns 2005, 26.
82. On the context of Droysen's work, see the fine preface by Payen 2005, 31–36.
83. Droysen 1980, 12.
84. In the preface to the first German edition of vol. 3 of the *Histoire de l'Hellénisme* (which does not appear in the French translation), Droysen wrote as follows: "Who can fail to admire the Athens of Themistocles and Pericles? But why forget that the city founded a tyranny, extended it to cover half the Greek world and administered it quite harshly, knowing full well that this was tyranny" (author's translation), Droysen 1980, XXI.
85. Böckh 1886, 710 (the passage is not reproduced in the English edition). He reproached the Athenians in particular for having paid citizens for their public responsibilities and services (Böckh 1842, 226–227).
86. Böckh 1842, 195.
87. Ibid., 228–232.
88. Beloch 1967, iv. See also Beloch 1913, 13: "However, for Grote, the Greeks are basically simply the English of the mid-nineteenth century in disguise; the democrats are the liberals, the oligarchs the conservatives, and since the author is a liberal, the Greek democrats are always in the right, the oligarchs always in the wrong; Grote's history thus becomes a magnification of the Athenian democracy. That is a reaction that is altogether legitimate and useful to the hitherto prevailing under-estimation of democracy; only it is just as unhistorical as the opposite view." ("Dabei sind die Griechen für Grote im Grunde nichts weiter, als verkleidete Engländer aus der Mitte des XIX. Jahrhunderts; die Demokraten sind die Liberalen, die Oligarchen die Konservativen, und da der Verfasser zu den Liberalen gehörte, haben die griechischen Demokraten immer Recht, und die Oligarchen immer Unrecht; Grotes Geschichte wird so zu einer Verherrlichung der athenischen Demokratie. Das war als Reaktion gegen die bis dahin herrschende Unterschätzung dieser

Demokratie ganz berechtigt und nützlich; nur ist es ebenso unhistorisch, wie die entgegengesetzte Auffassung.").

89. Beloch 1914, 154–155.

90. Ibid., 319–310 (author's translation): "Aber der Spruch sollte auch nicht den Verwaltungs-beamten treffen, sondern den Politiker, der aus persönlichen Motiven den hellenischen Bruderkrieg entzündet und sich damit des größten Verbrechens schuldig gemacht hatte, das die ganze griechische Geschichte kennt." See also Beloch 1967, 19 f. and the commentaries by Christ 1999, 92.

91. Burckhardt 2002, 78.

92. Ibid., 77.

93. Drerup 1916, 1–4. A few years later, the historian returned to this theme in order, this time, to attack the politicians of the Weimar Republic. He lamented the fact that "in our country formerly so proud, here too a Republic of lawyers had been established, a Republic of the streets and demagogues, of which a Cleon and Aristophanes' sausage-merchant would have been proud" (Drerup 1923, 1).

94. See Pernot 2006.

95. On *Phi-Phi*, see *L'encyclopédie multimedia de la comédie musicale théâtrale en France (1918–1940)*, which offers an opportunity to listen to this work, available at http://194.254.96.55/cm/?for=fic&cleoeuvre=258 (accessed 23 August 2013).

96. "Pericles on the Athenians" (1915), advertisement published by the *Underground Electric Railway Company*. See Turner 1981, 187.

97. See Zimmern 1911, 202. The citation is taken from Thucydides, 2.43.4. Zimmern may possibly have put in a word of his own on the subject of this affair, for he was entrusted with various responsibilities on the Board of Education.

98. Müller 1824.

99. See the illuminating remarks of Hansen 2005, 15.

100. See Churchill 1951, 81 (citation taken from Thucydides, 2.64.6).

101. Churchill, "A Speech to the House of Commons, June 4, 1940," in Churchill 1953, 195. See Kagan 1991, 275.

102. Murray 1946, 202, cited by Roberts 1989, 204.

103. See Murray 1946, 200–201, who compares Demosthenes' *Philippics* to Churchill's famous "Arms and the League." See Rougemont 1996.

104. See Jones 1978, 109–110.

105. Most 1995, 438–440.

106. Andurand 2010.

107. Pohlenz 1920, 69 (author's translation).

108. Jaeger 1965, 407–409.

109. Ibid., 409 (author's italics).

110. Ibid., 409.

111. See Näf 1992, 125–146.

112. Among the many examples of this kind of slanted history, see in particular Berve 1937; John 1939; Lüdemann 1939; and Brake 1939. To take but one example, Berve praised Sparta for "the education of its young, its community spirit, its military form of life and the way in which the individual was integrated and proved his worth by his brave deeds," and finally for the "type of

Herrenmensch" (superior being), who emerged from "natural selection" and "shared blood" (Berve 1937, 7, 39, and 45).

113. Chapoutot 2008, 265–281 (citation pp. 276–277).

114. A. Hitler, speech of 4 August 1929, in Hitler 1992, vol. 2, 2, 348.

115. Arminius had been exalted as the first Germanic hero ever since *The Battle of Arminius* (*Die Hermannsschlacht*) by Heinrich von Kleist (1809), as was Vercingétorix celebrated in France.

116. Schachermeyr 1933, 41. See the close analyses by Chapoutot 2008, 323–324.

117. Brauer 1943, 131–136, cited by Näf 1986, 161.

118. Brauer 1943, 135.

119. Speer 1976, 110. See also Speer 1980, 20 April 1947. The former Nazi dignitary recorded a conversation with Hitler on 20 April 1943, when Hitler held forth on the action of great men in history and, in particular, on Pericles.

120. Hitler 1926, 289–290, cited by Chapoutot 2008, 298.

121. Speer 1976, 110.

122. See Scobie 1990, 15–16.

123. Zschietzschmann 1940, 14 and 16.

124. Berve 1940, 21. On Berve, Hitler, and Pericles, see Christ 1999, 249; and Chapoutot 2008, 324–326.

125. On the career of Berve, see Nippel 2010, 278–279.

126. Chapoutot 2008, 326. Germania was the name given by Hitler to the project of the urban renewal of the German capital.

127. Berve 1940, 21.

128. Ibid., 25: "er war auch während der vergangenen 15 Jahre in einem Stahlbad gehärtet, so dass er nun erst recht gegenüber inneren Anfeindungen und äußeren Schwierigkeiten eine schwer zu brechende Widerstandskraft besaß." See Christ 1999, 195 and 244.

129. Churchill was not alone in admiring the *stratēgos*. The members of the French Resistance had likewise made Pericles one of their heroes; the Mouvements Unis de Résistance (MUR) had given the *stratēgos*'s name to their network for training maquis cadres. See Dabdab Trabulsi 2011, 13.

130. Glotz 1931, 170. See "Périclès et l'impérialisme pacifique" (pp. 166–214); "le socialisme d'Etat" (pp. 178–187).

131. De Sanctis 1944. I am here following the line of thought suggested by Dabdab Trabulsi 2011, 21–38 and 197–199.

132. De Sanctis 1944, 184; Dabdab Trabulsi 2011, 31.

133. De Sanctis 1944, 218.

134. Ibid., 274.

135. Ibid., 131: "L'imperialismo pacifico di Pericle."

136. See Canfora 1976.

137. Homo 1954.

138. Ibid., 66.

139. Ibid., 97. On directed democracy, see ibid., 124–128.

140. Ibid., 78.

141. Châtelet 1982, 17 and 21.

142. Lévêque 1964, 265–266. See Châtelet 1982, 163–166; and Delcourt 1939, 171, n. 1. See the illuminating remarks of Mossé 2005, 240–242.

143. Lévêque 1964, 265–266.
144. Homo 1954 and Châtelet 1982. The publication date of the biography by Marie Delcourt was prewar 1939.
145. Lévêque and Vidal-Naquet 1996; and Loraux 2002.
146. See Roberts 1994, 265–270. As early as 1959, Finley was describing the advance "of slavery and freedom, hand in hand" (Finley 1959, 164).
147. Keuls 1993, 88. See, earlier, Pomeroy 1975.
148. Delcourt 1939. See Dabdab Trabulsi 2011, 87–109 (esp. 98–99).
149. Delcourt 1939, 118. The cleruchies are thus judged to be just a "simple instrument of domination," at the same time as a "financial expedient" (p. 120).
150. See, for example, Strasburger 1958, according to whom Thucydides more or less secretly condemned the imperialism embodied by Pericles. See Nicolai 1996.
151. Ehrenberg 1968, 238.
152. Starr 1974, 306. In the writings of Peter Green, then a professor of classics at the University of Texas and the author of numerous popular works on the ancient world, this critique reached its climax. According to him, Pericles was a quasi-dictator who had subjected the Athenian *demos* to a veritable brainwashing; and the democratic regime owed its survival only to the rabble-rousing leaders who followed. See Green 1972.
153. Hornblower 1994, 174.
154. Samons II 2004, 55–56 and 62. After deploring the coldness of Pericles and his lack of compassion (pp. 64–65), he also attacks the *misthos*, which undermined civic values (p. 173), in keeping with the purest Plutarchian tradition. See the review by Mossé 2006/2007, 467–470.
155. Samons II 2004, 130–131 and 190.
156. Luginbill 2011, 256.
157. See earlier, chapter 4; and Dabdab Trabulsi 2011, 113–137 ["Un Périclès du Nouveau Monde. Donald Kagan et son Périclès US"].
158. Mattingly 1966, 212–213: "None of the inscriptional evidence for fully organized Athenian imperialism can be dated before 431 B.C."
159. Bengtson 1983, 109 f., here 142 (author's translation). See also Weber 1985.
160. Admittedly, official instructions now encourage one to turn away from an idealized history, emphasizing "the restrictive concept of citizenship developed in fifth-century Athens, and . . . the limits of Athenian democracy: citizenship founded on birth-rights (but denied to women), which excluded foreigners and slaves and the functioning of which was flawed" (*Bulletin Officiel du ministère de l'Education Nationale et du ministère de la Recherche*, HS no. 6, 31 August 2000). Nevertheless, whenever it is a matter of considering the political or artistic history of the Greek world, the *stratēgos* continues to attract most of the attention.
161. See for example Nemo 1988.
162. Yourcenar 1989, 14.
163. See Wyke 1997 and Aziza 2008.
164. The only exceptions are a cinema adaptation of the operetta, *Phi-Phi*, in 1926, by Georges Pallu *alias* Demetrios Saixi (Isis Film-Les Productions Nathan, France) and, even more marginally, a Greek film, *Hippocrates and Democracy*

(*Ippocratis kè Dhimokratia*), by Dimis Dadiras, in 1972—in which Hippocrates tries to fight the 430 "plague" in Athens, and in the course of his peregrinations encounters Socrates, Phidias, Euripides, and Pericles. See Dumont 2009, 223–224.

165. An analysis of the situation has been carried out via www.gamekult.com (accessed 23 August 2013). It reveals several definite trends in the use of Antiquity. Games involving war and conquest predominate, some of which are spinoffs from the cinema (such as *The Three Hundred* and *Gladiator*) or from comic strips (for example, the many *Asterix* volumes). Rome is also very much present, particularly in the successful series of *Rome: Total War*. There are also a number of *Alexander* games—involving strategies for conquering the whole world—and a few games that use Sparta as a framework (*Spartan: Total Warrior*, which was produced in 2005 and sold widely).

166. Martin 2000.

BIBLIOGRAPHY

ABBREVIATIONS

ATL = Meritt, B. D., H. T. Wade-Gery, and M. F. McGregor. 1939–1953. *The Athenian Tribute Lists*, 4 vols. Cambridge, MA: Harvard University Press.

Brun = Brun, P. 2005. *Impérialisme et démocratie. Inscriptions de l'époque classique*. Paris: Armand Colin.

FGrHist = Jacoby, F., ed. 1922–1958. *Die Fragmente der griechischen Historiker*. Berlin: Weidmann [new ed. 15 vols., 1968–1969. Leiden: Brill].

Fornara = Fornara, C. W. 1983. *Archaic Times to the End of the Peloponnesian War*, 2nd ed. Cambridge/London/New York: Cambridge University Press [1st ed. 1977].

Gigon = Gigon, O. 1987. *Aristotelis Opera*, vol. 3. Berlin: W. de Gruyter.

IG I³ = Lewis, D. M., ed. 1981–1998. *Inscriptiones Graecae*, vol. I (3rd ed.), *Inscriptiones Atticae Euclidis Anno Anteriores*, 3 vols. Berlin: W. de Gruyter.

IG II² = Kirchner, J., ed. 1913–1940. *Inscriptiones Graecae*, vol. II (2nd ed.), *Inscriptiones Atticae Euclidis Anno Posteriores*, 5 vols. Berlin: W. de Gruyter.

K.-A. = Kassel, R., and C. Austin, ed. 1984–. *Poetae Comici Graeci*. Berlin: W. de Gruyter.

ML = Meiggs, R., and D. Lewis, ed. 1989. *A Selection of Greek Historical Inscriptions: To the End of the Fifth Century BC*, vol. 1. Oxford, UK: Oxford University Press [1st ed. 1969].

SSR = Giannantoni, G., ed. 1990. *Socratis et Socraticorum Reliquiae*, 4 vols. Naples: Bibliopolis.

*Syll.*³ = von Gärtringen, H. ed. 1915–1924. *Sylloge inscriptionum graecarum* (3rd ed.), 3 vols. Leipzig: S. Hirzel.

Thalheim = Thalheim, T., and F. Blass, eds. 1914. *Antiphon, orationes et fragmenta*. Leipzig: Teubner.

Wehrli = Wehrli, F., ed. 1944–1945. *Die Schule des Aristoteles*, vol. 1 [Dikaiarchos] and vol. 2 [Aristoxenos]. Basel: Schwabe & Co.

Adair, D. C. 1955. "A note on certain of Hamilton's pseudonyms." *William and Mary Quarterly*, series 3, 12: 282–297.

Aizpurua, P., ed. 1994. *Frédéric II de Prusse. De la littérature allemande*. Paris: Le Promeneur.

Allen, D. S. 2000. *The World of Prometheus: The Politics of Punishing in Democratic Athens*. Princeton, NJ: Princeton University Press.

Ampolo, C. 1997. *Storie greche. La formazione della moderna storiografia sugli antichi greci*. Turin: G. Einaudi.

Andurand, A. 2010. "Lectures allemandes de l'oraison funèbre de Périclès (1850–1930)," in *Ombres de Thucydide. La réception de l'historien depuis l'Antiquité jusqu'au début du XXᵉ siècle*, ed. V. Fromentin, S. Gotteland, and P. Payen. Bordeaux: Ausonius, 573–586.

Arnaud-Lindet, M.-P. 2001. *Histoire et politique à Rome. Les historiens romains (IIIe av. J.C.–V^e ap. J.C.)*. Rosny: Bréal.

Aubenque, P. 1986. *La prudence chez Aristote*, 3rd ed. Paris: Vrin.

Austin, M., and P. Vidal-Naquet 1977. *Economic and Social History of Ancient Greece: An Introduction*. London: B. T. Batsford [1st French ed. 1972].

Avlami, C. 2001. "L'écriture de l'histoire grecque en France au XIXe siècle: temporalités historiques et enjeux politiques." *Romantisme*, 113: 61–85.

Aziza, C. 2008. *Guide de l'Antiquité imaginaire. Roman, cinéma, bande dessinée*. Paris: Les Belles Lettres.

Azoulay, V. 2004. *Xénophon et les grâces du pouvoir*. Paris: Publications de la Sorbonne.

———. 2009. "La gloire et l'outrage. Heurs et malheurs des statues honorifiques de Démétrios de Phalère." *Annales HSS*, 64, 2: 303–340.

———. 2011. "Les métamorphoses du *koinon* athénien: autour du *Contre Léocrate* de Lycurgue," in *Clisthène et Lycurgue d'Athènes. Autour du politique dans la cité classique*, ed. Id. and P. Ismard. Paris: Publications de la Sorbonne, 191–217.

Bakola, E. 2010. *Cratinus and the Art of Comedy*. Oxford, UK: Oxford University Press.

Balot, R. 2001a. *Greed and Injustice in Classical Athens*. Princeton, NJ: Princeton University Press.

———. 2001b. "Pericles' anatomy of Democratic courage." *American Journal of Philology*, 122: 505–525.

Banfi, A. 1999. "I processi contro Anassagora, Pericle, Fidia ed Aspasia e la questione del 'circolo di Pericle': note di cronologia e di storia." *Annali dell'Istituto Italiano per gli Studi Storici*, 16: 3–85.

———. 2003. *Il governo della città: Pericle nel pensiero antico*. Bologna: Il Mulino.

Baron, H. 1968. *From Petrarch to Leonardo Bruni: Studies in Humanistic and Political Literature*. Chicago/London: University of Chicago Press.

Barron, J. P. 1964. "Religious propaganda of the Delian League." *Journal of Hellenic Studies*, 84: 35–48.

———. 1966. *The Silver Coins of Samos*. London: Athlone Press.

Barthélemy, J.-J. 1806. *Travels of Anacharsis the Younger in Greece: During the Middle of the Fourth Century before the Christian Era*, vol. 1. London: J. Johnson [1st French ed. 1788].

Basch, L. 1987. *Musée imaginaire de la marine antique*. Athens: Institut hellénique pour la préservation de la tradition nautique.

Baudot, M.-A. 1893. *Notes historiques sur la Convention Nationale, le Directoire, l'Empire et l'exil des votants*. Published by Mme. Vve. E. Quinet. Paris: D. Jouaust.

Behr, C. A. 1986. *P. Aelius Aristides: The Complete Works*, vol. 1. Leiden: Brill.

Beloch, K. J. 1913. *Griechische Geschichte*, vol. I, 2 [*Die Zeit vor der Perserkriegen*]. Strasbourg: K. J. Trübner [1st ed. 1893–1904].

———. 1914. *Griechische Geschichte*, vol. II, 1 [*Erste Abteilung Bis auf die sophistische Bewegung und den Peloponnesischen Krieg*]. Berlin/Leipzig: W. de Gruyter [1st ed. 1893–1904].

———. 1967. *Die attische Politik seit Perikles*. Darmstadt: Wissenschaftliche Buchgesellschaft [1st ed. 1884].

Bengtson, H. 1983. *Griechische Staatsmänner des 5. und. 4. Jahrhunderts v. Chr.* Munich: C. H. Beck.

Bers, V. 1985. "Dikastic *thorubos*," in *Crux: Essays in Greek History Presented to G.E.M. de Sainte Croix on His 75th Birthday*, ed. P. Cartledge and F. D. Harvey. London: Duckworth, 1–15.

Bertrand, J.-M. 1999. *De l'écriture à l'oralité. Lectures des Lois de Platon.* Paris: Publications de la Sorbonne.

Berve, H. 1937. *Sparta.* Leipzig: Bibliographisches Institut.

———. 1940. *Perikles*, vol. 2. Leipzig: Leipziger Universitätsreden.

Bicknell, P. J. 1982. "*Axiochus Alkibiadou*, Aspasia and Aspasios." *L'Antiquité Classique*, 51: 240–250.

Bloedow, E. F. 2000. "The implications of a major contradiction in Pericles' career." *Hermes*, 128, 3: 295–309.

Blok, J. H. 2009. "Perikles' citizenship law: a new perspective." *Historia*, 58, 2: 141–170.

Bloomer, W. M. 2005. "A rhetorical Pericles," in *Periklean Athens and Its Legacy: Problems and Perspectives*, ed. J. Barringer and J. Hurwit. Austin: University of Texas, 217–232.

Böckh, A. 1842. *The Public Economy of Athens.* London: J. W. Parker [1st German ed. 1817].

———. 1886. *Die Staatshaushaltung der Athener* [1817], vol. 1. Berlin: G. Reimer.

Bodin, J. 1606. *The Six Bookes of a Commonweale*, trans. R. Knolles. London: G. Bishop.

———. 1945. *Method for the Easy Comprehension of History* [1566], trans. B. Reynolds. New York: Columbia University Press.

———. 1986. *Les six livres de la République* [1576]. Paris: Fayard.

Boedeker, D. 2007. "Athenian religion in the age of Pericles," in *The Cambridge Companion to the Age of Pericles*, ed. L. J. Samons II. Cambridge, UK: Cambridge University Press, 46–69.

Bonnard, J.-B. 2002. "Phèdre sans inceste. À propos de la théorie de l'inceste du deuxième type et de ses applications en histoire grecque." *Revue Historique*, 304: 77–107.

Bouineau, J. 1986. *Les Toges du pouvoir, ou la révolution de droit antique (1789–1799).* Toulouse: Association des Publications de l'Université de Toulouse–Le Mirail and Editions Eché.

Bourriot, F. 1976. *Recherches sur la nature du genos. Étude d'histoire sociale athénienne—périodes archaïque et classique*, 2 vols. Lille: Atelier Reproduction des thèses; Paris: H. Champion.

Brake, J. 1939. *Spartanische Staatserziehung.* Hamburg: Hanseatische Verlagsanstalt.

Brauer, H. 1943. "Perikles und die Kriegsschuldfrage." *Die Deutsche Höhere Schule*, 10: 131–136.

Brenne, S. 1994. "*Ostraka* and the process of *Ostrakophoria*," in *The Archaeology of Athens and Attica under Democracy*, ed. W.D.E. Coulson et al. Oxford, UK: Oxbow Books, 13–24.

Bresson, A. 2000. *La cité marchande.* Bordeaux: Ausonius.

———. 2007. *L'économie de la Grèce des cités*, vol. 1, *Les structures de la production.* Paris: Armand Colin.

Briant, P. 2002. *From Cyrus to Alexander: A History of the Persian Empire*. Winona Lake, IN: Eisenbrauns [1st French ed. 1996].

Briant, P., P. Lévêque, P. Brulé, R. Descat, and M.-M. Mactoux. 1995. *Le monde grec au Ve siècle*. Paris: Presses Universitaires de France.

Bruhns, H. 2005. "Grecs, Romains et Germains au 19e siècle: quelle Antiquité pour l'État national allemand?" *Anabases*, 1: 17–43.

Bruit, L. 2005. *Les Grecs et leurs dieux*. Paris: Armand Colin.

Brulé, P. 1994. *Périclès: l'apogée d'Athènes*. Paris: Gallimard.

———. 2003. *Women of Ancient Greece*. Edinburgh: Edinburgh University Press [1st French ed. 2001].

Brun, P. 2000. *L'Orateur Démade. Essai d'histoire et d'historiographie*. Bordeaux: Ausonius.

———. 2003. *Le monde grec à l'époque classique. 500–323 av. J.-C*. Paris: Armand Colin.

———. 2005a. *Impérialisme et démocratie. Inscriptions de l'époque classique*. Paris: Armand Colin.

———. 2005b. "Lycurgue d'Athènes: un législateur?" in *Le législateur et la loi dans l'Antiquité. Hommages à Françoise Ruzé*, ed. P. Sineux. Caen: Presses universitaires de Caen, 187–199.

Bruni, L. 2000. *Laudatio Florentine Urbis*, ed. S. Baldassarri. Florence: SISMEL.

Buchez, P.-J.-B., and P.-C. Roux. 1834. *Histoire parlementaire de la Révolution française, journal des assemblées nationales, depuis 1789 jusqu'en 1815*, vol. 6. Paris: J. Hetzel.

———. 1836. *Histoire parlementaire de la Révolution française, journal des assemblées nationales, depuis 1789 jusqu'en 1815*, vol. 26. Paris: J. Hetzel.

Buonarroti, P. 1828. *Conspiration pour l'égalité, dite de Babeuf*. Bruxelles: Librairie romantique.

Burckhardt, J. 2002. *History of Greek Culture*. Mineola, NY: Dover Publications [1st German ed. 1898].

Burn, A. R. 1948. *Pericles and Athens*. London: Hodder & Stoughton.

Calame, C. 1999. *The Poetics of Eros in Ancient Greece*. Princeton, NJ: Princeton University Press [1st Italian ed. 1992].

Calvié, L. 1999. "Antiquité et Révolution française dans la pensée et les lettres allemandes à la fin du XVIIIe siècle." *Annales historiques de la Révolution française*, 317: 455–476.

Cambiano, G. 1974. "Montesquieu e le antiche republiche greche." *Rivista di Filosofia*, 65: 93–144.

———. 2003. *Polis. Histoire d'un modèle politique*. Paris: Flammarion [1st Italian ed. 2000].

Camp, J. M. 1986. *The Athenian Agora: Excavations in the Heart of Classical Athens*. London: Thames and Hudson.

Canfora, L. 1976. "Classicismo e fascismo." *Quaderni di Storia*, 17: 15–48.

Cartledge, P. 1990. "Fowl Play: a curious lawsuit in Classical Athens (Antiphon frr. 57–59 Thalheim)," in *NOMOS: Essays in Athenian Law, Politics and Society*, ed. P. Cartledge, P. Millett, and S. Todd. Cambridge, UK: Cambridge University Press, 41–61.

Castellaneta, C., and E. Camesasca. 1969. *L'Opera completa del Perugino*. Milan: Rizzoli.

Ceccarelli, P. 1996. "L'Athènes de Périclès: un pays de Cocagne." *QUCC*, 54: 109–159.

Chapoutot, J. 2008. *Le national-socialisme et l'Antiquité*. Paris: Presses universitaires de France.

Châtelet, F. 1982. *Périclès*. Brussels: Complexe [1st ed. 1960].

Chauvelon, E. 1902. "La république athénienne de Gambetta." *Revue de l'enseignement primaire*, 13, 9: 97–99.

Christ, K. 1999. *Hellas. Griechische Geschichte und deutsche Geschichtswissenschaft*. Munich: Beck.

Christ, M. R. 1998. *The Litigious Athenian*. Baltimore: Johns Hopkins University Press.

Churchill, W. 1951. *The Hinge of Fate*, vol. 4. London: Cassell.

Cloché, P. 1949. *Le siècle de Périclès*. Paris: Presses Universitaires de France.

Condillac, É. (Bonnot de) 1798. *Cours d'études pour l'instruction du prince de Parme* [1775], in *Œuvres*, vol. IX. Paris: Ch. Houel.

Connor, W. R. 1963. "Two notes on Diopeithes the Seer." *Classical Philology*, 58, 2: 115–118.

———. 1992. *The New Politicians of Fifth-Century Athens*. Indianapolis: Hackett [1st ed. 1971].

Conwell, D. 2008. *Connecting a City to the Sea: The History of the Athenian Long Walls*. Leiden: Brill.

Cox, C. 1989. "Incest, inheritance and the political forum in fifth-century Athens." *Classical Journal*, 85: 34–46.

Cox, G. 1874. *History of Greece*, vol. 1, *From the Earliest Period to the End of the Persian War*. London: Longmans, Green.

Csapo, E. 2010. *Actors and Icons of the Ancient Theater*. Chichester, UK/Malden, MA: Wiley-Blackwell.

Curtius, E. 1857–1867. *Griechische Geschichte*, 3 vols. Berlin: Weidmannsche buchhandlung.

———. 1868–1873. *History of Greece*, trans. A. W. Ward. New York: Charles Scribner [vol. 2, 1871].

———. 1880–1883. *Histoire grecque*, trans. A. Bouché-Leclercq, 5 vols. Paris: E. Leroux [vol. 3, 1883].

Dabdab Trabulsi, J. A. 2006. *Participation directe et démocratie grecque. Une histoire exemplaire?* Besançon: Presses Universitaires de Franche-Comté.

———. 2011. *Le Présent dans le Passé. Autour de quelques Périclès du xxᵉ siècle et de la possibilité d'une vérité en histoire*. Besançon: Presses Universitaires de Franche-Comté.

D'Alembert, J. le Rond. 1893. *Discours préliminaire de l'Encyclopédie*. Paris: Ch. Delagrave [1st ed. 1751].

Davies, J. K. 1971. *Athenian Propertied Families 600–300 B.C.* Oxford, UK: Oxford University Press.

Decultot, E. 2000. *Johann Joachim Winckelmann. Enquête sur la genèse de l'histoire de l'art*. Paris: Presses Universitaires de France.

Delcourt, M. 1939. *Périclès*. Paris: Gallimard.

Deniaux, E., and P. Schmitt-Pantel. 1987–1989. "La relation patron-client en Grèce et à Rome." *Opus*, 6–8: 147–164.

Derenne, E. 1930. *Les procès d'impiété intentés aux philosophes à Athènes au Ve et IVe siècle av. J.-C.* Liège: Imp. H. Vaillant-Carmanne; Paris: Champion.

De Sanctis, G. 1944. *Pericle*, Milan: G. Principato.

Descat, R. 1995. "L'*Économie antique* et la cité grecque. Un modèle en question." *Annales HSS*, 5: 961–989.

Desmoulins, C. 1825. *Collection des mémoires relatifs à la Révolution française. Camille Desmoulins, Joachim Vilate et Charles André Méda.* Paris/Brussels: Baudouin Frères.

Detienne, M. 2003. *The Writing of Orpheus: Greek Myth in Cultural Context.* Baltimore: Johns Hopkins University Press [1st French ed. 1989].

Detienne, M. and J.-P. Vernant 1991. *Cunning Intelligence in Greek Culture and Society.* Chicago: University of Chicago Press [1st French ed. 1974].

Develin, R. 1989. *Athenian Officials 684–321 BC.* Cambridge, UK: Cambridge University Press.

D'Hautcourt, A. 2006. "Alexis, les prostituées et Aphrodite à Samos." *Kernos*, 19: 313–317.

Dillon, M. J. 1996. "The importance of the water supply at Athens: the role of the ἐπιμελητὴς τῶν κρηνῶν." *Hermes*, 124, 2: 192–204.

Dilts, M. R. 1971. *Heraclidis Lembi Excerpta politiarum.* Durham, NC: Duke University.

Dodds, E. R. 1959. *Plato. Gorgias.* Oxford, UK: Clarendon Press.

Donnay, G. 1968. "La date du procès de Phidias." *Antiquité Classique*, 37: 19–36.

Dosse, F. 2005. *Le pari biographique. Écrire une vie.* Paris: La Découverte.

Dover, K. J. 1960. "Dekatos autos." *Journal of Hellenic Studies*, 80: 61–77.

———. 1978. *Greek Homosexuality.* London: Duckworth.

———. 1988a. "Anecdotes, gossip and scandal," in *The Greeks and Their Legacy: Prose Literature, History, Society, Transmission, Influence, Collected Papers*, vol. 2. Oxford, UK: Blackwell, 45–52.

———. 1988b. "The freedom of the intellectual in Greek society," in *The Greeks and Their Legacy: Prose Literature, History, Society, Transmission, Influence, Collected Papers*, vol. 2. Oxford, UK: Blackwell, 135–158.

———. 1989. *Aristophanes Clouds: Introduction and Commentary.* Oxford, UK: Clarendon Press [1st ed. 1968].

Drerup, E. 1916. *Aus einer alten Advokaten-republik. Demosthenes und seine Zeit.* Paderborn: F. Schöningh.

———. 1923. *Demosthenes im Urteile des Altertums von Theopomp biz Tzetzes. Geschichte, Roman, Legende.* Würzburg: C. J. Becker.

Droysen, J. G. 1957. *Histoire d'Alexandre le grand.* Paris: Le Club du Meilleur Livre [1st ed. 1833].

———. 1980. *Geschichte des Hellenismus*, 3 vols. [*Geschichte der Epigonen*]. Munich: Deutscher Taschenbuch-Verlag [1st ed. 1843].

Dubuisson, M. 1989. "La Révolution française et l'Antiquité." *Cahiers de Clio*, 100: 29–42.

Dumont, H. 2009. *L'Antiquité au Cinéma. Vérités, légendes et manipulations.* Paris: Nouveau monde; Lausanne: Cinémathèque suisse.

Duplouy, A. 2006. *Le prestige des élites. Recherches sur les modes de reconnaissance sociale en Grèce entre X^e et Ve siècles avant J.-C.* Paris: Les Belles Lettres.

Duruy, V. 1867. *Histoire grecque,* 6th ed. Paris: Hachette [1st ed. 1851].

Edmonds, J. M. 1957. *Fragments of Attic Comedy,* vol 1. Leiden: Brill.

Ehrenberg, V. 1945. "Pericles and his colleagues between 441 and 429 B.C." *American Journal of Philology,* 66, 2: 113–134.

———. 1968. *From Solon to Socrates: Greek History and Civilization during the Sixth and Fifth Centuries B.C.* London: Methuen & Co. [repr. with foreword by P. Millett, London: Routledge, 2011]

Étienne, R. 2004. *Athènes, espaces urbains et histoire. Des origines à la fin du IIIe siècle après J.-C.* Paris: Hachette supérieur.

Fénelon, F. 1760. *Dialogues of the Dead.* London: D. Browne, J. Jackson, & A. and C. Corbett.

Feyel, Chr. 2006. *Les artisans dans les sanctuaires grecs à travers la documentation financière en Grèce.* Paris/Athens: Ecole française d'Athènes.

Figueira, T. J. 1991. *Athens and Aigina in the Age of Imperial Colonization.* Baltimore: Johns Hopkins University Press.

Filleul, E. 1874–1875. *Das Zeitalter des Perikles.* Leipzig: Teubner.

Finley, M. I. 1959. "Was Greek civilization based on slave labour?" *Historia,* 8: 145–164.

———. 1981. "Land, debt and the man of property in Classical Athens," [1953] in *Economy and Society in Ancient Greece,* ed. R. Saller and B. Shaw. London: Chatto & Windus, 62–76.

Flacelière, R. 1966. *La vie quotidienne en Grèce au siècle de Périclès.* Paris: Hachette.

Fontenelle (de), B. 1730. *New Dialogues of the Dead* [1683]. London: J. Tonson.

Fornara, C. W. 1971. *The Athenian Board of Generals from 501 to 404.* Wiesbaden: Franz Steiner.

Fornara, C. W. and L. J. Samons II 1991. *Athens from Cleisthenes to Pericles.* Berkeley/Los Angeles/Oxford, UK: University of California Press.

Foster, E. 2010. *Thucydides, Pericles, and Periclean Imperialism.* Cambridge, UK: Cambridge University Press.

Foxhall, L., and H. A. Forbes 1982. "*Sitometreia*: the role of grain as a staple food in Classical Greece." *Chiron,* 12: 41–90.

Frederick II of Prussia. 1846–1856. *Œuvres de Frédéric le Grand,* ed. J.D.E. Preuss, 30 vols. Berlin: R. Decker.

French, A. 1994. "Pericles' citizenship law." *Ancient History Bulletin,* 8: 71–75.

Fröhlich, P. 2000. "Remarques sur la reddition de comptes des stratèges athéniens." *Dikè,* 3: 81–111.

Gabrielsen, V. 1994. *Financing the Athenian Fleet: Public Taxation and Social Relations.* Baltimore/London: Johns Hopkins University Press.

Gantz, T. 1993. *Early Greek Myth: A Guide to Literary and Artistic Sources.* Baltimore/London: Johns Hopkins University Press.

Garnsey, P. 1989. *Famine and Food Supply in the Graeco-Roman World: Responses to Risk and Crisis.* Cambridge, UK: Cambridge University Press.

Gast, J. 1753. *The Rudiments of the Grecian History.* Dublin: S. Powell.

Gauthier, Ph. 1973. "À propos des clérouquies athéniennes du V siècle," in *Problèmes de la terre en Grèce ancienne,* ed. M. I. Finley. Paris/Leiden: Mouton, 163–178.

Geddes, A. 2007. "Ion of Chios and politics," in *The World of Ion of Chios*, ed. V. Jennings and A. Katsaros. Leiden: Brill, 110–138.

Gernet, L. 1981. "Marriages of tyrants," in *The Anthropology of Ancient Greece*. Baltimore: Johns Hopkins University Press, 289–302 [1st French ed. 1968].

———. 1983. *Les Grecs sans miracle*, ed. Riccardo di Donato. Paris: La Découverte.

Gillies, J. 1820. *The History of Ancient Greece, Its Colonies and Conquests* [1786], 4 vols. London: T. Cadell and W. Davies.

Giovannini, A. 1990. "Le Parthénon, le trésor d'Athènes et le tribut des Alliés." *Historia*, 39: 129–148.

———. 1997. "La participation des alliés au financement du Parthénon: *aparkhè* ou tribut?" *Historia*, 46: 145–157.

Glotz, G. 1931. *Histoire grecque*, vol. 2. Paris: Presses Universitaires de France.

Golden, M. 1984. "Slavery and homosexuality at Athens." *Phoenix*, 38: 308–324.

Gomme, A. W. 1956. *Historical Commentary on Thucydides*, vol. 2. Oxford, UK: Clarendon Press.

Green, P. 1972. "In the shadow of the Parthenon," in *The Shadow of the Parthenon: Studies in Ancient History and Literature*. Berkeley: Maurice Temple Smith Limited, 11–46.

Grégoire, H. 1977. *Œuvres. Grégoire, député à la convention nationale*, vol. 2. Nendeln, Liechtenstein: KTO Press [reprint of *L'ancien Moniteur: seule histoire authentique et inaltérée de la révolution française depuis la réunion des États-généraux jusqu'au consulat (mai 1789–novembre 1799)*, vol. 22. Paris (1862)].

Grell, C. 1993. *L'Histoire entre érudition et philosophie. Étude sur la connaissance historique à l'âge des Lumières*. Paris: Presses Universitaires de France.

———. 1995. *Le dix-huitième siècle et l'antiquité en France 1680–1789*, 2 vols. Oxford, UK: Voltaire Foundation.

Grell, C., and C. Michel 1988. *L'École des princes ou Alexandre disgracié. Essai sur la mythologie monarchique de la France absolutiste*. Paris: Les Belles Lettres.

Gribble, D. 2006. "Individuals in Thucydides," in *Brill's Companion to Thucydides*, ed. A. Rengakos and A. Tsakmakis. Leiden: Brill, 439–468.

Grote, G. 1869–1870. *A History of Greece from the Earliest Period to the Close of the Generation Contemporary with Alexander the Great*, 12 vols. London: J. Murray [1st ed. 1846–1856].

Grunchec, P. 1983. *Le Grand Prix de peinture, les concours des prix de Rome de 1797 à 1863*. Paris: École nationale supérieure des beaux-arts.

Guerci, L. 1979. *Libertà degli antichi e libertà dei moderni. Sparta, Atene e i philosophes nella Francia del Settecento*. Naples: Guida.

Guicciardini, F. 1867. *Consolatoria, Accusatoria, Difensoria* [1527], in *Opere inedite di Francesco Guicciardini. Ricordi autobiografici e di famiglia e scritti vari*. Florence: Cellini.

Hall, E. 2006. *The Theatrical Cast of Athens. Interactions between Ancient Greek Drama and Society*. Oxford, UK: Oxford University Press.

Halliwell, S. 1991. "Comic satire and freedom of speech in Classical Athens." *Journal of Hellenic Studies*, 111: 48–70.

Halperin, D. 1990. *One Hundred Years of Homosexuality and Other Essays on Greek Love*. New York/London: Routledge.

Hamel, D. 1995. "*Stratēgoi* on the *Bema*: the separation of political and military authority in fourth-century Athens." *Ancient History Bulletin*, 9: 25–39.

———. 1998. *Athenian Generals: Military Authority in the Classical Period*. Leiden: Brill.

Hansen, M. H. 1991. *The Athenian Democracy in the Age of Demosthenes*. Oxford, UK/Cambridge, MA: Blackwell.

———. 1992. "The tradition of the Athenian democracy A.D. 1750–1990." *Greece & Rome*, 39, 1: 14–30.

———. 2005. *The Tradition of Ancient Greek Democracy and Its Importance for Modern Democracy*. Copenhagen: Det Kongelige Danske Videnskabernes Selskab.

Harding, Ph. 1994. *Androtion and the Atthis*. Oxford, UK: Clarendon Press.

Harris, E. M. 1990. "Did the Athenians regard seduction as a worse crime than rape?" *Classical Quarterly*, 40: 370–377.

Hartog, F. 2005. *Anciens, Modernes, Sauvages*. Paris: Galaade.

Haslam, M. 1990. "Pericles *poeta*." *Classical Philology*, 85: 33.

Hegel, G.W.F. 1902. *Lectures on Philosophy of History*, trans. J. Sibree. New York: P. F. Collier and Son [1st German ed. 1822–1831].

Henderson, J. 1975. *The Maculate Muse: Obscene Language in Attic Comedy*. New Haven, CT: Yale University Press [2nd ed. Oxford, UK: Oxford University Press, 1991].

Henry, M. M. 1995. *Prisoner of History: Aspasia of Miletus and Her Biographical Tradition*. Oxford, UK: Oxford University Press.

Herder, J. G. von 1800. *Outlines of a Philosophy of the History of Man*, trans. T. O. Churchill. New York: Bergman Publishers [1st German ed. 1791].

Héritier, F., B. Cyrulnik, and A. Naouri. 1994. *De l'inceste*. Paris: Odile Jacob.

Herman, G. 1987. *Ritualised Friendship and the Greek City*. Cambridge, UK: Cambridge University Press.

———. 2006. *Morality and Behavior in Democratic Athens: A Social History*. Cambridge, UK: Cambridge University Press.

Hesk, J. 1999. "The rhetoric of anti-rhetoric in Athenian oratory," in *Performance Culture and Athenian Democracy*, ed. S. Goldhill and R. Osborne. Cambridge, UK: Cambridge University Press, 201–230.

Hitler, A. 1926. *Mein Kampf*. Munich: F. Eher.

———. 1992. *Hitler. Reden, Schriften, Anordnungen*, 12 vols. Munich/London/Paris: K. G. Saur.

Hobbes, T. 1839. *The Latin Works*, vol. 1, ed. W. Molesworth. London: J. Bohn.

———. 1989 [1629]. *The Peloponnesian War, Thucydides: The Complete Hobbes Translation*, notes and intr. D. Grene. Chicago: University of Chicago Press.

Hölscher, T. 1975. "Die Aufstellung des Perikles-Bildnisses und ihre Bedeutung." *Würzburger Jahrbücher für die Altertumswissenschaft*, 1: 187–199.

Holtzmann, B. 2003. *L'Acropole d'Athènes. Monuments, cultes et histoire du sanctuaire d'Athèna Polias*. Paris: Picard.

Homo, L. 1954. *Périclès: une expérience de démocratie dirigée*. Paris: R. Laffont.

Hornblower, S. 1994. *Thucydides*. Baltimore: Johns Hopkins University Press [2nd ed. revised; 1st ed. 1987].

Hunter, V. 1993. *Policing Athens: Social Control in the Attic Lawsuits, 420–320 B.C.* Princeton, NJ: Princeton University Press.

Hurwit, J. M. 2004. *The Acropolis in the Age of Pericles.* Cambridge, UK: Cambridge University Press.

Ildefonse, F. 2005. "Notes sur la divination, le rationnel et l'irrationnel," in *Le rationnel et l'irrationnel dans l'Antiquité,* ed. L. Mouze. Toulouse: Presses Universitaires du Mirail, 227–234.

Isaac, B. 2004. *The Invention of Racism in Classical Antiquity.* Princeton, NJ: Princeton University Press.

Jaeger, W. 1965. *Paideia: The Ideals of Greek Culture,* vol. 1, *Archaic Greece: The Mind of Athens* [1934]. Oxford, UK: Oxford University Press.

Jennings, V., and A. Katsaros, eds. 2007. *The World of Ion of Chios.* Leiden: Brill.

John, H. 1939. *Von Werden des Spartanischen Staatsgedankens.* Breslau: Märtin.

Johnson, H. C. 1992. "Spartan simplicity versus decadent luxury." *Proceedings of the Annual Meeting of the Western Society of French History,* 19: 149–157.

Johnson, L. M. 1993. *Thucydides, Hobbes and the Interpretation of Realism.* Dekalb, IL: Northern Illinois University Press.

Jones, C. P. 1987. "Tattooing and branding in Graeco-Roman Antiquity." *Journal of Roman Studies,* 77: 139–155.

Jones, R. V. 1978. *Most Secret War: British Scientific Intelligence (1939–1945).* London: Hutchinson.

Jouanna, D. 2005. *Aspasie de Milet, égérie de Périclès.* Paris: Fayard.

Jouanna, J. 2007. *Sophocle.* Paris: Fayard.

Kagan, D. 1991. *Pericles of Athens and the Birth of Democracy.* London/New York/Sydney/Toronto: Gild Publishing.

Kallet, L. 2009. "Democracy, empire and epigraphy in the twentieth century," in *Interpreting the Athenian Empire,* ed. J. Ma, N. Papazarkadas, and R. Parker. London: Duckworth, 43–66.

Kallet-Marx, L. 1989. "Did tribute fund the Parthenon?" *Classical Antiquity,* 8: 252–266.

Kassel, R., and C. Austin, eds. 1983. *Poetae Comici Graeci,* vol. IV, *Aristophon-Crobylus.* Berlin: W. de Gruyter.

Keesling, C. M. 2003. *The Votive Statues of the Athenian Acropolis.* Cambridge, UK: Cambridge University Press.

Keuls, E. 1993. *The Reign of the Phallus: Sexual Politics in Ancient Athens.* Berkeley: University of California Press [2nd ed., revised; 1st ed. New York: Harper and Row, 1985].

Krentz, P. 1997. "The strategic culture of Periclean Athens," in *Polis and Polemos: Essays on Politics, War, and History in Ancient Greece, in Honor of Donald Kagan,* ed. C. Hamilton. Claremont, CA: Regina Books, 55–72.

Kurke, L. 1999. *Coins, Bodies, Games, and Gold: The Politics of Meaning in Archaic Greece.* Princeton, NJ: Princeton University Press.

Lahire, B. 1999. "De la théorie de l'*habitus* à une sociologie psychologique," in *Le travail sociologique de P. Bourdieu,* ed. B. Lahire. Paris: La Découverte, 121–152.

Leduc, C. 1994–1995. "Citoyenneté et parenté dans la cité des Athéniens. De Solon à Périclès." *Métis,* 9–10: 51–68.

———. 2003. "Ego et ses trois sœurs (germaine, utérine et consanguine). Athènes et Sparte, VIᵉ s.– IVᵉ s. av. J.-C.," in *Histoire, Espaces et Marges de l'Antiquité.*

Hommages à Monique Clavel-Lévêque, vol. 1, ed. M. Garrido-Hory and A. Gonzalès. Besançon: Presses Universitaires de Franche-Comté, 249–291.

Lehmann, G. A. 2008. *Perikles. Staatsmann und Stratege im klassischen Athen: eine Biographie*. Munich: C. H. Beck.

Lenfant, D. 2002. "Protagoras et son procès d'impiété: peut-on soutenir une thèse et son contraire?" *Ktèma*, 27: 135–154.

———. 2003a. "De l'usage des comiques comme source historique: les *Vies* de Plutarque et la Comédie Ancienne," in *Grecs et Romains aux prises avec l'histoire. Représentations, récits et idéologie*, ed. G. Lachenaud and D. Longrée. Rennes: Presses Universitaires de Rennes, 391–414.

———. 2003b. "Des décrets contre la satire: une invention de scholiaste? (Pseudo-Xén. II, 18, schol. Ach. 67, schol. Av. 1297)." *Ktèma*, 28: 5–31.

Lévêque, P. 1964. *L'aventure grecque*. Paris: Armand Colin.

Lévêque, P., et P. Vidal-Naquet 1996. *Cleisthenes the Athenian: An Essay on the Representation of Space and Time in Greek Political Thought from the End of the Sixth Century to the Death of Plato*. Atlantic Highlands, NJ: Humanities Press [1st French ed. 1964].

Leventi, I. 2003. *Hygieia in Classical Greek Art*. Athens: A. A. Lemos and E. Simantoni-Bournia.

Lévesque, C. 1811. *Études d'histoire ancienne et de celle de la Grèce*, 5 vols. Paris: Fournier Frères.

Lévy, E. 1976. *Athènes devant la défaite de 404. Histoire d'une crise idéologique*. Paris/Athens: École française d'Athènes.

Lewis, D. M. 1992. "The Thirty Years' peace," in *The Cambridge Ancient History*, 2nd ed., vol. 5, *The Fifth Century BC*, ed. D. M. Lewis, J. Boardman, J. K. Davies, and M. Ostwald. Cambridge, UK: Cambridge University Press, 121–146.

Lissarrague, F. 1990. "The sexual life of satyrs," in *Before Sexuality: The Construction of Erotic Experience in the Ancient Greek World*, ed. D. M. Halperin, J. J. Winkler, and F. I. Zeitlin. Princeton, NJ: Princeton University Press, 53–81.

Loraux, N. 1986. *The Invention of Athens: The Funeral Oration in the Classical City*. Cambridge, MA: Harvard University Press [1st French ed. 1981].

———. 1993a. "Éloge de l'anachronisme en histoire." *Le genre humain*, 27: 23–39.

———. 1993b. *The Children of Athena: Athenian Ideas about Citizenship and the Division between the Sexes*. Princeton, NJ: Princeton University Press [1st French ed. 1981].

———. 2002. *The Divided City: On Memory and Forgetting in Ancient Athens*. New York: Zone Books [1st French ed. 1997].

———. 2003. "Aspasie, l'étrangère, l'intellectuelle," in *La Grèce au féminin*, ed. N. Loraux. Paris: Les Belles Lettres, 133–164.

———. 2011. "Thucydides is not a colleague" [1980], in *Greek and Roman Historiography: Oxford Readings in Classical Studies*, ed. J. Marincola. Oxford/New York: Oxford University Press, 19–38.

Lüdemann, H. 1939. *Sparta. Lebensordnung und Schicksal*. Leipzig: B. G. Teubner.

Ludwig, P. 2002. *Eros and Polis. Desire and Community in Greek Political Theory*. Cambridge, UK: Cambridge University Press.

Luginbill, R. D. 2011. *Author of Illusions: Thucydides' Rewriting of the History of the Peloponnesian War*. Newcastle upon Tyne, UK: Cambridge Scholars Publishing.

Lyttleton, G. 1760. *Dialogues of the Dead*. London: W. Sandby.

Mably, de (G. Bonnot). 1769. *Phocion's Conversations, or, The Relation between Morality and Politics*. London: Mr. Dodsley [1st French ed. 1763].

———. 1784. *Observations on the Manners, Government, and Policy of the Greeks*, trans. J. and J. Fletcher, D. Prince, J. Cooke, and S. Arnold. Oxford, UK: W. Jackson [1st French ed. 1766].

MacDowell, D. 1978. *The Law in Classical Athens*. Ithaca, NY: Cornell University Press.

Machiavelli, N. 1882. *Discourses on the First Ten Books of Titus Livius* [1512–1517], in *The Historical, Political and Diplomatic Writings of Niccolo Machiavelli*, 4 vols., trans. C. E. Detmold. Boston: J. R. Osgood.

———. 1965. *The History of Florence* [1525], in *Machiavelli: The Chief Works and Others*, ed. A. Gilbert. Durham, NC: Duke University Press.

Maffre, J.-J. 1994. *Le siècle de Périclès*. Paris: Presses Universitaires de France.

Mann, C. 2007. *Die Demagogen und das Volk. Zur politischen Kommunikation im Athen des 5. Jahrhunderts v. Chr.* Berlin: Akademie Verlag.

Martin, J. 2000. *Les aventures d'Orion*, vol. 2, *Le Styx*. Paris: Casterman.

Mat-Hasquin, M. 1981. *Voltaire et l'Antiquité grecque* (Studies on Voltaire and the Eighteenth Century 197). Oxford, UK: Voltaire Foundation.

Mattingly, H. B. 1961. "The Athenian coinage decree." *Historia: Zeitschrift für Alte Geschichte*, 10, 2: 148–188.

———. 1966. "Periclean imperialism," in *Ancient Society and Institutions: Studies Presented to Victor Ehrenberg on His 75th Birthday*, ed. E. Badian. Oxford, UK: Basil Blackwell, 193–223.

———. 1977. "Poets and politicians in fifth-century Greece," in *Greece and the Eastern Mediterranean in Ancient History and Prehistory: Studies Presented to Fritz Schachermeyr on the Occasion of His Eightieth Birthday*, ed. K. H. Kinzl. Berlin/New York: Walter de Gruyter, 231–245.

———. 1992. "Epigraphy and the Athenian Empire." *Historia*, 41: 129–138.

———. 1996. *Athenian Empire Restored: Epigraphic and Historical Studies*. Ann Arbor: University of Michigan Press.

Mazzarino, S. 1990. *Il Pensiero Storico Classico*, vol. 3. Rome/Bari: Laterza [1st ed. 1983].

McGlew, J. 2002. *Citizens on Stage: Comedy and Political Culture in the Athenian Democracy*. Ann Arbor: University of Michigan Press.

———. 2006. "The comic Pericles," in *Ancient Tyranny*, ed. S. Lewis. Edinburgh: Edinburgh University Press, 164–177.

Mérimée, P. 1868. "De l'histoire ancienne de la Grèce" [1848], in *Mélanges historiques et littéraires*. Paris: Michel Lévy frères, 109–219.

Meritt, B. D. 1984. "The Samian revolt from Athens in 440–439 B.C." *Proceedings of the American Philosophical Society*, 128, 2: 123–133.

Miller, M. C. 1997. *Athens and Persia in the Fifth Century BC: A Study in Cultural Receptivity*. Cambridge, UK: Cambridge University Press.

Mitchell, L. G. 1998. *Greeks Bearing Gifts: The Public Use of Private Relationships in the Greek World, 435–323 BC*. Cambridge, UK: Cambridge University Press.

Mitford, W. 1814. *The History of Greece*, vol. 3. London: T. Cadell and W. Davies.

Momigliano, A. 1966. "George Grote and the study of greek history," [1952] in *Studies in Historiography*. London: Weidenfeld and Nicolson, 56–74.

Monoson, S. 2000. *Plato's Democratic Entanglements: Athenian Politics and the Practice of Philosophy*. Princeton, NJ: Princeton University Press.

Montaigne, M. de. 1877. *Essays*, 3 vols., trans. C. Cotton and ed. W. C. Hazlitt. London: Reeves and Turner [1st French ed. 1595].

Montepaone, C., G. Imbruglia, M. Catarzi, and M. L. Silvestre. 1994. *Tucidide nella Storiografia Moderna. G. B. Niebuhr, L. V. Ranke, W. Roscher, E. Meyer*. Naples: Morano.

Montesquieu (de Secondat, C.-L.) 1989. *The Spirit of the Laws*, ed. and trans. A. M. Cohler, B. C. Miller, H. S. Stone. Cambridge, UK: Cambridge University Press [1st French ed. 1748].

Montuori, M. 1981. "Di Aspasia Milesia," in *Corolla Londinensis* 1 (*London Studies in Classical Philology*, 8), ed. G. Giangrande. Amsterdam: J. C. Gieben, 87–109.

Moreno, A. 2007. *Feeding the Democracy. The Athenian Grain Supply in the Fifth and Fourth Centuries BC*. Oxford, UK: Oxford University Press.

———. 2009. " 'The Attic neighbour': The cleruchy in the Athenian Empire," in *Interpreting the Athenian Empire*, ed. J. Ma, N. Papazarkadas, and R. Parker. London: Duckworth, 211–221.

Mortgat-Longuet, E. 2006. "Du siècle d'Auguste au siècle de Louis XIV: quelques réflexions sur le concept de 'siècle' du début du dix-septième siècle à Voltaire." in *Voltaire et le Grand Siècle*, ed. J. Dagen et al. Oxford, UK: Voltaire Foundation, 97–116.

Mossé, C. 1971. "Le 'siècle' de Périclès," in *Histoire d'une démocratie: Athènes*. Paris: Seuil, 43–66.

———. 1989. *L'Antiquité dans la Révolution française*. Paris: Albin Michel.

———. 2005. *Périclès. L'inventeur de la démocratie*. Paris: Payot.

———. 2006/2007. "Review of Samons II, L. J., *What's Wrong with Democracy? From Athenian Practice to American Worship*. Berkeley and Los Angeles. 2004." *International Journal of the Classical Tradition*, 13: 467–470.

Most, G. W. 1995. "Perikles in Gettysburg. Antike Beredsamkeit und neue Humanität bei Abraham Lincoln." *Ein Bücher-Tagebuch. Buchbesprechungen aus der Frankfurter Allgemeinen Zeitung*. Frankfurt: Frankfurter Allgemeine, 438–440.

Müller, K. O. 1824. *Die Dorier*, 2 vols. Breslau: Josef Max und Komp.

Murari Pires, F. 2006. "Thucydidean modernities: history between science and art," in *Brill's Companion to Thucydides*, ed. A. Rengakos and A. Tsakmakis. Leiden/Boston: Brill, 811–838.

Murray, G. 1946. "Greece and England," in *Greek Studies*. Oxford, UK: Clarendon Press, 192–201.

Murray, O. 1990. "The affair of the Mysteries: democracy and the drinking group," in *Sympotica. A Symposium on the Symposion*, ed. O. Murray. Oxford, UK: Clarendon Press, 149–161.

———. 1993. "L'homme grec et les formes de socialité," in *L'homme grec*, ed. J.-P. Vernant. Paris: Seuil, 303–348.

———. 2010. "Modern perceptions of ancient realities from Montesquieu to Mill," in *Démocratie athénienne—démocratie moderne: tradition et influences*, Entretiens sur l'Antiquité Classique, 56, ed. M. H. Hansen. Geneva: Fondation Hardt, 137–166.

Näf, B. 1986. *Von Perikles zu Hitler? Die athenische demokratie und die deutsche althistorie bis 1945*. Bern: Lang.

———. 1992. "Werner Jaegers *Paideia:* Entstehung, Kulturpolitische Absichten und Rezeption," in *Werner Jaeger Reconsidered*, ed. W. M. Calder III. Atlanta: Scholars Press, 125–146.

Nagy, G. 1996. *Poetry as Performance: Homer and Beyond*. Cambridge, UK: Cambridge University Press.

Neils, J. 1992. *Goddess and Polis: The Panathenaic Festival in Ancient Athens*. Princeton, NJ: Princeton University Press.

Nelson, E. 2004. *The Greek Tradition in Republican Thought*. Cambridge, UK: Cambridge University Press.

Nemo, P. 1988. "Athènes, Rome, Jérusalem: trois piliers de l'identité européenne," in *L'Union européenne et les États-nations, The European Union and the Nation-States*, ed. P. Nemo. Paris: ESCP.

Nick, G. 2002. *Die Athena Parthenos. Studien zum griechischen Kultbild und seiner Rezeption*. Mainz: P. von Zabern.

Nicolai, W. 1996. "Thukydides und die perikleische Machtpolitik." *Hermes*, 124: 264–281.

Niebuhr, B. G. 1852a. *Lectures on Ancient History, from the Earliest Times to the Taking of Alexandria by Octavianus*, 3 vols. Philadelphia: Blanchard and Lee [1st German ed. 1829–1830].

———. 1852b. *The Life and Letters of Barthold Georg Niebuhr*, vol. 2, ed. and trans. S. Winkworth. London: Chapman and Hall.

Nippel, W. 2010. *Liberté antique, liberté moderne. Les fondements de la démocratie de l'Antiquité à nos jours*. Toulouse: Presses Universitaires du Mirail [1st German ed. 2008].

Nisard, C. 1851. "*Histoire grecque*, par M. Victor Duruy." *Journal général de l'Instruction publique et des cultes*, 557–560.

Noiriel, G. 2001. *État, nation et immigration. Vers une histoire du pouvoir*. Paris: Belin.

Noussia, M. 2003. "The language of tyranny in Cratinus, *PCG* 258." *Proceedings of the Cambridge Philological Society*, 49: 74–88.

Ober, J. 1985. "Thucydides, Pericles, and the strategy of defense," in *The Craft of the Ancient Historian: Essays in Honor of Chester G. Starr*, ed. J. W. Eadie and J. Ober. Lanham, MD: University Press of America, 171–188.

———. 1989. *Mass and Elite in Democratic Athens: Rhetoric, Ideology, and the Power of the People*. Princeton, NJ: Princeton University Press.

———. 1996. *The Athenian Revolution: Essays on Ancient Greek Democracy and Political Theory*. Princeton, NJ: Princeton University Press.

———. 1998. *Political Dissent in Democratic Athens: Intellectual Critics of Popular Rule*. Princeton, NJ: Princeton University Press.

Oliver, G. J. 2007. *War, Food and Politics in Early Hellenistic Athens*. Oxford, UK: Oxford University Press.

Osborne, R. 1990. "Vexatious litigation in Classical Athens: sykophancy and the sykophant," in *NOMOS: Essays in Athenian Law, Politics, and Society*, ed. P. Cartledge et al. Cambridge, UK: Cambridge University Press, 83–102.

Ostwald, M. 1986. *From Popular Sovereignty to the Sovereignty of the Law: Law, Society, and Politics in Fifth-Century Athens.* Berkeley: University of California Press.

Papazarkadas, N. 2009. "Epigraphy and the Athenian Empire: reshuffling the chronological cards," in *Interpreting the Athenian Empire*, ed. J. Ma, N. Papazarkadas, and R. Parker. London: Duckworth, 67–88.

Parker, R. 1996. *Athenian Religion: A History.* Oxford, UK: Oxford University Press.

Patterson, C. B. 1981. *Pericles' Citizenship Law of 451–50 B.C.* Salem, NH: The Ayer Company.

———. 1998. *The Family in Greek History.* Cambridge, MA: Harvard University Press.

Payen, P. 2005. "Johann Gustav Droysen et l'Histoire de l'Hellénisme. L'époque hellénistique entre Alexandre et la Prusse," in *Histoire de l'Hellénisme*, 2 vols., ed. J. G. Droysen. Grenoble: J. Millon, vol. 1, 5–54.

———. 2007a. "D'Ephialte à Socrate. Construction et déni d'une 'cause démocratique' à Athènes," in *Affaires, scandales et grandes causes. De Socrate à Pinochet*, ed. L. Boltanski et al. Paris: Stock, 21–40.

———. 2007b. "L'autorité des Grecs dans l'*Histoire ancienne* de Rollin," in *Les Autorités. Dynamiques et mutations d'une figure de référence à l'Antiquité*, ed. D. Foucault and P. Payen. Grenoble: J. Millon, 171–194.

———. 2010. "Thucydide et Rollin: émergence du paradigme athénien au XVIIIe siècle," in *Ombres de Thucydide. La réception de l'historien depuis l'Antiquité jusqu'au début du XXe siècle*, ed. V. Fromentin, S. Gotteland, and P. Payen. Bordeaux: Ausonius, 613–634.

Pébarthe, C. 2005. "Clisthène a-t-il été archonte en 525/4? Mémoire et histoire des Athéniens à l'époque classique." *Revue Belge de Philologie et d'Histoire*, 83: 25–53.

———. 2007. "La question de la clientèle en Grèce ancienne: Cimon *versus* Périclès, patronage privé contre patronage communautaire?" in *Clientèle guerrière, clientèle foncière et clientèle électorale*, ed. V. Lécrivain. Dijon: Éditions universitaires de Dijon, 173–197.

———. 2010a. "La vie politique des Athéniens illustres au Ve siècle. Périclès, Thucydide et Plutarque," in *La cité et ses élites. Pratiques et représentation des formes de domination et de contrôle social dans les cités grecques*, ed. L. Capdetrey and Y. Lafond. Bordeaux: Ausonius, 273–290.

———. 2010b. "Périclès, au-delà de Thucydide," in *Ombres de Thucydide. La réception de l'historien depuis l'Antiquité jusqu'au début du XXe siècle*, ed. V. Fromentin, S. Gotteland, and P. Payen. Bordeaux: Ausonius, 463–490.

Pelling, C. 2002. *Plutarch and History.* Swansea, UK: Classical Press of Wales; London: Duckworth.

Perlman, S. 1963. "The politicians in the Athenian democracy of the fourth century B.C." *Athenaeum*, 41: 327–355.

Pernot, L. 2006. *L'Ombre du tigre. Recherches sur la réception de Démosthène.* Naples: M. D'Auria.

Perrault, C. 1693. *Parallèle des anciens et des modernes*, vol. 1. Paris: J.-B. Coignard [2nd ed.].

———. 1697. *Parallèle des anciens et des modernes*, vol. 4. Paris: J.-B. Coignard.

Pesely, G. E. 1989. "Hagnon." *Athenaeum*, 67: 191–209.

Planeaux, C. 2000–2001. "The date of Bendis' entry into Attica." *Classical Journal*, 96: 165–192.

Podlecki, A. J. 1966. *The Political Background of Aeschylean Tragedy*. Ann Arbor: University of Michigan Press.

———. 1998. *Perikles and His Circle*. London/New York: Routledge.

Pohlenz, M. 1920. "Thukydides und wir." *Neue Jahrbücher für das klassische Altertum, Geschichte und deutsche Literatur und für Pädagogik*, 23, 46: 57–72.

Pomeroy, S. 1975. *Goddesses, Whores, Wives, and Slaves*. New York: Schocken Books.

Pontier, P. 2010. "Grote et la réception de Thucydide en France sous la IIe République et le Second Empire," in *Ombres de Thucydide. La réception de l'historien depuis l'Antiquité jusqu'au début du XXe siècle*, ed. V. Fromentin, S. Gotteland, and P. Payen. Bordeaux: Ausonius, 635–648.

Pritchett, W. K. 1971. *The Greek State at War*, vol 1. Berkeley: University of California Press.

Raaflaub, K. A. 2003. "The alleged ostracism of Damon," in *Gestures: Essays in Ancient History, Literature, and Philosophy Presented to Alan L. Boegehold*, ed. G. W. Bakewell and J. Sickinger. Oxford, UK: Oxbow Books, 317–331.

———. 2004. *The Discovery of Freedom in Ancient Greece*. Chicago: University of Chicago Press [1st German ed. 1985].

———. 2009. "Learning from the Enemy: Athenian and Persian 'Instruments of Empire,'" in *Interpreting the Athenian Empire*, ed. J. Ma, N. Papazarkadas, and R. Parker. London: Duckworth, 89–124.

Ranke, L. von. 1867–1890. *Sämtliche Werke*, vol. 53/54. Leipzig: Duncker und Humblot.

———. 1975. *Vorlesungseinleitungen*, vol. 4, *Aus Werk und Nachlass*. Munich: R. Oldenbourg.

Rawson, E. 1969. *The Spartan Tradition in European Thought*. Oxford, UK: Clarendon Press.

Reden, S. von. 1997. "Money, law and exchange: coinage in the Greek *polis*." *Journal of Hellenic Studies*, 117: 154–176.

Renan, E. 1929. *Recollections of My Youth*. London: Routledge [1st French ed. 1883].

Rhodes, P. J. 1988. *Thucydides, History II*. Warminster, UK: Aris and Phillips.

———. 1993. *A Commentary on the Aristotelian Athenaion Politeia*. Oxford, UK: Clarendon Press [rev. ed., 1st ed. 1981].

———. 2006. *A History of the Classical Greek World, 478–323 B.C.* Malden, MA: Blackwell.

Rico, F. 2002. *Le rêve de l'humanisme*. Paris: Les Belles Lettres.

Roberts, J. T. 1989. "Athenians on the Sceptered Isle." *Classical Journal*, 84, 3: 193–205.

———. 1994. *Athens on Trial: The Antidemocratic Tradition in Western Thought*. Princeton, NJ: Princeton University Press.

Robespierre, M. 1967. *Œuvres. Discours. 5e partie: 27 juillet 1793–27 juillet 1794*, vol. 5, ed. M. Bouloiseau and A. Soboul. Paris: Presses Universitaires de France.

Robinson, C. A. 1959. *Athens in the Age of Pericles*. Norman: University of Oklahoma Press.

Roisman, J. 2004. "Speaker-audience interaction in Athens: a power struggle," in *Free Speech in Classical Antiquity*, ed. I. Sluiter and R. M. Rosen. Leiden: Brill, 261–278.

Rolley, C. 1999. *La Sculpture grecque*, vol. 2. Paris: Picard.

Rollin, C. 1790. *The Ancient History of the Egyptians, Carthaginians, Assyrians, Babylonians, Medes and Persians, Macedonians and Grecians*, 8 vols. Edinburgh, UK: A. Guthrie [1st French ed. 1731–1738].

Romilly, J. de 2000. *La Grèce antique contre la violence*. Paris: De Fallois.

Rosivach, V. 1987. "Autochthony and the Athenians." *Classical Quarterly*, 37: 294–305.

Ross, E. 1975. "The Debate on Luxury in Eighteenth-Century France: A Study in the Language of Opposition to Change." PhD Thesis, University of Chicago.

Rougemont, G. 1996. "Histoire grecque et 'actualisme' politique. Démosthène, *alias* Churchill?" *Topoi. Orient-Occident* 6: 275–281.

Rousseau, J. J. 1997a. *"The Discourses" and Other Early Political Writings*, ed. and trans. V. Gourevitch, vol. 1, Cambridge Texts in the History of Political Thought. Cambridge, UK: Cambridge University Press.

———. 1997b. *"The Social Contract" and Other Later Political Writings*, ed. and trans. V. Gourevitch, vol. 2, Cambridge Texts in the History of Political Thought. Cambridge, UK: Cambridge University Press.

Rudhardt, J. 1960. "La définition du délit d'impiété d'après la législation attique." *Museum Helveticum*, 17: 87–105.

Saetta Cottone, R. 2005. *Aristofane e la poetica dell'ingiuria*. Rome: Carocci.

Saint-Just, de, L.-A. 1791. *L'Esprit de la révolution et de la constitution de la France*. Paris: Beuvin.

Saint-Lambert, de, J.-F. 1765. "Luxe," in *Encyclopédie, ou Dictionnaire Raisonné des Sciences, des Arts et des Métiers*, vol. IX, ed. D. Diderot and J. le Rond d'Alembert. Paris: Briasson, David, Le Breton, Durand, col. 763a–771b.

Saladin, J.-C. 2000. *La bataille du grec à la Renaissance*. Paris: Les Belles Lettres.

Saller, R. 2005. "Framing the debate over growth in the ancient economy," in *The Ancient Economy: Evidence and Models*, ed. J. G. Manning and I. Morris. Stanford, CA: Stanford University Press, 223–238.

Samons II, L. J. 1993. "Athenian finance and the treasury of Athena." *Historia*, 42: 129–138.

———. 2004. *What's Wrong with Democracy? From Athenian Practice to American Worship*. Berkeley/Los Angeles: University of California Press.

———, ed. 2007. *The Cambridge Companion to the Age of Pericles*. Cambridge, UK: Cambridge University Press.

Schachermeyr, F. 1933. "Die nordische Führerpersönlichkeit im Altertum," in *Humanistische Bildung im Nationalsozialistischen Staate, Neue Wege zur Antike*, ed. H. Gieselbusch. Leipzig/Berlin: Teubner, 36–43.

———. 1968. *Religionspolitik und Religiosität bei Pericles*. Vienna: Böhlau in Kommission.

Schelle, G. 1913. *Œuvres de Turgot et documents le concernant*, vol. 1. Paris: F. Alcan.

Schiappa, E. 1990. "Did Plato coin *Rhetorikè*?" *American Journal of Philology*, 111: 457–470.

Schlatter, R. 1945. "Thomas Hobbes and Thucydides." *Journal of the History of Ideas*, 6, 3: 350–362.

———, ed. 1975. *Hobbes's Thucydides*. New Brunswick, NJ: Rutgers University Press.

Schmidt, W. A. 1877–1879. *Das perikleische Zeitalter: Darstellungen und Forschungen*, 2 vols. Jena: H. Duft.

Schmitt Pantel, P. 1992. *La cité au banquet. Histoire des repas publics dans les cités grecques*. Rome: Ecole française de Rome.

———. 2007. "Aspasie, la nouvelle Omphale," in *Athènes et le politique. Dans le sillage de Claude Mossé*, ed. P. Schmitt Pantel and F. de Polignac. Paris: Albin Michel, 199–221.

———. 2009. *Hommes illustres. Mœurs et politique à Athènes au Ve siècle*. Paris: Aubier.

Scholtz, A. 2007. *Concordia Discors: Eros and Dialogue in Classical Athenian Literature*. Washington, DC/Cambridge, MA/London: Harvard University Press.

Schubert, C. 1994. *Perikles*. Darmstadt: Wissenschaftliche Buchgesellschaft.

Schwartz, J. 1969. "Hérodote et Périclès." *Historia*, 18: 367–370.

Schwarze, J. 1971. *Die Beurteilung des Perikles durch die attische Komödie und ihre historische und historiographische Bedeutung*. Munich: C. H. Beck.

Scobie, A. 1990. *Hitler's State Architecture: The Impact of Classical Antiquity*. University Park, PA: Pennsylvania State University Press.

Seaford, R. 1994. *Reciprocity and Ritual: Homer and Tragedy in the Developing City-State*. Oxford, UK: Clarendon Press.

Sebillotte Cuchet, V. 2006. *Libérez la patrie! Patriotisme et politique en Grèce ancienne*. Paris: Belin.

Shapiro, H. A. 1996. "Athena, Apollo and the religious propaganda of the Athenian Empire," in *Religion and Power in the Ancient Greek World*, ed. P. Hellström and B. Alroth. Uppsala: Almqvist and Wiksell International, 101–114.

Shipley, G. 1987. *A History of Samos, 800–188 BC*. Oxford, UK: Clarendon Press.

Shipton, K.M.W. 2000. *Leasing and Lending: The Cash Economy in Fourth-Century BC Athens*. London: Institute of Classical Studies.

Siewert, P., ed. 2002. *Ostrakismos-Testimonien I*. Stuttgart: F. Steiner.

Sigonio, C. 1593. *Caroli Sigonii De Antiqvo Ivre Civivm Romanorvm, Italiae Provinciarvm, Ac Romanae Ivrisprvdentiae Ivdiciis. Libri XI. Eivsdem, De Republica Atheniensium, eorumq[ue] ac Lacedaemoniorum temporibus, libri quinque. Quibus adiecti nunc sunt eiusdem de Republicae Hebraeorum, libri septem*. Frankfurt: Ed. Wechelus.

Sinclair, R. 1988. *Democracy and Participation in Athens*. Cambridge, UK: Cambridge University Press.

Sinos, R. H. 1993. "Divine selection: epiphany and politics in archaic Greece," in *Cultural Poetics in Archaic Greece: Cult, Performance, Politics*, ed. C. Dougherty and L. Kurke. Cambridge, UK: Cambridge University Press, 73–91.

Sommerstein, A. H. 1990. *Aristophanes: "Peace."* Warminster, UK: Aris and Phillips.

———. 2004. "Harassing the satirist: the alleged attempts to prosecute Aristophanes," in *Free Speech in Classical Antiquity*, ed. I. Sluiter and R. M. Rosen. Leiden: Brill, 145–174.

Sourvinou-Inwood, C. 1990. "What is *polis* religion?" in *The Greek City from Homer to Alexander*, ed. O. Murray and S. Price. Oxford, UK: Clarendon Press, 295–322.

Speer, A. 1976. *Erinnerungen*. Frankfurt: Ullstein.

———. 1980. *Spandauer Tagebücher*. Berlin: Propyläen.

Spon, J. 1678. *Voyage d'Italie, de Dalmatie, de Grèce et du Levant, fait aux années 1675 & 1676*, 3 vols. Lyon: Antoine Cellier le fils.

Stadter, P. 1989. *A Commentary on Plutarch's Pericles*. Chapel Hill: University of North Carolina Press.

———. 1991. "Pericles among the intellectuals." *Illinois Classical Studies*, 16, 1: 111–124.

Stark, I. 2004. *Die Hämische Muse. Spott als soziale und mentale Kontrolle in der griechischen Komödie*. Munich: C. H. Beck.

Starobinski, J. 1985. *Montaigne in Motion*. Chicago: University of Chicago Press [1st French ed. 1982].

Starr, C. G. 1974. *A History of the Ancient World*. Oxford, UK: Oxford University Press.

Storey, I. C. 2003. *Eupolis: Poet of Old Comedy*. Oxford, UK: Oxford University Press.

Strasburger, H. 1955. "Herodot und das perikleische Athen." *Historia*, 4: 1–25.

———. 1958. "Thukydides und die politische Selbstdarstellung der Athener." *Hermes*, 86: 17–40.

Tacon, J. 2001. "Ecclesiastic 'Thorubos': interventions, interruptions, and popular involvement in the Athenian assembly." *Greece & Rome*, 48, 2: 173–192.

Tanner, J. 2006. *The Invention of Art History in Ancient Greece*. Cambridge, UK: Cambridge University Press.

Tatti, A. 1986. "Le *Dionysalexandros* de Cratinos." *Métis*, 1: 325–332.

Taylor, M. 2010. *Thucydides, Pericles, and the Idea of Athens in the Peloponnesian War*. Cambridge, UK: Cambridge University Press.

Thirlwall, C. 1835–1844. *History of Greece*, 8 vols. London: Longman et al.

Thomas, R. 1989. *Oral Tradition and Written Record in Classical Athens*. Cambridge, UK: Cambridge University Press.

Tracy, S. V. 2002. "Herodotus and Xanthippus, father of Pericles," in *Noctes Atticae: Studies Presented to Jorgen Mejer*, ed. B. Amden et al. Copenhagen: Museum Tusculanum Press, 315–319.

———. 2009. *Pericles: A Sourcebook and Reader*. Berkeley, CA/London: University of California Press.

Tsakmakis, A. 2006. "Leaders, crowds, and the power of the image: political communication in Thucydides," in *Brill's Companion to Thucydides*, ed. A. Rengakos and A. Tsakmakis. Leiden: Brill, 161–187.

Tuplin, C. J. 1985. "Imperial tyranny: some reflections on a classical Greek political metaphor," in *CRUX: Essays in Greek History Presented to G.E.M de Ste. Croix*, ed. P. Cartledge and F. D. Harvey. London: Duckworth, 348–375.

Turgot, A.R.J. 1913. *Œuvres de Turgot et Documents le concernant, avec biographies et notes par Gustave Schelle*, vol. 1. Paris: Librairie Félix Alcan.

Turner, F. M. 1981. *The Greek Heritage in Victorian Britain*. New Haven, CT: Yale University Press.

Valdes Guia, M. 2009. "Bouzyges nomothetes: purification et exégèse des lois sacrées à Athènes," in *La norme en matière religieuse en Grèce ancienne, Kernos* suppl. 21, ed. P. Brulé. Liège: Centre international d'étude de la religion grecque antique, 293–320.

Verilhac, A.-M. and C. Vial 1998. *Le Mariage grec du VIe a. C. à l'époque d'Auguste,* *BCH* suppl. 32. Athens/Paris: Ecole française d'Athènes.

Vernant, J.-P. 1990. *Figures, idoles, masques.* Paris: Julliard.

Vickers, M. 1997. *Pericles on Stage: Political Comedy in Aristophanes' Early Plays.* Austin: University of Texas Press.

Vidal-Naquet, P. 1995. *Politics Ancient and Modern.* Cambridge, UK: Polity Press [1st French ed. 1990].

———. 2000. *Les Grecs, les historiens, la démocratie. Le grand écart.* Paris: La Découverte.

Villacèque, N. 2013. *Spectateurs de paroles! Délibération démocratique et théâtre à Athènes à l'époque classique.* Rennes: Presses Universitaires de Rennes.

Volney, C. F. 1800. *Lectures on History Delivered in the Normal School of Paris* [1795]. London: J. Ridgway.

Voltaire [Arouet, F.-M.]. 1765. *Nouveaux mélanges philosophiques, historiques, critiques, etc.* Genève: s.n.

———. 1784–1789. *Œuvres complètes de Voltaire,* 70 vols. Paris/Kehl: Société Typographique.

———. 1901. *The Works of Voltaire: A Contemporary Version,* 21 vols., ed. and trans. J. Morley, T. Smollett, and W. F. Fleming. New York: E. R. DuMont.

Wade-Gery, H. T. 1932–1933. "Studies in Attic inscriptions of the fifth century B.C." *Annual of the British School at Athens,* 33: 101–136.

Wallace, R. W. 2004a. "Damon of Oa: a music theorist ostracized?" in *Music and the Muses: The Culture of Mousikē in the Classical Athenian City,* ed. P. Murray and P. Wilson. Oxford, UK: Oxford University Press, 249–268.

———2004b. "The power to speak—and not to listen—in Ancient Athens," in *Freedom of Speech in Ancient Athens,* ed. R. Rosen and I. Sluiter. Leiden: Brill, 221–232.

Watkiss Lloyd, W. 1875. *The Age of Pericles: A History of the Politics and Arts of Greece from the Persian to the Peloponnesian War.* London: Macmillan and Co.

Weber, C. W. 1985. *Perikles. Das goldene Zeitalter von Athen.* Munich: Ullstein Taschenbuchverlag.

Wilgaux, J. 2010. "Le mariage des élites dans le monde grec des cités," in *La cité et ses élites. Pratiques et représentation des formes de domination et de contrôle social dans les cités grecques,* ed. L. Capdetrey and Y. Lafond. Bordeaux: Ausonius, 345–358.

Will, É. 1972. *Le monde grec et l'orient,* vol. 1. Paris: Presses Universitaires de France.

Will, W. 1995. *Perikles.* Hamburg: Rowohlt.

Williams, G. M. E. 1980. "The image of the Alcmeonidai between 490 and 487/6 B.C." *Historia,* 29: 106–110.

Wilson, P. 2000. *The Athenian Institution of the Khorēgia: The Chorus, the City and the Stage.* Cambridge, UK: Cambridge University Press.

Winckelmann, J. J. 2005. *Essays on the Philosophy and History of Art,* 3 vols. London: Continuum International Publishing.

Winkler, J. J. 1990. *The Constraints of Desire: The Anthropology of Sex and Gender in Ancient Greece.* New York/London: Routledge.

Wohl, V. 2002. *Love among the Ruins: The Erotics of Democracy in Classical Athens.* Princeton, NJ: Princeton University Press.

————. 2009. "Rhetoric of the Athenian citizen," in *The Cambridge Companion to Ancient Rhetoric*, ed. E. Gunderson. Cambridge, UK: Cambridge University Press, 162–177.

Woodbury, L. 1981. "Anaxagoras and Athens." *Phoenix*, 35: 295–315.

Woodhead, A. G. 1973–1974. "The date of the Springhouse Decree (IG I² 54)." *Archeologia classica*, 25–26: 751–761.

Wyke, M. 1997. *Projecting the Past, Ancient Rome, Cinema, and History*. New York/London: Routledge.

Young, W. 1786. *The History of Athens Politically and Philosophically Considered with the View to an Investigation of the Immediate Causes of Elevation, and of Decline, Operative in a Free and Commercial State*. London: J. Robson [1st ed. 1777].

Yourcenar, M. 1989. *En pèlerin et en étranger: Essais*. Paris: Gallimard.

Zimmern, A. E. 1911. *The Greek Commonwealth: Politics and Economics in Fifth-Century Athens*. Oxford, UK: Clarendon Press [5th ed. 1931].

Zschietzschmann, W. 1940. *Die Blütezeit der griechischen Kunst. Akademische Rede zur Jahresfeier der Ludwigs-Universität am 1. Juni 1940*. Giessen: Münchow.

INDEX